John Playford

The Whole Book of Psalms

With the usual hymns and spiritual songs ; together with all the ancient and proper tunes sung in churches, with some of later use

John Playford

The Whole Book of Psalms
With the usual hymns and spiritual songs ; together with all the ancient and proper tunes sung in churches, with some of later use

ISBN/EAN: 9783337467951

Printed in Europe, USA, Canada, Australia, Japan

Cover: Foto ©Lupo / pixelio.de

More available books at **www.hansebooks.com**

THE
WHOLE BOOK
OF
PSALMS:
WITH THE
Uſual *HYMNS* and Spiritual *SONGS*:
TOGETHER
With all the *Ancient* and *Proper* TUNES ſung in *Churches*, with ſome of *Later Uſe*.

Compoſed in THREE PARTS,
CANTUS, MEDIUS, & BASSUS:
In a more Plain and Uſeful Method than hath been formerly Publiſhed.

By JOHN PLAYFORD.

The Second Edition, Corrected and Amended.

PSAL. xlvii. Verſ. 7.
God is King of all the Earth, ſing ye Praiſes with Underſtanding.
EPHES. v. Verſ. 19.
Speaking to your ſelves in Pſalms and Hymns, and Spiritual Songs, ſinging and making melody in your hearts unto the Lord.

In the SAVOY,
Printed by *Edw. Jones*, for the Company of STATIONERS. And are to be ſold by *Henry Playford* at his Shop near the *Temple* Church, and at his Houſe in *Arundel-Street* in the *Strand*: 1695.

THE
PREFACE:
SHEWING THE
Antiquity of Singing PSALMS and HYMNS; with an Account of this *Book*, and the Use thereof.

THE Praising of GOD by *Psalms* and *Hymns*, as it seems a part of Natural Religion owned and used by all Mankind, so we find the Practice of it very early in the Church of God. There can be no just cause to doubt, but that it was at least contemporary with Instrumental Musick; a thing as ancient as the Times of *Adam*, invented by *Jubal*, who was *the Father of all such as handle the Harp and Organ*, Gen. 4, 21. But we need not build upon Conjectures, where we have clear Evidence. After the famous Deliverance which God gave the *Israelites* at the *Red-Sea*, they celebrated the Mercy with a Song of Triumph; and *Josephus* says, They spent the whole night in Hymns and Mirth: *Then sang Moses and the children of Israel this song unto the Lord*, Exod. 15. 1. which is there upon Record, composed (as *Josephus* adds) in Hexameter Verse; and that it was conjoyned with Instrumental Musick is plain, *verf.* 20, 21. *And Miriam the prophetess, the sister of Aaron, took a timbrel in her hand, and all the women went out after her with timbrels and with dances: And Miriam answered them, Sing ye to the Lord, for he hath triumphed gloriously*, &c. But the first that established singing Psalms and Hymns, as a fix'd and constant part of God's publick Worship in the solemn Assemblies of the *Jewish* Church, was King *David*; whose zeal for God's Glory (before the House of God was built) set himself to compose divers Psalms for that service, as we read in 1 *Chron.* 16. 7. and *ch.* 25. *v.* 6, 7. and to chuse out Men skilful in Song to perform the same to the praise of Almighty God. When his Son *Salomon* had finished the Temple, at the Dedication thereof, you may read in 2 *Chron.* 5. 12, 13, 14. how the Praises of the Lord were sounded forth with Voices and Instruments, and also how acceptable it was to the Lord. This being established, the Priests and *Levites* continued

A

The Preface.

tinued this solemn Worship during the time of the First and Second Temple, even till the Destruction thereof, foretold by our blessed Saviour, who saw the Glory thereof, and frequented that place, as he acknowledgeth, *Luke* 22. 53. *I was daily with you in the Temple.* And (as a Learned Divine observes) it is not credible, that our blessed Saviour, who so often quoted *David's* Psalms for the confirmation of his Doctrine, would neglect that part of Worship then in force, and who did himself say, That it became him to *fulfil all righteousness*; which he further testified, when together with his Disciples he sung a *Psalm* or *Hymn* at the end of the Celebration of his *Last Supper.* After his Ascension, his Disciples gave testimony of their Approbation, *Acts* 2. 46, 47. *They were daily with one accord in the temple praising God,* &c. And *Acts* 3. 1. mentions, that *Peter* and *John* went up together into the temple at the hour of prayer; which was the set time for the Celebration of publick Worship.

The Use of Singing *Psalms* and *Hymns* was continued with great Reverence and Devotion among the Primitive Christians; those who consult the Writings of the Primitive Fathers, shall scarce meet with one that makes not mention thereof. An account hereof I find learnedly discoursed by Dr. *Cave* in his *Primitive Christianity,* Part 1. p. 276, 277. where, speaking of reading the appointed Lessons, he hath these words: *About this part of the Service it was that they sung* Hymns *and* Psalms, *a considerable part of the Divine Worship,* (*as it had ever been accounted both amongst* Jews *and* Gentiles) *and more immediately serviceable for Celebrating the Honour of God, and lifting up the Minds of Men to Divine and Heavenly Raptures.*

But to come nearer our Times: In our late Forefathers days, (upon the Restauration of our Church to its Primitive Purity and Discipline) it was, That some holy and godly Men brought the present use and manner of singing Psalms into the Publick Service of our Church, following herein the Examples of the *Reformed Churches* in *France* and *Germany*: But Time and long Use hath much abated the wonted Reverence and Estimation it had for about 100 Years after this Establishment. It was the Saying of a Learned Divine in his Sermon on this Subject, *That* Prayer *shall cease, and* Preaching *shall cease, but* Praising *of* GOD *shall never cease, neither in this world, nor in that which is to come.* To sing Praises to God, is an Angelic Office; it is a taste of the First Fruits of Heaven while we are on Earth. *MUSICK* (the Learned say) is the Handmaid to Divinity; and there is no Science, except That, admitted into the Service of the Church.

To conclude; I have made it my Endeavour so to perfect and finish this Work, that nothing should be wanting to render it useful to the End it is designed, The Glory of GOD, and the Publick Service of the Church: And for that reason, (with the Judgment of some of the best skill'd in Musick) I have Composed all the Musical Tunes into Three Parts, *viz. Cantus, Medius,* and *Bassus*: The *Church Tune* is placed in the *Treble* Part,

The Preface.

Part, (which is the *Cantus*,) with the *Bass* under it, as most proper to joyn Voice and Instrument together, according to holy *David*'s prescription, *Psal.* 144. 9. And since many of our Churches are lately furnished with Organs, it will also be useful for the Organist; and likewise for such Students in the Universities as shall practise Song, to sing to a Lute or Viol. The *Medius* Part is composed (as is proper) not to rise above the Church Tune, to cloud or obscure the Ayre thereof, except in such places as it could not be well avoided. The *Bass* is composed in such a compass of Notes, as will sute an indifferent Voice both below and above. All Three Parts may as properly be sung by Men, as by Boys or Women: And to that end, the two Upper Parts are constant in the G *fol re ut* Cliff, and the Bass in the F *fa ut* (its proper) Cliff; all Three Parts moving together in Solemn way of Counterpoint, and also every *Tune* put in such *Keys* as is most sutable to the Ayre thereof. Lastly, you will find every *Psalm* fitted to Tunes sutable and proper to the Matter: Psalms of Prayer and Confession, to solemn grave *Flat Tunes*; Psalms of Thanksgiving and Praise, to lively chearful *Sharp Tunes*. Likewise all such Psalms and Hymns whose Tunes are long, and may seem difficult to some, have Directions over them to be sung to other short Common Tunes. Also there is affixed before the Book, a Table of the first Line of the *Treble-Tunes* of all the *Psalms*, with the Names alphabetically set over each Tune; and under, what Psalms are sung to them: And a Table of *Hymns* in a Page by themselves. As for *Instructions* to the Singing of them, I refer you to my *Introduction to the Skill of Musick*, in 8º.

I have no more to add, but as the *Glory* of GOD, and the *Service* of his Church, was my sole End and Aim; so I shall account my Labour and Pains herein sufficiently recompensed, if it prove Useful to such as so endeavour to sing the Praises of their Creator here on Earth in *Psalms* and *Hymns*, that hereafter they may eternally sing *Hallelujahs* among the blessed Choir of Saints and Angels. Which is the hearty Prayer of

Your Faithful Servant,

John Playford.

Of the Virtue and Efficacy of the PSALMS.

IN the Psalms are described the *rewards* of good, the *punishments* of evil men, the *rudiments* of beginners, the *progress* of proficients, and *consummation* of perfect men.

The Singing of Psalms *comforteth* the sorrowful, *pacifieth* the angry, *strengtheneth* the weak, *humbleth* the proud, *gladdeth* the humble, *stirreth up* the slow, *reconcileth* enemies, *lifteth up* the heart to heavenly things, and *uniteth* the Creature to his Creator; for whatsoever is in the Psalms, conduceth to the *edification, benefit,* and *consolation* of mankind.

If thou would'st make a *confession*, and repent thee of thy sins; then with remorse and humility sing the 7 Penitential Psalms of *David, viz.* Psal. 6, 32, 38, 51, 102, 130, 143. and thou shalt feel the sweet mercies of God, and thy mind refreshed with spiritual joy.

If thou would'st pray; then pour forth thy soul in Psal. 25, 54, 67, 70, 72, 86, 143. for the soul of man cannot either feelingly express its misery, tribulation, and anguish of temptation, or more powerfully call upon the mercy of God, than in these Psalms.

If thou would'st praise the Majesty of God, or give him thanks for all his benefits; then sing Psal. 103, 104, 105, 106, 107, 108, 111, 113, 144, 145, 146, 147, 148, 149, 150.

If thou art so far afflicted with outward and inward temptations, that thou seemest to be forsaken; then sing heartily Psal. 22, 64, 69.

If this present life be tedious unto thee, and that with an ardent desire thou waitest to see God; then sing Psal. 42, 63, 84.

If thou find thy self quite dejected, and (as it were) forlorn in trouble; then with compunction of heart sing Psal. 13, 31, 44, 54, 56. And if thou hast found ease and rest unto thy soul, then sing to the praise of God Psal. 30, 34, 103, 104. And always (whether in time of *adversity* or *prosperity*) sing out the *Song of the 3 holy Children*, wherein every creature is invited to praise God.

If thou desirest to exercise thy self in God's divine praises and precepts; then sing Psal. 119. wherein if thou search even all thou canst, yet thou wilt never perfectly understand the *virtues* and *excellencies*, or reach to the *heights* and *depths* comprehended in it; for hardly is there a Verse, wherein is not mention made of God's *Law, Commandments, Testimonies,* or *Precepts.*

In a word, he that gives these heavenly *Hymns* their due, had need to compose a Psalm in *praise* of the Psalms, that so the devout and joyful soul might, with looking up to God, reflect upon its own work, and transport it self unto the Choir of Angels and Saints, whose perpetual task is to sing their concording Parts without pause, redoubling and descanting, *Holy, Holy, Holy, Lord God of Hosts.* And if *Vocal Musick* be not enough, let the *Instrumental* be added, *Rev.* 15. 2, 3. *They have in their hands the harps of God, and sing the song of Moses, and the song of the Lamb, saying, Great and marvellous are thy works, Lord God Almighty.* Amen. *A* Table

A Table *of the first Line of the* Trebles *of all the* PSALMS, *with the* Names *Alphabetically set over each Tune; and under, what* Psalms *are sung to them.*

Cantus.   *Bristol Tune.*
PSALM 6, 60, 83.

Cambridge Tune.
Psalm 2, 10, 36, 49, 2ᵈ Metre of Ps. 51,
Psalm 62, 80, 117.

Canterbury Tune.
Psalm 12, 23, 105, 146.

St. David's Tune.
Psalm 43, 95, 106, 147.

Exeter Tune.
Psalm 48, 59, 72, 99.

Glastenbury Tune.
Psalm 11, 54, 69.

Glocester Tune.
Psalm 9, 73, 140.

Hereford Tune.
Psalm 20, 35, 87.

Lichfield Tune.
Psalm 31, 52.

Cantus.   *London Tune*
Psalm 5, 16, 2ᵈ Metre of Psal. 23,
Psalm 42, 57, 66, 101, 110, 128.

London new Tune.
Psalm 47, 93, 150.

Magnificat Tune.
Psalm 33.

Manchester Tune.
Psalm 55, 88, 102, 143.

St. Mary's Tune.
Psalm 8, 32, 91, 142.

Martyrs Tune.
Psalm 15, 34, 63, 92, 108, 118, 138, 149.

Norwich Tune.
Psalm 27, 29, 58, 109, 129.

Nunc Dimittis Tune.
Psalm 46.

Oxford Tune.
Psalm 4.

Peter-

The TABLE.

Cant.	
Peterborough Tune. — Psalm 44, 94.	*Proper Tune.* — Psalm 71.
St. Peter's Tune. — Psalm 45.	*77 Psalm Tune.* — Psalm 77, 141.
Proper Tune. — Psalm 1.	*81 Psalm Tune.* — Psalm 81, 98, 135.
Proper Tune. — Psalm 3.	*Proper Tune.* — Psalm 86.
Proper Tune. — Psalm 18.	*100 Psalm Tune.* — Psalm 100, 136.
Proper Tune. — Psalm 21.	*Proper Tune.* — Psalm 103.
Proper Tune. — Psalm 30.	*Proper Tune.* — Psalm 104.
Proper Tune. — Psalm 38.	*Proper Tune.* — Psalm 111.
Proper Tune. — Psalm 50.	*112 Psalm Tune.* — Psalm 112, 127.
Proper Tune. — Psalm 51.	*Proper Tune.* — Psalm 113.
Proper Tune. — Psalm 68.	*Proper Tune.* — Psalm 116.

The TABLE.

Cantus. 119 Psalm Tune.
Psalm 61, 89, 119, 145.

Proper Tune.
Psalm 120.

Proper Tune.
Psalm 121.

Proper Tune.
Psalm 122.

Proper Tune.
Psalm 124.

Proper Tune.
Psalm 125.

Proper Tune.
Psalm 126.

Proper Tune.
Psalm 130.

Proper Tune.
Psalm 137.

148 Psalm Tune.
2d Metre of Ps. 136, Psal 148.

Rochester Tune.
Psalm 13, 24, 37, 82, 139.

Cantus. Salisbury Tune.
Psalm 22, 56, 64, 79.

Southwel Tune.
Psalm 25, 2d Metre of Psal. 50,
Psalm 67, 70, 134.

Te Deum Tune.
Psalm 41.

Ten Commandment Tune.
2d Metre of Psalm 125.

Veni Creator Tune.
Psalm 132.

Westminster Tune.
Psalm 40, 76, 97, 115.

Winchester Tune.
Psalm 84, 96, 107, 133.

Windsor Tune.
Psalm 17, 26, 39, 74, 85, 90, 123, 131.

Worcester Tune.
Psalm 7, 75, 114.

York Tune.
Psalm 14, 19, 28, 53, 65, 78, 144.

The TABLE.

A Table *of the first Line of the* Trebles *of all the* HYMNS *in this Book, and in what Page you may find them.*

Cantus.   *Proper Tune.*
Hymn at Consecr. of Priests, *pag.* 263.

Proper Tune.
Veni Creator, *p.* 264.

Proper Tune.
Te Deum, *p.* 266.

Proper Tune.
Benedictus, *p.* 268.

Proper Tune.
Magnificat, *p.* 270.

Proper Tune.
Nunc Dimittis, *p.* 272.

112 *Psalm Tune.*
The LORD's Prayer, *p.* 273.

St. Mary's Tune.
The Creed, *p.* 274.

Proper Tune.
The 10 Commandments, *p.* 275.

Cantus.   *Proper Tune.*
Song of the 3 H. Children, *p.* 277.

38 *Psalm Tune.*
Humble Suit of a Sinner, *p.* 279.

Martyrs Tune.
Lamentation of a Sinner, *p.* 281.

Proper Tune.
A Penitential Hymn, *p.* 282.

Proper Tune.
Hymn after H. Communion, *p.* 284.

Proper Tune.
An Hymn for Sunday, *p.* 285.

100 *Psalm Tune.*
A Morning Hymn, *p.* 286.

Proper Tune.
An Hymn on the Divine Use of MUSICK, *p.* 287.

(1)

The PSALMS of DAVID in Metre.

Cantus & Bassus.   PSALM I.   *Or to York Tune.*

He man is blest that hath not bent, to ill advise his ear:

Nor led his life as sinners do, nor sate in scorners chair.

But in the law of God the Lord, doth set his whole delight:

And in that law doth exercise himself both day and night.

Medius.   Psalm 1.   *A. 3. Voc.*

THe man is blest that hath not bent, to ill advise his ear:

Nor led his life as sinners do, nor sate in scorners chair.

But in the law of God the Lord, doth set his whole delight:

And in that law doth exercise himself both day and night.

B.1.

Bassus.  *A. 3. Voc.*

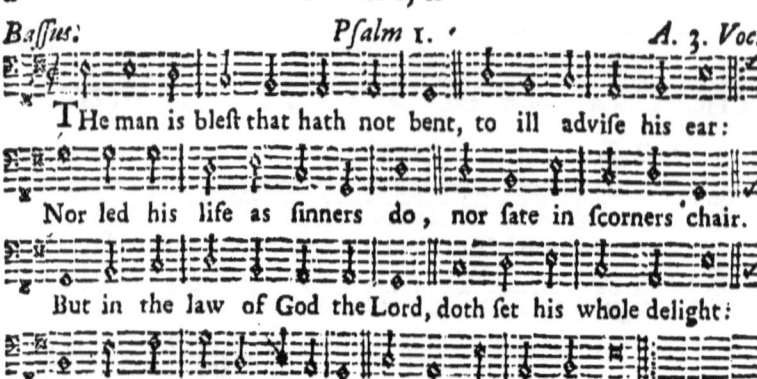

THe man is blest that hath not bent, to ill advise his ear:

Nor led his life as sinners do, nor sate in scorners chair.

But in the law of God the Lord, doth set his whole delight:

And in that law doth exercise himself both day and night.

3 He shall be like the tree that grows
  fast by the river side;
Which bringeth forth most pleasant
  in her due time and tide.   (fruit
Whose leaf shall never fade nor fall,
  but flourish still and stand:
Ev'n so all things shall prosper well,
  that this man takes in hand.

4 So shall not the ungodly men,
  they shall be nothing so:
But as the dust which from the earth
  the wind drives to and fro.

5 Therefore shall not the wicked men
  in judgment stand upright:
Nor yet the sinners with the just
  shall come in place or sight.

6 For why? the way of godly men
  unto the Lord is known:
And eke the way of wicked men
  shall quite be overthrown.

To Father, Son, and Holy Ghost,
  all glory be therefore:
As in beginning was, is now,
  and shall be evermore.

Cantus & Bassus.   P S A L M II.   *Cambridge Tune.*

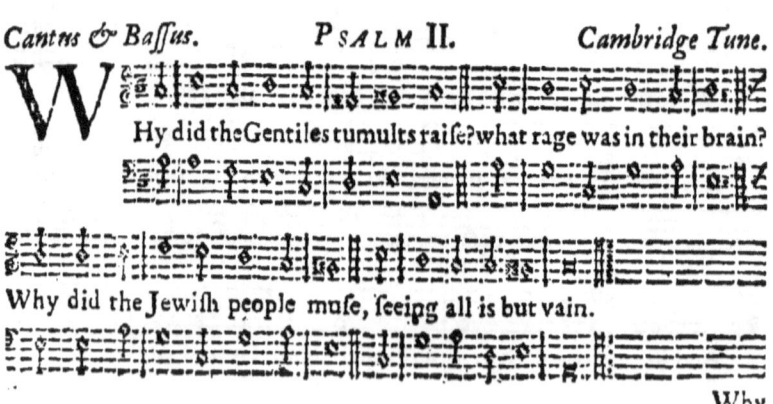

WHy did the Gentiles tumults raise? what rage was in their brain?

Why did the Jewish people muse, seeing all is but vain.

Why

Psalm ii. 3

Medius.   *Psalm* 2.   *A. 3. Voc.*

WHy did the Gentiles tumults raise? what rage was in their brain?

Why did the Jewish people muse, seeing all is but vain?

Bassus.   *Psalm* 2.   *A. 3. Voc.*

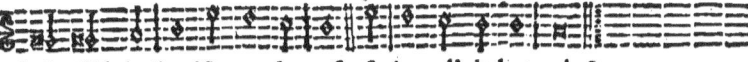

WHy did the Gentiles tumults raise? what rage was in their brain?

Why did the Jewish people muse, seeing all is but vain?

2 The Kings and Rulers of the earth
conspire, and are all bent
Against the Lord and Christ his Son,
which he among us sent.

3 Shall we be bound to them, say they?
let all their bonds be broke:
And of their doctrine and their law
let us reject the yoke.

4 But he that in the heaven dwells,
their doings will deride:
And make them all as mocking stocks
throughout the world so wide.

5 For in his wrath the Lord will say
to them upon a day:
And in his fury trouble them,
and then the Lord will say:

6 I have anointed him my King
upon my holy hill:
I will therefore, Lord, preach thy law,
and else declare thy will.

7 For in this wise the Lord himself
did say to me I wot,
Thou art my dear and only Son,
to day I thee begot.

8 All people I will give to thee,
as heirs at thy request:
The ends and coasts of all the earth
by thee shall be possest.

9 And thou shalt break them migh-
as with an iron rod: (tily,
And as a Potters vessel thou
shalt dash them all abroad.

10 Now ye, O Kings and Rulers all,
be wise therefore, and learn'd,
By whom the matters of the world
be judged and discern'd.

11 See that ye serve the Lord above
in trembling and in fear:
See that with rev'rence ye rejoyce
to him in like manner.

12 See that ye kiss, and eke embrace
His blessed Son, I say,
Lest in his wrath ye suddenly
perish in the mid-way.

13 If once his wrath never so small,
shall kindle in his breast:
O then all they that trust in Christ,
shall happy be, and blest.

Cantus & Bassus.   PSALM III.   Or to *Westminster Tune.*

O Lord, how are my foes increas'd, wch vex me more and more!

They kill my heart when as they say, God can him not restore.

But thou, O Lord, art my defence, when I am hard bestead:

My worship and mine honour both, and thou hold'st up my head.

Medius.   Psalm 3.   A. 3. Voc-

O Lord, how are my foes increas'd, which vex me more and more!

They kill my heart when as they say, God can him not restore.

Psalm iii, iv.

Bassus. *Psalm 3.* *A. 3. Voc.*

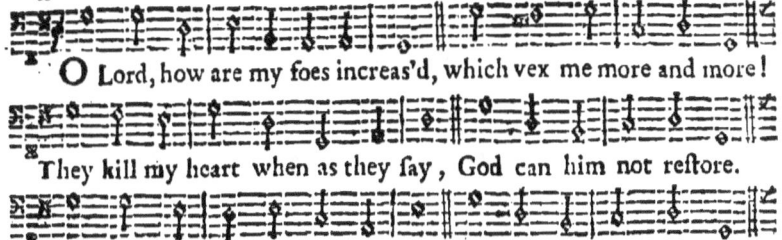

O Lord, how are my foes increas'd, which vex me more and more!

They kill my heart when as they say, God can him not restore.

But thou, O Lord, art my defence, when I am hard bestead:

My worship and mine honour both, and thou hold'st up my head.

4 Then with my voice upon the Lord
I did both call and cry:
And he out of his holy hill
did hear me speedily.

5 I laid me down, and quietly
I slept, and rose again :
For why ? I know assuredly
the Lord will me sustain.

6 If ten thousand had hem'd me in,
I could not be afraid :
For thou art still my Lord and God,
my Saviour and mine aid.

7 Rise up therefore, save me, my God,
for now to thee I call :   (teeth
For thou hast broke the cheeks and
of these wicked men all.

8 Salvation only doth belong
to thee, O Lord, above :
Thou dost bestow upon thy folk
thy blessing and thy love.

To Father, Son, and Holy Ghost,
all glory be therefore :
As in beginning was, is now,
and shall be evermore.

Cantus & Bassus. **PSALM IV.** *Oxford Tune.*

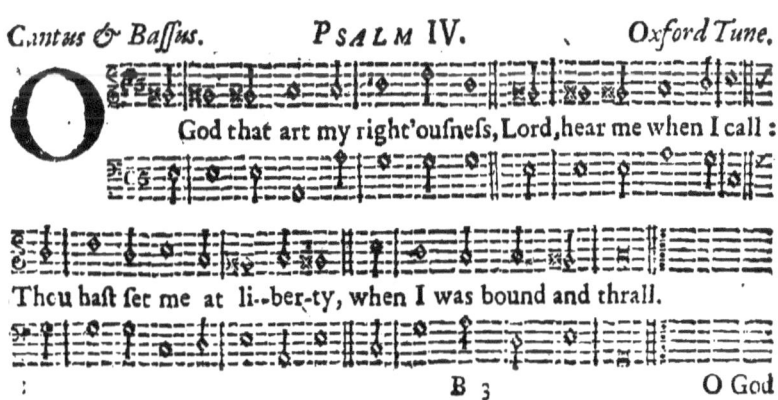

O God that art my right'ousness, Lord, hear me when I call :

Thou hast set me at li--ber-ty, when I was bound and thrall.

O God

6 Psalm iv, v.

Medius. Psalm 4. *A. 3. Voc.*

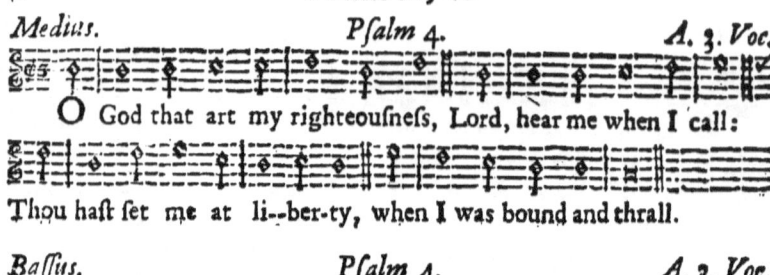

O God that art my righteousness, Lord, hear me when I call:
Thou hast set me at li--ber-ty, when I was bound and thrall.

Bassus. Psalm 4. *A. 3. Voc.*

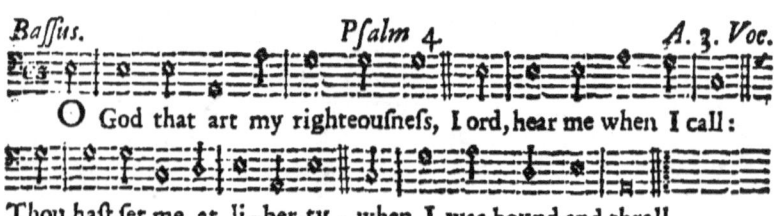

O God that art my righteousness, Lord, hear me when I call:
Thou hast set me at li-ber-ty, when I was bound and thrall.

2 Have mercy, Lord, therefore on me,
  and grant me my request:
For unto thee unceasantly,
  to cry I will not rest.

3 O mortal men, how long will ye
  my glory thus despise?
Why wander ye in vanity,
  and follow after lies?

4 Know ye that good and godly men
  the Lord doth take and chuse:
And when to him I make my plaint,
  he doth me not refuse.

5 Sin not, but stand in awe therefore,
  examine well your heart:
And in your chamber quietly,
  see you your selves convert.

6 Offer to God the sacrifice
  of righteousness, I say:
And look that in the living Lord
  you put your trust alway.

7 The greater sort crave worldly
  and riches do embrace: (goods,
But, Lord, grant us thy countenance,
  thy favour and thy grace.

8 For thou thereby shall make my
  more joyful and more glad, (heart
Than they that of their corn & wine
  full great increase have had.

9 In peace therefore lie down will I,
  taking my rest and sleep:
For thou only wilt me, O Lord,
  alone in safety keep.

Cantus & Bassus. PSALM V. *London Tune.*

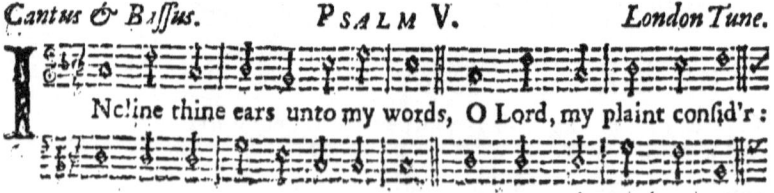

Incline thine ears unto my words, O Lord, my plaint consid'r:

And

Psalm v.

And hear my voice, my King, my God, to thee I make my pray'r.

Medius. *Psalm 5.* *A. 3. Voc.*

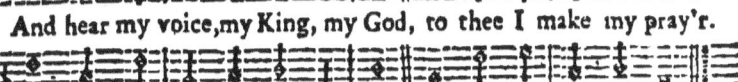

INcline thine ears un---to my words, O Lord, my plaint consid'r:

And hear my voice, my King, my God, to thee I make my pray'r.

Bassus. *Psalm 5.* *A. 3. Voc.*

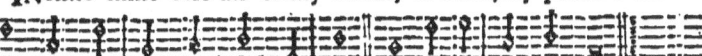

INcline thine ears un--to my words, O Lord, my plaint consid'r:

And hear my voice, my King, my God, to thee I make my pray'r.

3 Hear me betime, Lord, tarry not,
for I will have respect
My prayer early in the morn
to thee for to direct.

4 And I will trust through patience
in thee my God alone: (ness,
Thou art not pleas'd with wicked-
and ill with thee dwells none.

5 And in thy sight shall never stand
these cruel men, O Lord:
Vain workers of iniquity
thou hast always abhorr'd.

6 The liers and the flatterers
thou shalt destroy them than:
And God will hate the blood-thirsty,
and the deceitful man.

7 Therefore will I come to thine
trusting upon thy grace: (house,
And rev'rently will worship thee
toward thine holy place.

8 Lord, lead me in thy righteousness,
for to confound my foes:
And eke the way that I shall walk,
before my face disclose.
(truth,
9 For in their mouths there is no
their heart is foul and vain:
Their throat an open sepulchre,
their tongues do glose and fain.

10 Destroy their false conspiracies,
that they may come to nought:
Subvert them in their heaps of sin,
which have rebellion wrought.

11 But

Psalm v, vi.

11 But those that put their trust in
    let them be glad always: (thee,
And render thanks for thy defence,
    and give thy name the praise.

12 For thou with favour wilt increase
    the just and righteous still:
And with thy grace, as with a shield,
    defend him from all ill.

Cantus & Bassus.   PSALM VI.   *Bristol Tune.*

LOrd, in thy wrath reprove me not, thô I deserve thine ire:
Ne yet correct me in thy rage, O Lord, I thee desire.

Medius.   Psalm 6.   *A. 3. Voc.*

LOrd, in thy wrath reprove me not, thô I deserve thine ire:
Ne yet correct me in thy rage, O Lord, I thee desire.

Bassus.   Psalm 6.   *A. 3. Voc.*

LOrd, in thy wrath reprove me not, thô I deserve thine ire:
Ne yet correct me in thy rage, O Lord, I thee desire.

1 For I am weak, therefore, O Lord,
    of mercy me forbear, (know'st
And heal me, Lord, for why? thou
    my bones do quake for fear.

2 My soul is troubled very sore,
    and vexed veh'mently,

But, Lord, how long wilt thou delay
    to cure my misery!

4 Lord, turn thee to thy wonted
    my silly soul up take: (grace,
O save me not for my deserts,
    but for thy mercies sake.

5 For

5 For why? no man among the dead
 remembreth thee one whit:
Or who shall worship thee, O Lord,
 in the infernal pit?

6 So grievous is my plaint and moan,
 that I wax wondrous faint,
All the night long I wash my bed
 with tears of my complaint.

7 My sight is dim, and waxeth old
 with anguish of my heart:
For fear of those that be my foes,
 and would my soul subvert.

8 But now away from me, all ye
 that work iniquity:
For why? the Lord hath heard the voice
 of my complaint and cry.

9 He heard not only the request
 and prayer of my heart,
But it received at my hands,
 and took it in good part.

10 And now my foes that vexed me
 the Lord will soon defame,
And suddenly confound them all,
 to their rebuke and shame.

Cantus & Bassus.   PSALM VII.   *Worcester Tune.*

O Lord, my God, I put my trust and confidence in thee:

Save me from them that me pursue, and eke de--li--ver me.

Medius.   *Psalm 7.*   *A. 3. Voc.*

O Lord, my God, I put my trust and con--fi--dence in thee:

Save me from them that me pursue, and eke de--li--ver me.

Bassus.   *Psalm 7.*   *A. 3. Voc.*

O Lord, my God, I put my trust and con--fi--dence in thee:

Save me from them that me pursue, and eke de--li--ver me.

Psalm vii.

2 Lest like a Lion he me tear,
   and rend in pieces small:
While there is none to succour me,
   and rid me out of thrall.

3 O Lord, my God, if I have done
   the thing that is not right;
Or else if I be found in fault,
   or guilty in thy sight:

4 Or to my friend rewarded ill,
   or left him in distress,
Which me pursu'd most cruelly,
   and hated me causeless:

5 Then let my foes pursue my soul,
   and eke my life down thrust
Unto the earth, and also lay
   mine honour in the dust.

6 Start up, O Lord, now in thy wrath,
   and put my foes to pain:
Perform the kingdom promised
   to me, which wrong sustain.
               (thee,
7 Then shall great nations come to
   and know thee by this thing,
If thou declare for love of them,
   thy self as Lord and King.

8 And as thou art of all men judge,
   O Lord, now judge thou me
According to my righteousness,
   and mine integrity.

The second part.

9 Lord, cease the hate of wicked men,
   and be the just man's guide:
By whom the secrets of all hearts
   are searched and descri'd.

10 I take my help to come of God,
   in all my pain and smart;
That doth preserve all those that be
   of pure and perfect heart.
               (both,
11 The just man and the wicked
   God judgeth by his pow'r:
So that he feels his mighty hand,
   ev'n ev'ry day and hour.

12 Except he change his mind, I die:
   for ev'n as he should smite,
He whets his sword, his bow he bends,
   aiming where he may hit:
               (darts,
13 And doth prepare his mortal
   his arrows keen and sharp,
For them that do me persecute,
   while he doth mischief warp.

14 But lo! thô he in travel be
   of his dev'lish forecast,
And of his mischief once conceiv'd,
   yet brings forth nought at last.

15 He digs a ditch, and delves it deep,
   in hope to hurt his brother:
But he shall fall into the pit
   that he digg'd up for other.

16 Thus wrong returneth to the hurt
   of him in whom it bred:
And all the mischief that he wrought
   shall fall upon his head.

17 I will give thanks to God there-
   that judgeth righteously: (fore,
And with my song will praise the
   of him that is most high. (Name

Psalm viii.

Cantus & Bassus.   **P**sa**l**m **VIII.**   *St. Mary's Tune.*

O God our L^d, how wonderful are thy works ev'ry where;
Whose fame surmounts in dignity above the heavens clear!

Medius.   Psalm 8.   *A. 3. Voc.*

O God our Lord, how wonderful are thy works ev'ry where;
Whose fame surmounts in dignity above the heavens clear!

Bassus.   Psalm 8.   *A. 3. Voc.*

O God our Lord, how wonderful are thy works ev'ry where;
Whose fame surmounts in dignity above the heavens clear!

2 Ev'n by the mouth of sucking babes
   thou wilt confound thy foes:
For in those babes thy might is seen,
   thy graces they disclose.

3 And when I see the heavens high,
   the works of thine own hand:
The sun, the moon, and all the stars,
   in order as they stand :
                 (then,
4 What thing is man, Lord, think I
   that thou dost him remember?

Or what is man's posterity,
   that thou dost it consider ?

5 For thou hast made him little less
   than angels in degree :
And thou hast crowned him also
   with glory and dignity.

6 Thou hast preferr'd him to be lord
   of all thy works of wonder :
And at his feet hast set all things,
   that he should keep them under.

12 **Pſalm viii, ix.**

7 As ſheep and neat, and all beaſts elſe,
   that in the fields do feed:
8 Fowls of the air, fiſh in the ſea,
   and all that therein breed.

9 Therefore muſt I ſay once again,
   O God that art our Lord:
How famous, and how wonderful,
   are thy works through the world!

Cantus & Baſſus.   PSALM IX.   *Gloceſter Tune.*

With heart & mouth un'o the Lord, will I ſing laud and praiſe:

And ſpeak of all thy wondrous works, and them declare always.

Medius.   Pſalm 9.   *A. 3. Voc.*

With heart and mouth un---to the Lord, will I ſing laud and praiſe:

And ſpeak of all thy wondrous works, and them declare always.

Baſſus.   Pſalm 9.   *A. 3. Voc.*

With heart and mouth un---to the Lord, will I ſing laud and praiſe:

And ſpeak of all thy wondrous works, and them declare always.

2 I will be glad, and much rejoyce
   in thee, O God moſt high:
And make my ſongs extoll thy Name
   above the ſtarry sky.

3 For that my foes are driven back,
   and turned unto flight:

They fall down flat, and are deſtroy'd
   by thy great pow'r and might.

4 Thou haſt revenged all my wrong,
   my grief, and all my grudge:
Thou doſt with juſtice hear my cauſe,
   moſt like a righteous judge.

5 Thou

Psalm ix.

5 Thou doſt rebuke the heathen folſ,
  and wicked ſo confound :
That afterward the memory
  of them cannot be found.
                    (patch,
6 My foes thou haſt made good diſ-
  and all their towns deſtroy'd :
Thou haſt their fame with them de-
  thrô all the world ſo wide. (fac'd

7 Know thou, that he which is above,
  for evermore ſhall reign :
And in the ſeat of equity
  true judgment will maintain.

8 With juſtice he will keep & guide
  the world and ev'ry wight :
And ſo will yield with equity
  to ev'ry man his right.

9 He is protector of the poor,
  what time they be oppreſt :
He is in all adverſity
  their refuge and their reſt.
                    (Name,
10 And they that know thy holy
   therefore ſhall truſt in thee :
For thou forſakeſt not their ſuit
  in their neceſſity.

The ſecond part.
11 Sing Pſalms therefore unto the
   that dwells in Sion hill :   (Lord,
Publiſh among all Nations
  his noble acts and will.

12 For he is mindful of the blood
   of thoſe that be oppreſt :
Forgetting not th' afflicted heart,
  that ſeeks to him for reſt.

13 Have mercy L^d on me poor wretch
   whoſe en'mies ſtill remain :
Which from the gates of death are
  to raiſe me up again.   (wont

14 In Sion that I might ſet forth
   thy praiſe with heart and voice :
And that in thy ſalvation, Lord,
  my ſoul might ſtill rejoyce.

15 The heathen ſtick faſt in the pit
   that they themſelves prepar'd :
And in the net that they did ſet,
  their own feet faſt are ſnar'd.
                    (were good,
16 God ſhews his judgments which
   for ev'ry man to mark :
When as ye ſee the wicked man
  lie trapt in his own wark.

17 The wicked and deceitful men
   go down to hell for ever :
And all the people of the world
  that will not God remember.

18 But ſure the Lord will not forget
   the poor man's grief and pain :
The patient people never look
  for help of God in vain.

19 O Lord, ariſe, leſt men prevail
   that be of worldly might :
And let the heathen folk receive
  their judgment in thy ſight.

20 Lord, ſtrike ſuch terror, fear and
   into the hearts of them : (dread,
That they may know aſſuredly,
  they be but mortal men.

PSALM

Psalm x.

Cantus & Bassus.   PSALM X.   *Cambridge Tune.*

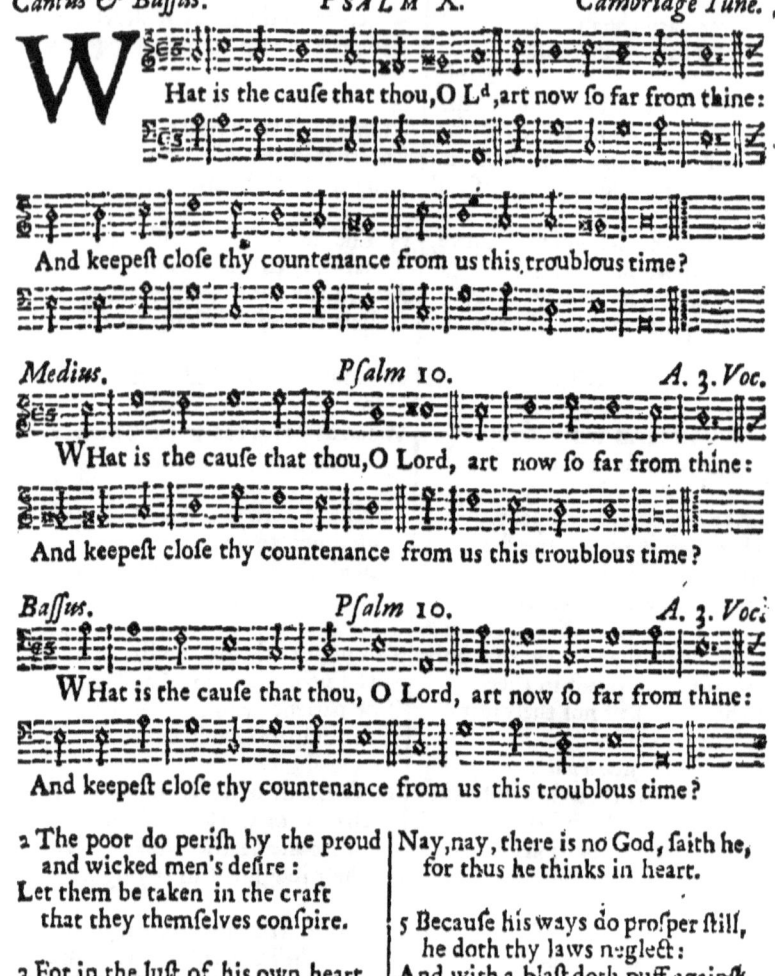

WHat is the cause that thou, O L^d, art now so far from thine:
And keepest close thy countenance from us this troublous time?

Medius.   Psalm 10.   *A. 3. Voc.*

WHat is the cause that thou, O Lord, art now so far from thine:
And keepest close thy countenance from us this troublous time?

Bassus.   Psalm 10.   *A. 3. Voc.*

WHat is the cause that thou, O Lord, art now so far from thine:
And keepest close thy countenance from us this troublous time?

2 The poor do perish by the proud
and wicked men's desire:
Let them be taken in the craft
that they themselves conspire.

3 For in the lust of his own heart
th'ungodly doth delight:
So doth the wicked praise himself,
and doth the Lord despight.

4 He is so proud, that right & wrong
he setteth all apart:

Nay, nay, there is no God, saith he,
for thus he thinks in heart.

5 Because his ways do prosper still,
he doth thy laws neglect:
And with a blast doth puff against
such as would him correct.

6 Tush, tush, saith he, I have no dread
lest mine estate should change:
And why? for all adversity
to him is very strange.

7 His

Pſalm x, xi.

7 His mouth is full of curſedneſs,
of fraud, deceit, and guile:
Under his tongue doth miſchief ſit,
and travel all the while.

8 He lieth hid in ways and holes,
to ſlay the innocent:
Againſt the poor that paſs him by,
his cruel eyes are bent.

9 And, like a lion, privily
lies lurking in his den:
If he may ſnare them in his net,
to ſpoil poor ſimple men.

10 And for the nonce full craftily
he coucheth down, I ſay:
So are great heaps of poor men made
by his ſtrong pow'r his prey.

The ſecond part.

11 Tuſh, God forgetteth this, ſaith he,
therefore I may be bold:
His countenance is caſt aſide,
he doth it not behold.

12 Ariſe, O Lord, O God, in whom
the poor man's hope doth reſt:
Lift up thine hand, forget not, Lord,
the poor that be oppreſt.

13 What blaſphemy is this to thee,
Lord, doſt thou not abhor't?
To hear the wicked in their heart
ſay, Tuſh, thou car'ſt not for't?

14 But thou feeſt all their wickedneſs,
and well doſt underſtand,
That friendleſs and poor fatherleſs
are left into thy hand.

15 Of wicked and malicious men,
then break the pow'r for ev'r:
That they with their iniquity
may periſh altogether.

16 The Lord ſhall reign for evermore
as King and God alone:
And he will chaſe the heathen folk
out of the land each one.
(plaint,

17 Thou hear'ſt, O L^d, the poor men's
their prayers and requeſt:
Their hearts thou wilt confirm, until
thine ears to hear be preſt.

18 To judge the poor and fatherleſs,
and help them to their right:
That they may be no more oppreſt
by men of worldly might.

Cantus & Baſſus. P SALM XI. *Glaſtenbury Tune.*

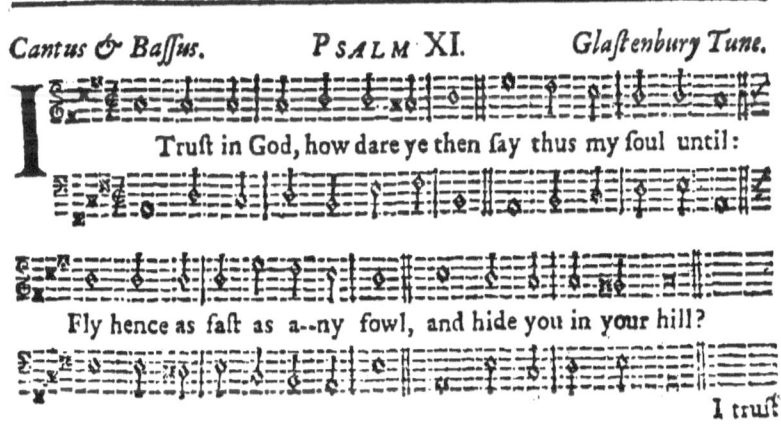

Truſt in God, how dare ye then ſay thus my ſoul until:

Fly hence as faſt as a--ny fowl, and hide you in your hill?

I truſt

Psalm xi, xii.

Medius.   Psalm 11.   *A. 3. Voc.*

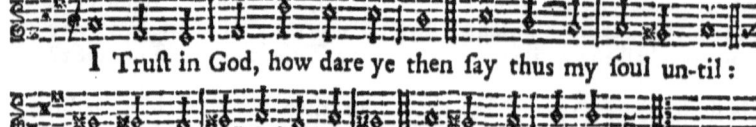

I Trust in God, how dare ye then say thus my soul un-til:

Fly hence as fast as a--ny fowl, and hide you in your hill?

Bassus.   Psalm 11.   *A. 3. Voc.*

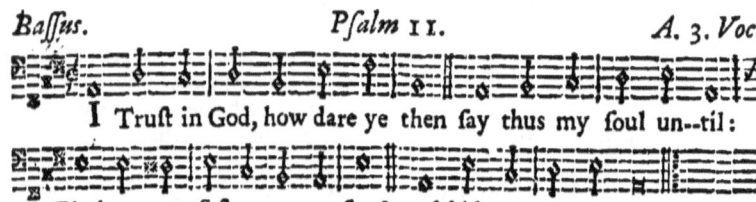

I Trust in God, how dare ye then say thus my soul un--til:

Fly hence as fast as a--ny fowl, and hide you in your hill?

2 Behold the wicked bend their bows,
and make their arrows prest:
To shoot in secret, and to hurt
the sound and harmless breast.

3 Of worldly hope all stays were (shrunk,
and clearly brought to nought:
Alas, the just and righteous man,
what evil hath he wrought?

4 But he that in his Temple is
most holy and most high:
And in the heavens hath his seat
of Royal Majesty.

The poor and simple man's estate
consid'reth in his mind:
And searcheth out full narrowly
the manners of mankind.

5 And with a chearful countenance
the righteous man will use:
But in his heart he doth abhor
all such as mischief muse.

6 And on the sinners casteth snares,
as thick as any rain:
Fire and brimstone, and whirlwinds (thick,
appointed for their pain.

7 Yee see then how a righteous God
doth righteousness embrace:
And to the just and upright men
shews forth his pleasant face.

Cantus & Bassus.   PSALM XII.   *Canterbury Tune.*

Help, Lord, for good and godly men do perish and decay;

Psalm xii.

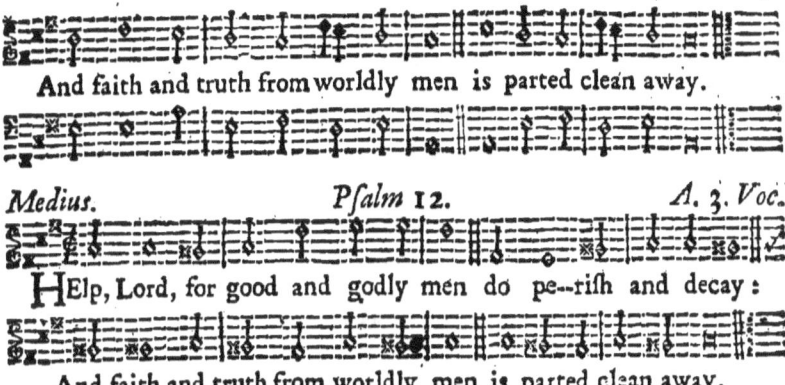

And faith and truth from worldly men is parted clean away.

Medius.   *Psalm* 12.   *A.* 3. *Voc.*

HElp, Lord, for good and godly men do pe-rish and decay:

And faith and truth from worldly men is parted clean away.

Bassus.   *Psalm* 12.   *A.* 3. *Voc.*

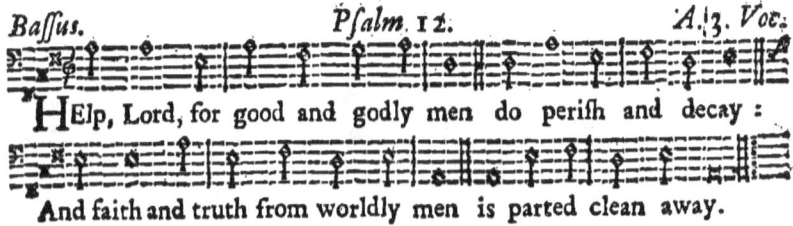

HElp, Lord, for good and godly men do perish and decay:

And faith and truth from worldly men is parted clean away.

2 Whoso doth with his neighbour
  his talk is all but vain: (talk,
For ev'ry man bethinketh how
  to flatter, lie, and fain.

3 But flatt'ring and deceitful lips,
  & tongues that be so stout: (brags,
To speak proud words, & make great
  the Lord soon cuts them out.

4 For they say still, We will prevail,
  our tongues shall us extol: (speak,
Our tongues are ours, we ought to
  what Lord shall us control?

5 But for the great complaint and cry
  of poor and men opprest:

Arise will I now, saith the Lord,
  and them restore to rest.

6 God's Word is like the silver pure,
  that from the earth is tri'd:
And hath no less than seven times
  in fire been purifi'd.

7 Now sith thy promise is to help,
  Lord, keep thy promise then:
And save us now, and evermore,
  from this ill kind of men.

8 For now the wicked world is full
  of mischiefs manifold:
When vanity with worldly men
  so highly is extoll'd.

Psalm xiii.

Cantus & Bassus. PSALM XIII. *Rochester Tune.*

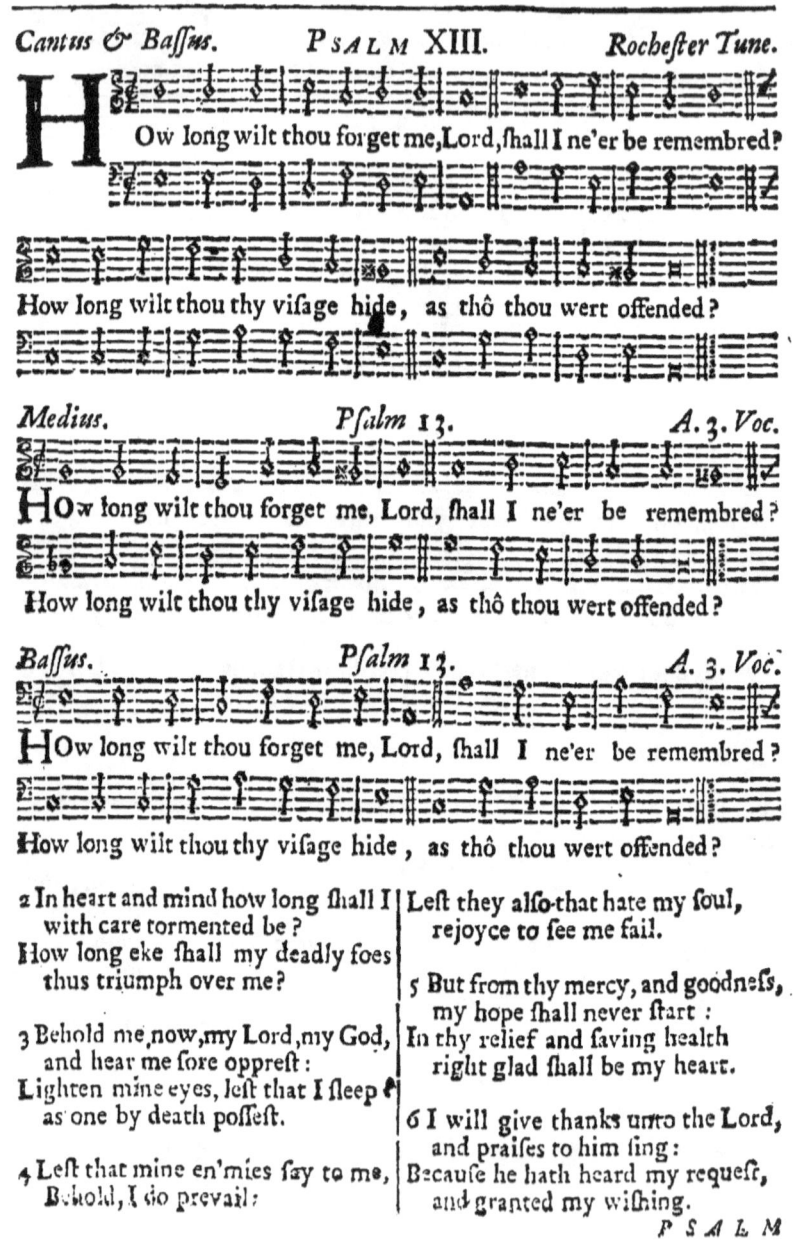

How long wilt thou forget me, Lord, shall I ne'er be remembered?

How long wilt thou thy visage hide, as thô thou wert offended?

Medius. Psalm 13. *A. 3. Voc.*

How long wilt thou forget me, Lord, shall I ne'er be remembered?

How long wilt thou thy visage hide, as thô thou wert offended?

Bassus. Psalm 13. *A. 3. Voc.*

How long wilt thou forget me, Lord, shall I ne'er be remembered?

How long wilt thou thy visage hide, as thô thou wert offended?

2 In heart and mind how long shall I
   with care tormented be?
How long eke shall my deadly foes
   thus triumph over me?

3 Behold me, now, my Lord, my God,
   and hear me sore opprest:
Lighten mine eyes, lest that I sleep
   as one by death possest.

4 Lest that mine en'mies say to me,
   Behold, I do prevail:

Lest they also that hate my soul,
   rejoyce to see me fail.

5 But from thy mercy, and goodness,
   my hope shall never start:
In thy relief and saving health
   right glad shall be my heart.

6 I will give thanks unto the Lord,
   and praises to him sing:
Because he hath heard my request,
   and granted my wishing.

PSALM

Psalm xiv.

Cantus & Bassus. **PSALM XIV.** *York Tune.*

THere is no God, as foolish men affirm and do conclude:

Their drifts are all corrupt and vain, not one of them doth good.

Medius. *Psalm 14.* *A. 3. Voc.*

THere is no God, as foolish men affirm and do conclude:

Their drifts are all corrupt and vain, not one of them doth good.

Bassus. *Psalm 14.* *A. 3. Voc.*

THere is no God, as foolish men affirm and do conclude:

Their drifts are all corrupt and vain, not one of them doth good.

2 The Lord beheld from heaven high
  the whole race of mankind :
And saw not one that sought indeed
  the living God to find.

3 They went all wide, and were cor-
  and truly there was none (rupt,
That in the world did any good,
  I say, there was not one.

4 Is all their judgment so far lost,
that all work mischief still?

Eating my people ev'n as bread,
  not one to seek God's will?

5 When they thus rage, then suddenly
  great fear on them shall fall:
For God doth love the righteous men,
  and will maintain them all.

6 Ye mock the doings of the poor,
  to their reproach and shame:
Because they put their trust in God,
  and call upon his Name.

7 But

20   Pſalm xiv, xv.

7 But who ſhall give thy people
and when wilt thou fulfil (health,
Thy promiſe made to Iſrael,
from out of Sion hill?

8 Ev'n when thou ſhalt reſtore again
ſuch as were captive led:
Then Jacob ſhall therein rejoyce,
and Iſrael ſhall be glad.

Cantus & Baſſus.   PSALM XV.   *Martyrs Tune.*

O Lord, in thy Tabernacle, who ſhall in-ha-bit ſtill?

Or whom wilt thou receive to dwell in thy moſt holy hill?

Medius.   *Pſalm 15.*   *A. 3. Voc.*

O Lord, in thy Ta--ber--na-cle, who ſhall in--ha--bit ſtill?

Or whom wilt thou receive to dwell in thy moſt holy hill?

Baſſus.   *Pſalm 15.*   *A. 3. Voc.*

O Lord, in thy Ta--ber--na--cle, who ſhall in--ha--bit ſtill?

Or whom wilt thou receive to dwell in thy moſt holy hill?

2 The man whoſe life is uncorrupt,
whoſe works are juſt and ſtraight:
Whoſe heart doth think the very truth,
whoſe tongue ſpeaks no deceit.

3 Nor to his neighbour doth none ill,
in body, goods, or name:

Nor willingly doth move falſe tales,
which might impair the ſame.

4 That in his heart regardeth not
malicious wicked men:
But thoſe that love and fear the Lord,
he maketh much of them.

Psalm xv, xvi.

5 His oath, and all his promises,
that keepeth faithfully:
Althô he make his cov'nant so
that he doth lose thereby.

6 That putteth not to usury
his money and his coin:

Nor for to hurt the innocent
doth bribe, or else purloin.

7 Whoso doth all things as you see,
that here is to be done,
Shall never perish in this world,
nor in the world to come.

Cantus & Bassus. PSALM XVI. *London Tune.*

LOrd, keep me, for I trust in thee, and do confess indeed,

Thou art my God, and of my goods, O Lord, thou hast no need.

Medius. Psalm 16. A. 3. Voc.

LOrd, keep me, for I trust in thee, and do confess indeed,

Thou art my God, and of my goods, O Lord, thou hast no need.

Bassus. Psalm 16. A. 3. Voc.

LOrd, keep me, for I trust in thee, and do confess indeed,

Thou art my God, and of my goods, O Lord, thou hast no need.

2 I give my goods unto the saints
that in the world do dwell:
And namely, to the faithful flock
in virtue that excell.

3 Their sorrows shall be multipli'd,
that vex themselves in vain:
And to make haste to other Gods,
in blind zeal take great pain.

Psalm xvi, xvii.

4 As for their bloody sacrifice,
   and off'rings of that sort,
I will not touch, nor yet thereof
   my lips shall make report,

5 For why? the Lord the portion is
   of mine inheritance:
And thou art he that dost maintain
   my rent, my lot, my chance.

6 The place wherein my lot did fall,
   in beauty did excell:
Mine heritage assign'd to me,
   doth please me wondrous well.

7 I thank the Lord that caused me
   to understand the right:
For by his means my secret thoughts
   doth teach me ev'ry night.

8 I set the Lord still in my sight,
   and trust him over all:
For he doth stand on my right hand,
   therefore I shall not fall.

9 Wherefore my heart and tongue
   do both rejoyce together: (also
My flesh and body rest in hope,
   When I this thing consider.
                    (grave,
10 Thou wilt not leave my soul in
   for, Lord, thou lovest me:
Nor yet wilt give thy holy One
   corruption for to see.

11 But wilt me teach the way to life,
   for all treasure and store
Of perfect joy are in thy face,
   and pow'r for evermore.

Cantus & Bassus.   P SALM XVII.   *Windsor Tune.*

O Lord, give ear to my just cause, attend when I complain:

And hear the pray'r that I put forth, with lips that do not feign.

Medius.   Psalm 17.   A. 3. Voc.

O Lord, give ear to my just cause, attend when I complain:

And hear the pray'r that I put forth, with lips that do not feign.

O Lord,

Psalm xvii.

Bassus.   Psalm 17.   *A. 3. Voc.*

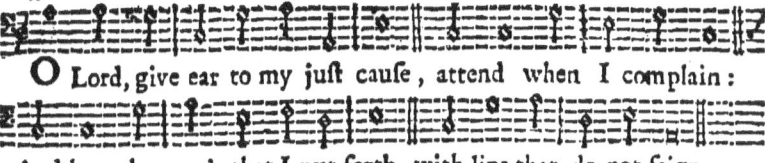

O Lord, give ear to my just cause, attend when I complain:

And hear the pray'r that I put forth, with lips that do not feign.

2 And let the judgment of my cause
proceed always from thee:
And let thine eyes behold, and clear
this my simplicity.
             (night,
3 Thou hast well tri'd me in the
and yet could'st nothing find
That I have spoken with my tongue,
that was not in my mind.

4 As for the works of wicked men,
and paths perverse and ill:
For love of thy most holy Name,
I have refrained still.
             (pure,
5 Then in thy paths that be most
stay me, Lord, and preserve:
That from the way wherein I walk,
my steps may never swerve.

6 For I do call to thee, O Lord,
surely thou wilt me aid: (well
Then hear my pray'r, & weigh right
the words that I have said.

7 O thou the Saviour of all them
that put their trust in thee,
Declare thy strength on them that
against thy Majesty.   (kick

8 O keep me as thou wouldest keep
the apple of thine eye:
And under covert of thy wings
defend me secretly.

The second part.
9 From wicked men that trouble me,
and daily me annoy:
And from my foes that go about
my soul for to destroy.
            (wealth,
10 Which wallow in their worldly
so full and eke so fat:
That in their pride they do not spare
to speak they care not what.
            (pass,
11 They lie in wait where I should
with craft me to confound:
And musing mischief in their minds,
to cast me to the ground.

12 Much like a lion greedily
that would his prey embrace:
Or lurking like a lion's whelp,
within some secret place.

13 Up, Lord, in haste prevent my foe,
and cast him at thy feet:
Save thou my soul from the ill man,
and with thy sword him smite.

14 Deliver me, Lord, by thy pow'r,
out of these tyrants hands:
Which now so long time reigned
and kept us in their bands. (have,

15 I mean from worldly men, to whom
all worldly goods are rife:
That have no hope, nor part of joy,
but in this present life.

Psalm xvii, xviii.

16 Thou of thy store their bellies fill'st
    with pleasure to their mind:
    Their Children have enough, and
    to theirs the rest behind. (leave

17 But I shall with pure conscience
    behold thy gracious face:
    So when I wake, I shall be full
    of thine image and grace.

Cantus & Bassus.   P SALM XVIII.   *Or to Windsor Tune.*

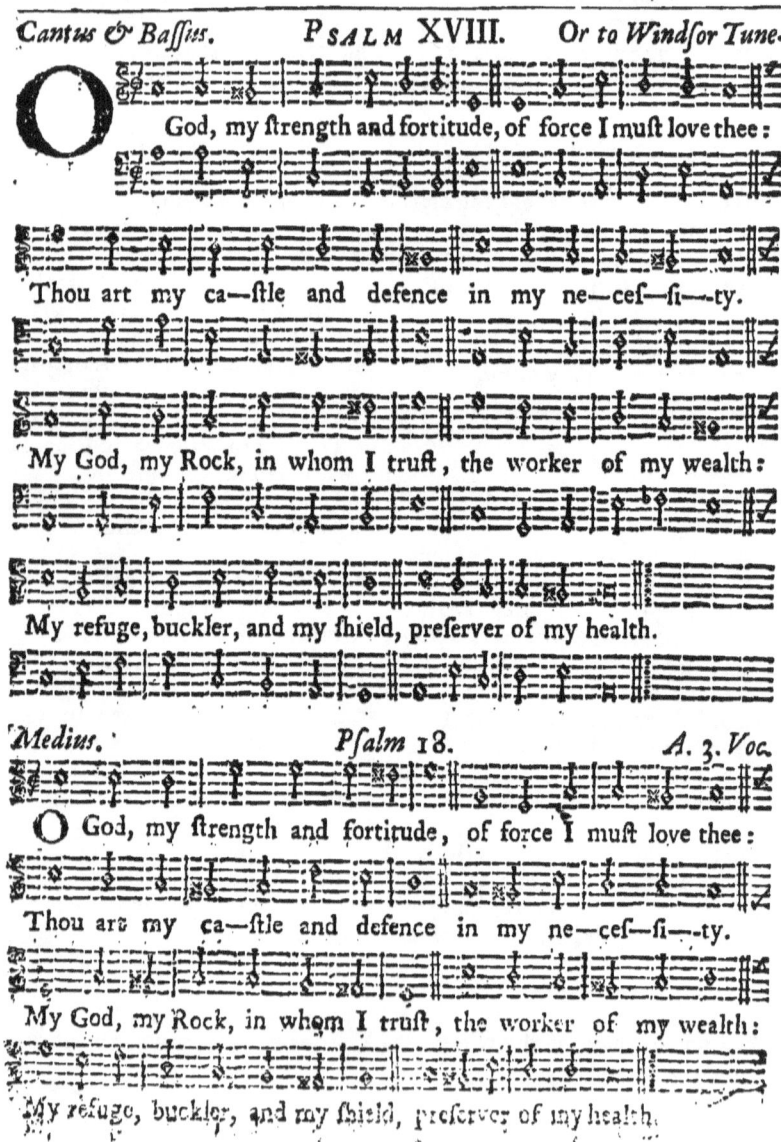

O God, my strength and fortitude, of force I must love thee:

Thou art my ca—stle and defence in my ne—cef—si—ty.

My God, my Rock, in whom I trust, the worker of my wealth:

My refuge, buckler, and my shield, preserver of my health.

Medius.   Psalm 18.   A. 3. Voc.

O God, my strength and fortitude, of force I must love thee:

Thou art my ca—stle and defence in my ne—cef—si—ty.

My God, my Rock, in whom I trust, the worker of my wealth:

My refuge, buckler, and my shield, preserver of my health.

Psalm xviii.

Bassus. Psalm 18. A. 3. Voc.

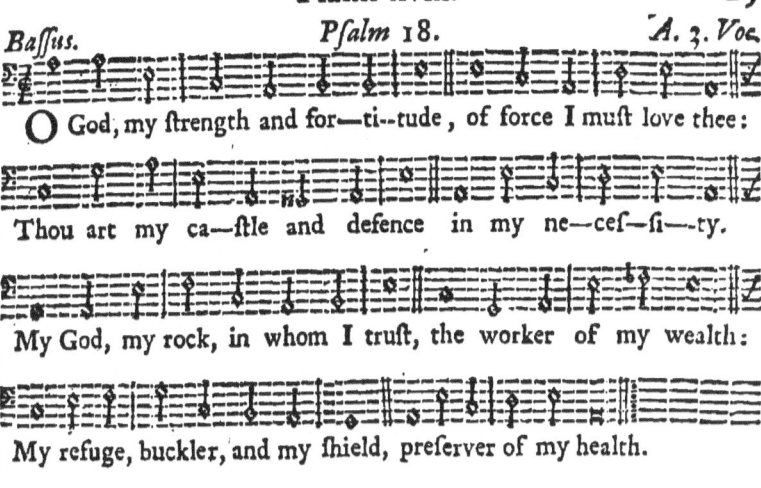

O God, my strength and for—ti--tude, of force I must love thee:

Thou art my ca—stle and defence in my ne—cef—si—ty.

My God, my rock, in whom I trust, the worker of my wealth:

My refuge, buckler, and my shield, preserver of my health.

3 When I sing laud unto the Lord,
    most worthy to be serv'd:
Then from my foes I am right sure
    that I shall be preserv'd.
4 The pangs of death did compass me,
    and bound me ev'ry where:
The flowing waves of wickedness
    did put me in great fear.

5 The sly and subtle snares of hell
    were round about me set:
And for my death, there was prepar'd
    a deadly trapping net.
6 I thus beset with pain and grief,
    did pray to God for grace:
And he forthwith did hear my plaint
    out of his holy place.

7 Such is his pow'r, that in his wrath
    he made the earth to quake:
Yea, the foundation of the mount
    of Basan for to shake.
8 And from his nostrils came a smoke,
    when kindled was his ire:
And from his mouth came kindled
    of hot consuming fire.   (coals

9 The Lord descended from above,
    and bow'd the heavens high:
And underneath his feet he cast
    the darkness of the sky.
10 On Cherubs, and on Cherubins,
    full royally he rode:
And on the wings of all the winds
    came flying all abroad.

The second part.

11 And like a den most dark he made
    his hid and secret place:
With waters black, and airy clouds,
    environed he was.
12 But when the presence of his face
    in brightness shall appear:
Then clouds consume, & in their stead
    come hail and coals of fire.

13 The fiery darts and thunderbolts
    disperse them here and there:
And with his often lightnings,
    he puts them in great fear.
14 Lord, at thy wrath & threatenings,
    and at thy chiding chear,
The springs and the foundations
    of all the world appear.

15 And

15 And from above the Lord sent
   to fetch me from below: (down
And pluck'd me out of waters great,
   that would me overflow.
16 And me deliver'd from my foes
   that would have made me thrall:
Yea, from such foes as were too strong
   for me to deal withal.

17 They did prevent me to oppress
   in time of my great grief:
But yet the Lord was my defence,
   my succour and relief.
18 He brought me forth in open place,
   whereas I might be free:
And kept me safe, because he had
   a favour unto me.

19 And as I was an innocent,
   so did he me regard:
And to the cleanness of my hands
   he gave me my reward.
20 For that I walked in his ways,
   and in his paths have trod:
And have not waver'd wickedly
   against my Lord and God.

The third part.

21 But evermore I have respect
   to his law and decree:
His statutes and commandements
   I cast not out from me.
22 But pure, and clean, & uncorrupt,
   appear'd before his face:
And did refrain from wickedness
   and sin in any case.

23 The Lord will therefore me re-
   as I have done aright: (ward,
And to the cleanness of my hands,
   appearing in his sight.
24 For, Lord, with him that holy is,
   wilt thou be holy too:
And with the good and virtuous men
   right virtuously wilt do.

25 And to the
   thy love thou
And thou wilt
   as wicked m
26 For thou dost
   in trouble w
And dost bring
   of them that

27 The Lord w
   that it shall
The Lord my
   my darkness
28 For by thy
   discomfit, Lo
By thee I scale
   the strength

29 Unspotted a
   his word is p
He is a sure de
   as in his fait
30 For who is G
   for other the
Or else, who is
   saving our G

The

31 The God th
   is he that I d
That all the w
   did evermore
32 That made
   in swiftness c
And for my sur
   into an open

33 He did in o
   to battel and
To break in sun
   he gave mine
34 Thou teach
   thy right hand
Thy love and f
   doth still inc

Psalm xviii.

hou makeſt plain by thee: my feet ling free.	43 A people ſtrange, to me unknown, and yet they ſhall me ſerve: And at the firſt obey my word, whereas mine own will ſwerve.
urſue, and take annoy'd: do not return, ſtroy'd.	44 I ſhall be irkſom to mine own, they will not ſee my light: But wander wide out of the way, and hide them out of ſight.
I wound my foes, è no more: fall down flat, ſo ſore.	45 But bleſſed be the living Lord, moſt worthy of all praiſe: That is my rock and ſaving health, praiſed be he always.
rd me with thy wiſe, (ſtrength ıtter'd abroad ıe riſe.	46 For God it is that gave me pow'r revenged for to be: And with his holy word ſubdu'd the people unto me.
ut into my hands es yoke: ou doſt divide ıy ſtroke. (ear,	47 And from my foes deliver'd me, and ſet me above thoſe That cruel and ungodly were, and up againſt me roſe.
lp, but none gave ith relief: ıy call'd for help, their grief.	48 And for this cauſe, O Lord my God, to thee give thanks I ſhall: And ſing out praiſes to thy Name among the Gentiles all.
part. before the wind, er feet: ıt like filthy clay he ſtreet. (folk, e from ſeditious are led: he heathen folk head.	49 Thou gaveſt great proſperity unto the King, I ſay: To David thine anointed King, and to his ſeed for aye. *To Father, Son, and Holy Ghoſt, all glory be therefore: As in beginning was, is now, and ſhall be evermore.*

PSALM

Psalm xix.

Cantus & Bassus.   PSALM XIX.   *York Tune.*

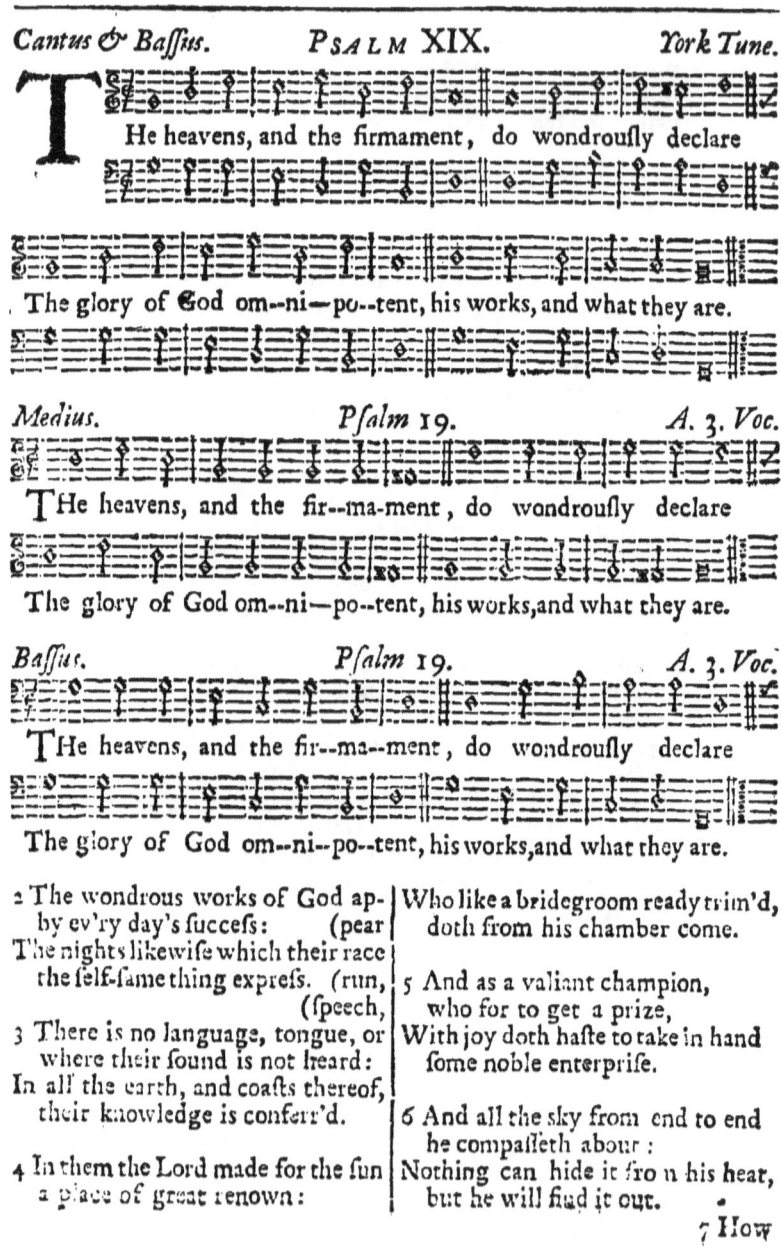

THe heavens, and the firmament, do wondrously declare
The glory of God om-ni-po-tent, his works, and what they are.

Medius.   Psalm 19.   A. 3. Voc.

THe heavens, and the fir-ma-ment, do wondrously declare
The glory of God om-ni-po-tent, his works, and what they are.

Bassus.   Psalm 19.   A. 3. Voc.

THe heavens, and the fir-ma-ment, do wondrously declare
The glory of God om-ni-po-tent, his works, and what they are.

2 The wondrous works of God ap-
   by ev'ry day's succefs: (pear
The nights likewife which their race
   the felf-fame thing exprefs. (run,
                                (fpeech,

3 There is no language, tongue, or
   where their found is not heard:
In all the earth, and coafts thereof,
   their knowledge is conferr'd.

4 In them the Lord made for the fun
   a place of great renown:

Who like a bridegroom ready trim'd,
   doth from his chamber come.

5 And as a valiant champion,
   who for to get a prize,
With joy doth hafte to take in hand
   fome noble enterprife.

6 And all the sky from end to end
   he compafleth about :
Nothing can hide it from his heat,
   but he will find it out.

7 How

Pſalm xix, xx.

7 How perfect is the law of God,
how is his cov'nant ſure:
Converting ſouls, and making wiſe
the ſimple and obſcure!
                (ments,
8 Juſt are the Lord's commande-
and glad both heart and mind:
His precepts pure, and giveth light
to eyes that be full blind.

9 The fear of God is excellent,
and doth endure for ever:
The judgments of the Lord are true,
and righteous altogether.

10 And more to be embrac'd alway
than fined gold, I ſay:
The hony, and the hony-comb,
are not ſo ſweet as they.

11 By them thy ſervant is forewarn'd
to have God in regard:
And in performance of the ſame,
there ſhall be great reward.

12 But, Lord, what earthly man doth
the errors of his life? (know
Then cleanſe me from my ſecret ſins,
which are in me moſt rife.

13 And keep me that preſumptuous
prevail not over me: (ſins
And ſo ſhall I be innocent,
and great offences flee.

14 Accept my mouth, & eke my heart,
my words and thoughts each one:
For my redeemer and my ſtrength,
O Lord, thou art alone.

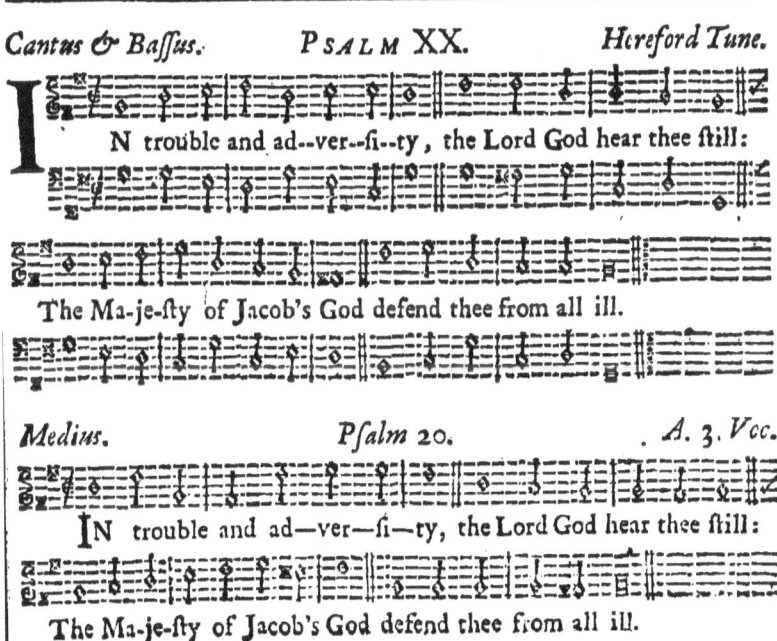

Cantus & Baſſus.   PSALM XX.   *Hereford Tune.*

IN trouble and ad--ver--ſi--ty, the Lord God hear thee ſtill:

The Ma-je-ſty of Jacob's God defend thee from all ill.

Medius.   *Pſalm 20.*   *A. 3. Vcc.*

IN trouble and ad—ver—ſi—ty, the Lord God hear thee ſtill:

The Ma-je-ſty of Jacob's God defend thee from all ill.

In

Psalm xx, xxi.

Bassus.   *Psalm* 20.   *A.* 3. *Voc.*

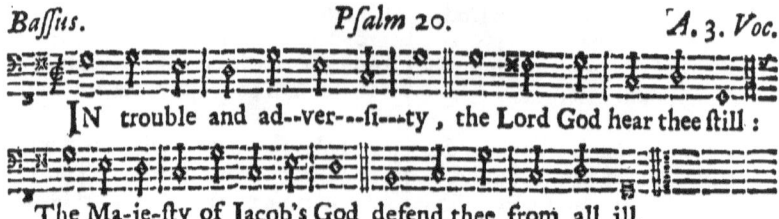

IN trouble and ad--ver---si---ty, the Lord God hear thee still:

The Ma-je-sty of Jacob's God defend thee from all ill.

2 And send thee from his holy place
   his help at ev'ry need:
And so in Sion stablish thee,
   and make thee strong indeed.

3 Remembring well the sacrifice
   that now to him is done,
And so receive right thankfully
   thy burnt-off'rings each one.

4 According to thy heart's desire,
   the Lord grant unto thee:
And all thy councel and advice
   full well perform may he.
                   (sav'st,
5 We shall rejoyce when thou us
   and our banners display:

Unto the Lord, which thy requests
   fulfilled hath alway.

6 The Lord will his anointed save,
   I know well by his grace:
And send him help by his right hand,
   out of his holy place.

7 In chariots some put confidence,
   and some in horses trust:
But we remember God our Lord,
   that keepeth promise just.

8 They fall down flat, but we do rise,
   and stand up stedfastly: (King,
9 Now save and help us, Lord and
   on thee when we do cry.

Cantus & Bassus.   P SALM XXI. *Or to St. David's Tune.*

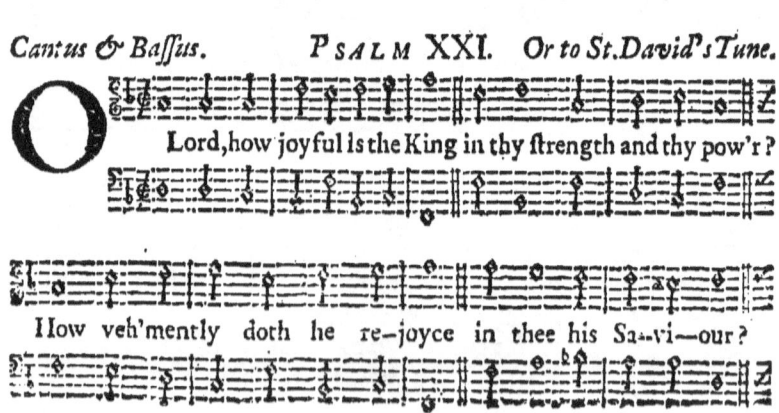

O Lord, how joyful is the King in thy strength and thy pow'r?

How veh'mently doth he re-joyce in thee his Sa--vi—our?

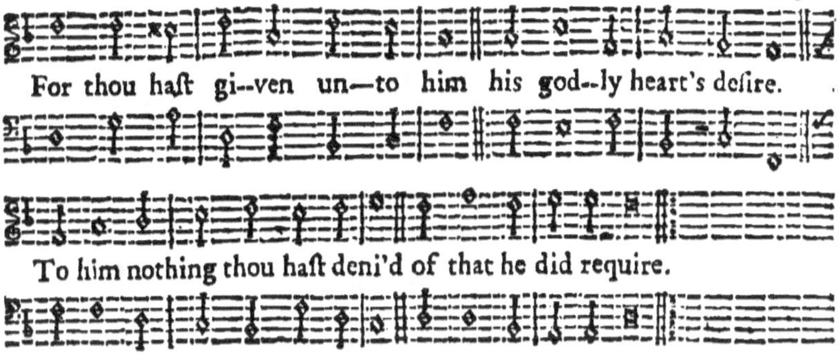

Psalm xxi. 31

For thou hast gi--ven un—to him his god--ly heart's desire.

To him nothing thou hast deni'd of that he did require.

Medius.   *Psalm 21.*   *A. 3. Voc.*

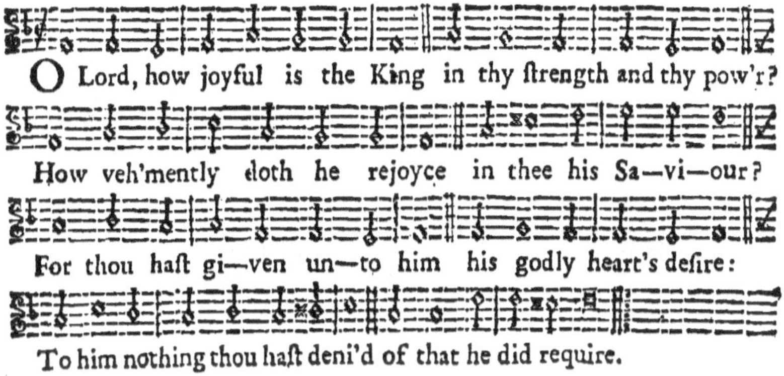

O Lord, how joyful is the King in thy strength and thy pow'r?

How veh'mently doth he rejoyce in thee his Sa—vi—our?

For thou hast gi—ven un—to him his godly heart's desire:

To him nothing thou hast deni'd of that he did require.

Basses.   *Psalm 21.*   *A. 3. Voc.*

O Lord, how joyful is the King in thy strength and thy pow'r?

How veh'mently doth he rejoyce in thee his Sa—vi—our?

For thou hast gi—ven un—to him his godly heart's desire:

To him nothing thou hast deni'd of that he did require.

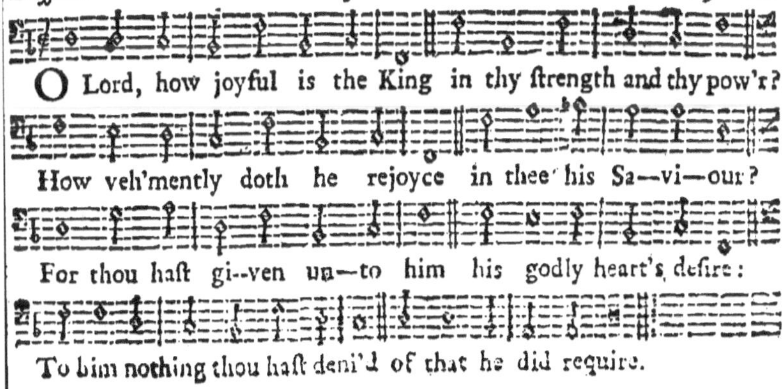

3 Then

Pſalm xxi, xxii.

3 Thou didſt prevent him with thy
  and bleſſings manifold: (gifts,
And thou haſt ſet upon his head
  a crown of perfect gold.
4 And when he asked life of thee,
  thereof thou mad'ſt him ſure:
To have long life, yea ſuch a life
  as ever ſhall endure.

5 Great is his glory by thy help,
  thy benefit and aid:
Great worſhip and great honor both,
  thou haſt upon him laid.
6 Thou wilt give him felicity
  that never ſhall decay:
And with thy chearful countenance,
  wilt comfort him alway.

7 For why? the King doth ſtrongly
  in God for to prevail: (truſt
Wherefore his goodneſs & his grace
  will not that he ſhall fail.
8 But let thy en'mies feel thy force,
  and thoſe that thee withſtand:
Find out thy foes, and let them feel
  the pow'r of thy right hand.

9 And like an oven burn them, Lord,
  in fiery flame and fume:
Thine anger ſhall deſtroy them all,
  and fire ſhall them conſume. (earth
10 And thou ſhalt root out of the
  their fruit that ſhould increaſe:
And from the number of thy folk,
  their ſeed ſhall end and ceaſe.

11 For why? much miſchief did they
  againſt thy holy Name: (muſe
Yet did they fail, and had no pow'r
  for to perform the ſame.
12 But as a mark thou ſhalt them ſet
  in a moſt open place:
And charge thy bow-ſtrings readily
  againſt thine en'mies face.

13 Be thou exalted, Lord, therefore,
  in thy ſtrength ev'ry hour:
So ſhall we ſing right ſolemnly,
  praiſing thy might and pow'r.
To Father, Son, and Holy Ghoſt,
  immortal Glory be:
As was, is now, and ſhall be ſtill,
  to all Eternitie.

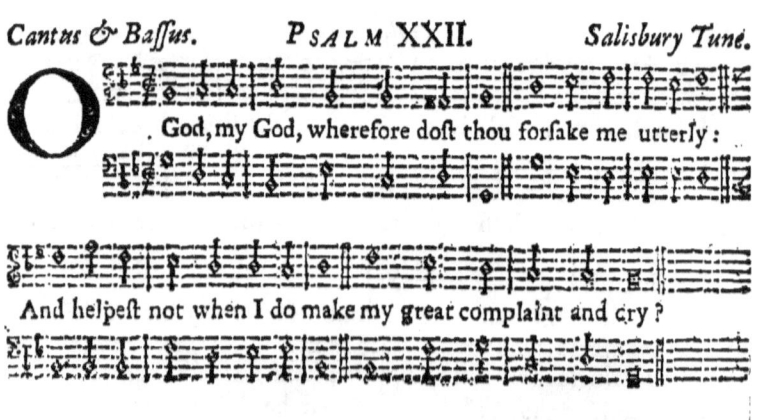

Cantus & Baſſus.   PSALM XXII.   *Salisbury Tune.*

O God, my God, wherefore doſt thou forſake me utterly:

And helpeſt not when I do make my great complaint and cry?

Psalm xxii.

Medius.   *Psalm 22.*   *A. 3. Voc.*

O God, my God, wherefore dost thou forsake me ut—ter--ly:

And helpest not when I do make my great complaint and cry?

Bassus.   *Psalm 22.*   *A. 3. Voc.*

O God, my God, wherefore dost thou forsake me ut—ter--ly:

And helpest not when I do make my great complaint and cry?

2 To thee my God, ev'n all day long
   I do both cry and call :
 I cease not all the night, and yet
   thou hearest not at all.

3 Ev'n thou that in thy sanctuary
   and holy place dost dwell:
 Thou art the comfort, and the joy,
   and glory of Israel.

4 And he, in whom our fathers old
   had all their hope for ever: (thee,
 And when they put their trust in
   thou didst them aye deliver.

5 They were deliver'd ever when
   they called on thy Name:
 And for the faith they had in thee,
   they were not put to shame.

6 But I am now become a worm,
   more like than any man :
 An out-cast, whom the people scorn,
   with all the spite they can.

7 All men despise, as they behold
   me walking on the way:
 They shoot the lip, & shake the head,
   and on this wise they say:

8 This man did glory in the Lord,
   his favour and his love :
 Let him redeem and help him now,
   his pow'r if he will prove.

9 But from the prison of the womb
   I was by thee releas'd :
 Thou didst preserve me still in hope,
   while I did suck the breast.

10 I was committed from my birth,
   with thee to have abode :
 Since I was in my mother's womb,
   thou hast been e'er my God.

The second part.

11 Then, Lord, depart not now from
   in this my present grief: (me
 Since I have none to be my help,
   my succour and relief.

Pſalm xxii.

12 So many bulls do compaſs me,
   that be full ſtrong of head:
Yea, bulls ſo fat, as thô they had
   in Baſan field been fed.

13 They gape upon me greedily,
   as thô they would me ſlay:
Much like a lion roaring out,
   and ramping for his prey.

14 But I drop down like water ſhed,
   my joynts in ſunder break,
My heart doth in my body melt
   like wax, I am ſo weak.
                (dry,
15 My ſtrength doth like a potſherd
   my tongue it cleaveth faſt
Unto my jaws, and I am brought
   to duſt of death at laſt.

16 And many dogs do compaſs me,
   in council they do meet:
Conſpiring ſtill againſt my life,
   piercing my hands and feet.

17 I was tormented, ſo that I
   might all my bones have told:
Yet ſtill upon me they do look,
   and ſtill they me behold.

18 My garments they divided have
   in parts among them all:
And for my coat they did caſt lots,
   to whom it might befall.

19 Therefore, I pray thee, be not far
   from me at my great need:
But rather, ſith thou art my ſtrength,
   to help me, Lord, make ſpeed.
                (ſoul
20 And from the ſword ſave thou my
   by thy might and thy pow'r:
And ever keep my darling dear
   from dogs that would devour.

21 And from the
   me all in ſund
And from the h
   Lord, ſafely me

22 Then ſhall I
   thy Majeſty r
And in thy Chu
   of thee the li
              The th
23 All ye that f
   thou Jacob, h
And all ye ſeed
   with rev'renc

24 For he deſpi
   he hideth not
His countenanc
   but hears the

25 Among the fo
   I will therefo
Thy praiſe, an
   for ſetting for

26 The poor ſhal
   and thoſe that
To know the L^d,
   their hearts ſ

27 The coaſts of
   the Lord, and
The heathen ſo
   before his ble

28 The kingdon
   the Lord ſha
And he ſhall be
   and King for

29 The rich me
   ſhall feed an
And in his preſ
   and bow thei

Pſalm xxii, xxiii. 35

30 And all that ſhall go down to duſt, of life by him ſhall taſte: A ſeed ſhall ſerve and worſhip him, while any world ſhall laſt.

31 They ſhall declare & plainly ſhew his truth and righteouſneſs, Unto a peoble yet unborn, who ſhall his Name confeſs.

Cantus & Baſſus.   PSALM XXIII.   *Canterbury Tune.*

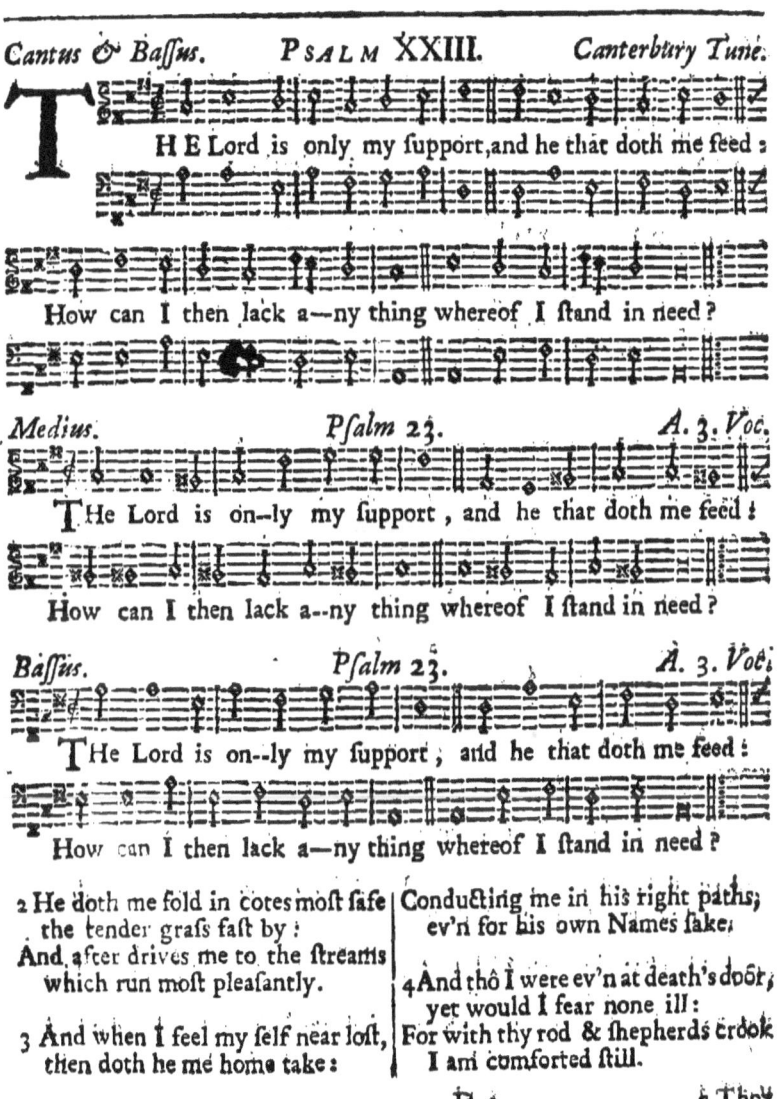

THE Lord is only my ſupport, and he that doth me feed:
How can I then lack a—ny thing whereof I ſtand in need?

Medius.   Pſalm 23.   *A. 3. Voc.*

THe Lord is on--ly my ſupport, and he that doth me feed:
How can I then lack a—ny thing whereof I ſtand in need?

Baſſus.   Pſalm 23.   *A. 3. Voc.*

THe Lord is on--ly my ſupport, and he that doth me feed:
How can I then lack a—ny thing whereof I ſtand in need?

2 He doth me fold in cotes moſt ſafe the tender graſs faſt by: And after drives me to the ſtreams which run moſt pleaſantly.

3 And when I feel my ſelf near loſt, then doth he me home take:

Conducting me in his right paths, ev'n for his own Names ſake.

4 And thô I were ev'n at death's door, yet would I fear none ill: For with thy rod & ſhepherds crook I am comforted ſtill.

Psalm xxiii, xxiv.

5 Thou haſt my table richly deck'd,
 in deſpite of my foe:
Thou haſt my head with balm re-
 my cup doth overflow. (freſh'd,

6 And finally, while breath doth laſt,
 thy grace ſhall me defend:
And in the houſe of God will I
 my life for ever ſpend.

Pſalm 23.   *By another Author.*   *Or to London Tune.*

MY ſhepherd is the living Lord,
 nothing therefore I need:
In paſtures fair, with waters calm,
 he ſets me forth to feed.

2 He did convert and glad my ſoul,
 and brought my mind in frame,
To walk in paths of righteouſneſs
 for his moſt holy Name.

3 Yea, thô I walk in vale of death,
 yet will I fear none ill:

Thy rod, thy ſtaff, doth comfort me,
 and thou art with me ſtill.

4 And in the preſence of my foes,
 my table thou ſhalt ſpread:
Thou ſhalt, O Lord, fill full my cup,
 and eke anoint my head.

5 Though all my life thy favour is
 ſo frankly ſhew'd to me,
That in thy houſe for evermore
 my dwelling place ſhall be.

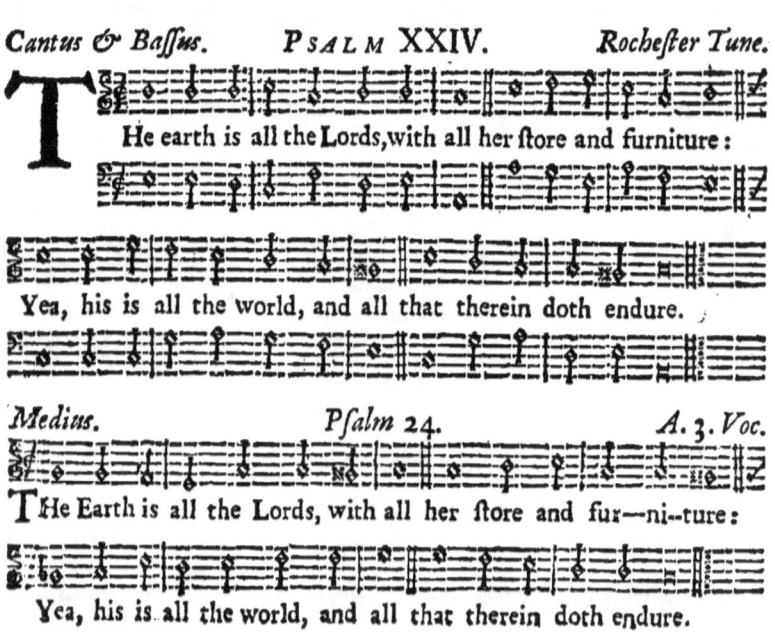

Cantus & Baſſus.   PSALM XXIV.   *Rocheſter Tune.*

THe earth is all the Lords, with all her ſtore and furniture:

Yea, his is all the world, and all that therein doth endure.

Medius.   *Pſalm 24.*   *A. 3. Voc.*

THe Earth is all the Lords, with all her ſtore and fur—ni-ture:

Yea, his is all the world, and all that therein doth endure.

Baſſus

Psalm xxiv, xxv.

Bassus.  *A. 3. Voc.*

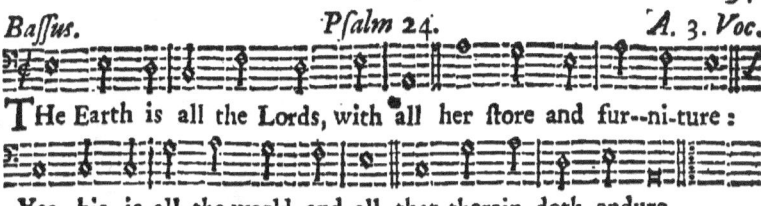

The Earth is all the Lords, with all her store and fur--ni-ture:

Yea, his is all the world, and all that therein doth endure.

2 For he hath fastly founded it
above the seas to stand:
And laid alow the liquid floods,
to flow beneath the land.

3 For who is he, O Lord, that shall
ascend into thy hill?
Or pass into thy holy place,
there to continue still?
     (heart
4 Whose hands are harmless,& whose
no spot there doth defile:
His soul not set on vanity,
who hath not sworn to guile.

5 Him that is such a one, the Lord
shall place in blissful plight:
And God, his God and Saviour,
shall yield to him his right:

6 This is the brood of travellers,
in seeking of his grace:

As Jacob did the Israelite.
in that time of his race.

7 Ye Princes, ope your gates, stand ope
the everlasting gate:
For there shall enter in thereby,
the King of glorious state.

8 Who is the King of glorious state?
The strong and mighty Lord:
The mighty Lord, in battle stout,
and trial of the sword.

9 Ye Princes, ope your gates, stand ope
the everlasting gate:
For there shall enter in thereby
the King of glorious state.

10 Who is the King of glorious state?
The Lord of hosts it is:
The kingdom and the royalty
of glorious state is his.

Cantus & Bassus.   PSALM XXV.   *Southwel Tune.*

I Lift my heart to thee, my God and guide most just:

Now suffer me to take no shame, for in thee do I trust.

Medius.

Psalm xxv.

Medius.   Psalm 25.   A. 3. Voc.

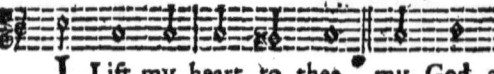

I Lift my heart to thee, my God and guide most just:
Now suffer me to take no shame, for in thee do I trust.

Bassus.   Psalm 25.   A. 3. Voc.

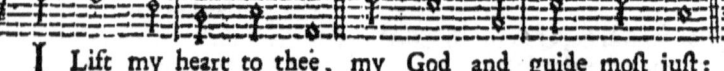

I Lift my heart to thee, my God and guide most just:
Now suffer me to take no shame, for in thee do I trust.

2 Let not my foes rejoyce,
  nor make a scorn of me:
And let them not be overthrown,
  that put their trust in thee.

3 But shame shall them befall
  which harm them wrongfully:
Therefore thy paths and thy right (ways
  unto me, Lord, descry.

4 Direct me in thy truth,
  and teach me I thee pray:
Thou art my God and Saviour,
  on thee I wait alway.

5 Thy mercies manifold
  remember, Lord, I pray:
Also thy pity plentiful,
  for they have been alway.

6 Remember not the faults
  and frailty of my youth:
Remember not how ignorant
  I have been of thy truth.

Nor after my deserts
  let me thy mercy find:
But of thine own benignity,
  Lord, have me in thy mind.

7 His mercy is full sweet,
  his truth a perfect guide:
Therefore the Lord will sinners (teach,
  and such as go aside.

8 The humble he will teach
  his precepts to obey:
He will direct in all his paths
  the lowly man alway.

9 For all the ways of God
  both truth and mercy are,
To them that do his covenant
  and statutes keep with care.

The second part.

10 Now for thy holy Name,
  O Lord, I thee intreat,
To grant me pardon for my sin,
  for it is wondrous great.

11 Who-

Psalm xxv, xxvi.

11 Whoso doth fear the Lord,
  by him he shall be kept,
To lead his life in such a way
  as he doth best accept.

12 His soul shall evermore
  in goodness dwell and stand,
His seed and his posterity
  inherit shall the land.

13 All those that fear the Lord,
  know his secret intent:
And unto them he doth declare
  his will and testament.

14 Mine eyes and thankful heart
  to him I will advance,
That pluck'd my feet out of the snare
  of sin and ignorance.

15 With mercy me behold,
  to thee I make my moan:
For I am poor and desolate,
  and comfortless alone.

16 The troubles of my heart
  are multipli'd indeed:

Bring me out of this misery,
  necessity and need.

17 Behold my poverty,
  mine anguish and my pain:
Remit my sin and mine offence,
  and make me clean again.

18 O Lord, behold my foes,
  how they do still increase:
Pursuing me with deadly hate,
  that fain would live in peace.

19 Preserve and keep my soul,
  and still deliver me:
And let me not be overthrown,
  because I trust in thee.

20 Let mine integrity
  and uprightness still be
My sure protection and defence,
  because I wait on thee.

21 Deliver, Lord, thy folk,
  and send them some relief,
I mean thy chosen Israel,
  from all their pain and grief.

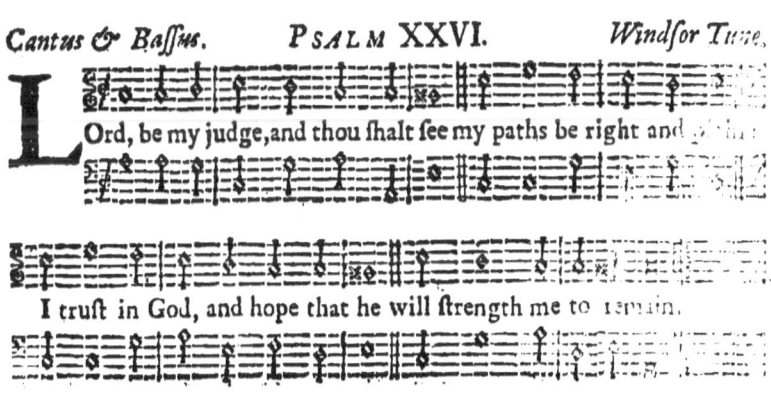

Cantus & Bassus. PSALM XXVI. Windsor Tune.

Lord, be my judge, and thou shalt see my paths be right and
I trust in God, and hope that he will strength me to remain.

Psalm xxvi.

Medius.   Psalm 26.   A. 3. Voc.

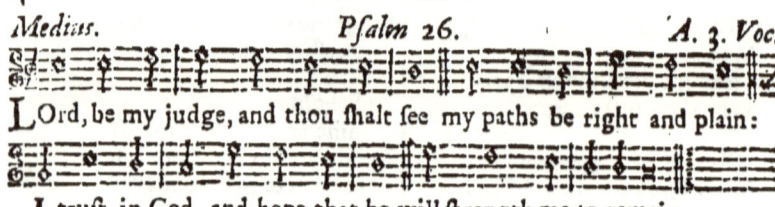

LOrd, be my judge, and thou shalt see my paths be right and plain:
I trust in God, and hope that he will strength me to remain.

Bassus.   Psalm 26.   A. 3. Voc.

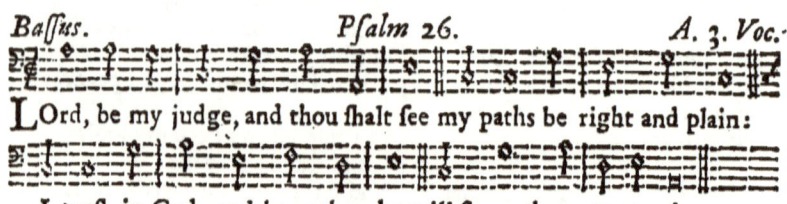

LOrd, be my judge, and thou shalt see my paths be right and plain:
I trust in God, and hope that he will strength me to remain.

2 Prove me, my God, I thee desire,
  my ways to search and try:
As men do prove their gold with fire,
  my reins and heart espy.

3 Thy goodness laid before my face,
  I do behold always:
For of thy truth I tread the path,
  and will do all my days.

4 I do not lust to haunt or use,
  with men whose deeds are vain:
To come in house I do refuse
  with the deceitful train.

5 I much abhor the wicked sort,
  their deeds I do despise:
I do not once to them resort,
  that wicked works devise.

6 My hands I wash, and do proceed
  in works to walk upright:
Then to thine altar I make speed,
  to offer there in sight:
              (praise,
7 That I may speak and preach the
  that doth belong to thee:

And so declare how wondrous ways
  thou hast been good to me.

8 O God, thy house I love most dear,
  to me it doth excell:
I have delight, and would be near
  whereas thy grace doth dwell.

9 O shut not up my soul with them
  in sin that take their fill:
Nor yet my life among those men
  that seek much blood to spill.
              (craft,
10 Whose hands and heart is full of
  much mischief there is found:
Corrupting Justice in its course,
  in bribes they do abound.

11 But I in righteousness intend
  my time and days to serve:
Have mercy, Lord, and me defend,
  so that I do not swerve.

12 My foot is staid for all assays,
  it standeth well and right:
Wherefore to God will I give praise,
  in all the peoples sight.

PSALM

Pſalm xxvii. 41

Cantus & Baſſus.   PSALM XXVII.   *Norwich Tune.*

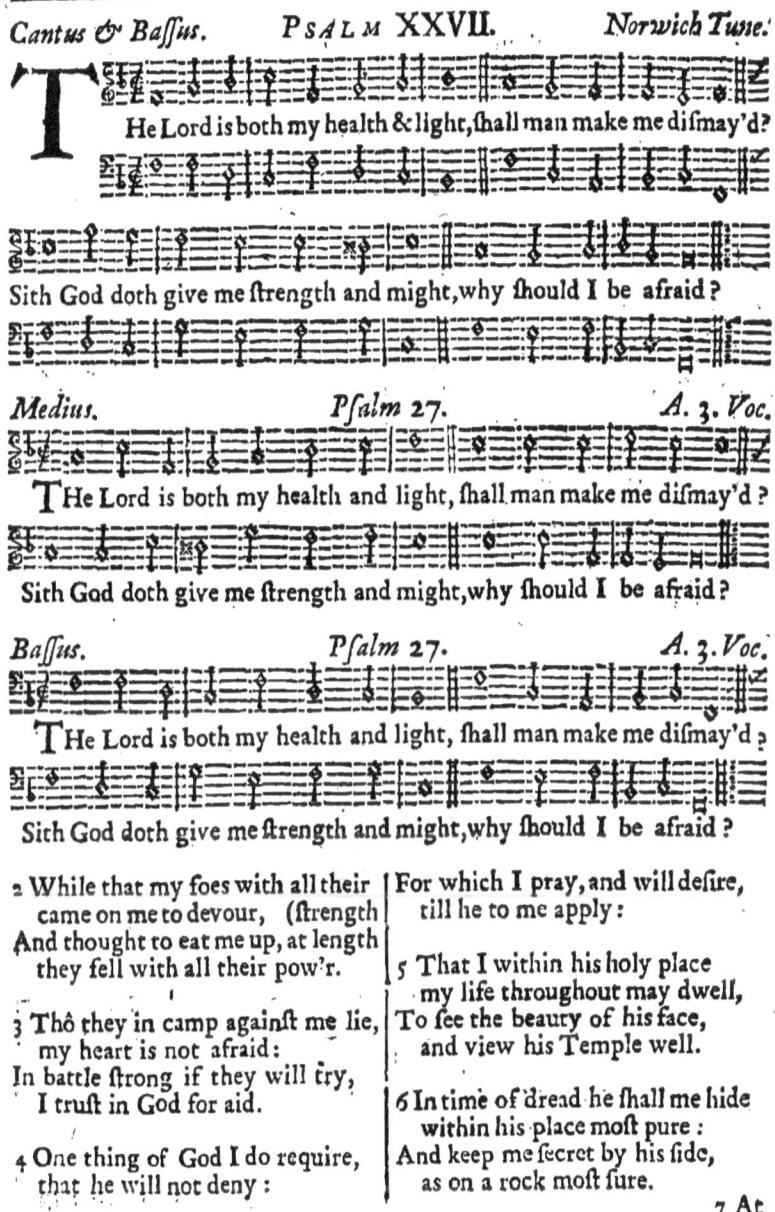

THe Lord is both my health & light, ſhall man make me diſmay'd?
Sith God doth give me ſtrength and might, why ſhould I be afraid?

Medius.   Pſalm 27.   *A. 3. Voc.*

THe Lord is both my health and light, ſhall man make me diſmay'd?
Sith God doth give me ſtrength and might, why ſhould I be afraid?

Baſſus.   Pſalm 27.   *A. 3. Voc.*

THe Lord is both my health and light, ſhall man make me diſmay'd?
Sith God doth give me ſtrength and might, why ſhould I be afraid?

2 While that my foes with all their
   came on me to devour, (ſtrength
And thought to eat me up, at length
   they fell with all their pow'r.

3 Thô they in camp againſt me lie,
   my heart is not afraid:
In battle ſtrong if they will try,
   I truſt in God for aid.

4 One thing of God I do require,
   that he will not deny:

For which I pray, and will deſire,
   till he to me apply:

5 That I within his holy place
   my life throughout may dwell,
To ſee the beauty of his face,
   and view his Temple well.

6 In time of dread he ſhall me hide
   within his place moſt pure:
And keep me ſecret by his ſide,
   as on a rock moſt ſure.

7 At

Pſalm xxvii, xxviii.

7 At length I know the L's good grace
 ſhall make me ſtrong and ſtout,
My foes to foil, and clean deface,
 that compaſs me about.

8 Therefore within his houſe will I
 give ſacrifice of praiſe:
With pſalms and ſongs I will apply
 to laud the Lord always.

The ſecond part.

9 Lord, hear the voice of my requeſt,
 for which to thee I cry:
Have mercy, Lord, on me oppreſs'd,
 and help me ſpeedily.

10 My heart confeſſeth unto thee,
 I ſue to have thy grace:
Then ſeek my face, ſaid'ſt thou to me,
 Lord, I will ſeek thy face.

11 In wrath turn not thy face away,
 nor ſuffer me to ſlide:
Thou art my help ſtill to this day,
 be ſtill my God and guide.

12 My parents both their ſon forſook,
 and caſt me off at large:
Yet then the Lord himſelf did take
 of me the care and charge.

13 Teach me, O Lord, the way to thee,
 and lead me on forth right,
For fear of ſuch as watch for me,
 to trap me if they might.

14 O leave me not unto the will
 of them that be my foes:
For they ſurmiſe againſt me ſtill
 falſe witneſs to depoſe.

15 I utterly ſhould faint, but that
 this hope ſupporteth me,
That in the land wherein I live,
 God's goodneſs I ſhall ſee.

16 Truſt ſtill in God, whoſe whole (thou art,
 his will abide thou muſt:
He will ſupport and eaſe thy heart,
 if thou in him do truſt.

Cantus & Baſſus. PSALM XXVIII. York Tune.

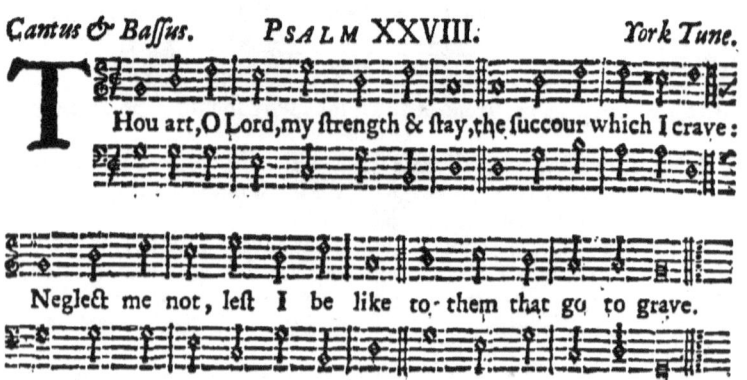

Hou art, O Lord, my ſtrength & ſtay, the ſuccour which I crave:

Neglect me not, left I be like to them that go to grave.

Medius.

Psalm xxviii.

Medius.   *Psalm 28.*   *A. 3. Voc.*

THou art, O Lord, my strength and stay, the succour which I crave:

Neglect me not, lest I be like to them that go to grave.

Bassus.   *Psalm 28.*   *A. 3. Voc.*

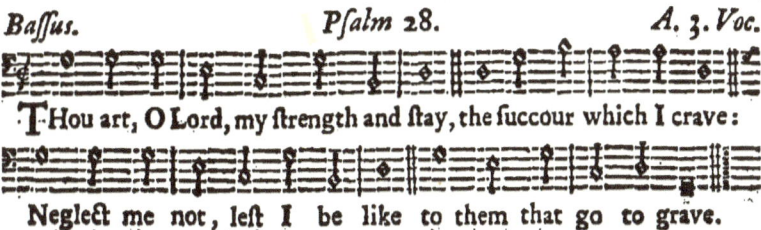

THou art, O Lord, my strength and stay, the succour which I crave:

Neglect me not, lest I be like to them that go to grave.

2 My voice and supplications hear,
  when unto thee I cry,
When I lift up my hands unto
  thy holy ark most high,

3 Repute me not among those men
  in sin that take their fill :
That speak right fair unto their
  but think in heart full ill. (friends,

4 According to those wicked deeds
  which they did most regard :
And after their inventions
  let them receive reward.

5 Because they never mind the words
  of God, he will therefore,
In stead of building of them up,
  destroy them evermore.

6 To render thanks unto the Lord,
  how great a cause have I,
My voice, my pray'r, and my com-
  that heard so willingly ! (plaint,

7 He is my shield and fortitude,
  my buckler in distress :
My hope, my help, my heart's relief,
  my song shall him confess.

8 He is our strength and our defence,
  our foes for to resist :
The health and the salvation
  of his elect be Christ.

9 Thy people and thine heritage,
  Lord, bless, guide, and preserve :
Increase them, L^d, & rule their hearts
  that they may never swerve.

Cantus & Bassus. PSALM XXIX. *Norwich Tune*

Give to the Lord, ye Potentates, ye Rulers of the world:

Give ye all praise, honour, and strength, unto the living Lord.

Medius. Psalm 29. *A. 3. Voc*

Give to the Lord, ye Po-ten--tates, ye Rulers of the world:

Give ye all praise, honour, and strength, unto the living Lord.

Bassus. Psalm 29. *A. 3. Voc*

Give to the Lord, ye Po-ten--tates, ye Rulers of the world:

Give ye all praise, honour, and strength, unto the living Lord.

2 Give glory to his holy Name,
  and honour him alone:
Worship him in his Majesty,
  within his holy throne.

3 His voice doth rule the waters all,
  ev'n as himself doth please:
He doth prepare the thunder-claps,
  and governs all the seas.

4 The voice of God is of great force,
  and wondrous excellent:

It is most mighty in effect,
  and most magnificent.

5 The voice of God doth rend and break
  the Cedar-trees so long:
The Cedar-trees of Lebanon,
  which are most high and strong.

6 And makes them leap like as a calf,
  or else the unicorn:
Not only trees, but mountains great,
  whereon the trees are born.

7 His

Psalm xxix, xxx. 45

7 His voice divides the flames of fire,
and shakes the wilderness:
8 It makes the desert quake for fear,
that called is Cades.

9 It makes the hinds for fear to calve,
and makes the coverts plain:
Then in his Temple ev'ry man
his glory doth proclaim.

10 The Lord was set above the floods,
ruling the raging sea:
So shall he reign as Lord and King
for ever and for aye.
                          (pow'r,
11 The Lord will give his people
in virtue to increase:
The Lord will bless his chosen flock
with everlasting peace.

Cantus & Bassus.   P SAL M XXX.   *Or to Rochester Tune.*

A LL laud & praise with heart & voice, O Lord, I give to thee:

Which didst not make my foes rejoyce, but hast ex—al—ted me:

O Lord, my God, to thee I cry'd in all my pain and grief:

Thou gav'st an ear, and didst provide to ease me with relief.

Medius.   *Psalm 30.*   *A. 3. Voc.*

A LL laud and praise with heart and voice, O Lord, I give to thee:

Which didst not make my foes rejoyce, but hast ex—al—ted me.

                                                O Lord,

Psalm xxx.

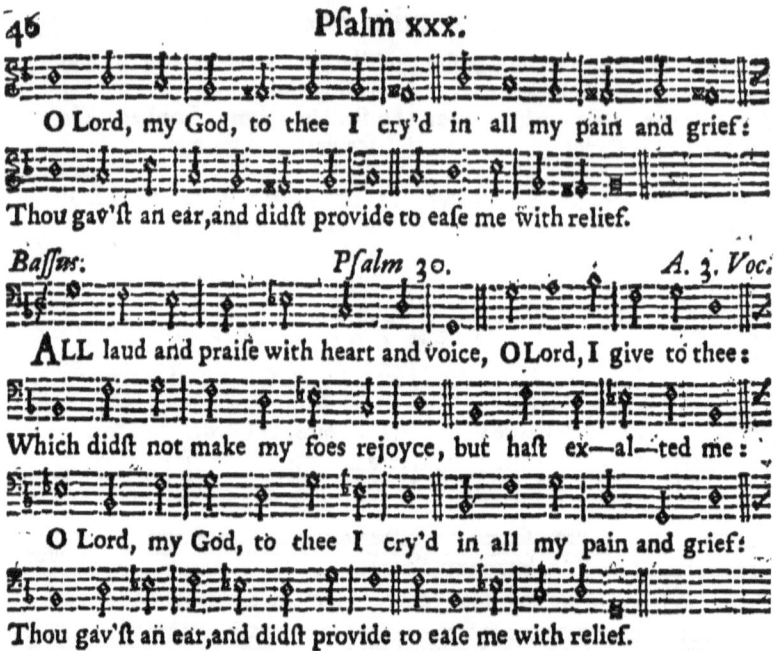

O Lord, my God, to thee I cry'd in all my pain and grief:
Thou gav'st an ear, and didst provide to ease me with relief.

Bassus: *Psalm 30.*   A. 3. Voc.

ALL laud and praise with heart and voice, O Lord, I give to thee:
Which didst not make my foes rejoyce, but hast ex—al—ted me:
O Lord, my God, to thee I cry'd in all my pain and grief:
Thou gav'st an ear, and didst provide to ease me with relief.

3 Of thy good will thou hast cal'd back
  my soul from hell to save: (lack,
Thou didst revive when strength did
  and kept'st me from the grave.

4 Sing praise, ye saints, that prove and
  the goodness of the Lord: (see
In memory of his Majesty
  rejoyce with one accord.

5 For why? his anger but a space
  doth last and slack again:
But in his favour and his grace
  always doth life remain.
Tho gripes of grief & pangs full sore
  abide with us all night,
The Lord to joy shall us restore
  before the day be light.

6 When I enjoy'd the world at will,
  thus would I boast and say.
Tush, I am sure to feel none ill,
  my wealth shall not decay.

7 For thou, O Lord, of thy good grace
  didst send me strength and aid:
But when thou turn'dst away thy face,
  my mind was sore dismay'd.

8 Wherefore again then did I cry
  to thee, O Lord of might:
And my complaints did multiply,
  praying both day and night.

9 What gain is in thy blood, said I,
  if death destroy my days?
Can dust declare thy Majesty,
  or give thy truth its praise?

10 Wherfore, my God, some pity take,
  O Lord, I thee desire:
Do not this simple soul forsake,
  of thee help I require. (woe

11 Then didst thou turn my grief and
  in a cheerful voice: (fro,
The mourning weed thou took'st me
  and mad'st me to rejoyce.

12 Where-

Pſalm xxx, xxxi. 47

12 Wherefore my ſoul inceſſantly
ſhall ſing unto thy praiſe:
My Lord, my God, to thee will I
give laud and thanks always.

To Father, Son, and Holy Ghoſt,
all glory be therefore:
As in beginning was, is now,
and ſhall be evermore.

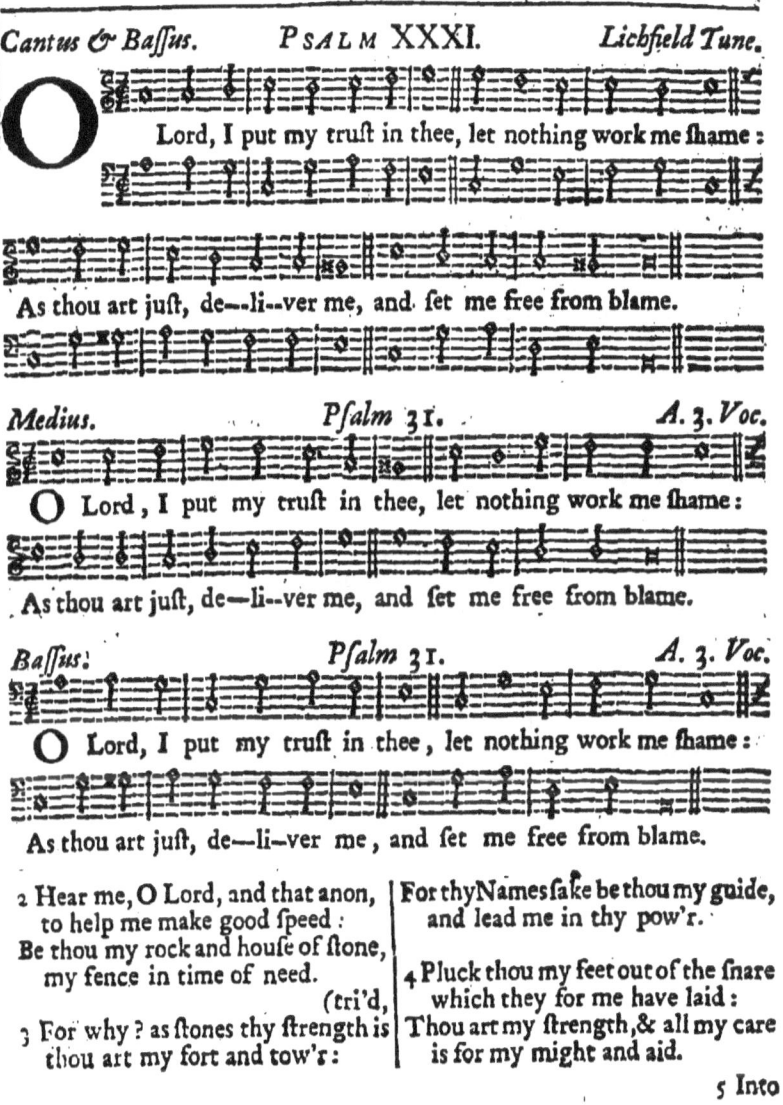

Cantus & Baſſus.   P SA L M XXXI.   *Lichfield Tune.*

O Lord, I put my truſt in thee, let nothing work me ſhame:

As thou art juſt, de—li--ver me, and ſet me free from blame.

Medius.   Pſalm 31.   *A. 3. Voc.*

O Lord, I put my truſt in thee, let nothing work me ſhame:

As thou art juſt, de—li--ver me, and ſet me free from blame.

Baſſus.   Pſalm 31.   *A. 3. Voc.*

O Lord, I put my truſt in thee, let nothing work me ſhame:

As thou art juſt, de—li--ver me, and ſet me free from blame.

2 Hear me, O Lord, and that anon,
to help me make good ſpeed:
Be thou my rock and houſe of ſtone,
my fence in time of need.
                              (tri'd,
3 For why? as ſtones thy ſtrength is
thou art my fort and tow'r:

For thy Names ſake be thou my guide,
and lead me in thy pow'r.

4 Pluck thou my feet out of the ſnare
which they for me have laid:
Thou art my ſtrength, & all my care
is for my might and aid.

5 Into

Pſalm xxxi.

5 Into thy hands, Lord, I commit
 my ſpirit, which is thy due:
For why? thou haſt redeemed it,
 O Lord my God moſt true.

6 I hate ſuch folk as will not part
 from things to be abhorr'd:
When they on trifles ſet their heart,
 my truſt is in the Lord.

7 For I will in thy mercy joy,
 I ſee it doth excell: (annoy,
Thou ſeeſt when ought would me
 and know'ſt my ſoul full well.

8 Thou haſt not left me in their hand,
 that would me over-charge:
But thou haſt ſet me out of band,
 to walk abroad at large.

The ſecond part.

9 Great grief, O Lord, doth me aſſail,
 ſome pity on me take: (fail,
Mine eyes wax dim, my ſight doth
 my womb for woe doth ake.

10 My life is worn with grief & pain,
 my years in woe are paſt: (dain
My ſtrength is gone, & through diſ-
 my bones corrupt and waſte.

11 Among my foes I am a ſcorn,
 my friends are all diſmay'd:
My neighbours and my kinſmen
 to ſee me are afraid. (born,

12 As men once dead are out of mind,
 ſo am I now forgot:
As ſmall effect in me they find,
 as in a broken pot.

13 I heard the brags of all the rout,
 their threats my mind did fray:
How they conſpir'd, and went about
 to take my life away.

14 But, Lord, I truſt in thee for aid,
 not to be over-trod:
For I confeſs, and ſtill have ſaid,
 thou art my Lord and God.

15 The length of all my life and age,
 O Lord, is in thy hand:
Defend me from the wrath and rage
 of them that me withſtand.

16 To me thy ſervant, Lord, expreſs
 and ſhew thy joyful face:
And ſave me, Lord, for thy goodneſs,
 thy mercy, and thy grace.

The third part.

17 Lord, let me not be put to blame,
 for that on thee I call:
But let the wicked bear the ſhame,
 and in the grave to fall.

18 O Lord, make dumb their lips out-
 which are addict to lies: (right,
And cruelly with pride and ſpight,
 againſt the juſt deviſe.

19 O how great good haſt thou in
 laid up full ſafe for them (ſtore,
That fear and truſt in thee therefore,
 before the ſons of men! (guide

20 Thy preſence ſhall them fence and
 from all proud brags and wrongs:
Within thy place thou ſhalt them hide
 from all the ſtrife of tongues.

21 Thanks to the Lord that hath de-
 on me his grace ſo far: (clar'd
Me to defend with watch and ward,
 as in a town of war.

22 Thus did I ſay both day & night,
 when I was ſore oppreſt:
Lo, I was clean caſt out of ſight,
 yet heard'ſt thou my requeſt.

23 Ye

Psalm xxxi, xxxii. 49

23 Ye saints, love ye the Lord alway,
the faithful he doth guide:
And to the proud he doth repay
according to their pride.

24 Be of good courage evermore,
on God your strength depend:
For those that put their trust in him,
he ever will defend.

Cantus & Bassus.   PSALM XXXII.   *St. Mary's Tunes*

He man is blest whose wickedness the Lord doth clean pass by:

And he whose sin is likewise hid, and cover'd se-cret-ly.

Medius.   *Psalm 32.*   *A. 3. Voc.*

THe man is blest, whose wickedness the Lord doth clean pass by:

And he whose sin is likewise hid, and cover'd secretly.

Bassus.   *Psalm 32.*   *A. 3. Voc.*

THe man is blest, whose wickedness the Lord doth clean pass by:

And he whose sin is likewise hid, and cover'd secretly.

2 And blest is he to whom the Lord
imputeth not his sin:
Which in his heart hath hid no guile,
nor fraud is found therein.

3 For whilst that I kept close my sin
in silence and constraint,

My bones did wear and waste away
with daily moan and plaint.

4 For night and day thy hand on me
so grievous was and smart,
That all my blood and humors moist
to driness did convert.

5 I did

50   Pſalm xxxii, xxxiii.

5 I did therefore confeſs my fault,
   and all my ſins diſcover:
Then thou, O Lord, didſt me forgive,
   and all my ſins paſs over.
                              (fore,
6 The humble man ſhall pray there-
   and ſeek thee in due time:
So that the floods of waters great
   ſhall have no pow'r on him.

7 When trouble and adverſity
   do compaſs me about,
Thou art my refuge and my joy,
   and thou doſt rid me out.

8 Come hither, and I will thee teach
   how thou ſhalt walk aright:

I will thee guide as I my ſelf
   have learn'd by proof and ſight.

9 Be not ſo rude and ignorant
   as is the horſe and mule,
Whoſe mouth without a rein or bit
   from harm thou canſt not rule.

10 The wicked man ſhall manifold
   ſorrows and griefs ſuſtain:
But unto him that truſts in God,
   his goodneſs ſhall remain.

11 Be merry therefore in the Lord,
   ye juſt lift up your voice:
And ye of pure and perfect heart
   with chearfulneſs rejoyce.

Cantus & Baſſus.   PSALM XXXIII. Or to St. David's Tune.

YE right'ous in the Lord rejoyce, it is a ſeemly ſight,

That upright men with thankful voice ſhould praiſe the Lord of might.

Praiſe ye the Lord with harp and ſong, in pſalms and pleaſant things:

With lute and Inſtrument al--ſo that ſoundeth with ten ſtrings.

Ye

Pſalm xxxiii.

Medius.   Pſalm 33.   *A. 3. Voc.*

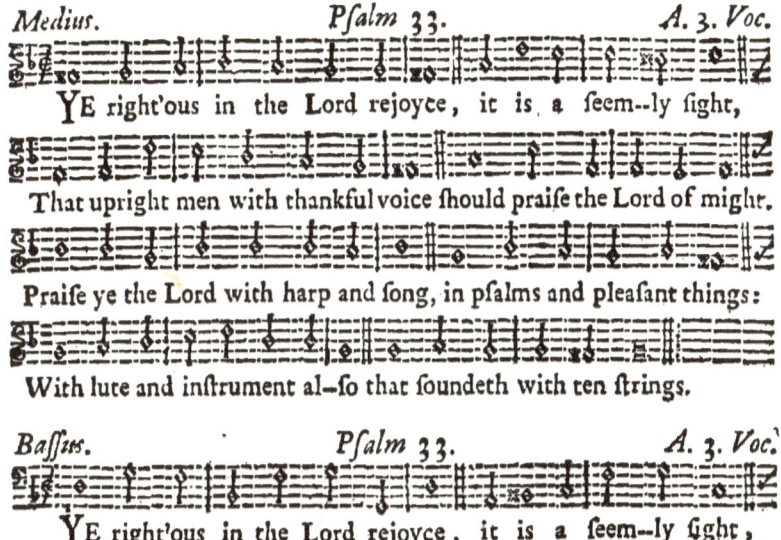

YE right'ous in the Lord rejoyce, it is a ſeem--ly ſight,

That upright men with thankful voice ſhould praiſe the Lord of might.

Praiſe ye the Lord with harp and ſong, in pſalms and pleaſant things:

With lute and inſtrument al--ſo that ſoundeth with ten ſtrings.

Baſſus.   Pſalm 33.   *A. 3. Voc.*

YE right'ous in the Lord rejoyce, it is a ſeem--ly ſight,

That upright men with thankful voice ſhould praiſe the Lord of might.

Praiſe ye the Lord with harp and ſong, in pſalms and pleaſant things:

With lute and inſtrument al--ſo that ſoundeth with ten ſtrings.

3 Sing to the Lord a ſong moſt new,
with courage give him praiſe:
4 For why? his word is ever true,
his works and all his ways.
5 To judgment, equity, and right,
he hath a great good will:
And with his gifts he doth delight
the earth throughout to fill,

6 For by the word of God alone
the heav'ns above were wrought:
Their hoſts and powers ev'ry one
his breath to paſs hath brought.

7 The waters great gather'd hath he
on heaps within the ſhore:
And hid them in the depth to be,
as in a houſe of ſtore,

8 All men on earth both ſmall & great
fear God and keep his law:
Ye that inhabit in each coaſt,
dread him and ſtand in awe.

9 What he commanded wrought it
at once with preſent ſpeed: (was
What he doth will is brought to paſs
with full effect indeed.

Psalm xxxiii, xxxiv.

10 The counsels of the nations rude
  the Lord doth bring to nought:
He doth defeat the multitude
  of their device and thought.
11 But his decrees continue still,
  they never slack nor swage:
The motions of his mind and will
  take place in ev'ry age.

The second part.

12 And blest are they to whom the L^d
  as God and guide is known:
Whom he doth chuse of meer accord
  to take them as his own.   (sight
13 The Lord from heav'n did cast his
  on men mortal by birth:
14 Beholding from his seat of might
  the dwellers on the earth.
               (wrought
15 The Lord, I say, whose hand hath
  man's heart, and doth it frame:
For he alone doth know the thought,
  and working of the same.
16 A king that trusteth in his host,
  shall nought prevail at length:
The man that of his might doth boast,
  shall fall from all his strength.

17 The troops of horsmen all shall fail,
  their sturdy steeds shall swerve:
The strength of horse shall not pre-
  the rider to preserve.   (vail
18 But lo, the eyes of God intend
  and watch to aid the just:
With such as fear him to offend,
  and on his goodness trust.

19 That he of death and great distress
  may set their souls from dread:
And if that dearth their land oppress,
  in hunger them to feed.   (pend
20 Wherfore our soul doth whole de-
  on God our strength and stay:
He is our shield us to defend,
  and drive all darts away.

21 Our joyful souls always proclaim
  his power and his might:
For why? in his most holy Name
  we hope and much delight.
22 Therfore let thy goodness, O Lord,
  still present with us be:
As we always with one accord
  do only trust in thee.

Cantus & Bassus.   PSALM XXXIV.   *Martyrs Tune.*

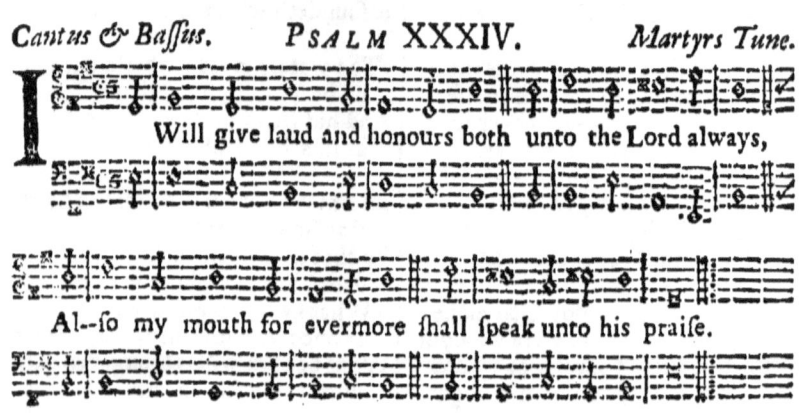

I Will give laud and honours both unto the Lord always,

Al-so my mouth for evermore shall speak unto his praise.

Psalm xxxiv. 53

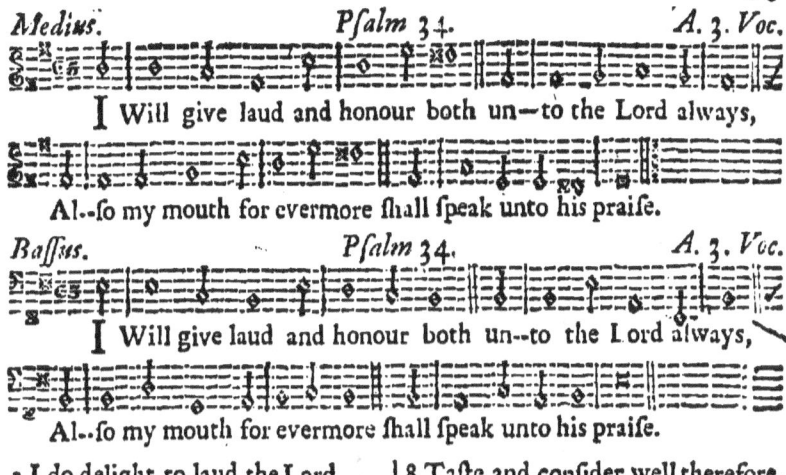

Medius.   *Psalm 34.*   *A. 3. Voc.*

I Will give laud and honour both un—to the Lord always,

Al..so my mouth for evermore shall speak unto his praise.

Bassus.   *Psalm 34.*   *A. 3. Voc.*

I Will give laud and honour both un--to the Lord always,

Al..so my mouth for evermore shall speak unto his praise.

2 I do delight to laud the Lord
in soul, in heart, and voice:
That humble men and mortifi'd
may hear, and so rejoyce.

3 Therefore see that ye magnifie
with me the living Lord,
Let us exalt his holy Name
always with one accord.

4 For I my self besought the Lord,
he answer'd me again,
And me deliver'd instantly
from all my fear and pain.

5 Whoso they be that him behold,
shall see his light most clear:
Their countenance shall not be dasht,
they need it not to fear.

6 This poor distressed man for help
unto the Lord did call:
Who did him hear without delay,
and rid him out of thrall.

7 The angel of the Lord doth pitch
his tents in ev'ry place,
To save all such as do him fear,
that nothing them deface.

8 Taste and consider well therefore,
that God is good and just:
O happy man that maketh him
his only stay and trust.

9 Fear ye the Lord, ye holy ones,
above all earthly thing:
For they that fear the living Lord,
are sure to lack nothing.

10 The Lions shall be hunger-bit,
and pin'd with famine much:
But as for them that fear the Lord,
no lack shall be to such.

The second part.

11 Come near to me, my children dear,
and to my words give ear:
I will you teach the perfect way,
how ye the Lord should fear.

12 Who is the man that would live
and lead a godly life? (long,
13 See thou refrain thy tongue & lips
from all deceit and strife.

14 Turn back thy face from doing ill,
and do the godly deed:
Enquire for peace and quietness,
and follow it with speed.

E 3   15 For

Psalm xxxiv, xxxv.

15 For why? the eyes of God above
upon the juſt are bent:
His ears likewiſe to hear the cry
of the poor innocent.

16 But he doth frown and bend his (brows
upon the wicked train:
And cuts away the memory
that ſhould of them remain.

17 But when the juſt do call and cry,
the Lord doth hear them ſo,
That out of pain and miſery
forthwith he lets them go.

18 The Lord is ever nigh to them
that broken-hearted are:
And for the contrite ſpirit he
ſalvation doth prepare.

19 Full many be the miſeries
that righteous men endure:
But of deliv'rance from them all
the Lord doth them ſecure.

20 The Lord doth ſo preſerve & keep
their very bones alway,
That not ſo much as one of them
do periſh or decay.

21 The ſin ſhall ſlay the wicked man,
which he himſelf hath wrought:
And ſuch as hate the righteous man,
ſhall ſoon be brought to nought.

22 But they that fear the living Lord,
are ever ſafe and found:
And as for thoſe that truſt in him,
nothing ſhall them confound.

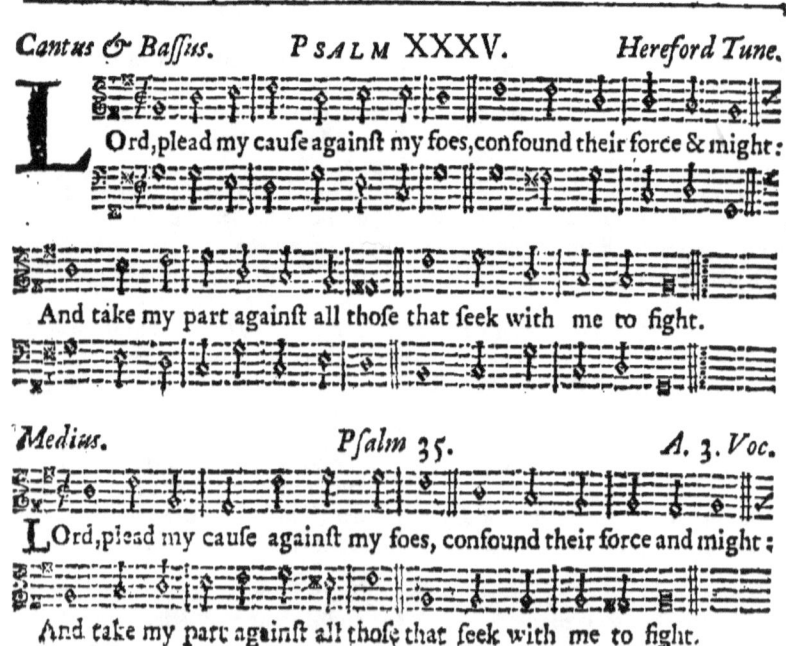

Cantus & Baſſus.   PSALM XXXV.   *Hereford Tune.*

Lord, plead my cauſe againſt my foes, confound their force & might:
And take my part againſt all thoſe that ſeek with me to fight.

Medius.   Pſalm 35.   A. 3. Voc.

Lord, plead my cauſe againſt my foes, confound their force and might:
And take my part againſt all thoſe that ſeek with me to fight.

Baſſus.

Psalm xxxv.   55

Bassus.   Psalm 35.   A. 3. Voc.

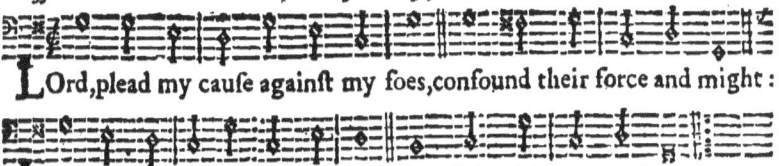

LOrd, plead my cause against my foes, confound their force and might:

And take my part against all those that seek with me to fight.

2 Lay hand upon the spear and shield,
thy self in armour dress:
Stand up for me and fight the field,
to help me from distress.

3 Gird on thy sword, & stop the way,
mine enemies withstand:
That thou unto my soul may'st say,
I am thy help at hand.
       (blame
4 Confound them with rebuke and
that seek my soul to spill:
Let them turn back and flee with
that seek to work me ill. (shame,

5 Let them disperse and flee abroad,
as wind doth drive the dust :
That so the angel of our God
their might away may thrust.

6 Let all their ways be void of light,
and slipp'ry like to fall :
And send thine angel with thy might,
to persecute them all.
       (have
7 For why? without my fault they
in secret set their gin :
And for no cause have digg'd a pit
to take my soul therein.
       (care,
8 When they think least, and have no
O Lord, destroy them all :
Let them be trapt in their own snare,
and in their mischief fall.

9 And let my soul, my heart & voice,
in God have joy and wealth :
That in the Lord I may rejoyce,
and in his saving health.
       (say,
10 Then all my bones shall speak and
my parts shall all agree :
O thou great God of heav'n & earth,
what man is like to thee ?
The second part.   (them
11 Thou dist defend the weak from
that are both stout and strong :
And rid the poor from wicked men
that spoil and do them wrong.

12 My cruel foes against me rise,
to witness things untrue :
And to accuse me they devise
of things I never knew.
       (will,
13 Where I to them did shew good
they quit me with disdain : (ill,
That they should pay my good with
my soul doth sore complain.
       (therefore,
14 When they were sick I mourn'd
my self in sackcloth clad :
With fasting did I faint full sore,
and pray'd with heart most sad.

15 As they had been my brethren dear
I did my self behave :
As one that mourneth heavily
about his mothers grave.

E 4   16 But

Pſalm xxxv, xxxvi.

16 But they in mine adverſity
did gather in a rout:
Yea, abject ſlaves reproachfully
at me did mock and flout.

17 The belly-gods, & flatt'ring train,
that all good things deride:
At me do grin with great diſdain,
and pluck their mouths aſide.

18 Lᵈ, when wilt thou for me appear?
why doſt thou ſtay and pauſe?
O rid my ſoul, mine only dear,
out of theſe lions claws.

19 And then will I give thanks to
before the Church always: (thee
And where moſt of the people be,
there will I ſhew thy praiſe.

20 Let not my foes prevail on me,
which hate me for no fault:
Nor let them wink or turn their eye,
that cauſeleſs me aſſault.

The third part.

21 Of peace no word they think or ſay,
their talk is all untrue:
They ſtill conſult, and would betray
all thoſe that peace enſue.

22 With open mouth they run at me,
their fury is like fire:
Well, well, ſay they, our eye doth ſee
the thing that we deſire.
(they take,
23 But, Lord, thou ſeeſt what ways
and what they do intend:

Be not far off, nor me forſake,
as men that fail their friend.

24 Awake, ariſe, and ſtir abroad,
defend me in my right:
Revenge my cauſe, O Lord my God,
and aid me with thy might.

25 According to thy righteouſneſs,
my Lord God, ſet me free:
And let them not their pride expreſs,
nor triumph over me.

26 Let not their hearts rejoyce & cry,
Ev'n ſo we would it have:
Nor give them cauſe to ſay on high,
He's ſunk into the grave.
(ſhame
27 Confound them with rebuke and
that joy when I do mourn:
And pay them home with ſpite and
that brag at me with ſcorn. (blame

28 Let them moſt heartily rejoyce,
which love mine upright way:
Let them all times with heart & voice
ſtill praiſe the Lord, and ſay,

29 Great is the Lord, and doth excell,
and he doth much delight
To ſee his ſervants proſper well,
it is his pleaſant ſight.

30 Wherefore my tongue I will apply
thy righteouſneſs to praiſe:
To thee the Lord my God, will I
give laud and thanks always.

Cantus & Baſſus.　　P ſ A L M　XXXVI.　　*Cambridge Tune.*

The wicked by his works unjuſt, doth thus perſwade my heart,

That

Psalm xxxvi.

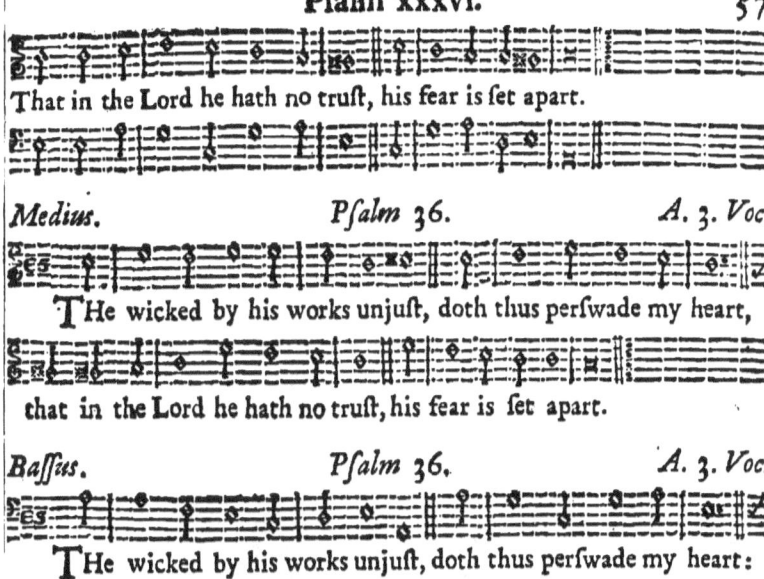

That in the Lord he hath no trust, his fear is set apart.

Medius.   Psalm 36.   *A. 3. Voc.*

THe wicked by his works unjust, doth thus perswade my heart,

that in the Lord he hath no trust, his fear is set apart.

Bassus.   Psalm 36.   *A. 3. Voc.*

THe wicked by his works unjust, doth thus perswade my heart:

That in the Lord he hath no trust, his fear is set apart.

2 Yet doth he joy in his estate,
to walk as he began:
So long till he deserve the hate
of God as well as man.

3 His words are wicked, vile & naught,
his tongue no truth doth tell:
Yet at no hand will he be taught
which way he may do well.

4 When he should sleep, then doth he
his mischief to fulfill? (muse,
No wicked ways doth he refuse,
nor any thing that's ill.

5 But, L^d, thy goodness doth ascend
above the heav'ns most high:
So doth thy truth it self extend
unto the cloudy sky.

6 Much more than hills so high and
thy justice is exprest : (steep,
Thy judgments like to seas most deep
thou sav'st both man and beast.

7 Thy mercy is above all things,
O God, it doth excell:
In trust whereof, as in thy wings,
the sons of men shall dwell.

8 Within thy house shall they be fed
with plenty at their will:
Of all delights they shall be sped,
and take thereof their fill.

9 Because the will of life most pure
doth ever flow from thee,
And in thy light we are full sure
the lasting light to see.

58   Psalm xxxvi, xxxvii.

10 From such as thee desire to know,
   let not thy grace depart:
   Thy righteousness declare and show
   to men of upright heart.

11 Let not the proud on me prevail,
   O Lord, of thy good grace:

Nor let the wicked me assail,
to throw me out of place.

12 But they in their device shall fall
   that wicked works maintain:
   They shall be certainly cast down,
   and never rise again.

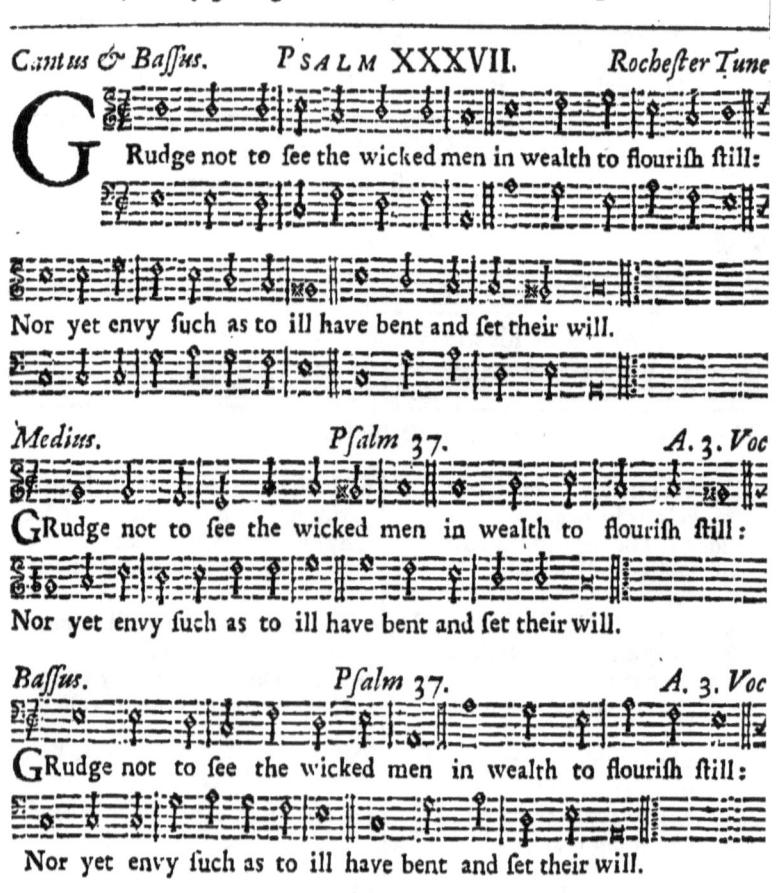

Cantus & Bassus.   P SALM XXXVII.   *Rochester Tune*

GRudge not to see the wicked men in wealth to flourish still:

Nor yet envy such as to ill have bent and set their will.

Medius.   Psalm 37.   A. 3. Voc

GRudge not to see the wicked men in wealth to flourish still:

Nor yet envy such as to ill have bent and set their will.

Bassus.   Psalm 37.   A. 3. Voc

GRudge not to see the wicked men in wealth to flourish still:

Nor yet envy such as to ill have bent and set their will.

2 For as green grass & the green herbs
  are cut and wither away:
  So shall their great prosperity
  soon pass, fade and decay.

3 Trust thou therefore in God alone
  to do well give thy mind:
  So shalt thou have the land as thine
  and there sure food shalt find.

4 In

Psalm xxxvii.

heart's delight,
ɔu wouldſt have,
ι all the world
ιt to crave.

and thine affairs
feᴄt truſt,
ʋith patience
e and juſt.

nd godly Name
ιe light:
at noon-day
If ſo bright.

ιnd ſtedfaſtly
vait then,
he proſp'rous
·d men. (ſtate

envy, and hate,
r riſe:
ιt be drawn into
rpriſe.

nan will God
ɜ and leſs:
him are ſure
ſſeſs.

& thou ſhalt ſee
ɜd train,
ouſe or place
l remain.
ɔart.
humble men
ι land:
y ſhall rejoyce,
hem withſtand.

ιd malicious
ιnſpire:
:h at him, as men
ɜ deſire.

13 But while ungodly men thus think,
    the Lord laughs them to ſcorn:
For he doth ſee their term approach,
    when they ſhall ſigh and mourn.

14 The wicked have their ſword out
    their bow alſo is bent, (drawn,
To overflow and kill the poor,
    whoſe life is innocent.
                        (their heart
15 But the ſame ſword ſhall pierce
    which was to kill the juſt:
So ſhall the bow in ſhivers break
    wherein they put their truſt.

11 Doubtleſs the juſt man's poor eſtate
    is to be valu'd more
Than all the lewd and wicked man's
    rich pomp and heaped ſtore.

17 For thô their power be moſt ſtrong,
    God will it overthrow:
Where contrary he doth preſerve
    the humble men and low.

18 He ſees by his great providence
    the good man's trade and way:
And will give them inheritance
    which never ſhall decay.

19 They ſhall not be diſcouraged,
    when ſome are hard beſted:
When others ſhall be hunger-bit,
    they ſhall be clad and fed.

20 For whoſover wicked is,
    and enemy to God,
Shall like the fat of lambs conſume,
    or ſmoak that flies abroad.
              The third part.
21 Behold the wicked borrows much,
    and never pays again:
Whereas the juſt by lib'ral gifts
    the needy doth ſuſtain.

22 For

22 For they whom God doth bless,
   the land for heritage: (shall have
   And they whom he doth curse, like-
   shall perish in his rage. (wise

23 The Lord the just mans steps doth
   and all his works doth bless:(guide,
   To ev'ry thing he takes in hand
   he giveth good success.

24 Thô he do fall, yet is he sure
   not utterly to sink:
   For God upholds him with his hand,
   and from him will not shrink.

25 I have been young, but now am old,
   yet did I never see
   The just man left, nor yet his seed
   to beg for misery:

26 He gives always most lib'rally,
   and lends where there is need:
   By which he doth from God secure
   a blessing to his seed.

27 Flee vice therefore & wickedness,
   and virtue do embrace:
   So God shall grant thee long to have
   on earth a dwelling-place.

28 For God so loveth equity,
   and shews to his such grace,
   That he preserveth them, but doth
   cut off the wicked race.

29 Whereas the good and godly men
   inherit shall the land,
   Having as lords all things therein
   in their own pow'r and hand.
   (speak

30 The just man's mouth doth ever
   of matters wise and high:
   His tongue doth talk of judgment, &
   of truth and equity.

31 For in his heart the law of God
   his Lord doth still abide:
   So that wherever he doth go,
   his foot shall never slide.

32 The wicked like a greedy wolf
   the just man doth beset,
   By all means seeking him to kill,
   and take him in his net.

The fourth part.

33 But thô he fall into his hands,
   yet God will succour send:
   Thô men against him sentence give
   God will him yet defend.

34 Wait thou on God, & keep his way
   he shall preserve thee then
   The earth to rule, and thou shalt see
   destroy'd these wicked men.
   (strong

35 The wicked have I seen most
   and plac'd in high degree,
   Flourishing in all wealth and store
   as doth the laurel-tree.

36 But suddenly he pass'd away,
   and lo he was quite gone: (find
   Then I him sought, but could not
   the place where dwelt such one.

37 Mark and behold the perfect man,
   his God doth him increase:
   For the just man shall have at length
   great joy with rest and peace.

38 As for transgressors, wo to them,
   destroy'd they all shall be:
   God will cut off their budding race,
   and rich posterity.

39 But the salvation of the just
   doth come from God above:
   Who in their trouble sends them aid
   of his meer grace and love.

40 God

Pfalm xxxvii, xxxviii.   61

o God evermore delivers them | And ſtill will ſave them, whilſt that
from lewd men and unjuſt: | in him do put their truſt.   (they

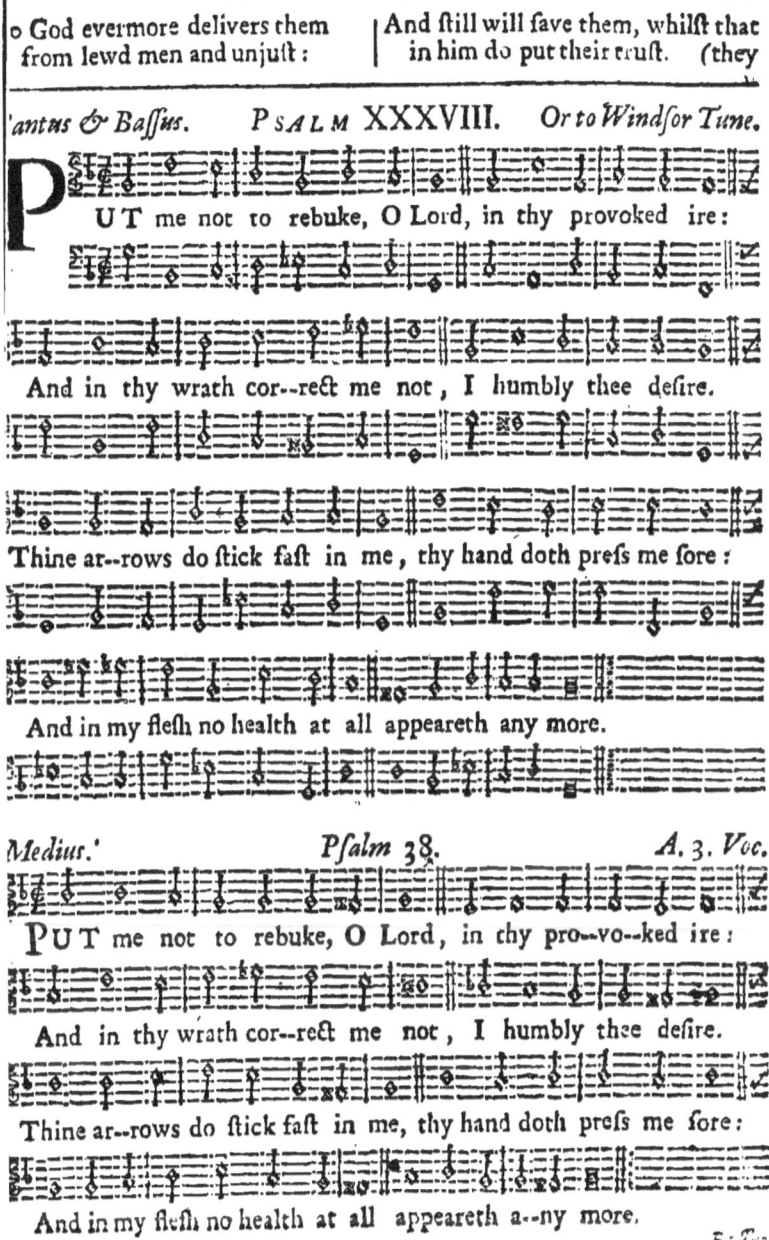

'antus & Baſſus.   PSALM XXXVIII.   Or to Windſor Tune.

PUT me not to rebuke, O Lord, in thy provoked ire:

And in thy wrath cor--rect me not, I humbly thee deſire.

Thine ar--rows do ſtick faſt in me, thy hand doth preſs me ſore:

And in my fleſh no health at all appeareth any more.

Medius.'   Pſalm 38.   A. 3. Voc.

PUT me not to rebuke, O Lord, in thy pro--vo--ked ire:

And in thy wrath cor--rect me not, I humbly thee deſire.

Thine ar--rows do ſtick faſt in me, thy hand doth preſs me ſore:

And in my fleſh no health at all appeareth a--ny more.

Eaſtus.

Bassus. Psalm 38. A. 3. Voc.

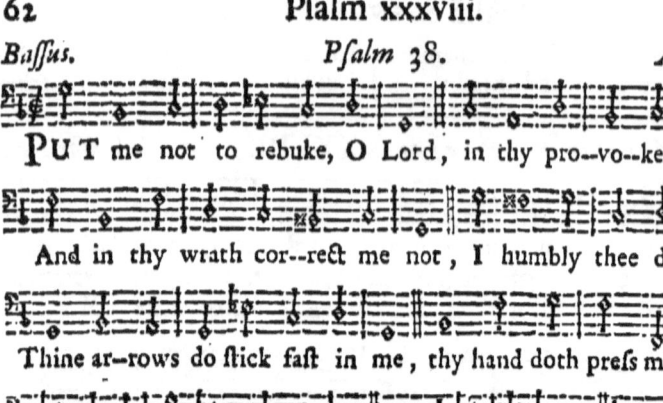

PUT me not to rebuke, O Lord, in thy pro--vo--ked ire:

And in thy wrath cor--rect me not, I humbly thee desire.

Thine ar--rows do stick fast in me, thy hand doth press me sore;

And in my flesh no health at all appeareth any more.

3 And all this is by reason of
thy wrath that I am in:
Nor any rest is in my bones,
by reason of my sin.
4 For lo, my wicked doings, Lord,
above my head are gone:
A greater load than I can bear,
they lie me sore upon.

5 My wounds do stink, & are corrupt,
and loathsom are to see: (ness
Which all through mine own foolish-
doth happen unto me.
6 And I in careful wise am brought
into such great distress,
That I go wailing all the day
in doleful heaviness.

7 My loyns are fill'd with fore disease,
my flesh hath no whole part:
8 I feeble am and broken sore,
and roar for grief of heart. (grones
9 Thou know'st, Lord, my desire, my
are open in thy sight: (doth fail,
10 My heart doth pant, my strength
mine eyes have lost their light.

11 My lovers and my wonted friends
stand looking on my wo:
Also my kinsmen far away
are me departed fro. (snares,
12 They that do seek my life, lay
and they that go the way
To do me hurt, speak lies, and think
on mischief all the day.

The second part.

13 But as a deaf man I became,
that cannot hear at all;
14 And as one dumb, that opens not
his mouth to speak withal.
15 For all my confidence, O Lord,
is wholly set on thee:
Therefore, O Lord, that art my God,
do thou give ear to me.

16 This do I crave, that they my foes
triumph not over me:
For when my foot doth slip, then they
rejoyce my fall to see.
17 And I am ready for to halt,
I cannot stand upright:
Also my grievous heaviness
is ever in my sight.

Pſalm xxxviii, xxxix.   63

8 For while that I my wickedneſs
   in humble wiſe confeſs,
And while I for my ſinful deeds
   my ſorrows do expreſs:
9 My foes do ſtill remain alive,
   and mighty are alſo:
And they that hate me wrongfully,
   in number hugely grow.

20 They ſtand againſt me, that my
    with evil do repay: (good,
Becauſe that good and honeſt things
    I do enſue alway.
21 Forſake me not, O Lord my God,
    be thou not far away:
22 Haſte me to help, my Lord my
    my ſafety and my ſtay.   (God,

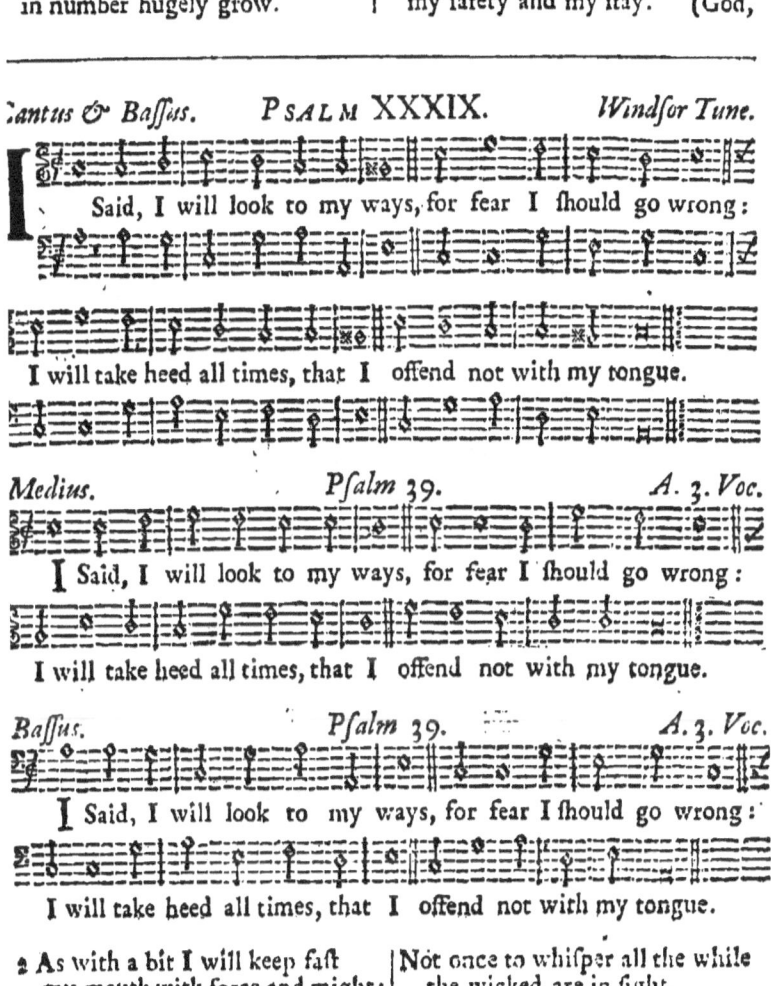

Cantus & Baſſus.   PSALM XXXIX.   Windſor Tune.

Said, I will look to my ways, for fear I ſhould go wrong:

I will take heed all times, that I offend not with my tongue.

Medius.   Pſalm 39.   A. 3. Voc.

I Said, I will look to my ways, for fear I ſhould go wrong:

I will take heed all times, that I offend not with my tongue.

Baſſus.   Pſalm 39.   A. 3. Voc.

I Said, I will look to my ways, for fear I ſhould go wrong:

I will take heed all times, that I offend not with my tongue.

2 As with a bit I will keep faſt
   my mouth with force and might:

Not once to whiſper all the while
   the wicked are in ſight.

3 I held

Pſalm xxxix, xl.

3 I held my tongue,& ſpake no word,
   but kept me cloſe and ſtill:
Yea, from good talk I did refrain,
   but ſore againſt my will.
                            (breaſt

4 My heart wax'd hot within my
   with muſing,thought,and doubt,
Which did increaſe and ſtir the fire:
   at laſt theſe words burſt out;

5 Lord,number out my life and days
   which yet I have not paſt,
So that I may be certiſi'd
   how long my life ſhall laſt.
                            (life

6 Lord, thou haſt pointed out my
   in length much like a ſpan:
Mine age is nothing unto thee,
   ſo vain is ev'ry man.

7 Man walketh like a ſhade,and doth
   in vain himſelf annoy,
In gettting goods, and cannot tell
   who ſhall the ſame enjoy.
                            (for?

8 Therefore now,Lord, what wait I
   what help do I deſire?
Of truth my help depends on thee,
   I nothing elſe require.

The ſecond part.

9 From all the ſins that I have done,
   Lord, quit me out of hand,
And make me not a ſcorn to fools
   that nothing underſtand.

10 I was as dumb, and to complain
   no trouble might me move:
Becauſe I knew it was thy work,
   my patience for to prove.
                            (plague,

11 Lord,take from me thy ſcourge and
   I can them not withſtand:
I faint and pine away for fear
   of thy moſt heavy hand.
                            (buke,

12 When thou for ſin doſt man re-
   he waxeth woe and wan,
As doth a cloth that moths have fret,
   ſo vain a thing is man.
                            (heed,

13 Lord,hear my ſuit,and give good
   regard my tears that fall:
I ſojourn like a ſtranger here,
   as did my fathers all.

14 O ſpare a little, give me ſpace
   my ſtrength for to reſtore,
Before I go away from hence,
   and ſhall be ſeen no more.

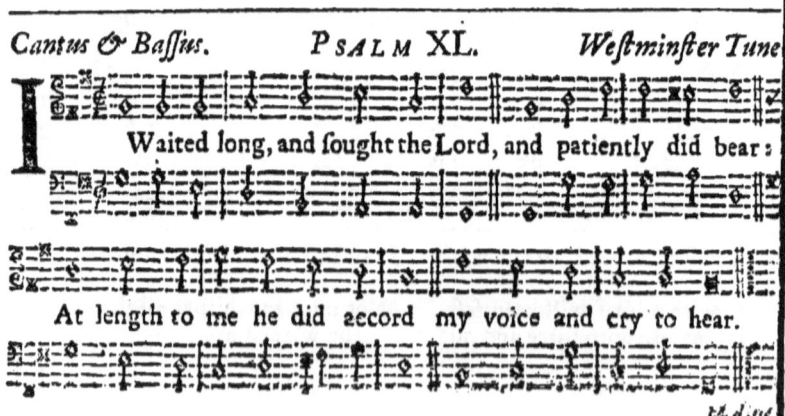

Cantus & Baſſus.   P S A L M   XL.   *Weſtminſter Tune*

Waited long, and ſought the Lord, and patiently did bear:

At length to me he did accord my voice and cry to hear.

Psalm xl. 65

Medius. Psalm 40. *A. 3. Voc.*

I Waited long, and sought the Lord, and patiently did bear:
At length to me he did accord my voice and cry to hear.

Bassus. Psalm 40. *A. 3. Voc.*

I Waited long, and sought the Lord, and patiently did bear:
At length to me he did accord my voice and cry to hear.

1 He pluck'd me from the lake so deep
out of the mire and clay:
Upon a rock he set my feet,
and he did guide my way.

3 To me he taught a psalm of praise,
which I must shew abroad:
And sing new songs of thanks always
unto the Lord our God.

4 When all the folk these things shall
as people much afraid, (see,
Then they unto the Lord will flee,
and trust upon his aid.

5 O blest is he whose hope and heart
doth in the Lord remain,
That with the proud doth take no
nor such as lies maintain. (part,

6 For, L^d my God, thy wondrous deeds
in greatness far do pass:
Thy favour towards us exceeds
all things that ever was.

7 When I intend and do devise
thy works abroad to show,
To such a reckning they do rise,
thereof no end I know.

8 Burnt-off'rings thou delight'st not
I know thy whole desire, (in,
With sacrifice to purge his sin
thou dost no man require.

9 Meat-offerings and sacrifice
thou would'st not have at all:
But thou, O Lord, hast open made
mine ears to hear withal.

10 But then said I, Behold and look,
I come with heart most free:
For in the volume of thy book
thus it is said of me.

11 That I, O God, should do thy mind,
which thing doth please me well:
For in my heart thy law I find
fast placed there to dwell.

12 Thy righteousness and justice I
in great assemblies tell:
Behold, my tongue no time doth cease,
O Lord, thou know'st full well.

The second part.

13 I have not hid within my breast
thy goodness as by stealth:
But I declare and have exprest
thy truth and saving health.

66 Pſalm xl, xli.

14 I kept not cloſe thy loving mind,
  that no man ſhould it know:
The truſt that in thy truth I find,
  to all the Church I ſhow.

15 Thy tender mercy, Lord, from me
  withdraw thou not away:
But let thy love and verity
  preſerve me ev'ry day.

16 For I with many troubles am
  encompaſſed about:
My ſins ſo greatly do increaſe,
  I cannot ſpy them out.

17 For why? in number they exceed
  the hairs upon my head:
My heart doth faint for very fear,
  that I am almoſt dead.

18 With ſpeed ſend help, and ſet me
  O Lord, I thee require: (free,
Make haſte with aid to ſuccour me,
  O Lord, at my deſire.

19 Confound them with rebuke and
  that ſeek my ſoul to ſpill: (ſhame
Drive back my foes, & them defame,
  that wiſh me any ill.

20 For their ill feats do them deſcry
  that would deface my name:
Always at me they rail and cry,
  Fie on him, fie for ſhame.

21 Let them in thee have joy & wealth
  the ſeek to thee always:
That thoſe that love thy ſaving health
  may ſay, To God be praiſe.

22 But as for me, I am but poor,
  oppreſt and brought full low:
Yet thou, O Lord, wilt me reſtore
  to health, full well I know.

23 For why? thou art my hope and
  my refuge, help and ſtay: (truſt
Wherefore, my God, as thou art juſt
  with me no time delay.

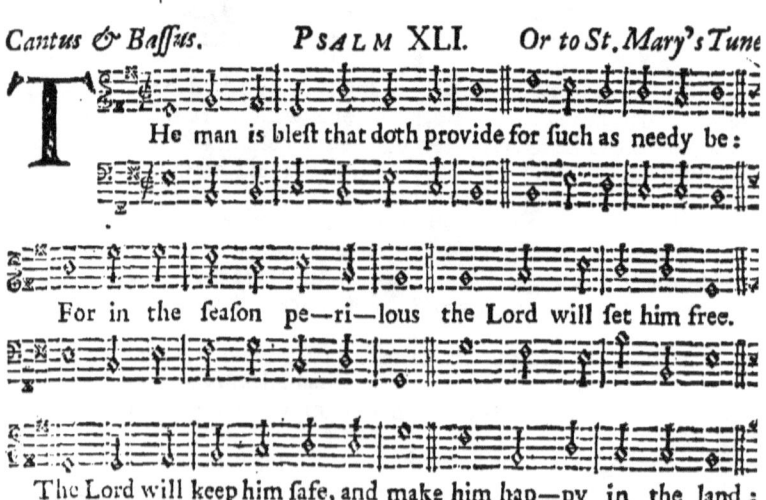

Cantus & Baſſus.   PSALM XLI.   Or to St. Mary's Tune

He man is bleſt that doth provide for ſuch as needy be:

For in the ſeaſon pe—ri—lous the Lord will ſet him free.

The Lord will keep him ſafe, and make him hap—py in the land:

Psalm xli. 67

And not de—li--ver him in--to his e--ne--mies strong hand.

Medius. *Psalm 41.* *A. 3. Voc.*

THe man is blest that doth provide for such as needy be:

For in the season pe—ri—lous the Lord will set him free:

The Lord will keep him safe, and make him happy in the land:

And not de—li--ver him in--to his e—ne--mies strong hand.

Bassus. *Psalm 41.* *A. 3. Voc.*

THe man is blest that doth provide for such as needy be:

For in the season pe—ri—lous the Lord will set him free.

The Lord will keep him safe, and make him happy in the land:

And not de—li--ver him in--to his e—ne--mies strong hand.

¶ And from his bed of languishing the Lord will him restore: For thou, O Lord, wilt turn to health his sickness and his sore.

4 Then in my sickness thus said I, have mercy, Lord, on me, And heal my soul which is full woe that I offended thee.

5 My foes did wish me ill in heart,
  and thus of me did say,
When shall he die, that so his name
  may perish quite away?
6 And when they come to visit me,
  they ask if I do well: (hatch,
But in their hearts they mischief
  and then abroad it tell.

7 All they that hate me do conspire
  against me craftily:
And still devise how to procure
  my ruine secretly.   (him to
8 Some grievous sin hath brought
  this sickness, say they plain:
He is so low, that without doubt
  he cannot rise again.

9 The man also that I did trust,
  with me did use deceit:
Who at my table eat my bread,
  the same for me laid wait.

10 Have mercy, Lord, on me therfore,
   and let me be preserv'd,
That I may render unto them
   the things they have deserv'd.

11 By this I know assuredly
   to be belov'd of thee,
Because my foes no power have
   to triumph over me.

12 But in my right thou hast me kept,
   and it maintained well:
And in thy presence place assign'd
   where I shall ever dwell.

13 The Lord the God of Israel
   be praised evermore:
Ev'n so be it, Lord, will I say,
   Praise ye the Lord therefore.

To *Father, Son, and Holy Ghost,*
   immortal Glory be:
As *was, is now, and shall be still,*
   to all Eternitie.

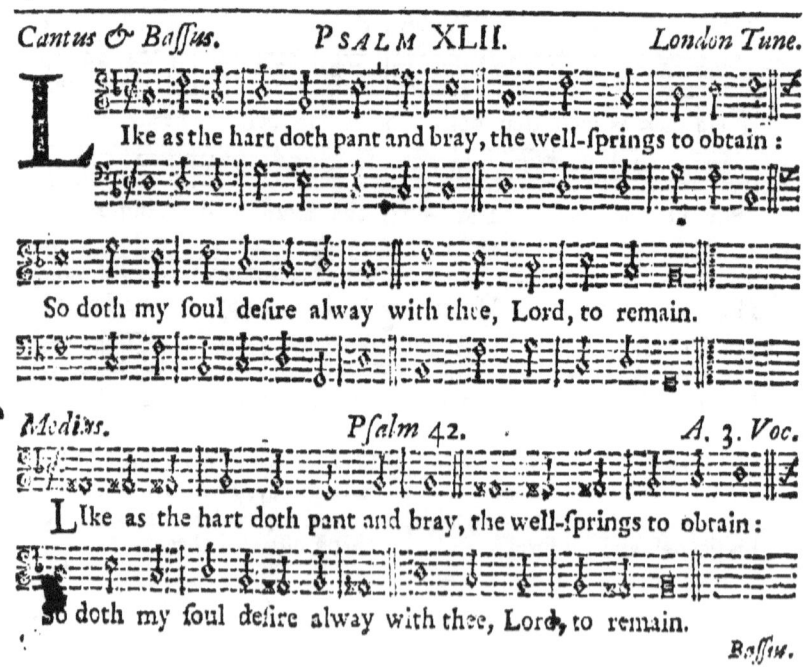

Cantus & Bassus.   PSALM XLII.   *London Tune.*

Like as the hart doth pant and bray, the well-springs to obtain:

So doth my soul desire alway with thee, Lord, to remain.

Medius.   Psalm 42.   *A. 3. Voc.*

Like as the hart doth pant and bray, the well-springs to obtain:

So doth my soul desire alway with thee, Lord, to remain.

Bassus.

Psalm xlii.

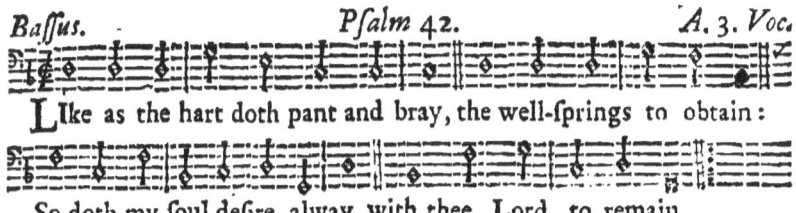

Bassus.   Psalm 42.   A. 3. Voc.

Like as the hart doth pant and bray, the well-springs to obtain:

So doth my soul desire alway with thee, Lord, to remain.

                 (draw near
2 My soul doth thirst, and would
   the living God of might:
Oh when shall I come and appear
   in presence of his sight.

3 The tears all times are my repast
   which from mine eyes do slide:
Whilst wicked men cry out so fast,
   Where now is God thy guide?

4 Alas, what grief is it to think
   what freedom once I had!
Therefore my soul, as at pit's brink,
   most heavy is and sad.

For I did march in good array,
   with joyful company:
Unto the temple was our way,
   to praise the Lord most High.

5 My soul, why art thou sad always,
   and frett'st thus in my breast?
Trust still in God, for him to praise
   I hold it ever best.

By him I have succour at need,
   against all pain and grief:
He is my God, which with all speed
   doth haste to send relief.

6 My soul within me is cast down,
   therefore, O Lord, I will
Remember thee from Jordan's land,
   and Hermon's little hill.

The second part.
7 One grief another in doth call,
   as clouds burst out their voice:
The floods of evil that do fall,
   run over me with noise.

8 Yet I by day felt his goodness,
   and help at all assays:
Likewise by night I did not cease
   the living God to praise.

9 I am perswaded thus to say
   to him with reverence,
O Lord, thou art my guide and stay,
   my rock and sure defence.

Why do I then in pensiveness
   hanging the head thus walk,
While that mine enemies oppress,
   and vex me with their talk?
                    (parts
10 For why? they pierce my inward
   with pains to be abhor'd, (hearts,
When they cry out with stubborn
   Where is thy God the Lord?
                    (faint,
11 So soon, my soul, why dost thou
   with pain and grief opprest?
Why do sad thoughts without re-
   thus rage within my breast? (straint

12 Trust in the Lord thy God always,
   and thou the time shalt see
To give him thanks with laud and
   for health restor'd to thee. (praise,

Pſalm xliii.

Cantus & Baſſus.   PSALM XLIII.   *St. David's Tune.*

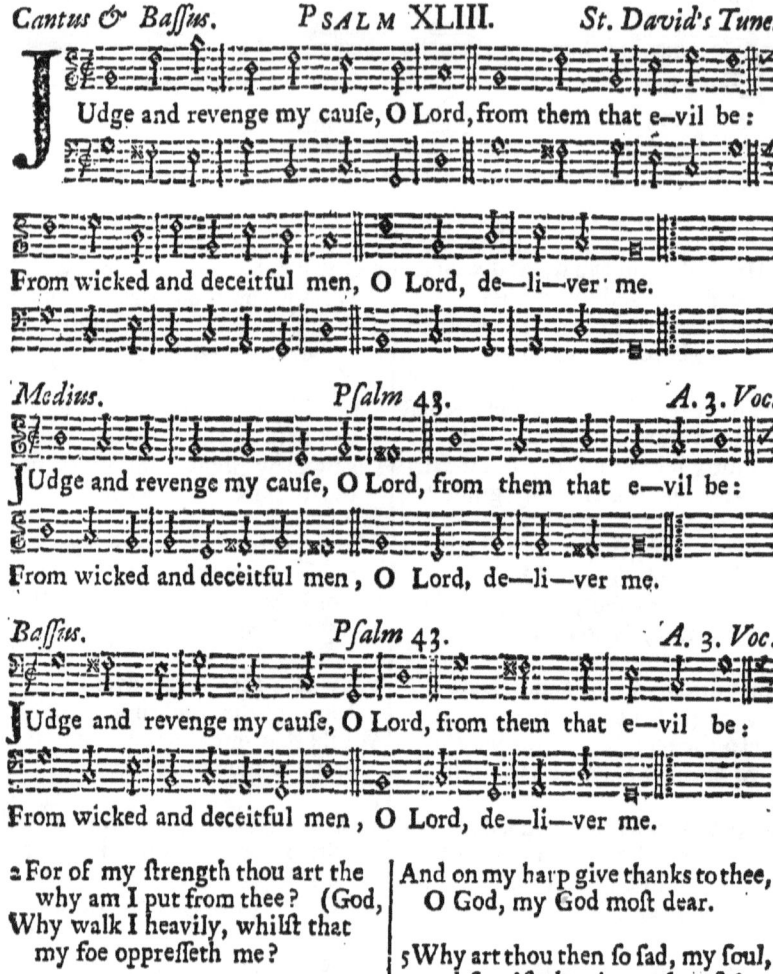

Judge and revenge my cauſe, O Lord, from them that e—vil be:

From wicked and deceitful men, O Lord, de—li—ver me.

Medius.   Pſalm 43.   *A. 3. Voc.*

Judge and revenge my cauſe, O Lord, from them that e—vil be:

From wicked and deceitful men, O Lord, de—li—ver me.

Baſſus.   Pſalm 43.   *A. 3. Voc.*

Judge and revenge my cauſe, O Lord, from them that e—vil be:

From wicked and deceitful men, O Lord, de—li—ver me.

2 For of my ſtrength thou art the God,
why am I put from thee?
Why walk I heavily, whilſt that
my foe oppreſſeth me?

3 O Lord, ſend out thy light & truth,
and lead me with thy grace,
Which may conduct me to thy hill,
and to thy dwelling-place.

4 Then ſhall I to thine altar go
with joy to worſhip there:
And on my harp give thanks to thee,
O God, my God moſt dear.

5 Why art thou then ſo ſad, my ſoul,
and frett'ſt thus in my breaſt?
Still truſt in God: for him to praiſe
I hold it always beſt.

6 By him I have deliverance
againſt all pain and grief:
He is my God, which doth alway
at need ſend me relief.

PSALM

Pſalm xliv. 71

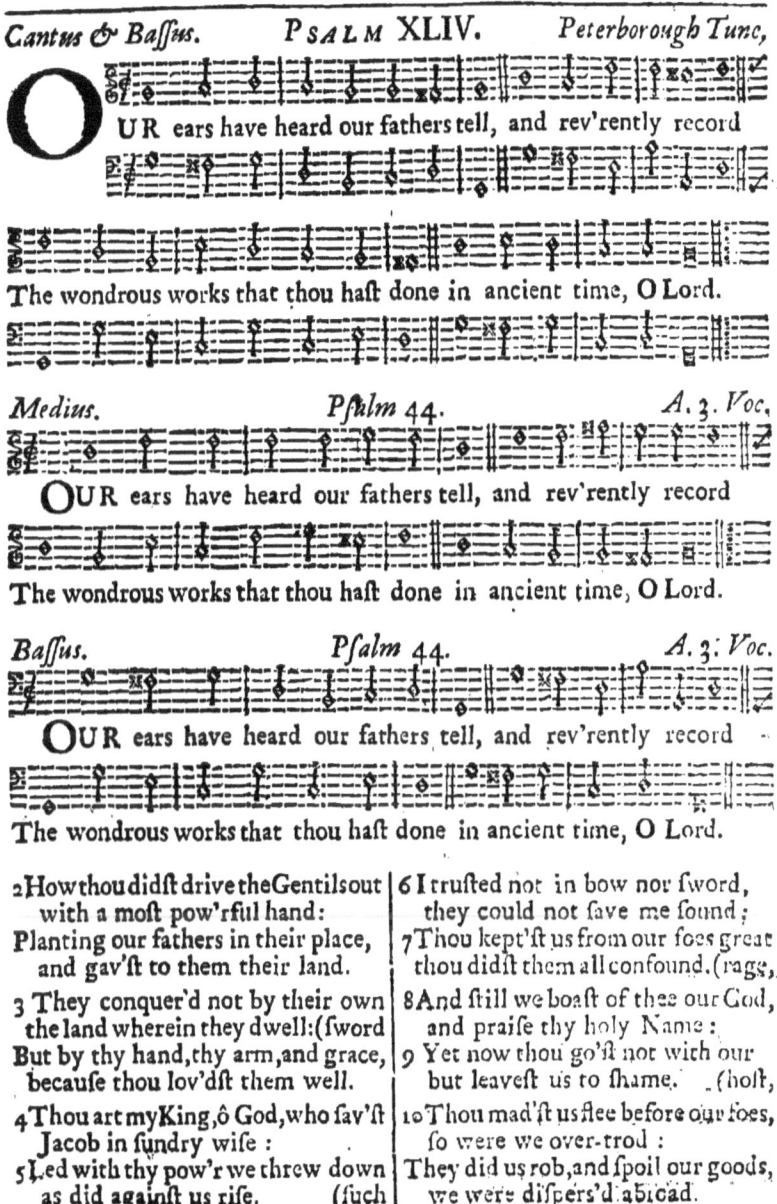

Cantus & Baſſus. PSALM XLIV. *Peterborough Tune,*

OUR ears have heard our fathers tell, and rev'rently record
The wondrous works that thou haſt done in ancient time, O Lord.

Medius. Pſalm 44. *A. 3. Voc.*

OUR ears have heard our fathers tell, and rev'rently record
The wondrous works that thou haſt done in ancient time, O Lord.

Baſſus. Pſalm 44. *A. 3. Voc.*

OUR ears have heard our fathers tell, and rev'rently record
The wondrous works that thou haſt done in ancient time, O Lord.

2 How thou didſt drive the Gentils out
  with a moſt pow'rful hand:
Planting our fathers in their place,
  and gav'ſt to them their land.
3 They conquer'd not by their own
  the land wherein they dwell:(ſword
But by thy hand, thy arm, and grace,
  becauſe thou lov'dſt them well.
4 Thou art my King, ô God, who ſav'ſt
  Jacob in ſundry wiſe :
5 Led with thy pow'r we threw down
  as did againſt us riſe. (ſuch

6 I truſted not in bow nor ſword,
  they could not ſave me found;
7 Thou kept'ſt us from our foes great
  thou didſt them all confound.(rage,
8 And ſtill we boaſt of thee our God,
  and praiſe thy holy Name :
9 Yet now thou go'ſt not with our
  but leaveſt us to ſhame. (hoſt,
10 Thou mad'ſt us flee before our foes,
  ſo were we over-trod :
They did us rob, and ſpoil our goods,
  we were diſpers'd abroad.

F 4   11 Thou

Psalm xliv, xlv.

11 Thou hast us given to our foes,
 as sheep for to be slain:
Amongst the heathen ev'ry where
 scatter'd we do remain.
12 Thy people thou hast sold like
 and as a thing of nought:(slaves,
For profit none thou hadst thereby,
 no gain at all was sought.
13 And to our neighbours thou hast
 of us a laughing-stock: (made
And those that round about us dwell,
 at us do grin and mock.
The second part.
14 Thus we serve for no other use,
 but for a common talk: (heads
They mock, they scorn, they nod their
 where-e'er they go or walk.
15 With shame and great confusion
 I am afflicted sore:
Yea so I blush that all my face
 with red is cover'd o'er.
16 For why? we hear such slandrous
 such false reports & lies: (words,
That death it is to see their wrongs,
 their threatnings and their cries.
17 For all this we forget not thee,
 nor yet thy cov'nant brake:

18 We turn not back our hearts from
 nor yet thy paths forsake. (thee,
19 Yet thou hast trod us down to dust,
 where dens of dragons be,
And cover'd us with shade of death,
 and great adversity.
20 If we God's Name forgotten have,
 and help of idols sought, (out,
21 Shall he not search and find this
 for he doth know our thought.
22 But 'tis for thy Name's sake, ô Lord,
 we always are slain thus:
As sheep unto the shambles sent,
 ev'n so they deal with us.
23 Up L^d, why sleepest thou? awake,
 for ever leave us not:
24 Why hidest thou thy countenance?
 our thrall thou hast forgot.
25 For down to dust our soul is
 our troubles come so fast:(brought,
Our belly, like as it were glu'd,
 unto the ground cleaves fast.
26 Rise up therefore for our defence,
 and help us, Lord, at need:
We thee beseech for thy goodness,
 to rescue us with speed.

Cantus & Bassus.   PSALM XLV.   *St. Peter's Tune.*

M Y heart doth take in hand some godly song to sing:
The praise that I shall shew therein, pertaineth to the King.

Medius.

Psalm xlv.

Medius.   Psalm 45.   *A. 3. Voc.*

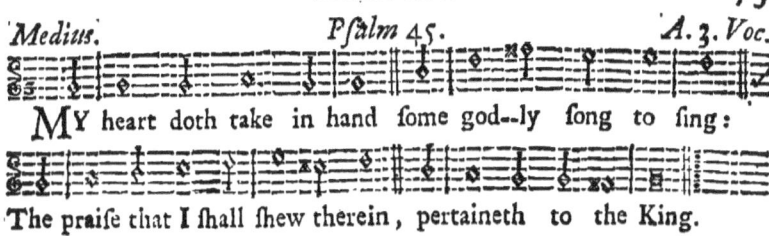

MY heart doth take in hand some god--ly song to sing:

The praise that I shall shew therein, pertaineth to the King.

Bassus.   Psalm 45.   *A. 3. Voc.*

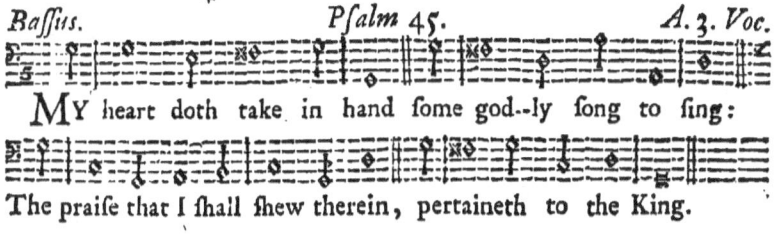

MY heart doth take in hand some god--ly song to sing:

The praise that I shall shew therein, pertaineth to the King.

2 My tongue shall be as quick
   his honour to indite,
As is the pen of any scribe
   that useth fast to write.

3 O fairest of all men,
   thy speech is pleasant pure:
For God hath blessed thee with gifts,
   for ever to endure.

4 About thee gird thy sword,
   O prince of might elect:
With honour, glory, and renown,
   thou art most richly deckt.

5 Go forth with godly speed,
   with meekness, truth and right:
And thy right hand shall thee instruct
   in works of dreadful might.

6 Thine arrows sharp and keen
   their hearts so sore shall sting:
That folk shall fall and kneel to thee,
   yea, all thy foes, O king.

7 Thy royal seat, O Lord,
   for ever shall remain:
Because the sceptre of thy realm
   doth righteousness maintain.

8 Because thou lov'st the right,
   and dost the ill detest,
Therefore hath God anointed thee
   with joy above the rest.

9 With mirth and favours sweet
   thy cloaths are all bespread:
When thou dost from thy palace
   thereby to make thee glad. (pass,

10 Kings daughters do attend
   in fine and rich array: (stand
At thy right hand the queen doth
   in gold and garments gay.

The second part.

11 O daughter, take good heed,
   incline and give good ear:
Thou must forget thy kindred all,
   and fathers house most dear.

12 Then shall the king desire
   thy beauty fair and trim:
For why? he is the Lord thy God,
   and thou must worship him.

13 The daughters then of Tyre,
   with gifts full rich to see,
And all the wealthy of the land
   shall make their suit to thee.

14 The

Psalm xlv, xlvi.

14 The daughter of the king
  is glorious to behold:
Within her closet she doth sit
  all deck'd in beaten gold.

15 In robes with needle wrought,
  and many pleasant thing:
With virgins fair on her to wait,
  she cometh to the king.

16 Thus are they brought with joy
  and mirth on ev'ry side,

Into the palace of the king,
  and there they do abide.

17 In stead of parents left,
  (O queen, the case so stands)
Thou shalt have sons whom thou
  as princes in all lands. (may'st set

18 Wherefore thy holy Name
  all ages shall record:
The people shall give thanks to thee
  for evermore, O Lord.

Cantus & Bassus.   PSALM XLVI.   *Or to Canterbury Tune.*

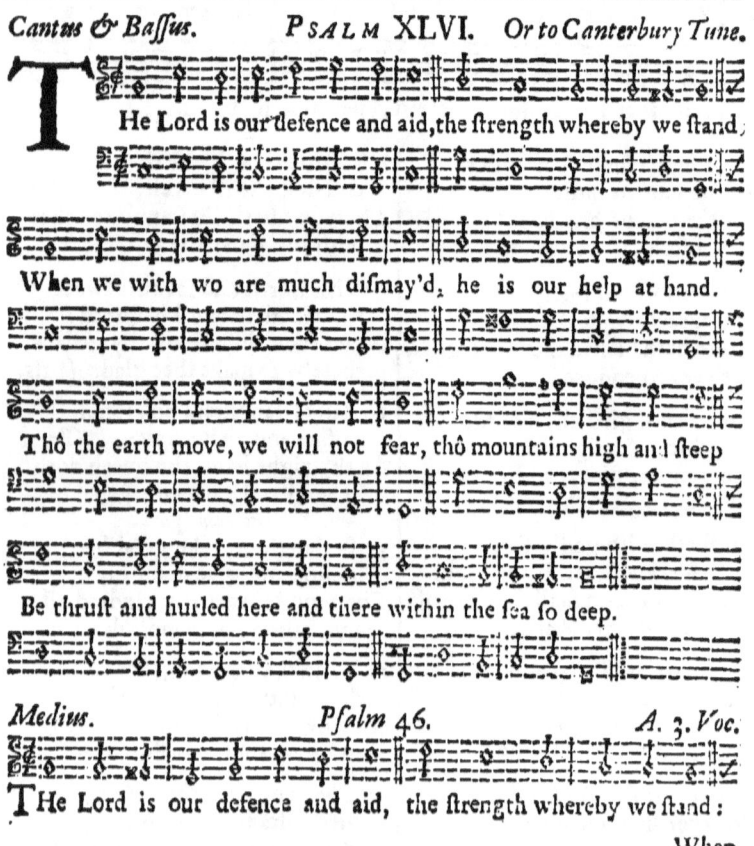

He Lord is our defence and aid, the strength whereby we stand,

When we with wo are much dismay'd, he is our help at hand.

Thô the earth move, we will not fear, thô mountains high and steep

Be thrust and hurled here and there within the sea so deep.

Medius.   Psalm 46.   *A. 3. Voc.*

The Lord is our defence and aid, the strength whereby we stand:

When

Psalm xlvi.

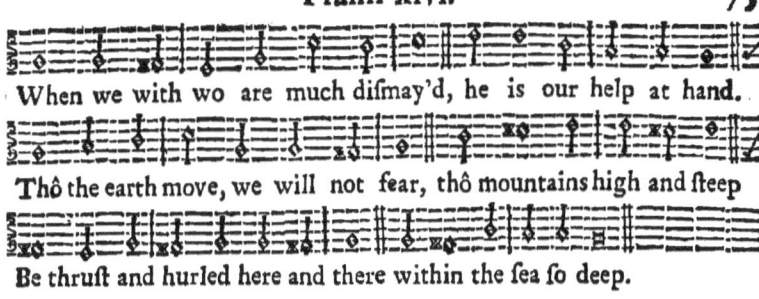

When we with wo are much difmay'd, he is our help at hand.

Thô the earth move, we will not fear, thô mountains high and fteep

Be thruft and hurled here and there within the fea fo deep.

Baffus.   *Pfalm 46.*   *A. 3. Voc.*

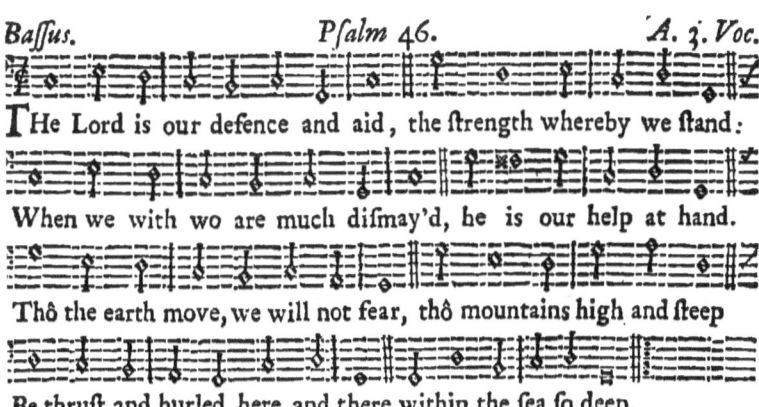

THe Lord is our defence and aid, the ftrength whereby we ftand:

When we with wo are much difmay'd, he is our help at hand.

Thô the earth move, we will not fear, thô mountains high and fteep

Be thruft and hurled here and there within the fea fo deep.

No, thô the fea do rage fo fore,
  that all the banks it fpills:
And thô it overflow the fhore,
  and beat down mighty hills.
For one fair flood doth fend abroad
  his pleafant ftreams apace,
To frefh the city of our God,
  and wafh his holy place.

In midft of her theLord doth dwell,
  fhe can no whit decay:
All things againft her that rebell
  the Lord will furely flay.
The heathen folk & kingdoms fear,
  the people make a noife:
The earth doth melt, and not appear,
  when God puts forth his voice.

7 The Lord of hofts did take our part,
  to us he hath an eye: (heart
Our hope of health with all our
  on Jacob's God doth lie. (thought
8 Come here and fee with mind and
  the working of our God:
What wonders he himfelf hath
  in all the world abroad. (wrought

9 By him all wars are hufh'd & gone,
  thô countries did confpire: (one,
Their bows and fpears he brake each
  their chariots burnt with fire.
10 Be ftill therefore, and know that I
  am God, and therefore will
Among the heathen people be
  highly exalted ftill.

Psalm xlvi, xlvii.

11 The Lord of hosts doth us defend,
he is our strength and tow'r:
On Jacob's God we do depend,
and on his might and pow'r.

To Father, Son, and Holy Ghost,
all glory be therefore:
As in beginning was, is now,
and shall be evermore.

Cantus & Bassus.   PSALM XLVII.   London new Tun

YE people all with one accord clap hands and much rejoyce:

Be glad and sing unto the Lord with sweet and pleasant voice.

Medius.   Psalm 47.   A. 3. Vo

YE people all with one accord clap hands and much rejoyce:

Be glad and sing unto the Lord with sweet and pleasant voice.

Bassus.   Psalm 47.   A. 3. Vo

YE people all with one accord clap hands and much rejoyce:

Be glad and sing unto the Lord with sweet and pleasant voice.

2 For high the Lord and dreadful is,
his wonders manifold:
A mighty King he is truly,
in all the earth extoll'd.

3 The people shall he make to be
unto our bondage thrall:

And underneath our feet shall he
the nations make to fall.

4 For us the heritage he chose
which we possess alone,
The excellency of Jacob,
his well-beloved one.

5 Ou

Psalm xlvii, xlviii. 77

Our God ascended up on high
with joy and pleasant noise,
The Lord goes up above the sky
with trumpets royal voice.

Sing praises to our God, sing praise,
sing praises to our King:
for God is King of all the earth,
all skilful praises sing.

7 God on the heathen reigns, and sits
upon his holy throne:
The princes of the people have
them joyned ev'ry one

8 To Abraham's people: for our God,
which is exalted high,
As with a buckler doth defend
the earth continually.

Cantus & Bassus.   PSALM XLVIII.   Exeter Tune.

GReat is the Lord, and with great praise to be advanced still

Within the Ci-ty of our God, upon his holy hill.

Medius.   Psalm 48.   A. 3. Voc.

GReat is the Lord, and with great praise to be ad--van--ced still

Within the City of our God, upon his holy hill.

Bassus.   Psalm 48.   A. 3. Voc.

GReat is the Lord, and with great praise to be ad--van--ced still

Within the City of our God, upon his holy hill.

2 Mount

2 Mount Sion is a pleasant place,
  it gladdeth all the land:
The City of the mighty King
  on her north-side doth stand.

3 Within the palaces thereof
  God is a refuge known:
For lo, the kings are gather'd, and
  together they are gone.

4 But when they did behold it so,
  they wondred, and they were
Astonish'd much, and suddenly
  were driven back with fear.

5 Great terror there on them did fall,
  for very wo they cry,
As doth a woman when she shall
  go travail instantly.

6 As thou with eastern wind the ships
  upon the sea dost break,
They were destroy'd: and ev'n as we
  have heard our fathers speak;

7 So in the city of our Lord
  we saw as it was told,
Yea, in the city which our God
  for ever will uphold.

8 O Lord, we wait and do dep
  on thy good help and grace
For which we do all times att
  within thy holy place.

9 O Lord, according to thy N
  for ever is thy praise:
And thy right hand, O Lord,
  of righteousness always.

10 Let, for thy judgments, Sion
  fulfilled be with joys:
Also of Judah grant, O Lor
  the daughters to rejoyce.

11 Go walk about all Sion hi
  yea, round about her go;
And tell the towers that ther
  are builded on a row.

12 And mark ye well her bulwa
  behold hers towers there:
That ye may tell thereof to t
  that after shall be here.

13 For this most mighty God, o
  for evermore is he:
Yea, and unto the death also
  our guider shall he be.

Cantus & Bassus.   PSALM XLIX.   *Cambridg*

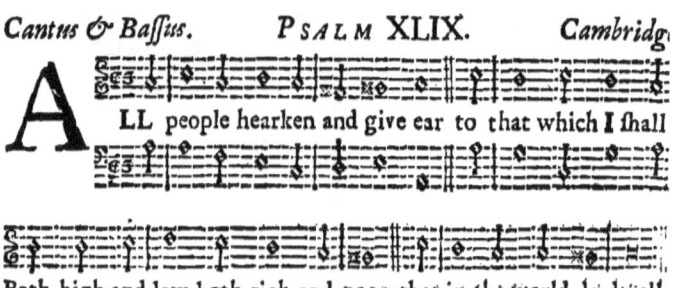

ALL people hearken and give ear to that which I shall
Both high and low, both rich and poor, that in the world do dwell.

Psalm xlix.   79

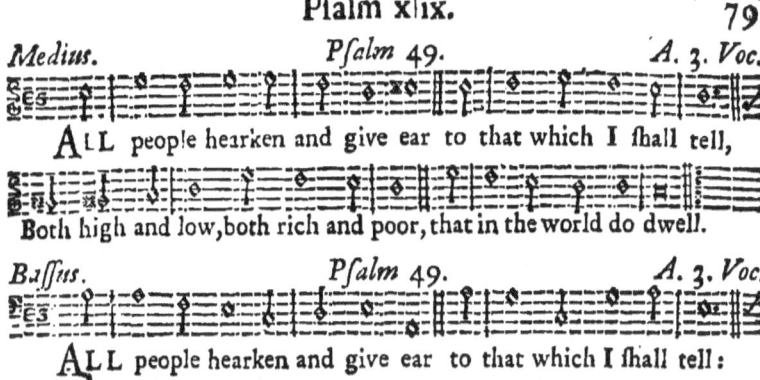

Medius.   *Psalm* 49.   *A. 3. Voc.*

ALL people hearken and give ear to that which I shall tell,

Both high and low, both rich and poor, that in the world do dwell.

Bassus.   *Psalm* 49.   *A. 3. Voc.*

ALL people hearken and give ear to that which I shall tell:

Both high and low, both rich and poor, that in the world do dwell.

3 For why? my mouth shall make dis-
of many things right wise: (course
In understanding shall mine heart
its study exercise.

4 I will incline mine ear to know
the parable so dark:
And open all my doubtful speech
in metre on my harp.

5 Why should I fear affliction,
or any careful toyl:
Or else my foes which at my heels
are prest my life to spoil?

6 For as for such as riches have,
wherein their trust is most;
And they which of their treasures
themselves do brag & boast. (great

7 There is not one of them that can
his brother's life redeem,
Or give a ransom unto God
sufficient for him.

8 It is too great a price to pay,
none can thereto attain:
So that he might his life prolong,
or not in grave remain.

9 They see wise men, as well as fools,
subject unto death's bands:
And being dead, strangers possess
their houses, goods and lands.

10 Their care is to build houses fair,
and so determine sure
To make their names upon the earth
for ever to endure.

11 Yet shall no man always enjoy
high honour, wealth and rest:
12 But shall at length taste of death's
as well as the brute beast. (cup,
The second part.

13 And thô they find their foolish
to be most lewd & vain: (thoughts
Their children yet approve their
and in like sin remain. (talk,

14 As sheep into the fold are brought,
they shall be laid in grave:
Death shall them eat, and in that day
the just shall lordship have.

15 Their beauty and their royal port
shall fade and quite decay,
When from their house unto the pit
with wo they pass away.

16 But

16 But God will surely me preserve
from death and endless pain,
Because he will of his good grace
my soul receive again.

17 If any man grow wondrous rich,
be not afraid therefore:
Althô the glory of his house
increaseth more and more.

18 For when he dies, of all these things
nothing shall he receive:
His glory will not follow him,
his pomp will take her leave.

19 Yet in this life he counts himself
the happi'st under sun:
And others likewise flatter him,
saying, All is well done.

20 But yet if he should live as long
as did his fathers old :   (place,
Yet must he needs at length give
and be brought to death's fold.

21 Man that in honour lives, and doth
not understand, may be
Compar'd unto the very beasts,
that perish utterly.

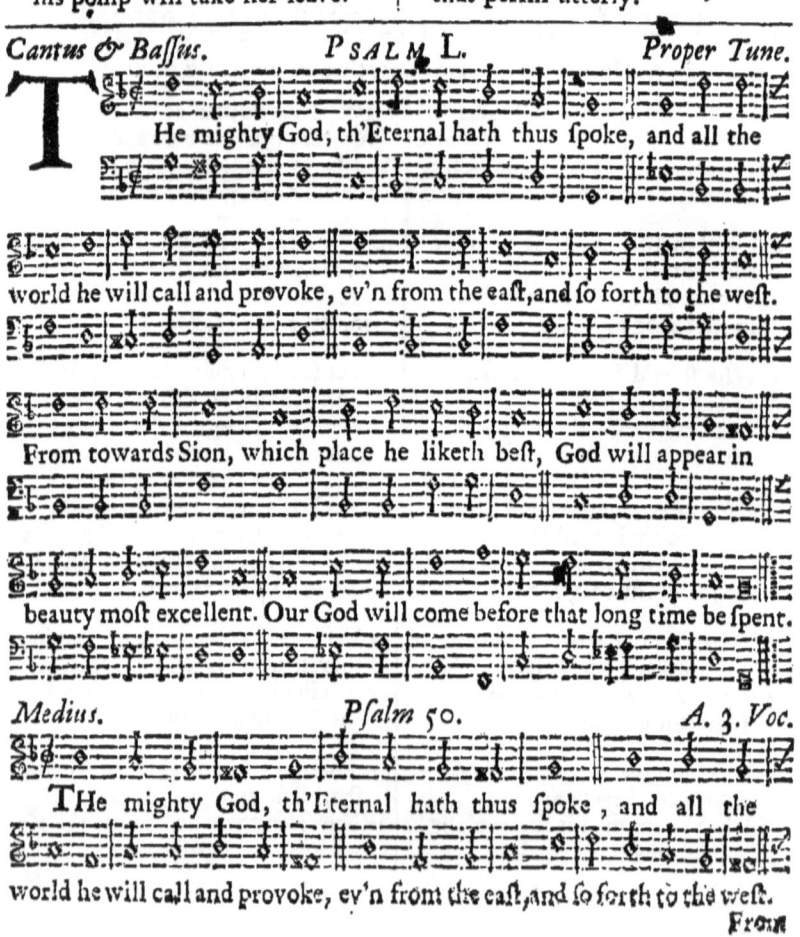

Cantus & Bassus.   PSALM L.   Proper Tune.

The mighty God, th'Eternal hath thus spoke, and all the world he will call and provoke, ev'n from the east, and so forth to the west. From towards Sion, which place he liketh best, God will appear in beauty most excellent. Our God will come before that long time be spent.

Medius.   Psalm 50.   A. 3. Voc.

The mighty God, th'Eternal hath thus spoke, and all the world he will call and provoke, ev'n from the east, and so forth to the west.

From

Psalm 1. 81

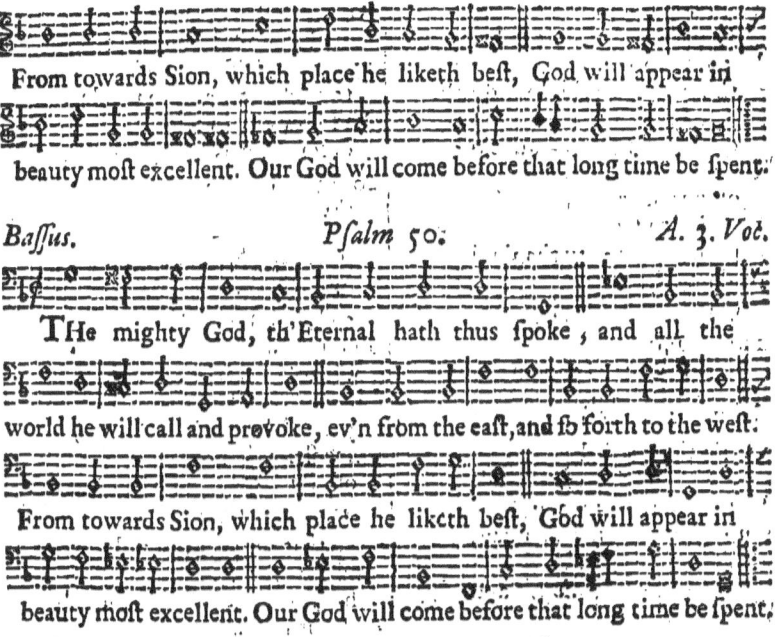

From towards Sion, which place he liketh best, God will appear in beauty most excellent. Our God will come before that long time be spent.

Bassus. — *Psalm 50.*   *A. 3. Voc.*

THe mighty God, th'Eternal hath thus spoke, and all the world he will call and provoke, ev'n from the east, and so forth to the west. From towards Sion, which place he liketh best, God will appear in beauty most excellent. Our God will come before that long time be spent.

Devouring fire
  shall go before his face;
A great tempest
  shall round about him trace.
4 Then shall he call
  the earth and heavens bright,
To judge his folk
  with equity and right:
5 Saying, Go to,
  and now my saints assemble:
My pact they keep,
  their gifts do not dissemble.
6 The heavens shall
  declare his righteousness:
For God is judge
  of all things more and less.
7 Hear my people,
  for I will now reveal;

Lift Israel,
  I'll from thee nought conceal.
Thy God, thy God
  am I, and will not blame thee
8 For giving not
  all manner offerings to me.
9 I have no need
  to take of thee at all
Goats of thy fold,
  or calf out of thy stall:
10 For all the beasts
  are mine within the woods:
On thousand hills
  cattel are mine own goods:
11 I know for mine
  all birds that are on mountains:
All beasts are mine   (tains.
  which haunt the fields and foun-

12 Hungry if I were,
  I would not thee it tell:
For all is mine
  that in the world doth dwell.
13 Eat I the flesh
  of great bulls, or bullocks?
Or drink the blood
  of goats, or of the flocks?
14 Offer to God
  praise and hearty thanksgiving,
And pay thy vows
  unto God everlasting.
15 Call upon me
  when troubled thou shalt be:
Then will I help,
  and thou shalt honour me.
16 To the wicked
  thus saith th'eternal God;
Why dost thou preach
  my laws and hests abroad,
17 Seeing thou hast
  them with thy mouth abused,
And har'st to be
  by discipline reformed?
My words, I say,
  thou dost reject and hate:
18 If that thou see
  a thief, as with thy mate,
Thou run'st with him,
  and so your prey seek out;
And art all one
  with the adult'rous rout.
19 Thou giv'st thy self
  to back-bite, and to slander:
And how thy tongue
  deceives, it is a wonder.
20 Thou sitt'st musing
  thy brother how to blame,
And how to put
  thy mothers son to shame.
21 These things thou didst,
  and whilst I held my tongue,
Thou didst me judge
  because I stay'd so long,
Like to thy self:
  yet tho I keep long silence,
Once shalt thou feel
  of thy wrongs just recompence.
22 Consider this
  ye that forget the Lord,
And fear not when
  he threatneth with his word:
Left without help
  I spoil you as a prey.
23 But he that thanks
  offereth, praiseth me aye,
Saith the Lord God:
  and he that walketh this trace,
I will him teach
  God's saving health to embrace.

Cantus & Bassus.   *Another of the same.*   *Southwel Tune.*

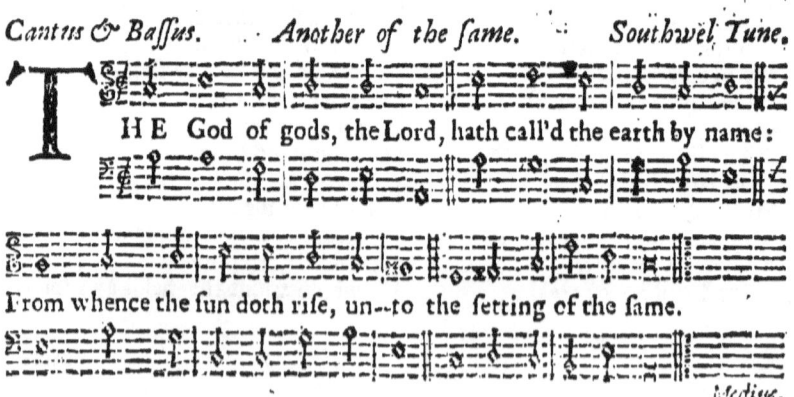

THE God of gods, the Lord, hath call'd the earth by name:
From whence the sun doth rise, un--to the setting of the same.

Medius.

Psalm I. 83

Medius. *Psalm 50.* *A. 3. Voc.*

THE God of gods, the Lord, hath call'd the earth by name:

From whence the sun doth rise, un--to the setting of the same.

Bassus. *Psalm 50.* *A. 3. Voc.*

THE God of gods, the Lord, hath call'd the earth by name:

From whence the sun doth rise, un--to the setting of the same.

2 From Sion his fair place,
  his glory bright and clear,
The perfect beauty of his grace,
  from thence it did appear.

3 Our God shall come in haste,
  to speak he shall not doubt:
Before him shall the fire waste,
  and tempest round about.

4 The heavens from on high,
  the earth below likewise
He will call forth to judge and try
  the people that are his.

5 Bring forth my saints, saith he,
  my faithful flock so dear:
Which are in band & league with me,
  my law to love and fear.

6 And when these things are tri'd,
  then shall the heav'ns record,
That God is just; and all must 'bide
  the judgment of the Lord.

7 My people, O give heed!
  Israel to thee I cry:
I am thy God, thy help at need,
  thou can'st it not deny.

8 I do not say to thee,
  thy sacrifice is slack:
Thou offer'st daily unto me
  much more than I do lack.

9 Think'st thou that I do need
  thy cattel young or old?
Or else so much desire to feed
  on goats out of thy fold?

10 Nay, all the beasts are mine
  in woods that eat their fills:
And thousands more of neat & kine
  that run wild on the hills.

The second part.

11 The birds that build on high,
  in hills and out of sight:
And beasts that in the fields do lie,
  are subject to my might.

12 Then tho' I hungred sore,
  what need I ought of thine,
Since that the earth with her great
  and all therein is mine? (store,

13 To bulls flesh have I mind
  to eat it dost thou think?
Or such a sweetness do I find
  the blood of goats to drink?

G 2 14 Give

Psalm l, li.

14 Give to the Lord his praise,
   with thanks to him apply:
And see thou pay thy vows always
   unto the God most high.
15 Then seek and call to me,
   when ought would work thee
And I will sure deliver thee, (blame
   that thou may'st praise my Name.
16 But to the wicked train,
   which talk of God each day:
And yet their works are fowl & vain,
   to them the Lord will say,
17 With what face darest thou
   my word once speak or name?
Why doth thy talk my law allow,
   thy deeds deny the same?
18 Whereas for to amend
   thy life thou art so slack:
My word the which thou dost pre-
   is cast behind thy back. (tend,

The third part.

19 When thou a thief dost see
   by theft to live in wealth,
With him thou runn'st & dost agree
   likewise to thrive by stealth.
20 When thou dost them behold
   that wives and maids defile:

Thou lik'st it well, and waxest bold
   to use that life most vile.
21 Thy lips thou dost apply
   to slander and defame: (lie,
Thy tongue doth teach to cheat and
   and still doth use the same.
22 Thou studi'st to revile
   thy friends to thee so near:
With slander thou wouldst needs de-
   thy mothers son most dear. (file
23 Hereat while I do wink,
   as thô I did not see,
Thou go'st on still, and so dost think
   that I am like to thee.
24 But sure I will not let
   to strike, when I begin:
Thy faults in order I will set,
   and open all thy sin.
25 Mark this I you require,
   that have not God in mind:
Lest when I plague you in mine ire,
   your help be far to find.
26 He that doth give to me
   the sacrifice of praise,
Doth please me well, and he shall see
   to walk in godly ways.

Cantus & Bassus.   **PSALM LI.**   *Proper Tune.*

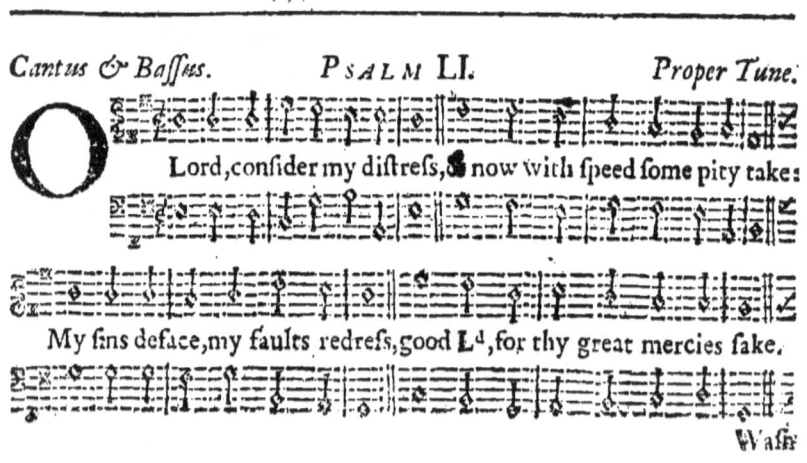

O Lord, consider my distress, & now with speed some pity take:
My sins deface, my faults redress, good L^d, for thy great mercies sake.

Wash

Psalm li. 85

Wash me, O Lord, and make me clean from this unjust and sinful act,

And pu--ri--fie me once again from this foul crime and bloody fact.

Medius.   *Psalm* 51.   *A. 3. Voc.*

O Lord, con--si--der my distress, and now with speed some pity take:

My sins deface, my faults redress, good Lord, for thy great mercies sake.

Wash me, O Lord, and make me clean from this unjust and sinful act,

And pu--ri--fie me once again from this foul crime and bloody fact.

Bassus.   *Psalm* 51.   *A. 3. Voc.*

O Lord, con--si--der my distress, and now with speed some pity take:

My sins deface, my faults redress, good Lord, for thy great mercies sake.

Wash me, O Lord, and make me clean from this unjust and sinful act,

And pu--ri--fie me once again from this foul crime and bloody fact.

G 3   3 Re-

Pſalm li.

3 Remorſe and ſorrow do conſtrain
  me to acknowledge mine exceſs:
My ſin, alas! doth ſtill remain
  before my face without releaſe.
4 Againſt thee only I have ſinn'd,
  committing evil in thy ſight:
And if I ſhould no mercy find,
  yet were thy judgments juſt &right.

5 It is too manifeſt, alas,
  that firſt I was conceiv'd in ſin:
Yea, of my mother ſo born was,
  and yet, vile wretch, remain therein.
6 Alſo behold, Lord, thou doſt love
  the inward truth of a pure heart:
Therefore thy wiſdom from above
  thou haſt reveal'd me to convert.

7 If thou with hyſſop purge this blot,
  I ſhall be cleaner than the glaſs:
And if thou waſh away my ſpot,
  the ſnow in whiteneſs ſhall I paſs.
8 Therfore, O Lord, ſuch joy me ſend,
that I may praiſe thee with my voice:
And that my ſtrenth may now amend,
  and broken bones alſo rejoyce.

9 Turn back thy face & frowning ire,
  for I have felt enough thy hand:
And purge my ſins I thee deſire,
  which do in number paſs the ſand.
10 Make new my heart within my
  & frame it to thy holy will:(breaſt,
And let thy ſpirit in me reſt,
  wch may my ſoul with comfort fill.

The ſecond part.

11 Caſt me not, L^d, out from thy ſight,
  but ſpeedily my torments end:
Take not from me thy holy ſpirit,
  wch may from dangers me defend.

12 Reſtore me to thoſe joys again
  which I was wont in thee to find:
Let me thy free Spirit retain,
  wch unto thee may ſtir my mind.
                  (know,
13 Thus when I ſhall thy mercies
  I ſhall inſtruct others therein:(low,
And men that are likewiſe brought
  by mine example ſhall flee ſin.
14 O God, that of my health art Lord,
  forgive me this my bloody vice:
My heart & tongue ſhall then accord
  to ſing thy mercies and juſtice.
                  (untie,
15 Touch thou my lips, my tongue
  O Lord, which art the only key:
And then my mouth ſhall teſtifie
  thy wondrous works & praiſe alway.
16 And as for outward ſacrifice,
  I would have offer'd many one:
But thou eſteem'ſt them of no price,
  and therein pleaſure takeſt none.

17 The heavy heart, the mind oppreſt,
  O Lord, thou never doſt reject:
Becauſe in truth, it is the beſt,
  and of all ſacrifice th' effect.
18 Lord, unto Sion turn thy face,
  pour out thy mercies on thy hill,
And on Jeruſalem thy grace,
  build up the walls, and love it ſtill.
                  (off'rings
19 Thou ſhalt accept then our
  of peace and right'ouſneſs alway,
Yea, calves, and many other things,
  upon thine altar will we lay.

To Father, Son, and Holy Ghoſt,
  all praiſe and glory be therefore:
As in beginning was, is now,
  and ſhall be evermore. Amen.

Another

Psalm li. 87

Cantus & Bassus.   *Another of the same.*   *Cambridge Tune.*

Have mercy on me, Lord, after thy great abounding grace:
After thy mercies mul-ti-tude, do thou my sins deface.

Medius.   *Psalm 51.*   *A. 3. Voc.*

Have mercy on me, Lord, after thy great abounding grace:
After thy mercies mul—ti--tude, do thou my sins deface.

Bassus.   *Psalm 51.*   *A. 3. Voc.*

Have mercy on me, Lord, after thy great abounding grace:
After thy mercies mul—ti--tude, do thou my sins deface.

2 Yea, wash me clean from mine of-
and mine iniquity: (fence,
For I do own my faults, and still
my sin is in mine eye.

3 Against thee, thee alone I have
offended in this case:
And evil have I done before
the presence of thy face.
                                (done,
4 That in the things which thou hast
upright thou may'st appear:

And when thou judgest, all may see
that thou art very clear,

5 Behold, in wickedness my kind
and shape I did receive:
My sinful mother at the first
in sin did me conceive.

6 But lo, truth in the inward parts
is pleasant unto thee;
And secrets of thy wisdom thou
revealed hast to me.

G 4   7 With

Psalm li, lii.

7 With hyssop, Lord, besprinkle (me,
   I shall be cleansed so :
Yea, wash thou me, and so I shall
   be whiter than the snow.

8 Of joy and gladness make thou me
   to hear the pleasant voice:
That so the bones wch thou, O Lord,
   hast broken, may rejoyce.

9 From the beholding of my sins,
   Lord, turn away thy face:
And all my deeds of wickedness
   do utterly deface.

10 O God, create in me a heart
    unspotted in thy sight:
Within my bowels, Lord, renew
    a firm and stable spirit.

11 Cast me not from thy sight, nor
    thy holy spirit away: (take
The comfort of thy saving health
    give me again, I pray.

12 With thy free spirit stablish me,
    and I will teach therefore
Sinners thy ways, that so they may
    turn to thee evermore.

The second part.

13 O God, that art God of my health,
    from blood deliver me:
That praises of thy righteousness
    my tongue may sing to thee.

14 My lips that yet fast closed be,
    do thou, O Lord, unloose:
The praises of thy Majesty
    my mouth shall then disclose.

15 I would have offer'd sacrifice,
    if that had pleased thee:
But pleased with burnt-offerings
    I know thou wilt not be.

16 A troubled spirit is sacrifice
    delightful in God's eyes:
A broken and an humble heart,
    Lord, thou wilt not despise.

17 In thy good will deal gently, Lord,
    to Sion, and withall,
Grant that of thy Jerusalem
    uprear'd may be the wall.

18 Burnt-off'rings, gifts, and sacrifice
    of justice, in that day
Thou shalt accept, and calves they
    upon thine altar lay. (shall

Cantus & Bassus.   **PSALM LII.**   *Lichfield Tune.*

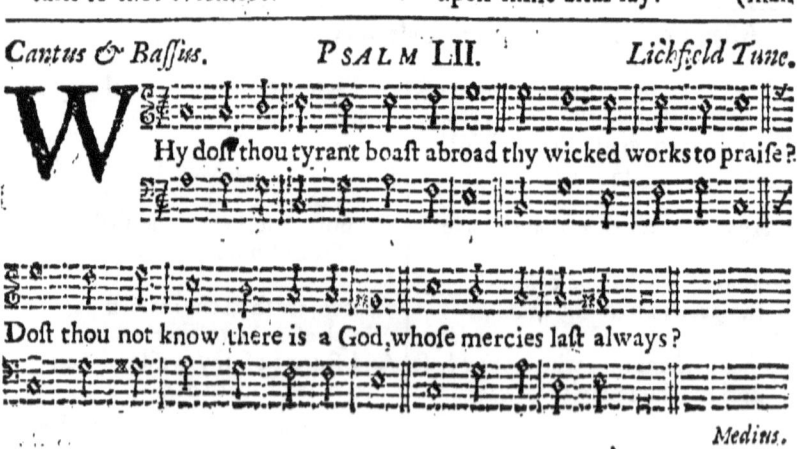

Why dost thou tyrant boast abroad thy wicked works to praise?

Dost thou not know there is a God, whose mercies last always?

Medius.

Doſt thou not know there is a God, whoſe mercies laſt always?

Baſſus.   *Pſalm* 52.   *A.* 3. *Voc.*

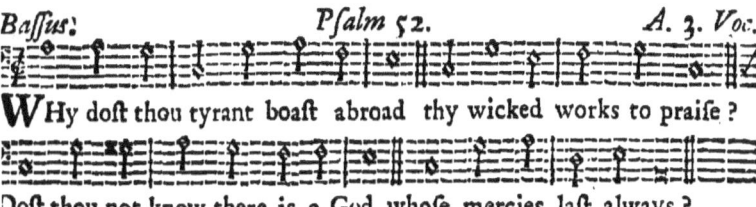

WHy doſt thou tyrant boaſt abroad thy wicked works to praiſe?

Doſt thou not know there is a God, whoſe mercies laſt always?

1 Why doth thy mind yet ſtill deviſe
ſuch wicked wiles to warp?
Thy tongue untrue in forging lies
is like a razor ſharp.   (mind,
3 On miſchief why ſett'ſt thou thy
and wilt not walk upright?
Thou haſt more luſt falſe tales to find,
than bring the truth to light.

4 Thou doſt delight in fraud & guile,
in miſchief, blood, and wrong:
Thy lips have learn'd the flatt'ring
O falſe deceitful tongue! (ſtyle,
 (found,
5 Therefore the Lord ſhall thee con-
and pluck thee from thy place:
Thy ſeed root out from off the
and utterly deface. (ground,

6 The juſt, when they behold thy fall,
with fear will praiſe the Lord,
And in reproach of thee withal
cry out with one accord,

7 Behold the man that would not take
the Lord for his defence:
But of his goods his God did make,
and truſt his corrupt ſenſe.

8 But I as olive freſh and green
ſhall ſpring and ſpread abroad:
For why? my truſt all times hath
upon the living God. (been

9 For this therefore will I give praiſe
to thee with heart and voice:
I will advance thy Name always,
wherein thy ſaints rejoyce.

Psalm liii.

Cantus & Bassus. **PSALM LIII.** *York Tun*

THe foolish man within his heart blasphemously hath said
There is not a—ny God at all, why should we be afraid?

Medius. *Psalm 53.* *A. 3. Vo*

THe foolish man within his heart blasphemously hath said,
There is not a—ny God at all, why should we be afraid?

Bassus. *Psalm 53.* *A. 3. Vo*

THe foolish man within his heart blaspemously hath said,
There is not a—ny God at all, why should we be afraid?

2 They are corrupt, and they also
a hainous work have wrought:
Among them all there is not one
of good that worketh ought.

3 The Lord look'd down from heav'n
the sons of men below, (upon
To see if any were that sought
the living God to know.

4 They are all gone out of the way,
they are corrupted all:
There is not any that doth good,
there is not one at all.

5 Do not all wicked workers know,
that they do feed upon
My people, as they fed on bread?
The Lord they call not on:

6 Ev'n there they were afraid, & stood
with trembling all dismay'd,
Whereas there was no cause at all
why they should be afraid.

7 For God his bones that thee besieg'd
hath scatter'd all abroad:
He hath confounded them, for the
rejected are of God.

8 O Lord, give thou thy people health
and thou, O Lord, fulfill
Thy promise made to Israel
from out of Sion hill.

9 When God his people shall restore
that once were captive led,
Then Jacob shall therein rejoyce,
and Israel be glad.

PSAL

Pſalm liv.   91

2 Regard, O Lord, and give an ear
 to me when I do pray:
Bow down thy ſelf to me, and hear
 the words that I do ſay.

3 For ſtrangers up againſt me riſe,
 and tyrants vex me ſtill:
Wch have not God before their eyes,
 they ſeek my ſoul to ſpill.

4 But lo, my God doth give me aid,
 the Lord is ſtraight at hand:
With them by whom my ſoul is ſtaid,
 the Lord doth ever ſtand.

5 With plagues repay again all thoſe
 for me that lie in wait:
And in thy truth deſtroy my foes
 with their own ſnare and bait.

6 An off'ring of free heart and will
 then I to thee ſhall make,
And praiſe thy Name, for therein ſtill
 great comfort I do take.

7 Thou, Ld, at length haſt ſet me free
 from them that craft conſpire:
And now mine eye with joy doth ſee
 on them my heart's deſire.

P S A L M

Psalm lv.

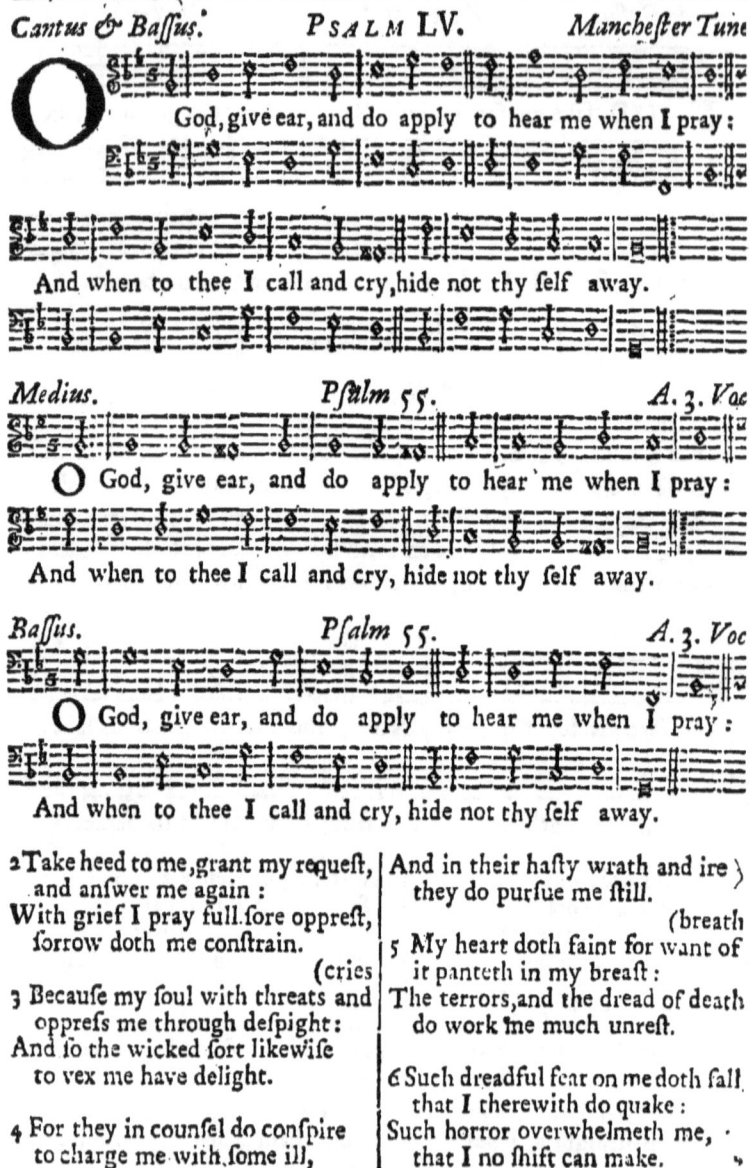

Cantus & Bassus. PSALM LV. *Manchester Tune*

O God, give ear, and do apply to hear me when I pray:
And when to thee I call and cry, hide not thy self away.

Medius. Psalm 55. A. 3. Voc

O God, give ear, and do apply to hear me when I pray:
And when to thee I call and cry, hide not thy self away.

Bassus. Psalm 55. A. 3. Voc

O God, give ear, and do apply to hear me when I pray:
And when to thee I call and cry, hide not thy self away.

2 Take heed to me, grant my request,
and answer me again :
With grief I pray full sore opprest,
sorrow doth me constrain.
      (cries
3 Because my soul with threats and
opprefs me through despight :
And so the wicked sort likewife
to vex me have delight.

4 For they in counfel do confpire
to charge me with some ill,

And in their hafty wrath and ire ⎫
they do pursue me still.
      (breath
5 My heart doth faint for want of
it panteth in my breaft :
The terrors, and the dread of death
do work me much unreft.

6 Such dreadful fear on me doth fall,
that I therewith do quake :
Such horror overwhelmeth me,
that I no fhift can make.
      7 But

Pſalm lv.

7 But I did ſay, Who will me give
   the ſwift and pleaſant wings
Of ſome fair dove, that I may flee.
   and reſt me from theſe things?
8 Lo, then I would go far away,
   to fly I would not ceaſe:
And I would hide my ſelf, and ſtay
   in ſome great wildernefs.
9 I would be gone in all the haſte,
   and not abide behind,
Till I were quit and overpaſt
   theſe blaſts of boiſtrous wind.
10 Divide them, Lord, and from them
   their falſe & double tongue: (pull
For I have ſpi'd their city full
   of rapine, ſtrife, and wrong.
11 Which things both night and day
   incloſe her as a wall: (throughout
In midſt of her is miſchief wrought,
   and ſorrow great withal.
12 Her inward parts are wicked plain,
   her deeds are much too vile:
And in her ſtreets there doth remain
   nothing but fraud and guile.

The ſecond part.

13 If that my foes did ſeek my ſhame,
   I might it well abide:
Becauſe from all their check & blame
   ſomewhere I could me hide.
14 But thou it was my fellow dear,
   which friendſhip did pretend,
And did my ſecret counſel hear,
   as my familiar friend.
15 With whom I had delight to talk
   in ſecret and abroad,
And we together oft did walk
   unto the houſe of God.
16 Let death in haſte upon them fall,
   and ſend them quick to hell:
For miſchief doth abide in all
   the places where they dwell.

17 But I unto my God will cry,
   to him for help I flee:
The Lord will help me inſtantly,
   and he will ſuccour me.
18 At morning, noon, & ev'ning-tide,
   unto the Lord I pray:
When I ſo conſtantly have cri'd,
   he did not ſay me nay.
19 To peace he ſhall reſtore me yet,
   thô war be now at hand:
Althô the number be full great
   that would againſt me ſtand.
20 The L^d that firſt & laſt doth reign
   both now and evermore,
Will hear when I to him complain,
   and puniſh them full ſore.
21 For ſure there is no hope that they
   to turn will once accord:
For why? they do not God obey,
   nor yet do fear the Lord.
22 Upon their friends they laid their
   wch were in cov'nant knit: (hands,
Of friendſhip to neglect the bands,
   they do not care one whit.
23 While they have war within their
   as butter are their words: (hearts,
And thô they were as ſoft as oyl,
   they cut as ſharp as ſwords.
24 Caſt thou thy care upon the Lord,
   and he ſhall nouriſh thee:
For in no wiſe he will accord
   the juſt in thrall to ſee.
25 But God ſhall caſt them deep in pit,
   that thirſt for blood always:
He will no guileful man permit
   to live out half his days.
26 Thô ſuch be quite deſtroy'd and
   on him is all my ſtay: (gone,
I will depend his grace upon
   with all my heart alway.

Psalm lvi.

Cantus & Bassus. PSALM LVI. *Salisbury Tune.*

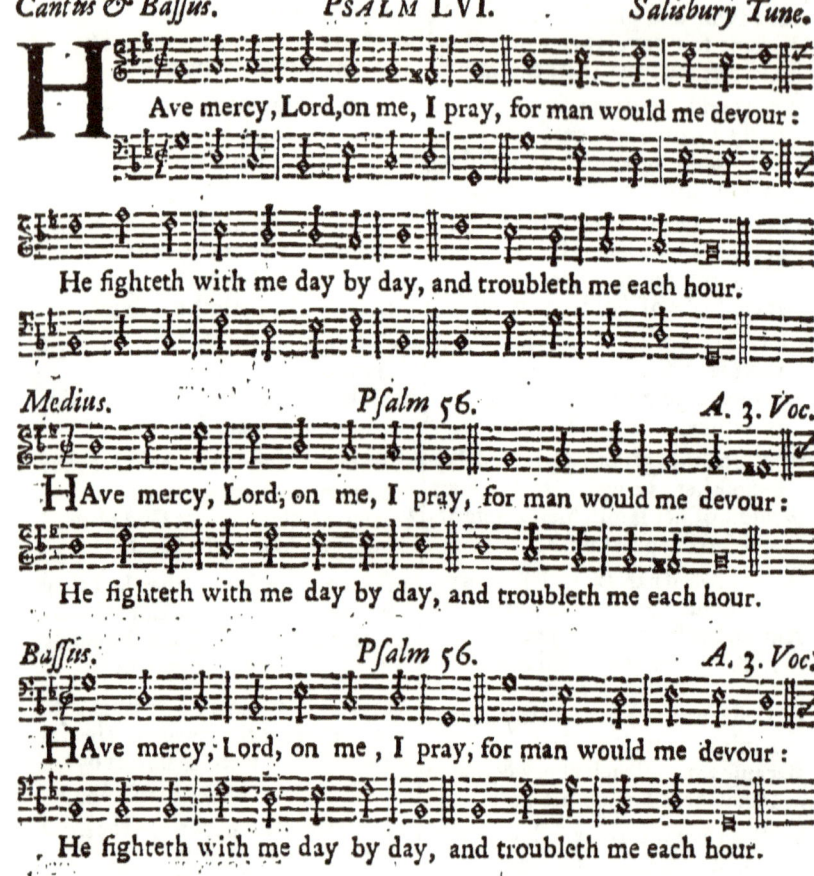

Have mercy, Lord, on me, I pray, for man would me devour:

He fighteth with me day by day, and troubleth me each hour.

Medius. Psalm 56. *A. 3. Voc.*

Have mercy, Lord, on me, I pray, for man would me devour:

He fighteth with me day by day, and troubleth me each hour.

Bassus. Psalm 56. *A. 3. Voc.*

Have mercy, Lord, on me, I pray, for man would me devour:

He fighteth with me day by day, and troubleth me each hour.

2 My foes do daily enterprise
  to swallow me out-right:
To fight against me many rise,
  O thou most High of might. (afraid

3 When they would make me most a-
  with beasts and brags of pride,
I trust in thee alone for aid,
  by thee I will abide.

4 God's promise I do mind & praise,
  O Lord, I stick to thee:
I do not care at all essays
  what flesh can do to me.

5 What things I either did or spake
  they wrest them at their will:
And all the counsel that they take,
  is how to work me ill.

6 They all consent themselves to hide
  close watch for me to lay: (tri'd
They spy my paths, and snares have
  to take my life away.

7 Shall they thus scape on mischief set:
  thou, God, on them wilt frown
For in thy wrath thou dost not let
  to throw whole kingdoms down

8 Thou

Psalm lvi, lvii.

Thou see'st how oft they made me
and on my tears dost look: (flee,
eserve them in a glass by thee,
and write them in thy book.

When I do call upon thy Name,
my foes away do start:
well perceive it by the same,
that God doth take my part.

I glory in the word of God,
to praise it I accord:
'ith joy I will declare abroad
the promise of the Lord.

11 I trust in God the Lord, and say,
as I before began,
The Lord he is my help and stay,
I do not care for man.

12 I will perform with heart most free
my vows to God always:
And I, O Lord, all times to thee
will offer thanks and praise.

13 My soul from death thou dost de-
and keep'st my feet upright:(fend,
That I before thee may ascend
with such as live in light.

antus & Bassus.   PSALM LVII.   *London Tune.*

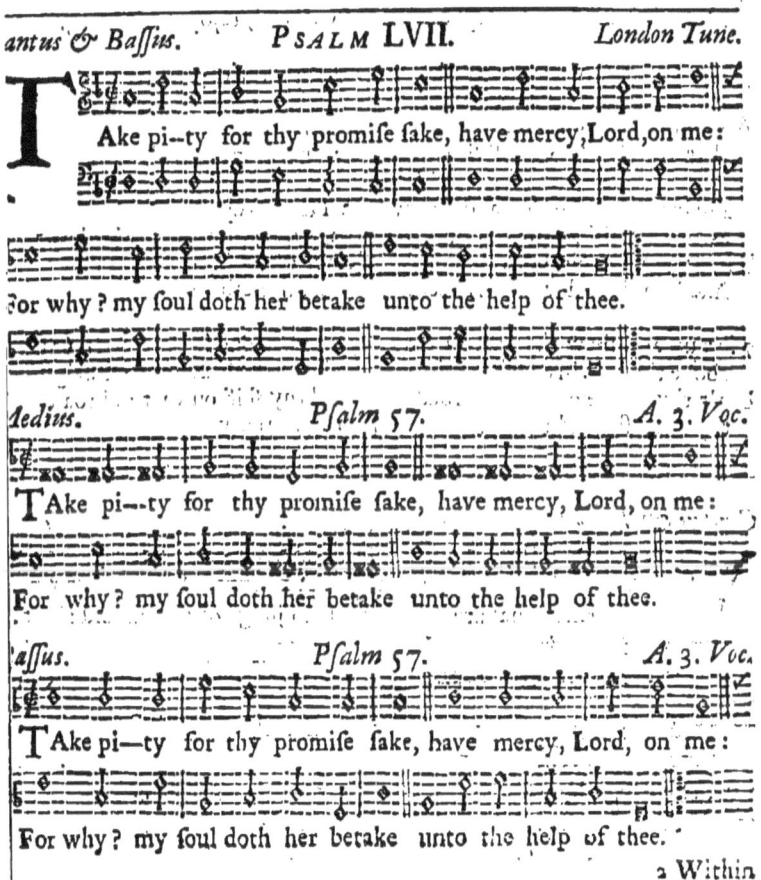

Take pi--ty for thy promise sake, have mercy, Lord, on me:

For why? my soul doth her betake unto the help of thee.

Medius.   Psalm 57.   *A. 3. Voc.*

Take pi--ty for thy promise sake, have mercy, Lord, on me:

For why? my soul doth her betake unto the help of thee.

Bassus.   Psalm 57.   *A. 3. Voc.*

Take pi--ty for thy promise sake, have mercy, Lord, on me:

For why? my soul doth her betake unto the help of thee.

a Within

Psalm lvii, lviii.

2 Within the shadow of thy wings
  I set my self full fast,
Till mischief, malice, and like things
  be gone and overpast.

3 I call upon the God most high,
  to whom I stick and stand:
I mean, the God that will stand by
  the cause I have in hand.

4 For he from heav'n hath sent his aid
  to save me from their spite,
That to devour me have essay'd
  his mercy, truth, and might.

5 I lead my life with lions fell,
  all set on wrath and ire:
And with such wicked men I dwell,
  that fret like flames of fire.
                              (long,
6 Their teeth are spears and arrows
  as sharp as I have seen: (tongue
They wound & cut with their quick
  like swords and weapons keen.

7 Set up and shew thy self, O God,
  above the heav'ns most bright:
Exalt thy praise on earth abroad,
  thy Majesty and might.

8 They laid their net, and did prepare
  a privy cave and pit:
Wherein they thought my soul to
  but they are fall'n in it. (snare,

9 My heart is set to laud the Lord,
  in him to joy always:
My heart doth ever well accord
  to sing his laud and praise.

10 Awake my soul, awake, I say,
  my lute, my harp, and string,
And I my self before the day,
  will rise, rejoyce, and sing.

11 Among the people I will tell
  the goodness of my God,
And shew his praise that doth excel
  in heathen lands abroad.

12 His mercy doth extend as far
  as the heav'ns all are high:
His truth as high as any star
  that shineth in the sky.

13 Set forth and shew thy self, O God
  above the heav'ns most bright;
Extol thy self on earth abroad,
  thy Majesty and might.

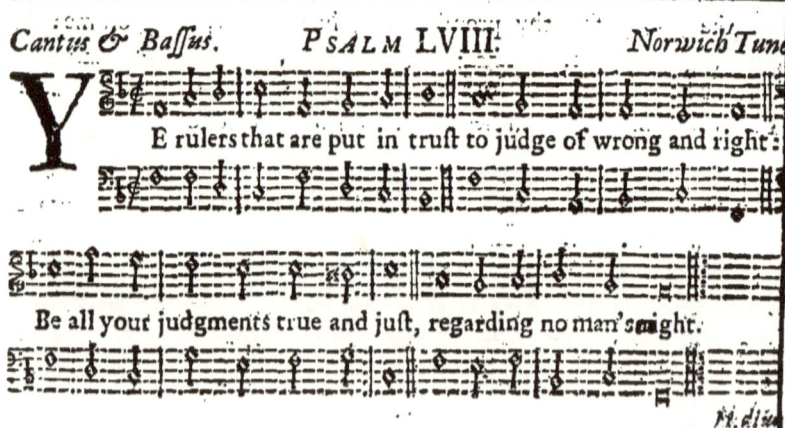

Cantus & Bassus.   PSALM LVIII.   Norwich Tune.

YE rulers that are put in trust to judge of wrong and right:

Be all your judgments true and just, regarding no man's might.

Psalm lviii.

Medius.   Psalm 58.   *A. 3. Voc.*

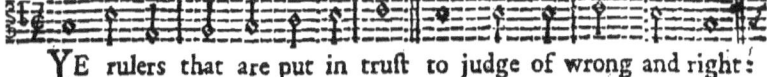

YE rulers that are put in trust to judge of wrong and right:

Be all your judgments true and just, regarding no man's might.

Bassus.   Psalm 58.   *A. 3. Voc.*

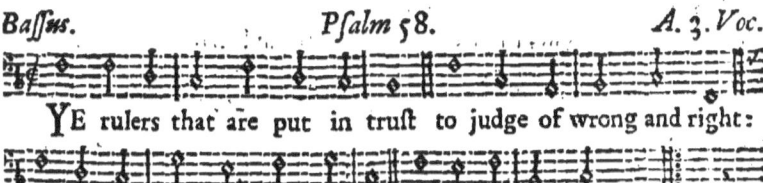

YE rulers that are put in trust to judge of wrong and right:

Be all your judgments true and just, regarding no man's might.

2 Nay, in your hearts ye mark & muse
 in mischief to consent:
And where ye should true justice use,
 your hands to bribes are bent.

3 The wicked sort from their birth
 have erred on this wise: (day
And from their mothers womb al-
 have used craft and lies. (way

4 In them the poyson and the breath
 of serpents do appear:
Yea, like the adder that is deaf,
 and fast doth stop his ear.

5 Because she will not hear the voice
 of one that charmeth well:
No, thô he were the chief of choice,
 and did therein excel.
 (set
6 The teeth, O Lord, which fast are
 in their mouth round about:
The lions teeth that are so great,
 do thou, Lord, break them out.

7 Let them consume away and waste,
 as water runs forth-right: (haste,
The shafts that they do shoot in
 let them be broke in flight.

8 As snails do waste within the shell,
 and unto slime do run:
As one before his time that fell,
 and never saw the sun.
 (young,
9 Before the thorns that now are
 to bushes big shall grow:
The storms of anger waxing strong,
 shall take them ere they know.
 (good,
10 The just shall joy, it doth them
 that God doth vengeance take:
And they shall wash their feet in
 of them that him forsake. (blood

11 Then shall the world shew forth &
 that good men have reward: (tell,
And that a God on earth doth dwell,
 that justice doth regard.

Pſalm lix.

Cantus & Baſſus.   P S A L M LIX.   *Exeter Tune.*

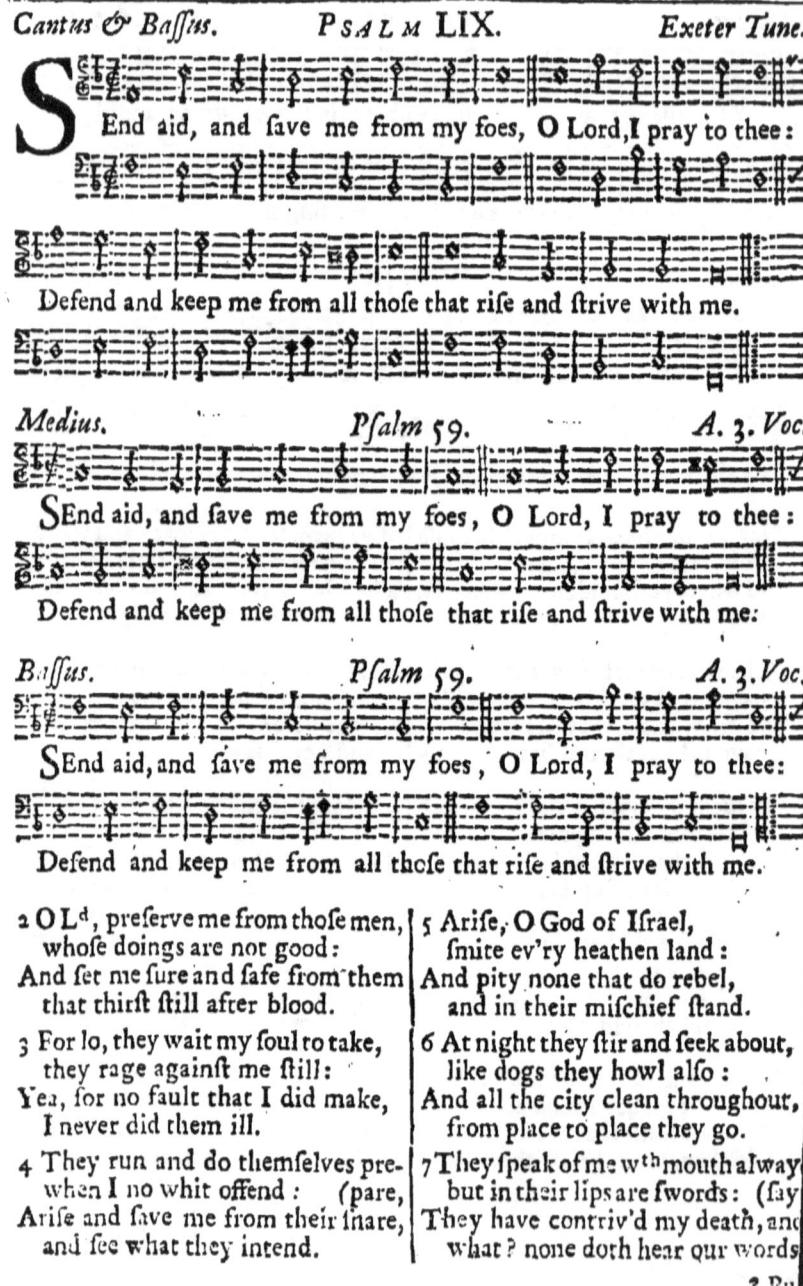

SEnd aid, and ſave me from my foes, O Lord, I pray to thee:

Defend and keep me from all thoſe that riſe and ſtrive with me.

Medius.   Pſalm 59.   *A. 3. Voc.*

SEnd aid, and ſave me from my foes, O Lord, I pray to thee:

Defend and keep me from all thoſe that riſe and ſtrive with me.

Baſſus.   Pſalm 59.   *A. 3. Voc.*

SEnd aid, and ſave me from my foes, O Lord, I pray to thee:

Defend and keep me from all thoſe that riſe and ſtrive with me.

2 O L^d, preſerve me from thoſe men,
   whoſe doings are not good:
And ſet me ſure and ſafe from them
   that thirſt ſtill after blood.

3 For lo, they wait my ſoul to take,
   they rage againſt me ſtill:
Yea, for no fault that I did make,
   I never did them ill.

4 They run and do themſelves pre-
   when I no whit offend : (pare,
Ariſe and ſave me from their ſnare,
   and ſee what they intend.

5 Ariſe, O God of Iſrael,
   ſmite ev'ry heathen land :
And pity none that do rebel,
   and in their miſchief ſtand.

6 At night they ſtir and ſeek about,
   like dogs they howl alſo :
And all the city clean throughout,
   from place to place they go.

7 They ſpeak of me wth mouth alway
   but in their lips are ſwords : (ſay
They have contriv'd my death, and
   what ? none doth hear our words

3 Bu

Psalm lix, lx.

8 But, L^d, thou hast their ways espi'd,
and thou shalt them disgrace:
The heathen folk thou dost deride,
and mock them to their face.
     (withstand,
9 The strength that doth our foes
O Lord, doth come from thee:
My God, he is my help at hand,
a fort and fence to me.
     (grace
10 The Lord to me doth shew his
in great abundance still;
That I may see my foes in case,
such as my heart doth will.

The second part.

11 Destroy them not at once, O Lord,
lest it from mind do fall: (broad,
But with thy strength drive them a-
and so consume them all.
     (tongue
12 For their ill words and truthless
confound them in their pride:
Their wicked oaths with lies and
let all the world deride. (wrong

13 Consume them in thy wrath, ô Lord,
that nought of them remain:
That men may know throughout the
that Jacob's God doth reign. (world

14 At ev'ning they return apace,
as dogs they grin and cry:
Throughout the streets in ev'ry place
they run about and spy.

15 They seek about for meat alway,
but let them not be fed:
Nor find a house wherein they may
be bold to put their head.
     (broad,
16 But I will shew thy strength a-
thy goodness I will praise:
For thou art my defence and God
at need in all essays.
     (stay'd,
17 Thou art my strength, thou hast me
O Lord, I sing to thee:
Thou art my fort, my fence, and aid,
a loving God to me.

Cantus & Bassus.   PSALM LX.   *Bristol Tune.*

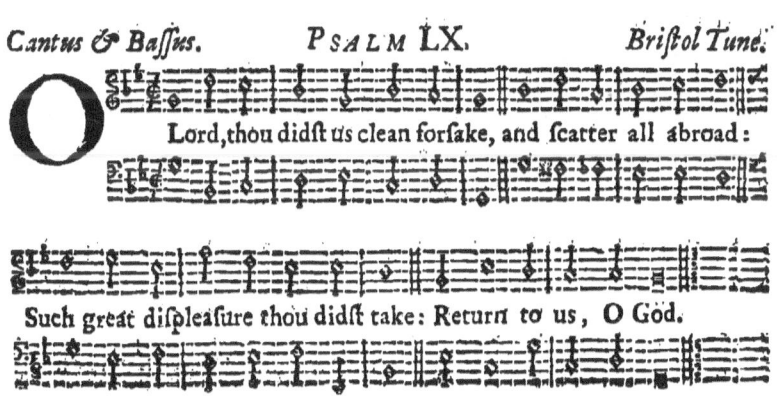

O Lord, thou didst us clean forsake, and scatter all abroad:

Such great displeasure thou didst take: Return to us, O God.

Psalm lx.

Medius.   Psalm 60.   A. 3. Voc.

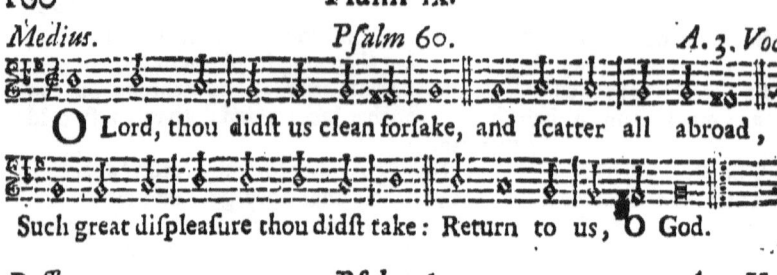

O Lord, thou didst us clean forsake, and scatter all abroad, Such great displeasure thou didst take: Return to us, O God.

Bassus.   Psalm 60.   A. 3. Voc.

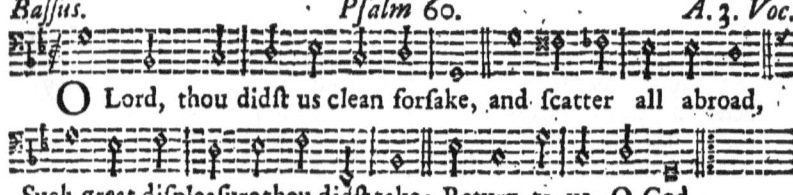

O Lord, thou didst us clean forsake, and scatter all abroad, Such great displeasure thou didst take: Return to us, O God.

2 Thy might did move the Land so
  that it in sunder brake: (sore,
The hurt thereof, O Lord, restore,
  for it doth bow and quake.

3 With heavy things thou plaguest
  the people that are thine: (thus
And thou hast given unto us
  a drink of deadly wine.

4 But yet to such as fear thy Name,
  a banner thou dost shew:
That they may triumph in the same,
  because thy Word is true.

5 So that thy might may keep and
  thy folk that favour thee: (save
That they thy help at hand may have,
  O Lord, grant this to me.

6 The Lord did speak from his own
  this was his joyful tale, (place,
I will divide Sichem by pace,
  and mete out Succoth's vale.

7 Gilead is given to my hand,
  Manasse's mine beside:

Ephraim the strength of all my land,
  my law doth Judah guide.

8 In Moab I will wash my feet,
  o'er Edom throw my shoe:
And thou Palestine ought'st to keep
  for favour me unto.

9 But who will bring me at this tide
  unto this city strong?
Or who to Edom will me guide,
  so that I go not wrong? .
                          (forsake
10 Lord, wilt not thou, which did'st
  thy folk, their land, and coasts?
Our wars in hand thou wouldst not
  nor walk among our hosts. (take,

11 Give aid, O Lord, and us relieve
  from them that us disdain:
The help that hosts of men can give,
  is all but weak and vain.
                          (have might
12 But through our God we shall
  to take great things in hand:
He will tread down and put to flight
  all those that us withstand.

PSALM

Psalm lxi. 101

Cantus & Bassus.   PSALM LXI.   *Or to Martyrs Tune.*

REgard, O Lord, for I complain, and make my suit to thee:

Let not my words return in vain, but give an ear to me.

From out the coasts and utmost parts of all the earth abroad,

In grief and anguish of my heart I cry to thee, O God.

Medius.   *Psalm 61.*   *A. 3. Voc.*

REgard, O Lord, for I complain, and make my suit to thee:

Let not my words return in vain, but give an ear to me:

From out the coasts and utmost parts of all the earth abroad,

In grief and anguish of my heart I cry to thee, O God.

H 3   *Bassus.*

Psalm lxi, lxii.

Bassus. Psalm 61. *A. 3. Voc.*

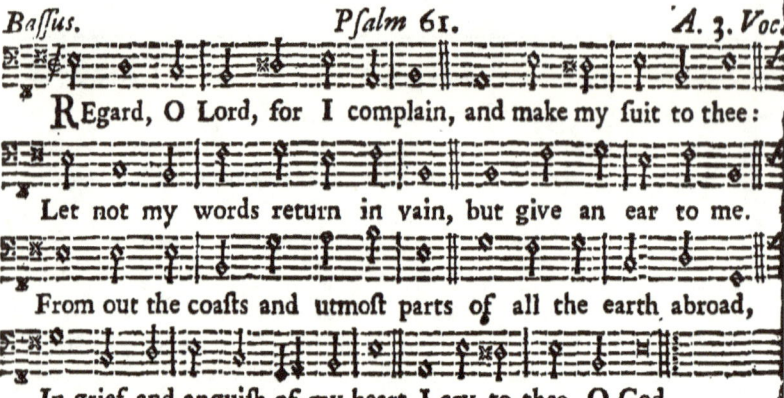

REgard, O Lord, for I complain, and make my suit to thee:

Let not my words return in vain, but give an ear to me.

From out the coasts and utmost parts of all the earth abroad,

In grief and anguish of my heart I cry to thee, O God.

3 Upon the rock of thy great pow'r
   my woful mind repose:
Thou art my hope, my fort, & tow'r,
   my fence against my foes.
4 Within thy tent I long to dwell,
   for ever to endure:
Under thy wings I know right well
   I shall be safe and sure.

5 The Lord doth my desire regard,
   and doth fulfil the same:
With riches great will he reward
   all those that fear his Name.

6 The king shall he in health main-
   and so prolong his days: (tain,
That he from age to age shall reign
   with honour great always.

7 That he may have a dwelling-place
   before the Lord alway:
O let thy mercy, truth, and grace,
   defend him from decay.
8 Then shall I sing for ever still
   with praise unto thy Name:
That all my vows I may fulfil,
   and daily pay the same.

Cantus & Bassus. PSALM LXII. *Cambridge Tune.*

Pſalm lxii.

Medius.   Pſalm 62.   *A. 3. Voc.*

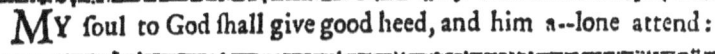

MY ſoul to God ſhall give good heed, and him a--lone attend:

For why? my health and hope to ſpeed doth whole on him depend.

Baſſus.   Pſalm 62.   *A. 3. Voc.*

MY ſoul to God ſhall give good heed, and him a--lone attend:

For why? my health and hope to ſpeed doth whole on him depend.

2 For he alone is my defence,
my rock, my health, and aid:
He is my ſtay, that no pretence
ſhall make me much diſmay'd.

3 O wicked folk, how long will ye
uſe craft? ſure ye muſt fall:
For as a rotten hedge ye be,
and like a tott'ring wall.
               (ways
4 Whom God doth love, ye ſeek al-
to put him to the worſe:
Ye love to lie, with mouth ye praiſe,
and yet your heart doth curſe.

5 Yet ſtill my ſoul doth whole depend
on God my chief deſire:
From all ill feats me to defend,
none but him I require.

6 He is my rock, my fort, and tow'r,
my health is of his grace:
He doth ſupport me, that no pow'r
can move me out of place.

7 My glory and ſalvation doth
on him alone depend:

He is my ſtrength, my ſtay, my wealth,
and ſtill doth me defend.

8 O have your truſt in him alway,
ye folk with one accord:
Pour out your hearts to him, and ſay,
Our truſt is in the Lord.

9 The ſons of men deceitful are,
on balance but a ſleight: (pare,
With things moſt vain do them com-
for they can hold no weight.

10 Truſt not in wrong and robbery,
let vain delights be gone:
Thô riches flow in ſuddenly,
ſet not your hearts thereon.
               (tell,
11 The Lord long ſince one thing did
which here to mind I call:
He ſpake it oft, I heard it well,
that he alone doth all:
               (kind,
12 And that thou, Lord, art good and
thy mercy doth exceed:
So that all ſorts with thee ſhall find
according to their deed.

And in this barren wildernefs,
 where waters there are none,
My flefh is parch'd for thought of
 for thee I wifh alone.   (thee,

2 This I might fee yet once again
 thy glory, ftrength, and might,
As I was wont it to behold
 within thy temple bright.

3 For why? thy mercies far furmount
 this life and wretched days:

My lips therefore fhall give to thee
 due honour, laud, and praife.

4 And whilft I live, I will not fail
 to worfhip thee alway:
And in thy Name I will lift up
 my hands when I do pray.

5 My foul is fill'd as with marrow,
 which is both fat and fweet:
My mouth therefore fhall fing fuch
 as are for thee moft meet. (fongs
                              6 When

Psalm lxiii, lxiv.

When in my bed I think on thee, and in the wakeful night;
And under covert of thy wings, rejoyce with great delight:
My soul doth surely stick to thee, thy right hand is my pow'r:
And those that seek my soul to slay, death shall them soon devour.

10 The sword shall them devour each their carcasses shall feed (one,
The hungry foxes, which do run their prey to seek at need.
11 The king & all men shall rejoyce, that do profess God's word:
For liars mouths shall then be stopt, and all their ways abhorr'd.

Cantus & Bassus.   PSALM LXIV.   Salisbury Tune.

O Lord, unto my voice give ear when I complain and pray:
And rid my life and soul from fear of foes that threat to slay.

Medius.   Psalm 64.   A. 3. Voc.

O Lord, un--to my voice give ear when I complain and pray:
And rid my life and soul from fear of foes that threat to slay.

Bassus.   Psalm 64.   A. 3. Voc.

O Lord, un--to my voice give ear when I complain and pray:
And rid my life and soul from fear of foes that threat to slay.

Defend me from that sort of men which in deceit do lurk:
And from the frowning face of them that all ill feats do work.

3 Who whet their tongues as we have men whet and sharp their swords:
They shoot abroad their arrows keen, I mean, most bitter words.

4 With (seen

106   Pſalm lxiv, lxv.

4 With privy ſleights ſhoot they their
   the upright man to hit: (ſhaft,
The innocent to ſtrike by craft,
   they care or fear no whit.

5 A wicked work they have decreed,
   in council thus they cry,
To uſe deceit let us not dread,
   what? who can it eſpy?
                     (muſe
6 What way to hurt they talk and
   all times within their heart:
They all conſult what feats to uſe,
   each doth invent his part.

7 But yet all this ſhall not prevail;
   when they think leaſt upon,

God with his dart ſhall ſure aſſail
   and wound them ev'ry one.
                     (with
8 Their crafts and their ill tongu
   ſhall work themſelves ſuch blam
That they which then behold the
   ſhall wonder at the ſame. (fa
                     we
9 And all that ſee ſhall know rigl
   that God the thing hath wrougl
And praiſe his wondrous works, & t(
   what he to paſs hath brought.

10 Yet ſhall the juſt in God rejoyc
   ſtill truſting in his might:
So ſhall they joy with mind & voic
   whoſe hearts are pure and right

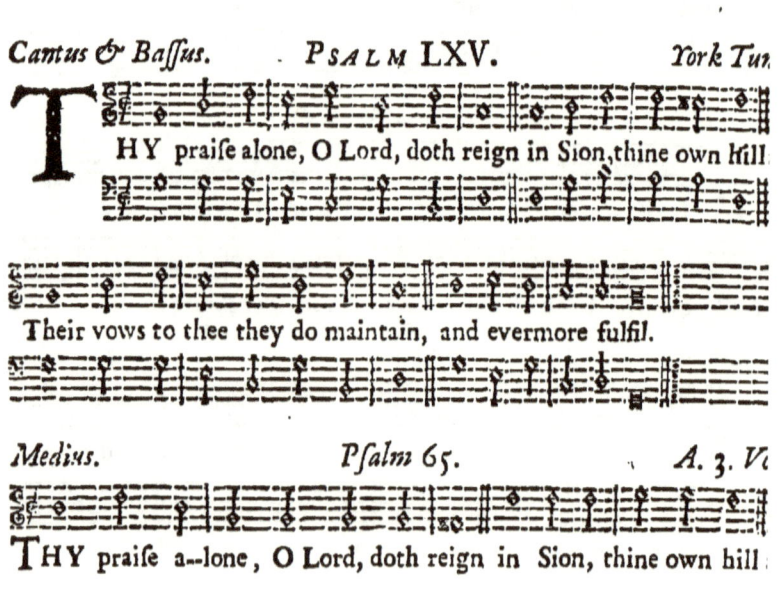

THY praife, a-lone, O Lord, doth reign in Sion, thine own hill:
Their vows to thee they do maintain, and evermore fulfil.

2 For that thou doſt their prayers
and doſt thereto agree: (hear,
The people all both far and near
with truſt ſhall come to thee.

3 Our wicked life ſo far exceeds,
that we ſhall fall therein: (deeds,
But, Lord, forgive our great mif-
and purge us from our ſin.
       (chufe
4 The man is bleſt whom thou doſt
within thy courts to dwell:
Thy houſe and temple he ſhall uſe
with pleaſures that excel.

5 Of thy great juſtice hear, O God,
our health of thee doth riſe:
The hope of all the earth abroad,
and the ſea-coaſts likewiſe.

6 With ſtrength thou art beſet about,
and compaſs'd with thy pow'r:
Thou mak'ſt the mountains ſtrong &
to ſtand in ev'ry ſhow'r. (ſtout,

7 The ſwelling ſeas thou doſt aſſwage,
making them very ſtill:
Thou doſt reſtrain the people's rage,
and rule them at thy will.
      (the earth
8 The folk that dwell throughout
ſhall dread thy ſigns to ſee:

Morning and ev'ning in great mirth
ſend praiſes up to thee.
       (dry,
9 When that the earth is chapt and
and thirſteth more and more,
Then with thy drops thou doſt ſup-
and much increaſe her ſtore. (ply,

10 The flood of God doth overflow,
and ſo doth cauſe to ſpring
The ſeed & corn which men do ſow,
for he doth guide the thing.

11 With wet thou doſt her furrows fill,
whereby her clods do fall:
Thy drops on her thou doſt diſtil,
and bleſs her fruit withal.
      (good grace
12 Thou deck'ſt the earth of thy
with fair and pleaſant crop:
Thy clouds diſtill their dew apace,
great plenty do they drop.

13 Whereby the defart ſhall begin
full great increaſe to bring,
The little hills ſhall joy therein,
much fruit in them ſhall ſpring.

14 In places plain the flocks ſhall feed,
and cover all the earth:
The vales with corn ſhall ſo exceed,
that men ſhall ſing for mirth.

PSALM

Psalm lxvi.

Cantus & Bassus.   PSALM LXVI.   *London Tune*

Ye men on earth, in God rejoyce, with praise set forth his Name

Extol his might with heart and voice, give glory to the same.

Medius.   Psalm 66.   *A. 3 Voc*

Ye men on earth, in God rejoyce, with praise set forth his Name

Extol his might with heart and voice, give glory to the same.

Bassus.   Psalm 66.   *A. 3 Voc*

Ye men on earth, in God rejoyce, with praise set forth his Name:

Extol his might with heart and voice, give glory to the same.

2 How wonderful, O Lord, say ye,
 in all thy works thou art!
Thy foes for fear shall seek to thee
 full sore against their heart.

3 All men that dwell the earth thrô-
 shall praise the Name of God: (out
The laud thereof the world about
 is shew'd and set abroad.

4 All folk come forth, behold and see
 what things the L^d hath wrought!
Mark well the wondrous works, that
 for man to pass hath brought. (he

5 He laid the sea like heaps on high
 therein a way they had
On foot to pass both fair and dry,
 whereof their hearts were glad.

6 His might doth rule the world al
 his eyes all things behold: (way
All such as shall him disobey,
 by him shall be controll'd.

7 Ye people, give unto our God
 due laud and thanks always:
With joyful voice declare abroad,
 and sing unto his praise:

8 Which

Pſalm lxvi, lxvii. 109

Which doth endue our ſoul with
and it preſerve withal: (life,
He ſtays our feet, ſo that no ſtrife
can make us ſlip, or fall.
9 The Lord doth prove our deeds with
if that they will abide: (fire,
As workmen do, when they deſire
to have their metals tri'd.
10 Altho thou ſuffer us ſo long
in priſon to be caſt,
And there with chains and fetters
to lie in bondage faſt. (ſtrong

The ſecond part.

11 Altho, I ſay, thou ſuffer men
on us to ride and reign:
Tho we through fire and water run
with very grief and pain:
12 Yet ſure thou doſt of thy good
diſpoſe it to the beſt, (grace
And bring us out into a place
to live in wealth and reſt.
13 Unto thy houſe reſort will I
to offer and to pray,
And there I will my ſelf apply
my vows to thee to pay:
14 The vows that with my mouth I
in all my grief and ſmart: (ſpake

The vows, I ſay, which I did make
in dolor of my heart.
15 Burnt off'rings I will give to thee
of oxen fat, and rams:
Yea, this my ſacrifice ſhall be
of bullocks, goats, and lambs.
16 Come forth and hearken here full
all ye that fear the Lord: (ſoon,
What he for my poor ſoul hath done
to you I will record.
17 Full oft I call to mind his grace,
this mouth to him doth cry:
And thou my tongue make ſpeed a-
to praiſe him inſtantly. (pace
18 But if I feel my heart within
in wicked works rejoyce:
Or if I have delight to ſin,
God will not hear my voice.
19 But ſurely God my voice hath
and what I do require: (heard,
My pray'r alſo he doth regard,
and granteth my deſire.
20 All praiſe to him that hath not
nor caſt me out of mind: (put
Nor yet his mercy from me ſhut,
which I do ever find.

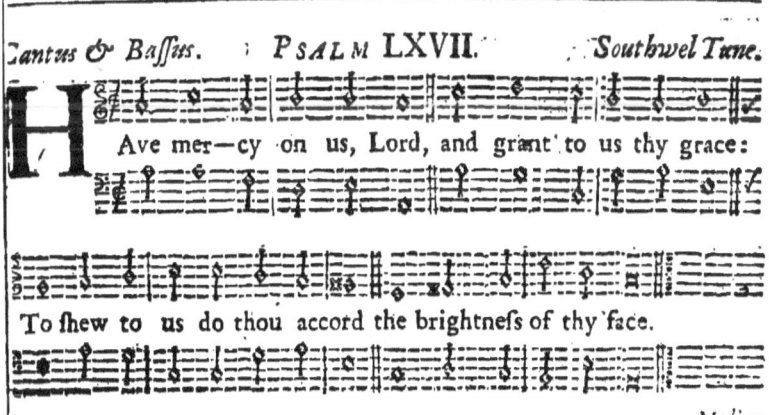

Cantus & Baſſus. Pſalm LXVII. Southwel Tune.

Have mer—cy on us, Lord, and grant to us thy grace:
To ſhew to us do thou accord the brightneſs of thy face.

Me'ius.

Medius.   Pſalm 67.   *A. 3. Voc.*

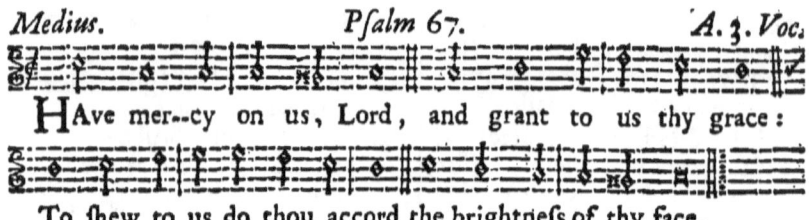

HAve mer--cy on us, Lord, and grant to us thy grace:
To ſhew to us do thou accord the brightneſs of thy face.

Baſſus.   Pſalm 67.   *A. 3. Voc.*

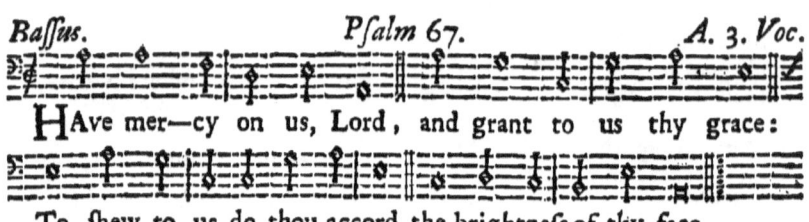

HAve mer—cy on us, Lord, and grant to us thy grace:
To ſhew to us do thou accord the brightneſs of thy face.

2 That all the earth may know
   the way to godly wealth:
And all the nations here below
   may ſee thy ſaving health.

3 Let all the world, O God,
   give praiſe unto thy Name:
And let the people all abroad
   extol and laud the ſame.

4 Throughout the world ſo wide
   let all rejoyce with mirth:
For thou with truth and right doſt guide
   the nations of the earth.

5 Let all the world, O God,
   give praiſe unto thy Name:
And let the people all abroad
   extol and laud the ſame.

6 Then ſhall the earth increaſe,
   great ſtore of fruit ſhall fall;
And then our God, the God of peace,
   ſhall ever bleſs us all.

7 God ſhall us greatly bleſs;
   and then both far and near,
The folk, which all the earth poſſeſs,
   of him ſhall ſtand in fear.

Cantus & Baſſus.   P S A L M LXVIII. Or to St. David's Tune

Psalm lxviii.   111

And as the fire doth melt the wax, and wind blows smoak away:

So in the presence of the Lord, the wicked shall decay.

Medius.   *Psalm 68.*   *A. 3. Voc.*

Let God arise, and then his foes will turn themselves to flight:

His e—ne--mies for fear shall run, and scatter out of sight.

And as the fire doth melt the wax, and wind blows smoak away:

So in the presence of the Lord, the wicked shall decay.

Bassus.   *Psalm 68.*   *A. 3. Voc.*

Let God arise, and then his foes will turn themselves to flight:

His e—ne--mies for fear shall run, and scatter out of sight.

And as the fire doth melt the wax, and wind blows smoak away:

So in the presence of the Lord the wicked shall decay.

3 But

Pſalm lxviii.

3 But righteous men before the Lord
 ſhall heartily rejoyce:
They ſhall be glad and merry all,
 and chearful in their voice.
4 Sing praiſe, ſing praiſe unto the
 who rideth on the sky: (Lord,
Extol the great Jehovah's Name,
 and him do magnifie.

5 The ſame is he that is above
 within his holy place,
That Father is of fatherleſs,
 and judge of widows caſe.
6 Houſes he gives, and iſſue both,
 unto the comfortleſs:
He bringeth bondmen out of thrall,
 and rebels to diſtreſs.
 (folk
7 When thou didſt march before thy
 th'Egyptians from among, (neſs
And brought'ſt them thrô the wilder-
 wch was both wide & long: (down,
8 The earth did quake, the rain pour'd
 heard were great claps of thunder:
Mount Sinai ſhook in ſuch a ſort,
 as if 'twould break in ſunder.

9 Thine heritage with drops of rain
 abundantly was waſh'd:
And if ſo be it barren wax'd,
 by thee it was refreſh'd. (main,
10 Thy choſen flock doth there re-
 thou haſt prepar'd that place:
And for the poor thou doſt provide
 of thine eſpecial grace.
 The ſecond part.
11 God will give women cauſes juſt
 to magnifie his Name,
When as his people triumphs make,
 and purchaſe mighty fame.
12 Puiſſant kings for all their pow'r
 ſhall flee and take the foil,
And women which remain at home
 ſhall help to part the ſpoil.

13 And thô ye were as black as pots,
 your hue ſhall paſs the dove,
Whoſe wings & feathers ſeem to have
 ſilver and gold above. (umph
14 When in this land God ſhall tri-
 o'er kings both high and low:
Then ſhall it be like Salmon hill,
 as white as any ſnow:

15 Thô Baſan be a fruitful hill,
 and in height others paſs:
Yet Sion, God's moſt holy hill,
 doth far excel in grace. (high,
16 Why leap ye thus, ye hills moſt
 and thus with pride do ſwell?
The hill of Sion God doth love,
 and there will ever dwell.

17 God's army is two millions
 of warriours great and ſtrong:
The Lord alſo in Sinai
 is preſent them among. (high,
18 Thou didſt, O Lord, aſcend on
 and captive led'ſt them all,
Which in times paſt thy choſen flock
 in bondage did inthrall.

Thou mad'ſt them tribute for to pay
 and ſuch as did repine, (dwell
Thou didſt ſubdue, that they might
 in thy temple divine.
19 Now praiſed be the Lord, for that
 he pours on us ſuch grace:
From day to day he is the God
 of our health and ſolace.
 The third part.
20 He is the God from whom alone
 ſalvation cometh plain:
He is the God by whom we ſcape
 all dangers, death, and pain.
21 But he will wound his en'mies
 and break the hairy ſcalp (head,
Of thoſe that in their wickedneſs
 continue ſtill to walk.

22 From

Pſalm lxviii.

(he,
22 From Baſan will I bring, ſaid
my people and my ſheep:
And all mine own, as I have done,
from dangers of the deep.
23 And make them dip their feet in
of thoſe that hate my Name:(blood
And dogs ſhall have their tongues
with licking of the ſame.(embrew'd

24 Thy goings they have ſeen,ô God,
unto their own diſgrace:
How thou my God and King doſt go
within thy holy place.
25 The ſingers go before with joy,
the minſtrels make no ſtay:
And in the midſt the damſels do
with timbrels ſweetly play.

26 Now in the congregation,
O Iſrael praiſe the Lord:
And Jacob's whole poſterity,
give thanks with one accord.
27 Their chief was little Benjamin,
but Judah made their hoſt,
With Zebulon and Nephthalim,
which dwelt about their coaſt.

28 As God hath given pow'r to thee,
ſo, Lord, make firm and ſure
The thing that thou haſt wrought in
for ever to endure.   (us,
29 Then in thy temple, gifts will we
offer to thee, O Lord:
And in thine own Jeruſalem
praiſe thee,with one accord.

The fourth part.

Yea,and ſtrange kings by us ſubdu'd
ſhall do like in thoſe days:
For unto thee they ſhall preſent
their gifts of laud & praiſe. (ranks,
30 He ſhall deſtroy the ſpear-men's
the calves and bulls of might:
And make them tribute pay,& daunt
all ſuch as love to fight.

31 Then ſhall the lords of Egypt come
and preſents with them bring:
The Moors moſt black ſhall ſtretch
to God their L^d &King.(their hands
32 Therfore ye kingdoms of the earth
give praiſe unto the Lord:
Sing pſalms to God with one con-
thereto let all accord.   (ſent,

33 For he doth ride, and ever did
above the heavens bright:
And by his fearful thunder-claps
men may well know his might.
34 Therefore the ſtrength of Iſrael
aſcribe to God on high,
Whoſe might and pow'r doth far ex-
above the cloudy sky.   (tend

35 O God, thy holineſs and pow'r
is dread for evermore:
The God of Iſrael gives us ſtrength,
praiſed be God therefore.
To Father, Son, and Holy Ghoſt,
immortal Glory be:
As was, is now, and ſhall be ſtill,
to all Eternitie.

Psalm lxix.

Cantus & Bassus. **PSALM LXIX.** *Glastenbury Tune.*

Save me, O God, and that with speed, the waters flow full fast:
So nigh my soul do they proceed, that I am sore agast.

Medius. **Psalm 69.** *A. 3. Voc.*

Save me, O God, and that with speed, the waters flow full fast:
So nigh my soul do they proceed, that I am sore agast.

Bassus. **Psalm 69.** *A. 3. Voc.*

Save me, O God, and that with speed, the waters flow full fast:
So nigh my soul do they proceed, that I am sore agast.

2 I sink full deep in mire and clay,
  where I can feel no ground:
And in deep waters, where I may
  most suddenly be drown'd.

3 With crying oft I weary am,
  my throat is hoarse and dry:
My sight doth fail with looking up
  for help to God on high.

4 My foes that guiltless do oppress
  my soul, with hate are led:
In number sure they are no less
  than hairs upon my head.

5 Thô for no cause they vex me sore,
  they prosper and are glad:
They do compel me to restore
  the things I never had.

6 What I have done for want of wit,
  thou, Lord, all times can'st tell:
And all the faults that I commit,
  to thee are known full well.

7 O God of hosts, defend and stay
  all those that trust in thee:
Let no man doubt or shrink away
  for ought that chanceth me.

8 It is for thee and for thy sake
  that I do bear this blame:
In spite to thee they would me make
  to hide my face for shame.

9 My mother's sons, my brethren all
  reject me with disgrace:
And as a stranger they me call,
  they will not know my face.

10 Unto

Psalm lxix.

10 Unto thy house such zeal I bear,
    that it doth vex me much:
Their checks and taunts at thee to
    my very heart doth grutch. (hear,

The second part.

11 Thô I do fast my flesh to chast,
    yea, if I weep and moan,
This in my teeth likewise is cast
    by scorners ev'ry one.

12 If I for grief and pain of heart
    in sackcloth use to walk,
Then they anon will it pervert,
    thereof they jest and talk.

13 Both high & low, & all the throng
    that sit within the gate,
They have me ever in their tongue,
    of me they talk and prate.

14 The drunkards which in wine de-
    it is their chief pastime, (light,
To seek wch way to work me spite,
    of me they sing and rhime.

15 But unto thee, O Lord, I pray,
    that when it pleaseth thee,
For thy great truth thou wilt alway
    send down thine aid to me.

16 Pluck thou my feet out of the mire,
    from drowning do me keep:
From such as owe me wrath and ire,
    and from the waters deep.

17 Lest with the waves I should be
    & depth my soul devour; (drown'd,
And that the pit should me confound,
    and shut me in her pow'r.

18 O Lord of hosts, to me give ear,
    as thou art good and kind:
And as thy mercy is most dear,
    Lord, have me in thy mind.

19 And do not from thy servant hide,
    nor turn thy face away:
I am opprest on ev'ry side,
    in haste give ear, I pray.

20 O Lord, unto my soul draw nigh,
    the same with aid repose:
Because of their great tyranny,
    acquit me from my foes.

The third part.

21 That I abide rebuke and shame,
    thou know'st and thou canst tell:
For those that seek & work the same,
    thou see'st them all full well.

22 When they with brags do break my
    some help I fain would see: (heart
But find no friends to ease my smart,
    not one to comfort me.

23 But in my meat they gave me gall,
    too cruel for to think:
And gave me in my thirst withal
    strong vinegar to drink.

24 Lord, turn their table to a snare
    to take themselves therein:
And when they think full well to fare,
    then trap them in their gin:

25 And let their eyes be dark & blind,
    that they may nothing see:
Bow down their backs, and do them
    in thraldom for to be.   (bind,

26 Pour out thy wrath as hot as fire,
    that it on them may fall:
Let thy displeasure in thine ire
    take hold upon them all.

27 As deserts dry their house disgrace,
    their seed do thou expel:
That none thereof possess their place,
    nor in their tents e'er dwell.

28 If thou dost strike the man to tame,
    on him they lay full sore:
And if that thou do wound the same,
    they seek to hurt him more.

29 Then let them heap up mischief
    since they are all pervert, (still,
That of thy favour and good will
    they never have a part.

Pſalm lxix, lxx.

30 And raſe them clean out of thy
    of life, of hope, and truſt : (book
That for their names they never look
    in number of the juſt.

The fourth part.

31 Thô I, O Lord, with wo and grief
    have been full ſore oppreſs'd :
Thy help ſhall give me ſuch relief,
    that all ſhall be redreſs'd.

32 That I may give thy name the
    that doth to thee belong : (praiſe
I will extol the ſame always
    with a thankſgiving ſong.

33 Which is more pleaſant unto thee,
    ſuch mind thy grace hath born,
Than either ox or calf can be,
    that hath both hoof and horn.

34 When ſimple folk do this behold,
    it ſhall rejoyce them ſure :
All ye that ſeek the Lord, your life
    for ever ſhall endure.
                      (hear
35 For why ? the Lord of hoſts doth
    the poor when they complain:
His pris'ners are to him full dear,
    he doth them not diſdain.

36 Wherfore the sky & earth below,
    the ſea, with flood and ſtream,
His praiſe they ſhall declare & ſhow,
    with all that live in them.

37 For ſure our God will Sion ſave,
    and Judah's cities build : (have,
38 Much folk poſſeſſion there ſhall
    her ſtreets ſhall all be fill'd.

His ſervants ſeed ſhall keep the ſame
    all ages out of mind : (Name,
39 And there all they that love his
    a dwelling-place ſhall find.

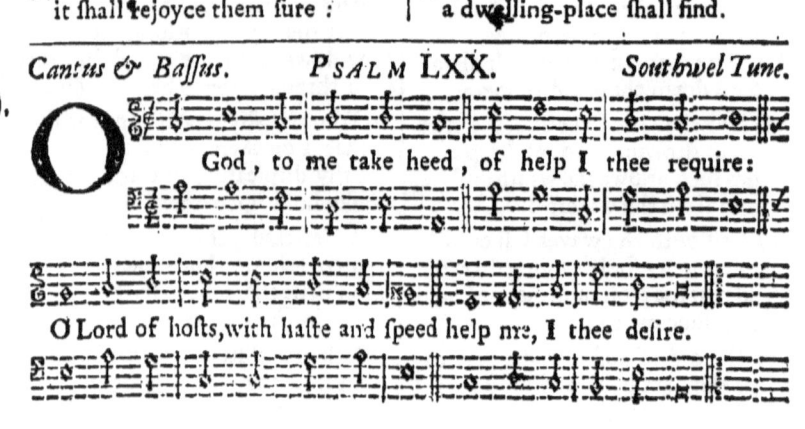

Cantus & Baſſus.   PSALM LXX.   *Southwel Tune.*

O God, to me take heed, of help I thee require:

O Lord of hoſts, with haſte and ſpeed help me, I thee deſire.

Psalm lxx, lxxi. 117

Bassus.   Psalm 70.   *A. 3. Voc.*

O God, to me take heed, of help I thee require:

O Lord of hosts, with haste and speed help me, I thee desire.

2 With shame confound them all, that seek my soul to spill: (fall
Rebuke them back with blame to that think and wish me ill.

3 Confound them that apply and seek to work me shame:
And at my harm do laugh, and cry, So, so, there goes the game.

4 But let them joyful be in thee with joy and wealth,

Which only trust and seek to thee, and to thy saving health.

5 That they may say always in mirth and one accord,
All glory, honour, laud, and praise, be giv'n to thee, O Lord.

6 But I am weak and poor, come, Lord, thine aid I lack:
Thou art my stay and help, therefore make speed, and be not slack.

Cantus & Bassus.   PSALM LXXI.   *Or to Windsor Tune.*

MY Lord, my God, in all distress my hope is whole in thee:

Then let no shame my soul oppress, nor once take hold on me.

As thou art just, defend me, Lord, and rid me out of dread:

Give ear, and to my suit accord, and send me help at need.

I 3   *Medius.*

Psalm lxxi.

Medius. — Psalm 71. — A. 3. Voc.

MY Lord, my God, in all diſtreſs my hope is whole in thee:
Then let no ſhame my ſoul oppreſs, nor once take hold on me.
As thou art juſt, defend me, Lord, and rid me out of dread:
Give ear and to my ſuit accord, and ſend me help at need.

Baſſus. — Psalm 71. — A. 3. Voc.

MY Lord, my God, in all diſtreſs my hope is whole in thee:
Then let no ſhame my ſoul oppreſs, nor once take hold on me.
As thou art juſt, defend me, Lord, and rid me out of dread:
Give ear, and to my ſuit accord, and ſend me help at need.

3 Be thou my rock, to whom I may
  for aid all times reſort:
Thy promiſe is to help alway,
  thou art my fence and fort.
4 Save me, my God, from wicked men,
  and from their ſtrength & pow'r:
From folk unjuſt, and alſo them
  that cruelly devour.

5 Thou art the ſtay whereon I reſt,
  thou Lord of hoſts art he:
Yea, from my youth I thought it beſt
  ſtill to depend on thee.

6 Thou haſt me kept ev'n from my
  and I thrô thee was born: (birth,
Wherefore I will thee praiſe with
  both ev'ning & at morn. (mirth,
7 As to a monſter ſeldom ſeen,
  much folk about me throng:
But thou art now, and ſtill haſt been
  my fence and aid moſt ſtrong.
8 Wherfore my mouth for ever ſhall
  be filled with thy praiſe:
Alſo my tongue ſhall never fail
  to honour thee always.

9 Refuſe

Pſalm lxxi.

9 Refuſe me not, O Lord, I pray,
  when age my limbs doth take :
And when my ſtrength doth waſte
  do not my ſoul forſake. (away,
10 Among themſelves my foes inquire
  to take me through deceit:
And they againſt me do conſpire,
  that for my ſoul lay wait.

The ſecond part.

11 Lay hand, & take him now, they ſay,
  for God from him is gone :
Diſpatch him quite, for to his aid
  moſt ſure there cometh none.
12 Do not abſent thy ſelf away,
  O Lord, when need ſhall be :
But that in time of grief I may
  in haſte have help from thee.

13 Wth ſhame confound & overthrow
  all thoſe that ſeek my life :
Suppreſs them with rebuke alſo
  that fain would work me ſtrife.
14 But I will patiently abide
  thy help at all eſſays :   (tide,
Still more and more, each time and
  I will ſet forth thy praiſe.

15 My mouth thy juſtice ſhall record,
  that daily help doth ſend :
For thy great benefits, O Lord,
  no numbers have, nor end.
16 Yet will I go and ſeek forth one,
  with thy good help, O God,
The ſaving health of thee alone
  to ſhew and ſet abroad.

16 For of my youth thou took'ſt the
  and doſt inſtruct me ſtill : (care,
Therefore thy wonders to declare
  I have great mind and will.

18 And as in youth from wanton rage
  thou didſt me keep and ſtay :
Forſake me not in mine old age,
  and when my head is gray.

The third part.

19 That I thy ſtrength & might may
  to them that now be here : (ſhow
And that our ſeed thy pow'r may
  hereafter many year.   (know
20 O Lord, thy juſtice doth exceed
  thy doings, all may ſee :
Thy works are wonderful indeed,
  Oh, who is like to thee !

21 Thou mad'ſt me feel affliction ſore,
  and yet thou didſt me ſave :
Yea, thou didſt help, and me reſtore,
  and took'ſt me from the grave.
22 And thou mine honour doſt in-
  my dignity maintain :   (creaſe,
Yea, thou doſt make all grief to ceaſe,
  and comfort'ſt me again.

23 Therfore thy faithfulneſs to praiſe
  I will with viol ſing :
My harp ſhall ſound thy laud always,
  O Iſr'els holy King.
24 My mouth will joy with pleaſant
  when I ſhall ſing to thee : (voice
Alſo my ſoul ſhall much rejoyce,
  for thou haſt made me free.

25 My tongue thy uprightneſs ſhall
  and ſpeak it daily ſtill : (ſound,
For grief & ſhame do them confound
  that ſeek to work me ill.

To Father, Son, and Holy Ghoſt,
  all glory be therefore :
As in beginning was, is now,
  and ſhall be evermore.

Psalm lxxii.

Cantus & Bassus. **PSALM LXXII.** *Exeter Tune.*

Lord, give thy judgments to the king, therein instruct them well:
And with his son, that princely thing, Lord, let thy justice dwell.

Medius. *Psalm 72.* *A. 3. Voc.*

Lord, give thy judgments to the king, therein instruct him well:
And with his son, that princely thing, Lord, let thy justice dwell.

Bassus. *Psalm 72.* *A. 3. Voc.*

Lord, give thy judgments to the king, therein instruct him well:
And with his son, that princely thing, Lord, let thy justice dwell.

2 That he may govern uprightly,
and rule thy folk aright:
And so defend through equity
the poor that have no might.
                (high,
3 And let the mountains that are
unto thy folk give peace:
Let little hills also apply
in justice to increase.
                (poor
4 That he may help the weak and
with aid, and make them strong:

And so destroy for evermore
all those that do them wrong.

5 And then from age to age shall
regard & fear thy might: (they
So long as sun doth shine by day,
or else the moon by night.

6 Lord, make the king unto the just
like rain to fields new mown:
And like to drops that lay the dust,
refreshing land new sown.

7 The

Pſalm lxxii.

7 The juſt ſhall flouriſh in his (days,
and all ſhall be at peace,
Until the moon ſhall leave to waſte,
to change, and to increaſe.

8 He ſhall be Lord, and have com- (mand
from ſhore to ſhore throughout:
And from the floods within the land,
through all the earth about.

9 The people that in deſarts dwell,
ſhall kneel to him full thick:
And all his foes that do rebel,
the earth and duſt ſhall lick.

10 The lords of all the iſles thereby
great gifts to him ſhall bring:
Arabia and Saba's kings
give many a coſtly thing.

The ſecond part.

11 All kings ſhall ſeek with one ac-
in his good grace to ſtand: (cord
And all the people of the world
obey at his command.

12 For he the needy ſort doth ſave,
that unto him do call:
Alſo the ſimple folk that have
no help of man at all.

13 He taketh pity on the poor
that are with ſpeed oppreſs'd:
He doth preſerve them evermore,
and bring their ſouls to reſt.

14 He ſhall redeem their lives from (dread,
from fraud, from wrong, & might:
Alſo the blood that they ſhall bleed
is precious in his ſight.

15 But he ſhall live, and they ſhall
to him of Saba's gold: (bring
He ſhall be honour'd as a king,
and daily be extoll'd.

16 The mighty mountains of his land
of corn ſhall bear ſuch throng,
That it like cedar-trees ſhall ſtand
in Libanus full long.

17 Their cities alſo well ſhall ſpeed,
the fruits thereof ſurpaſs:
In plenty it ſhall far exceed,
and ſpring as green as graſs.

18 For ever they ſhall praiſe his Name,
while that the ſun is light: (fame,
And think them happy through the
all folk ſhall bleſs his might.

19 Praiſe ye the Lord of hoſts, & ſing
to Iſr'els God each one:
For he doth ev'ry wondrous thing,
yea, he himſelf alone.

20 And bleſſed be his holy Name
all times eternally:
Let all the earth ſtill praiſe the ſame,
Amen, Amen, I ſay.

PSALM

Cantus & Bassus. PSALM LXXIII. *Glocester Tun*

Owe'er it be, yet God is good and kind to Is—ra—el:

And to all such as safely keep their conscience pure and well.

Medius. Psalm 73. A. 3. Vo

Howe'er it be, yet God is good and kind to Is—ra—el:

And to all such as safely keep their conscience pure and well.

Bassus. Psalm 73. A. 3. Vo

Howe'er it be, yet God is good and kind to Is—ra—el:

And to all such as safely keep their conscience pure and well.

2 But as for me, I almost slipt,
   my feet began to slide :
Before that I was well aware,
   my steps did turn aside.

3 For when I saw such foolish men,
   I grudg'd with great disdain,
That wicked men all things should
   without turmoil or pain. (have

4 They never suffer pangs nor grief,
   as if death should them smite :

Their bodies are both stout & strong
   and ever in good plight :

5 Always free from adversity,
   and ev'ry sad event :
With other men they take no part
   of plague or punishment.
               (brac
6 Therefore presumption doth err
   their necks as doth a chain :
They are ev'n wrapt as in a robe
   with rapine and disdain.

Pſalm lxxiii.

hat ev'n with fat	17 Until the time I went into
nes out ſtart:	thine holy place, and then
goods, they have	I underſtood right perfectly
'iſh their heart.	the end of all theſe men.

licentious, 18 Namely, how that thou fetteſt them
ith their tongue, upon a ſlipp'ry place:
and ſimple have And at thy pleaſure and thy will
:eat wrong. thou doſt them ſoon deface.

outh againſt the 19 Then all men muſe at that ſtrange
iheme: (heav'ns, to ſee how ſuddenly   (ſight,
ik of worldly They are deſtroyed, and conſum'd
ſteem. (things, to death ſo horribly.

ntimes turn back 20 Much like a dream when one a-
'rous ſtate: ſo ſhall their wealth decay: (wakes,
ie ſelf-ſame cup, Their famous names in all men's
me rate. ſhall fail and paſs away.   (ſight
part.   *The third part.*

at God, ſay they, 21 Yet thus my heart was grieved
inderſtand my mind was much oppreſt: (then,
gs, ſince wicked 22 So fond was I and ignorant,
l land? (men and in this point a beaſt.

iow wicked men 23 Nevertheleſs by my right hand
:eaſe, thou hold'ſt me always faſt:
i worldly goods, 24 And wth thy counſel doſt me guide
id peace. to glory at the laſt. \

o carefully 25 What thing is there that I can wiſh
refrain? but thee in heav'n above?
s in innocence, And in the earth there is nothing
eart in vain? like thee that I can love.

ges ev'ry day, 26 My fleſh and ſpirit both do fail,
lame: but God doth fail me never;
from my youth For of my health he is the ſtrength
d ſhame? and portion ev'n for ever.

t ſaid as they, 27 But lo, all ſuch as thee forſake
:ate: thou ſhalt deſtroy each one:
' children judge And thoſe that truſt in any thing,
:e. ſaving in thee alone.

me how I might 28 Therfore will I draw near to God,
ſtand: and ever with him dwell:
was too great In God alone I put me truſt,
hand: his wonders I will tell.

P S A L M

Psalm lxxiv.

Cantus & Bassus.   **PSALM LXXIV.**   *Windsor Tune*

WHY art thou, Lord, so long from us in all this danger deep

Why doth thine anger kindle thus at thine own pasture-sheep?

Medius.   *Psalm 74.*   *A. 3. Voc*

WHY art thou, Lord, so long from us in all this danger deep?

Why doth thine anger kindle thus at thine own pasture-sheep?

Bassus.   *Psalm 74.*   *A. 3. Voc*

WHY art thou, Lord, so long from us in all this danger deep?

Why doth thine anger kindle thus at thine own pasture-sheep?

2 Lord, call the people to thy thought
which have been thine so long,
The wch thou hast redeem'd & broght
from bondage sore and strong.

3 Have mind therfore & think upon,
remember it full well,
Thy pleasant place, thy mount Sion,
where thou wast wont to dwell.

4 Lift up thy feet and come in haste,
and all thy foes deface:

Which now at pleasure rob & waste
within thy holy place.

5 Amidst thy congregations all
thy foes do rore, O God:
They set as signs on ev'ry wall
banners display'd abroad.

6 As men with axes hew down trees
that on the hills do grow:
So shine the bills and swords of these
within thy temple now.

7 The

Psalm lxxiv.

7 The cieling saw'd, the carved (boards,
the goodly graven stones:
With axes, hammers, bills, & swords,
they beat them down at once.

8 Thy places they consume with (flame,
their rage doth so abound:
The house appointed to thy Name
they rase down to the ground.

9 And thus they say within their (hearts,
Dispatch them out of hand:
Then burn they up in ev'ry part
God's houses through the land.

10 Yet thou no sign of help dost send,
our prophets all are gone:
To tell when this our plague shall end
among us there is none.

11 How long, Lord, shall thine enemies
thus boldly thee defame?
Shall they for evermore blaspheme
thy great and holy Name?

12 Why dost thou thy right hand (withdraw
from us so long away?
Out of thy bosom pluck it forth
with speed thy foes to slay.

The second part.

13 O God, thou art our King & Lord,
and evermore hast been: (world
Yea, thy good grace throughout the
for our good help is seen.

14 The seas that are so deep and dead,
thy might did make them dry:
And thou didst break the serpent's (head,
that he therein did die.

15 Yea, thou didst break the heads so
of whales that are most fell: (great
And gav'st them to the folk to eat,
that in the desarts dwell.

16 Thou mad'st a spring with streams (to rise
from rocks both hard and high:
Thy mighty hand hath made like-
deep rivers to be dry.

17 Both day and night are also thine, (wise
by thee they were begun:
And thou likewise prepared hast
the light of moon and sun.

18 Thou didst appoint the ends and
of all the earth about: (coasts
Both summer-heats, & winter-frosts,
thy hand hath found them out.

19 Think on, O Lord, no time forget
thy foes that thee defame:
And how the foolish folk are set
to rail upon thy Name.

20 O let no cruel beasts devour
thy turtle that is true:
And always leave not in their pow'r
the poor that much do rue.

21 Regard, O Lord, thy covenant,
behold our misery:
All the dark places of the earth
are full of cruelty.

22 Let not the simple man therefore
be turned back with shame:
But let the needy evermore
give praise unto thy Name.

23 Arise, O Lord, and plead the cause
against thine enemies,
Who daily do reject thy laws,
and thee with scorn despise.

24 The voice forget not of thy foes,
for the presumption high
Is more and more increas'd of those
that hate thee spitefully.

PSALM

Pſalm lxxv.

Cantus & Baſſus.   PSALM LXXV.   *Worceſter Tune.*

To thee, O God, will we give thanks, we will give thanks to thee:
Since thy Name is ſo near, declare thy wondrous works will we.

Medius.   Pſalm 75.   *A. 3. Voc.*

To thee, O God, will we give thanks, we will give thanks to thee:
Since thy Name is ſo near, declare thy wondrous works will we.

Baſſus.   Pſalm 75.   *A. 3. Voc.*

To thee, O God, will we give thanks, we will give thanks to thee:
Since thy Name is ſo near, declare thy wondrous works will we.

2 I will uprightly judge when get
   convenient time I may:
The earth is weak, and all therein,
   but I her pillars ſtay.

3 I did to the mad people ſay,
   Deal not ſo furiouſly:
And unto the ungodly ones,
   Set not your horns on high;

4 I ſaid unto them, Set not up
   your raiſed horns on high;

And ſee that you do with ſtiff neck
   not ſpeak preſumptuouſly.

5 For neither from the eaſtern parts
   nor from the weſt likewiſe,
Nor from forſaken wilderneſs
   promotion doth ariſe.
          (earth

6 But God who rules both heav'n &
   that right'ous judge alone:
It's he that puts down one, and ſets
   another in the throne.

7 For

Psalm lxxv, lxxvi. 127

7 For why? a cup of mighty wine
is in the hand of God:
And all the mixture of the same
himself doth pour abroad.

8 As for the lees and filthy dregs
that do remain of it,
The wicked of the earth shall drink
and suck them ev'ry whit.

9 But I will talk of God alway,
and his great Name adore:

And will not cease to celebrate
his praise for evermore.

10 In sunder break the horns of all
ungodly men will I:
But then the horns of right'ous men
shall be exalted high.
Gloria Patri.
To Father, Son, and Holy Ghost,
all glory be therefore:
As in beginning was, is now,
and shall be evermore.

Cantus & Bassus.   PSALM LXXVI.   *Westminster Tune.*

TO all that now in Jewry dwell, the Lord is clearly known:

His Name is great in Is--ra--el, a people of his own.

Medius.   *Psalm 76.*   *A. 3. Voc.*

TO all that now in Jewry dwell, the Lord is clearly known:

His Name is great in Is--ra--el, a people of his own.

Bassus.   *Psalm 76.*   *A. 3. Voc.*

TO all that now in Jewry dwell, the Lord is clearly known:

His Name is great in Is--ra--el, a people of his own.

2 At Salem he hath pitch'd his tent,
  to tarry there a space:
In Sion also he is bent
  to fix his dwelling-place.
            (bow,
3 And there he brake both shaft and
  the sword, the spear, and shield:
His enemies did overthrow.
  in battel in the field.
            (Lord,
4 Thou art more worthy honour,
  more might in thee doth lie,
Than in the strongest of the world,
  that rob on mountains high.
            (through thee,
5 But now the proud are spoil'd
  and they are fall'n asleep:
Through men of war no help can be,
  themselves they could not keep.

6 At thy rebuke, O Jacob's God,
  when thou didst them reprove,
As half-asleep their chariots stood,
  no horseman once did move.

7 For thou art dreadful, Lord, indeed;
  what man the courage hath

To 'bide my sight, & doth not dread
  when thou art in thy wrath?
            (ments heard
8 When thou dost make thy judg-
  from heav'n unto the ground,
Then all the earth full sore afraid
  in silence shall be found.
            (stand
9 And that when thou, O God, dost
  in judgment for to speak,
To save th'afflicted of the land,
  on earth that are full weak.

10 The fury that in man doth reign,
  shall turn unto thy praise:
Hereafter, Lord, do thou restrain
  their wrath and threats always.

11 Make vows, & pay them to our God,
  ye folk that nigh him be:
Bring gifts, all ye that dwell abroad,
  for dreadful sure is he.
            (might
12 For he doth take both life and
  from princes great of birth:
And full of terrour is his sight
  to all the kings on earth.

Cantus & Bassus.   P s a l m LXXVII.   *Or to Martyrs Tune*

Pſalm lxxvii.   129

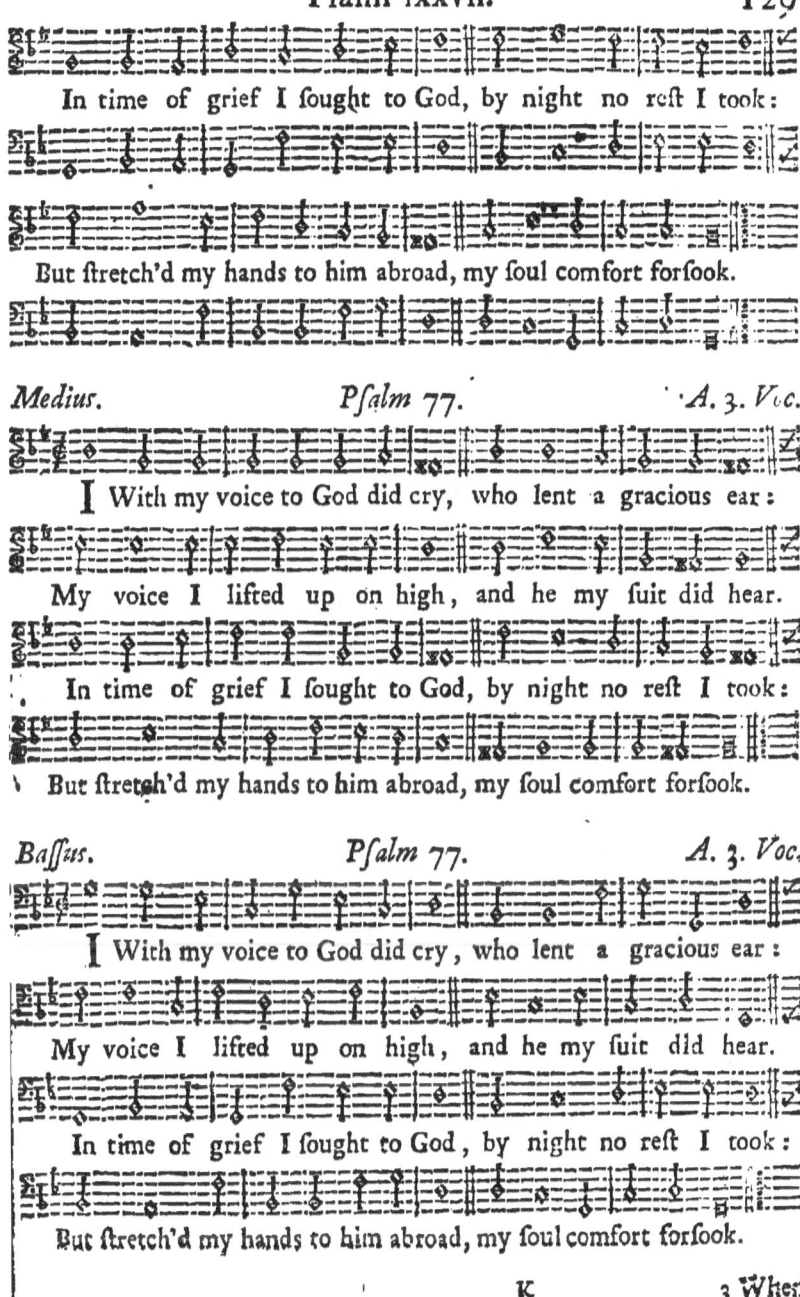

In time of grief I ſought to God, by night no reſt I took:

But ſtretch'd my hands to him abroad, my ſoul comfort forſook.

Medius.   Pſalm 77.   *A. 3. Voc.*

I With my voice to God did cry, who lent a gracious ear:

My voice I lifted up on high, and he my ſuit did hear.

In time of grief I ſought to God, by night no reſt I took:

But ſtretch'd my hands to him abroad, my ſoul comfort forſook.

Baſſus.   Pſalm 77.   *A. 3. Voc.*

I With my voice to God did cry, who lent a gracious ear:

My voice I lifted up on high, and he my ſuit did hear.

In time of grief I ſought to God, by night no reſt I took:

But ſtretch'd my hands to him abroad, my ſoul comfort forſook.

K   3 When

Psalm lxxvii.

3 When I to think on God in- (tend,
   my trouble then is more :
I fpake, but could not make an end,
   my breath was ftopt fo fore.
4 Thou doft mine eyes fo hold from
   that I always awake : (reft,
With fear I am fo fore oppreft,
   my fpeech doth me forfake.

5 The days of old in mind I caft,
   and oft do think upon
The times and ages that are paft
   full many years agone.
6 By night my fongs I call to mind,
   once made thy praife to fhow :
And with my heart much talk I find,
   my fpirits fearch to know.

7 Will God, faid I, at once for all
   caft off his people thus,
So that henceforth no time he fhall
   be friendly unto us ?
8 What ? is his goodnefs quite de-
   and paffed clean away ? (cay'd,
Or is his promife now delay'd,
   and doth his truth decay ?

9 And will the Lord our God forget
   his mercies manifold ?
Or fhall his wrath increafe fo hot,
   his mercies to withhold ?
10 At laft I faid, This furely is
    mine own infirmity :
But his right hand can help all this,
   and change it fpeedily.

The fecond part.

11 I Will regard and think upon
   the working of the Lord :
And all his wonders paft and gone
   I gladly will record.
12 Yea, all his works I will declare,
    and what he did devife :
To tell his facts I will not fpare,
    and all his counfel wife.

13 Thy works, O Lord, are all up- (right,
    and holy all abroad : (might
What one hath ftrength to match the
    of thee, O Lord our God ?
14 Thou art a God that doft forth
    thy wonders ev'ry hour : (fhow
And fo doft make the people know
    thy virtue and thy pow'r.

15 And thine own folk thou doft de- (fend
    with ftrength and ftretched arm,
Thofe that from Jacob did defcend,
    and Jofeph's feed from harm.
16 The waters, Lord, perceived thee,
    the waters faw thee well :
And they for fear away did flee,
    the depths on trembling fell.

17 The clouds that were both thick (and black,
    did rain full plenteoufly :
The thunder in the air did crack,
    thy fhafts abroad did fly.
18 Thy thunder in the air was heard,
    thy lightnings from above,
With flafhes great made men afraid,
    the earth did quake and move.

19 Thy ways within the fea do lie,
    thy paths in waters deep :
Yet none can there thy fteps efpy,
    nor know thy paths to keep.
20 Thou ledd'ft thy folk upon the
    as fheep on ev'ry fide : (land
By Mofes and by Aaron's hand
    thou didft them fafely guide.

Gloria Patri.

Glory to God the Father be,
Glory to God the Son,
Glory to God the Holy Ghoft,
myfterious Three in One :
As at the firft it was, is now,
and fhall for ever be ;
When this World ends, and the next World
puts on Eternitie.

PSALM

Pſalm lxxviii.   131

Cantus & Baſſus.   PSALM LXXVIII.   *York Tune.*

ATtend my people to my law, and to my words incline:
My mouth ſhall ſpeak ſtrange pa---ra--bles, and ſentences divine.

Medius.   Pſalm 78.   A. 3. Voc.

ATtend my people to my law, and to my words incline:
My mouth ſhall ſpeak ſtrange pa—ra--bles, and ſentences divine.

Baſſus.   Pſalm 78.   A. 3. Voc.

ATtend my people to my law, and to my words incline:
My mouth ſhall ſpeak ſtrange pa—ra—bles, and ſentences divine.

3 Which we ourſelves have heard &
ev'n of our fathers old,   (learn'd
And which for our inſtruction
our fathers have us told.

4 Becauſe we ſhould not keep it cloſe
from them that after came: (clare,
Who ſhould God's mighty pow'r de-
and wondrous works proclaim.

5 To Jacob he commandment gave
how Iſrael ſhould live,

Willing our fathers ſhould the ſame
unto their children give.

6 That they and their poſterity
that were not ſprung up then,
Should have the knowledg of the law,
and teach it their children.

7 That they might have the better
in God that is above: (hope
And not forget to keep his laws
and his precepts in love.

K 2   8 Not

Psalm lxxviii.

8 Not being as their fathers, who
rebelled in God's sight: (hearts
And would not frame their wicked
to know their God aright.

9 How went the sons of Ephraim
their neighbours for to spoil:
Shooting their darts in day of war,
and yet receiv'd the foil?

10 For why? they did not keep with
the cov'nant that was made, (God
Nor yet would walk or lead their
according as he said: (lives

11 But put into oblivion
his counsel and his will,
And all his works magnificent
which he declared still.

The second part.

12 What wonders to our forefathers
did he himself disclose
In Egypt land within the field
that call'd is Thaneos?

13 He did divide and part the sea,
through which he made a way
For them to pass, and on a heap
the waters made to stay.

14 He led them secret in a cloud
by day when it was bright:
And in the night when dark it was,
with fire he gave them light.

15 He brake the rocks in wilderness,
and gave the people drink:
As plentiful as when the deeps
do flow up to the brink.

16 He drew forth rivers out of rocks
that were both dry and hard,
Of such abundance, that no floods
to them might be compar'd.

17 Yet for all this against the Lord
their sin they did increase:
And stirr'd up him that is most high
to wrath in wilderness.

18 They tempted God within their
like people of mistrust; (hearts,
Requiring such a kind of meat
as served to their lust:

19 They spake against him, & thus said
in their unfaithfulness,
What! can this God prepare for us
a feast in wilderness?

20 Behold, he strake the stony rock,
and floods forthwith did flow:
But can he now give to his folk
both bread and flesh also?

21 When God heard this, he waxed
with Jacob and his seed: (wroth
So did his Indignation
'gainst Israel proceed.

The third part.

22 Because they did not faithfully
believe, and hope that he
Could always help and succour them
in their necessity. (clouds,

23 Wherefore he did command the
forthwith they brake in sunder,
24 And rain'd down manna for to eat,
a food of mighty wonder.

25 When earthly men with angels
were fed at their request, (food
26 He bad the east-wind blow away,
and brought in the south-west.

27 He rain'd down flesh as thick as
and fowls as thick as sand: (dust,
28 Which he did cast amidst the place
where all their tents did stand.

29 Then did they eat exceedingly,
and all men had their fills:
Yet more and more they did desire
to serve their lusts and wills.

30 But as the meat was in their mouths,
his wrath upon them fell,
31 And slew the strength of all their
and choice of Israel. (youth,

32 Yet

Pſalm lxxvii.

32 Yet fell they to their wonted ſin,
   and ſtill they did him grieve:
For all the wonders that he wrought,
   they would him not believe.

33 Their days therfore he ſhortened,
   and made their honour vain:
Their years did waſte & paſs away,
   with terrour and with pain.

34 But ever when he plagued them,
   they ſought him inſtantly,(ſtrength,
35 Remembring that he was their
   their help, and God moſt high.

36 Thô with their mouths they no-
   but flatter with the L^d : (thing did
And with their tongues,and in their
   diſſembled ev'ry word.   (hearts

The fourth part.

37 For why? their hearts were nothing
   to him, nor why he ſaid: (bent
Nor yet to keep or to perform
   the cov'nant that he made.

38 Yet was he ſtill ſo merciful
   when they deſerv'd to die,
That he forgave them their miſdeeds,
   and would not them deſtroy.

Yea, many a time he turn'd his wrath,
   and did them not ſurpriſe:
And would not ſuffer all his whole
   diſpleaſure to ariſe.

39 Conſidering they were but fleſh,
   or like to wind and rain
Paſſing away, and never doth
   return and come again.

40 How oftentimes in wildernefs
   did they the Lord provoke!
How did they move & ſtir the Lord
   to plague them with his ſtroke!

41 Yet did they turn again to ſin,
   and tempted him full ſoon;
Preſcribing to the mighty God
   what things they would have done.

42 Not thinking of his mighty hand,
   nor of the day when he
Deliver'd them out of the hands
   of the fierce enemy.

43 Nor how he wrought his miracles
   (as they themſelves beheld)
In Egypt, and the wonders that
   he did in Zoan field.

44 Nor how he turned by his pow'r
   their waters into blood:
That no man might receive his drink
   at river or at flood.   (of flies,

45 Nor how he ſent them ſwarms
   which did them ſore annoy:
And fill'd their country full of frogs,
   which did their land deſtroy.

The fifth part.

46 Nor how he did their fruits unto
   the caterpiller give:
And of the labour of their hands
   locuſts did them deprive.

47 With hailſtones he deſtroy'd their
   ſo that they all were loſt: (vines,
And alſo all their ſycamores
   did he conſume with froſt.

48 And yet with hailſtones once again
   the Lord their cattel ſmote,
And all their flocks & herds likewiſe
   with thunderbolts full hot.

49 He caſt upon them his fierce
   and indignation ſore: (wrath,
Amongſt them evil angels ſent,
   which troubled them yet more.

50 Then to his wrath he made a way,
   and ſpared not the leaſt,
But gave unto the peſtilence
   the man as well as beaſt.

51 He ſtrake alſo the firſt-born all
   that up in Egypt came:
And all the chief of men and beaſts
   within the tents of Ham.

Pſalm lxxviii.

52 But as for his own people dear,
   he did preſerve and keep :
And carri'd them thrô wilderneſs
   ev'n like a flock of ſheep.

53 Without all fear both ſafe & ſound
   he brought them out of thrall :
Whereas their foes with rage of ſeas
   were overwhelmed all.

54 And brought them out into the
   of his own holy land,   (coaſts
Ev'n to the mount which he had got
   by his ſtrong arm and hand.

55 And there caſt out the heathen
   and did their land divide : (folk,
And in their tents he ſet the tribes
   of Iſr'el to abide.

56 Yet for all this, their God moſt high
   they ſtirr'd and tempted ſtill,
And would not keep his teſtament,
   nor yet obey his will,

57 But as their fathers turned back,
   ev'n ſo they went aſtray,
Much like a bow that would not
   but ſlip and ſtart away.   (bend,

The ſixth part.

58 And griev'd him with their hill-
   with off'rings & with fire, (altars,
And with their idols grievouſly
   provoked him to ire.

59 For which his wrath began again
   to kindle in his breaſt :
The wickedneſs of Iſrael
   he did ſo much deteſt.

60 The tabernacle he forſook
   of Shilo, where he was
Right converſant with earthly men,
   ev'n as his dwelling-place.

61 Then ſuffer'd he his might and
   in bondage for to ſtand, (pow'r
And gave the honour of his ark
   into his en'mies hand.

62 And did commit them to the
   wroth with his heritage : (ſword,
63 Their young men were devour'd
   maids had no marriage. (with fire,
64 And with the ſword the prieſts
   did periſh ev'ry one :   (alſo
And not a widow left alive
   their death for to bemoan.

65 Then did the Lord awake as one
   whom ſleep could not confine :
And like a mighty giant that
   refreſhed is with wine.

66 With em'rods in the hinder parts
   his enemies he ſmote :
And put them unto ſuch a ſhame
   as ſhould not be forgot.

67 The tent and tabernacle he
   of Joſeph did refuſe :
Alſo the tribe of Ephraim
   he would in no wiſe chuſe :

68 But he the tribe of Judah choſe,
   that he therein might dwell :
Ev'n the moſt noble mount Sion,
   which he did love ſo well.

69 And there he did his temple build,
   both ſumpt'ouſly and ſure :
Like as the earth which he hath
   for ever to endure.   (made

70 Then choſe he David him to ſerve,
   his people for to keep ;
Whom he took up & brought away
   ev'n from the folds of ſheep.

71 As he did follow th' ews with
   the L^d did him advance (young,
To feed his people Iſrael,
   and his inheritance.

72 Thus David with a faithful heart
   his flock and charge did feed,
And prudently with all his pow'r
   did govern them indeed.

PSALM

Psalm lxxix.

Cantus & Bassus.   PSALM LXXIX.   *Salisbury Tune.*

O God, the Gentiles do invade thine he--ri--tage to spoil:
Je--ru--sa--lem an heap is made, thy temple they defile.

Medius.   Psalm 79.   A. 3. Voc.

O God, the Gentiles do invade thine he--ri--tage to spoil:
Je--ru--sa—lem an heap is made, thy temple they defile.

Bassus.   Psalm 79.   A. 3. Voc.

O God, the Gentiles do invade thine he--ri—tage to spoil:
Je--ru—sa--lem an heap is made, thy temple they defile.

2 The bodies of thy saints most dear
abroad to birds they cast:
The flesh of them that do thee fear,
the beasts devour and waste.

3 Their blood throughout Jerusalem
as water spilt they have:
So that there is not one of them
to lay their dead in grave.
     (flock

4 Thus are they made a laughing--
almost the world throughout:

The enemies do jest and mock
which dwell our coasts about.
     (tain

5 How long, O Lord, wilt thou re-
thine anger and thy rage?
And shall thy wrath and jealousie
not any more asswage?

6 Upon those people pour the same,
which did thee never know:
All realms wch call not on thy Name,
consume and overthrow.

K 4   7 For

7 For they have got the upper hand,
   and Jacob's seed destroy'd :
His habitation and his land
   they have laid waste and void.

8 Bear not in mind our former faults,
   with speed some pity show :
And aid us, Lord, in all assaults,
   for we are weak and low.

The second part.

9 O God, that giv'st all health and grace,
   on us declare the same :
Weigh not our works, our sins deface,
   for honour of thy Name.

10 Why shall the wicked still alway,
   to us as people dumb,
In thy reproach rejoyce, and say,
   Where is their God become ?

Require, O Lord, as thou see'st good
   before our eyes in sight,
Of all these folk thy servants blood
   which they spilt in despight.

11 Receive into thy sight in haste
   the clamours, grief, and wrong,
Of such as are in prison cast,
   and bound in irons strong.

Thy force and strength to celebrate,
   Lord, set them out of band :
Which unto death are destinate,
   and in their en'mies hand.

12 The nations wch have been so bold
   as to blaspheme thy Name,
Into their laps sev'n-fold do thou
   repay again the same.

13 So we thy flock and pasture-sheep
   will praise thee evermore,
And teach all ages for to keep
   for thee like praise in store.

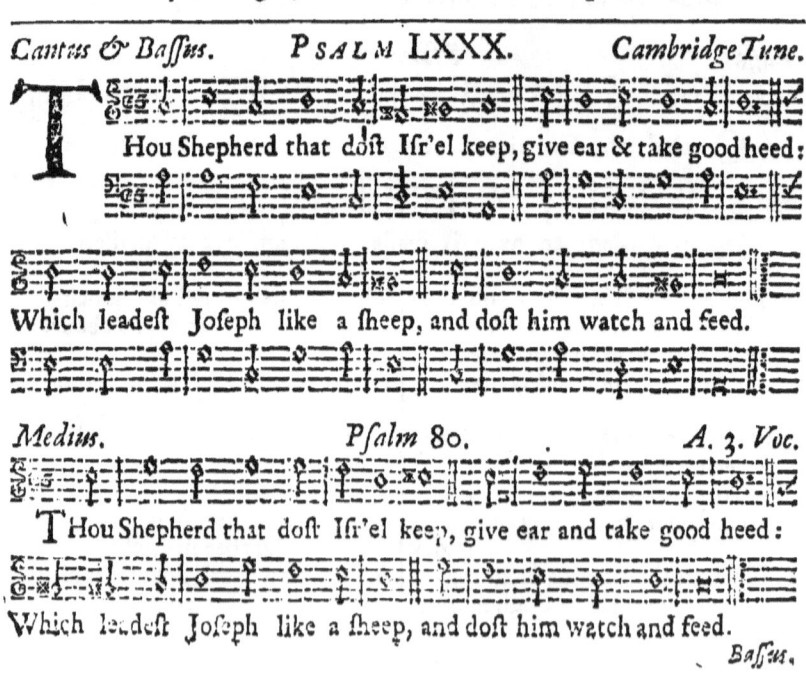

Cantus & Bassus.   P SAL M LXXX.   Cambridge Tune.

Thou Shepherd that dost Isr'el keep, give ear & take good heed:
Which leadest Joseph like a sheep, and dost him watch and feed.

Medius.   Psalm 80.   A. 3. Voc.

Thou Shepherd that dost Isr'el keep, give ear and take good heed:
Which leadest Joseph like a sheep, and dost him watch and feed.

Bassus.

Pſalm lxxx. 137

Baſſus.   *Pſalm* 80.   *A. 3. Voc.*

Thou Shepherd that doſt Iſr'el keep, give ear and take good heed:

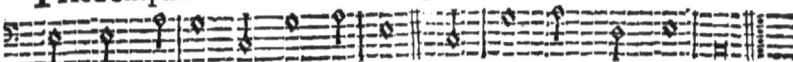

Which leadeſt Joſeph like a ſheep, and doſt him watch and feed.

2 And thou, O Lord, whoſe ſeat is ſet
on cherubims moſt bright,
Shew forth thy ſelf, and do not let,
ſend down thy beams of light.

3 Before Ephr'im and Benjamin,
Manaſſes in likewiſe,
To ſhew thy pow'r do thou begin;
come help us, Lord, ariſe.

4 Direct our hearts by thy good
convert us unto thee :   (grace,
Shew us the brightneſs of thy face,
and then full ſafe are we.

5 Lord God of hoſts of Iſrael,
how long wilt thou delay ?
And 'gainſt thy folk in anger ſwell,
& wilt not hear them pray?   (deep,

6 Thou doſt them feed with ſorrows
their bread with tears they eat :
And drink the tears that they do
in meaſure full & great.   (weep,

7 Thou haſt us made a very ſtrife
to thoſe that dwell about :
Wch much doth pleaſe our enemies,
they laugh and jeſt it out.

8 O take us, Lord, unto thy grace,
convert our hearts to thee :
Shew forth to us thy joyful face,
and we full ſafe ſhall be.

9 From Egypt where it grew not well
thou brought'ſt a vine full dear :
The heathen folk thou didſt expel,
and thou didſt plant it there.

10 Thou didſt prepare for it a place,
and ſet its roots full faſt :
That it did grow and ſpring apace,
and fill'd the land at laſt.

The ſecond part.

11 The hills were cover'd round about
with ſhade that from it came,
Alſo the cedars ſtrong and ſtout,
with branches of the ſame.   (ſtroy?

12 Why then didſt thou her walls de-
her hedge pluck'd up thou haſt :
That all the folk that paſs thereby
the ſame do ſpoil and waſte.

13 The boar out of the wood ſo wild
doth dig and root it out :
The furious beaſts out of the field
devour it all about.

14 O Lord of hoſts, return again,
from heav'n do thou look down :
Behold, and with thy help ſuſtain
thy vineyard overthrown.

15 Thy pleaſant vine, thine Iſrael,
which thy right hand hath ſet :
The ſame wch thou didſt love ſo well,
O Lord, do not forget.

16 They lop and cut it off apace,
they burn it down with fire :
And through the frowning of thy
we periſh in thine ire.   (face

17 Let thy right hand be with them
whom thou haſt kept ſo long : (now,
And with the Son of man whom thou
to thee haſt made ſo ſtrong.

18 And

Pfalm lxxx, lxxxi.

18 And so when thou hast set us free,
and saved us from shame:
Then will we never fall from thee,
but call upon thy Name.

19 O Lord of hosts, through thy good
convert us unto thee: (grace

Behold us with a pleasant face,
and then full safe are we.

Gloria Patri.

All Glory, Honour, Pow'r, and Praise,
to the Mysterious Three:
As at the first beginning was,
may now and ever be.

Cantus & Bassus.   PSALM LXXXI. *Or to London new Tune.*

BE light and glad, in God rejoyce, wch is our strength and stay:

Be joy--ful, and lift up your voice to Jacob's God alway.

Prepare your Instruments most meet, some joyful Psalm to sing:

Strike up with harp and lute most sweet, on ev'ry pleasant string.

Medius.   Psalm 81.   *A. 3. Voc.*

BE light and glad, in God rejoyce, which is our strength and stay:

Be joy--ful, and lift up your voice to Jacob's God alway.

Pre-

Pſalm lxxxi.

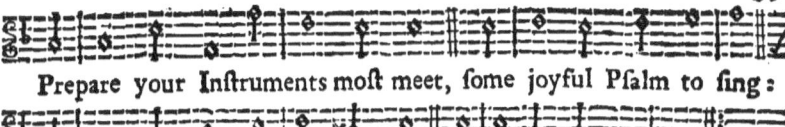
Prepare your Inſtruments moſt meet, ſome joyful Pſalm to ſing:
Strike up with harp and lute moſt ſweet, on ev'ry pleaſant ſtring.

Baſſus.   *Pſalm* 81.   *A.* 3, *Voc.*

BE light and glad, in God rejoyce, which is our ſtrength and ſtay:

Be joy--ful, and lift up your voice to Jacob's God alway.

Prepare your Inſtruments moſt meet, ſome joyful Pſalm to ſing:

Strike up with harp and lute moſt ſweet, on ev'ry pleaſant ſtring.

3 Blow as it were in the new-moon,
 with trumpets of the beſt:
As it is uſed to be done
 at any ſolemn feaſt.
4 For this is unto Iſrael
 a ſtatute, which was made
By Jacob's God, and muſt full well
 be evermore obey'd.   (creed
5 This clauſe with Joſeph was de-
 when he from Egypt came,
That as a witneſs all his ſeed
 ſhould ſtill obſerve the ſame.
6 When God himſelf had ſo prepar'd,
 to bring him from the land;
Whereas the ſpeech which he had
 he did not underſtand.   (heard,

7 I from his ſhoulder took (ſaith he)
 the burden clean away:
And from the furnace ſet him free
 from burning brick of clay.

8 When thou in grief didſt cry & call,
 I help'd thee inſtantly:
And I did anſwer thee withal
 in thunder ſecretly.

9 Yea, at the waters of diſcord
 I did thee tempt and prove:
Where thou the goodneſs of the Lord
 with murmering didſt move.
10 Hear, O my people Iſrael,
 and I'll aſſure it thee:
Regard & mark my words full well,
 if thou wilt cleave to me.
 The ſecond part.
11 Thou ſhalt no god in thee reſerve,
 of any land abroad:
Nor in no wiſe bow to or ſerve
 a ſtrange or foreign god.
12 I am the Lord thy God, and I
 from Egypt ſet thee free:
Then ask of me abundantly,
 and I will give it thee.

13 But

Psalm lxxxi, lxxxii.

13 But yet my people would not hear
 my voice when that I spake:
And Israel would not obey,
 but did me quite forsake. (will,
14 Then did I leave them to their
 in hardness of their heart:
To walk in their own counsels still,
 themselves they did pervert.

15 O that my people would have
 the words that I did say: (heard
And Israel with due reward
 had walked in my way!

16 How soon would I confound their
 & bring them down full low: (foes,
And turn my hand upon all those
 that would them overthrow.

17 And they that at the Lord do rage,
 as liars should be found:
But for his folk, their time and age
 should with great joy be crown'd.

18 I would have fed them with the
 and finest of the wheat: (crop,
And made the rock with hony drop,
 that they their fills should eat.

Cantus & Bassus.   PSALM LXXXII.   Rochester Tune.

A—Mid the press with men of might the Lord himself doth stand,

To plead the cause of truth and right with Judges of the land.

Medius.   Psalm 82.   A. 3. Voc.

A Mid the press with men of might the Lord himself doth stand,

To plead the cause of truth and right with Judges of the land.

Bassus.   Psalm 82.   A. 3. Voc.

A Mid the press with men of might the Lord himself doth stand:

To plead the cause of truth and right with Judges of the land.

2 How

Psalm lxxxii, lxxxiii.

2 How long, said he, will you proceed
 false judgment to award?
Why have you partially agreed
 the wicked to regard?

3 Whereas of due you should defend
 the fatherless and weak:
And when the poor man doth con-
 in judgment justly speak. (tend,

4 If ye be wise, defend the cause
 of poor men in their right:
And rid the needy from the claws
 of tyrants force and might.

5 But nothing will they know or
 in vain to them I talk: (learn,
They will not see or ought discern,
 but still in darkness walk.

6 For lo, ev'n now the time is come
 that all things fall to nought:
And laws likewise by ev'ry one
 for gain are sold and bought.

I had decreed it in my sight
 as gods to take you all:
Children also of the most High,
 for love I did you call.

7 But notwithstanding ye shall die
 as men, and so decay:
O tyrants, I shall you destroy,
 and pluck you quite away.
 (known,
8 Up, Lord, and let thy strength be
 and judge the world with might:
For why? all nations are thine own
 to take them as thy right.

Cantus & Bassus.   P S A L M LXXXIII.   *Bristol Tune.*

DO not, O God, refrain thy tongue, in silence do not stay:

Withhold not, Lord, thy self so long, and make no more delay.

Medius.   *Psalm 83.*   *A. 3. Voc.*

. Do not, O God, refrain thy tongue, in silence do not stay:

Withhold not, Lord, thy self so long, and make no more delay.

Bassus.

Psalm lxxxiii.

Bassus.   *Psalm 83.*   *A. 3. Voc.*

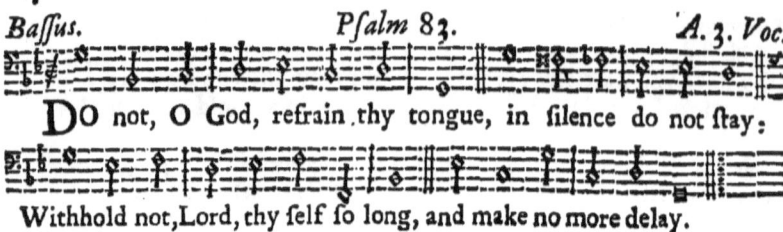

DO not, O God, refrain thy tongue, in silence do not stay:
Withhold not, Lord, thy self so long, and make no more delay.

2 For why? behold thy foes, and see
how they do rage and cry:
And those that bear an hate to thee,
hold up their heads on high.

3 Against thy folk they use deceit,
and craftily enquire:
For thine elect to lie in wait,
in council they conspire.

4 Come on, say they, let us expel
and pluck these folk away:
So that the name of Israel
may utterly decay.
                  (heart

5 They all conspire within their
how they may thee withstand:
Against the Lord to take a part
they are in league and band.

6 The tents of all the Edomites,
the Ismaelites likewise:
The Hagarenes and Moabites,
their plots do still devise.

7 Gebal and Ammon do likewise
with Amalek conspire:
The Philistines against thee rise,
with them that dwell in Tyre.

8 Assur is also joyn'd to them
in their conspiracy:
And is become a fence and aid
to Lot's posterity.

9 As thou didst to the Midianites,
so serve them, Lord, each one:

As unto Siser and Jabin,
beside the brook Kison.

10 Whom thou in Endor didst destroy,
& waste them through thy might:
That they like dung on earth did lie,
and that in open sight.

The second part.

11 Make them now and their lords
like Zeb and Oreb then: (appear
As Zebah and Zalmana were,
the kings of Midian.

12 Which said, Let us throughout the
in all the coasts abroad,   (land
Possess and take into our hand
the fair houses of God.
                  (fast

13 Turn them, O God, with storms as
as wheels that have no stay:
Or like the chaff which men do cast
with winds to flie away.

14 Like as the fire with rage & fume
the mighty forrests spills;
And as the flame doth quite consume
the mountains and the hills.

14 So let the tempest of thy wrath
upon their necks be laid:
And of thy stormy wind and showre,
Lord, make them all afraid.

16 Lord, bring them all, I thee desire,
to such rebuke and shame,
That it may cause them to enquire,
and learn to seek thy Name.

17 And

Psalm lxxxiii, lxxxiv.   143

17 And let them daily more and more
to shame and slander fall:
And in rebuke and obloquy
confound and sink them all.

18 That they may know & understand
thou art the God most high;
And that thou dost with mighty hand
the world rule constantly.

Cantus & Bassus. PSALM LXXXIV. *Winchester Tune.*

HOW pleasant is thy dwelling-place, O Lord of hosts, to me!

The ta--ber--na-cles of thy grace, how pleasant, Lord, they be!

Medius. *Psalm 84.* *A. 3. Voc.*

How pleasant is thy dwelling-place, O Lord of hosts, to me!

The ta--ber--na-cles of thy grace, how pleasant, Lord, they be!

Bassus. *Psalm 84.* *A. 3. Voc.*

How pleasant is thy dwelling-place, O Lord of hosts, to me!

The ta--ber--na--cles of thy grace, how pleasant, Lord, they be!

2 My soul doth long full sore to go
into thy courts abroad:
My heart and flesh cry out also
for thee the living God.

3 The sparrows find a room to rest,
and save themselves from wrong:

Also the swallow hath a nest
wherein to keep her young.

4 These birds full nigh thine altar
have place to sit and sing: (may
O Lord of hosts, thou art alway
my only God and King.

5 O

Psalm lxxxiv, lxxxv.

5 O they be blessed that may dwell
within thy house always:
For they all times thy facts do tell,
and ever give thee praise.

6 Yea, happy sure likewise are they,
whose stay and strength thou art,
W^{ch} to thy house do mind the way,
and seek it in their heart.

As they go through the vale of tears,
they dig up fountains still;
That as a spring it all appears,
and thou their pits dost fill.

7 From strength to strength they walk
no faintness there shall be: (full fast,
And so the God of gods at last
in Sion they do see.

8 O Lord of hosts, to me give heed,
and hearken to my cry:
And let it through thine ears pro-
O Jacob's God most high. (ceed,

8 O God, our shield, of thy good grace
regard, and so draw near:
Regard, O Lord, behold the face
of thine anointed dear.

10 For why? within thy courts one
is better to abide, (day
Than other where to keep or stay
a thousand days beside.

Much rather had I keep a door
within the house of God,
Than in the tents of wickedness,
to settle mine abode.

11 For God the Lord, light & defence
will grace and glory give:
And no good thing will he withhold
from them that purely live.

12 O Lord of hosts, that man is best,
and happy sure is he,
That is perswaded in his breast
to trust all times in thee.

Cantus & Bassus. P SALM LXXXV. *Windsor Tune.*

Thou hast been mer-ci—ful indeed, O Lord, unto thy land:

For thou restored'st Jacob's seed from thraldom, and from band.

Medius. Psalm 85. A. 3. Voc.

Thou hast been mer--ci—ful indeed, O Lord, unto thy land:

For thou restored'st Jacob's seed from thraldom, and from band.

Bassus

Psalm lxxxv. 145

Bassus. *Psalm 85.* *A. 3. Voc.*

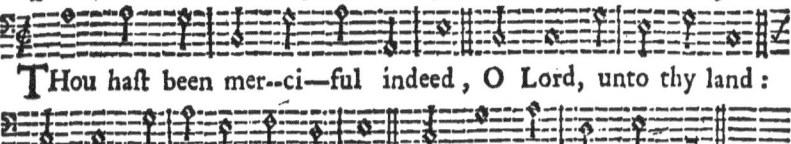

THou haſt been mer--ci—ful indeed, O Lord, unto thy land:
For thou reſtored'ſt Jacob's ſeed from thraldom, and from band.

2 The wicked ways that they were in,
thou didſt them clean remit:
And thou didſt hide thy people's ſin,
full cloſe thou cover'dſt it.

3 And thou thine anger didſt aſſwage,
that all thy wrath was gone:
And ſo didſt turn thee from thy rage,
with them to be at one.

4 O God our health, do now convert
thy people unto thee:
Put all thy wrath from us apart,
and angry ceaſe to be.

5 Shall thy fierce anger never end,
but ſtill be pour'd on us?
And ſhall thy wrath it ſelf extend
upon all ages thus?

6 Wilt thou not rather turn again,
and quicken us, that we
And all thy folk may evermore
be glad and joy in thee?

7 O Lord, on us do thou declare
thy goodneſs to our wealth:
Shew forth to us, and do not ſpare,
thine aid and ſaving health.

8 I'll hearken what God ſaith to me,
to his he ſpeaketh peace,

And to his ſaints, that never they
return to fooliſhneſs.

2 For why? his help is ſtill at hand
to ſuch as do him fear:
Whereby great glory in our land
ſhall dwell and flouriſh there.

10 For truth and mercy there ſhall
in one to take their place: (meet
And peace ſhall juſtice wth kiſs greet,
and there they ſhall embrace.

11 Truth from the earth ſhall ſpring
and flouriſh pleaſantly: (apace,
So right'ouſneſs ſhall ſhew her face,
and look from heav'n moſt high.

12 Yea, God himſelf doth take in hand
to give us each good thing:
And through the coaſts of all the land
the earth her fruit ſhall bring.

13 Before his face ſhall juſtice go
much like a guide or ſtay:
He ſhall direct his ſteps alſo,
and keep them in the way.

Gloria Patri.

To Father, Son, and Holy Ghoſt,
One God in Perſons Three:
All Honour, Praiſe, and Glory moſt,
both now and ever be.

L

146   Pſalm lxxxvi.

Cantus & Baſſus.   PSALM LXXXVI.   *Or to Windſor Tune.*

LOrd, bow thine ear to my requeſt, and hear me inſtantly:

For with great pain and grief oppreſs'd, full poor and weak am I.

Preſerve my ſoul, becauſe my ways and doings ho—ly be:

And ſave thy ſervant, O my God, that puts his truſt in thee.

Medius.   Pſalm 86.   *A. 3. Voc.*

LOrd, bow thine ear to my requeſt, and hear me inſtantly:

For with great pain and grief oppreſs'd, full poor and weak am I.

Preſerve my ſoul, becauſe my ways and doings ho—ly be:

And ſave thy ſervant, O my God, that puts his truſt in thee.

Baſſus.   Pſalm 86.   *A. 3. Voc.*

LOrd, bow thine ear to my requeſt, and hear me inſtantly:

For

Pſalm lxxxvi. 147

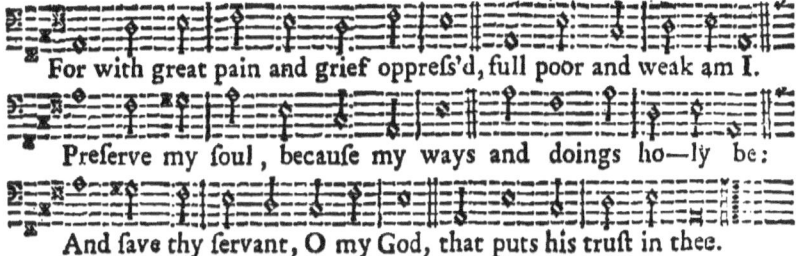

For with great pain and grief oppreſs'd, full poor and weak am I.
Preſerve my ſoul, becauſe my ways and doings ho—ly be:
And ſave thy ſervant, O my God, that puts his truſt in thee.

3 Thy mercy upon me expreſs,
and me defend alway:
For through the day I do not ceaſe
to thee, O Lord, to pray.
4 Comfort, O Lord, thy ſervant's ſoul
that now with pain is pin'd:
For unto thee I do exalt,
and lift my ſoul and mind.

5 For thou art good and bountiful,
thy gifts of grace are free:
Alſo thy mercy plentiful
to all that call on thee.
5 O Lord, likewiſe when I do pray,
regard and give an ear:
Mark well the words that I do ſay,
all my petitions hear.

7 In time when trouble doth me move,
to thee I do complain:
For why? I know and well do prove
thou anſwer'ſt me again.
8 Among the gods, O Lord, is none
with thee to be compar'd:
And none can do as thou haſt done,
the like hath not been heard.

The ſecond part.
9 The Gentiles and the people all
which thou didſt make and frame,
Before thy face on knees ſhall fall,
and glorifie thy Name.
10 For why? thou art ſo much of
all power is thine own: (might,
Thou workeſt wonders ſtill in ſight,
for thou art God alone.

11 O teach me, Lord, the way, and I
ſhall in thy truth proceed:
O joyn my heart to thee ſo nigh,
that I thy Name may dread.
12 To thee will I give thanks & praiſe,
O Lord, with all my heart:
And glorifie thy Name always,
becauſe my God thou art.

13 For why? thy mercy ſhew'd to me
is great, and doth excel:
Thou ſett'ſt my ſoul at liberty
out from the loweſt hell.
14 O Lord, the proud againſt me riſe,
and heaps of men of might:
They ſeek my ſoul, and in no wiſe
will have thee in their ſight.

15 Thou, Lord, art merciful and kind,
full ſlack and ſlow to wrath:
Thy goodneſs is full great, I find
thy truth no meaſure hath.
16 O turn to me, and mercy grant,
thy ſtrength to me apply:
O help and ſave thine own ſervant,
thy handmaid's ſon am I.

17 On me ſome ſign of favour ſhow,
that all my foes may ſee
And be aſham'd, becauſe, Lord, thou
doſt help and comfort me.
To Father, Son, and Holy Ghoſt,
all glory be therefore:
As in beginning was, is now,
and ſhall be evermore.

Psalm lxxxvii.

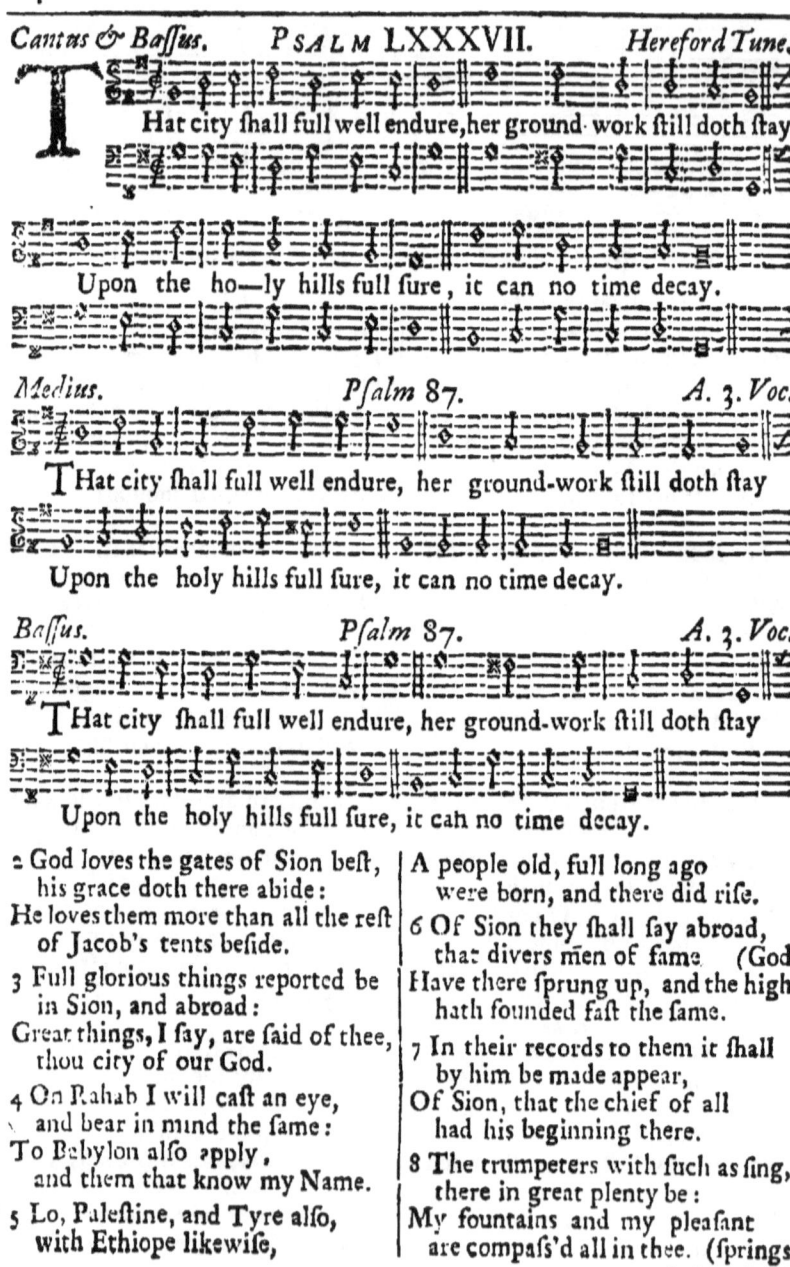

Cantus & Bassus. **PSALM LXXXVII.** *Hereford Tune.*

That city shall full well endure, her ground-work still doth stay
Upon the ho—ly hills full sure, it can no time decay.

Medius. Psalm 87. *A. 3. Voc.*

THat city shall full well endure, her ground-work still doth stay
Upon the holy hills full sure, it can no time decay.

Bassus. Psalm 87. *A. 3. Voc.*

THat city shall full well endure, her ground-work still doth stay
Upon the holy hills full sure, it can no time decay.

2 God loves the gates of Sion best,
  his grace doth there abide:
He loves them more than all the rest
  of Jacob's tents beside.

3 Full glorious things reported be
  in Sion, and abroad:
Great things, I say, are said of thee,
  thou city of our God.

4 On Rahab I will cast an eye,
  and bear in mind the same:
To Babylon also apply,
  and them that know my Name.

5 Lo, Palestine, and Tyre also,
  with Ethiope likewise,

A people old, full long ago
  were born, and there did rise.

6 Of Sion they shall say abroad,
  that divers men of fame (God
Have there sprung up, and the high
  hath founded fast the same.

7 In their records to them it shall
  by him be made appear,
Of Sion, that the chief of all
  had his beginning there.

8 The trumpeters with such as sing,
  there in great plenty be:
My fountains and my pleasant
  are compass'd all in thee. (springs

PSALM

Psalm lxxxviii.   149

Cantus & Bassus.   PSALM LXXXVIII.   *Manchester Tune.*

Lord God of health, the hope and stay thou art alone to me;

I call and cry throughout the day, and all the night to thee.

Medius.   Psalm 88.   *A. 3. Voc.*

Lord God of health, the hope and stay thou art alone to me;

I call and cry throughout the day, and all the night to thee.

Bassus.   Psalm 88.   *A. 3. Voc.*

Lord God of health, the hope and stay thou art alone to me;

I call and cry throughout the day, and all the night to thee.

2 O let my prayer soon ascend
   unto thy sight on high:
Incline thine ear, O Lord, attend,
   and hearken to my cry.

3 For why? with wo my heart is fill'd,
   and doth in trouble dwell:
My life & breath doth almost yield,
   and draweth nigh to hell.

4 I am esteem'd as one of them
   that in the pit do fall:

And made as one among those men
   that have no strength at all.

5 As one among the dead, and free
   from things that here remain:
It were more ease for me to be
   with them the which were slain.

6 As those that lie in grave, I say,
   whom thou hast clean forgot:
The which thy hand hath cut away,
   and thou regard'st them not.

L 3   7 Yea,

Psalm lxxxviii, lxxxix.

7 Yea, like to one shut up full sure
within the lower pit,
In places dark and all obscure,
and in the depth of it.

8 Thine anger & thy wrath likewise,
full sore on me doth lie:
And all thy storm against me rise,
my soul to vex and try.

9 Thou put'st my friends far off from
& mak'st them hate me sore: (me,
I am shut up in prison fast,
and can come forth no more.

10 My sight doth fail thrô grief & wo,
I call to thee, O God:
Throughout the day my hands also
to thee I stretch abroad.

The second part.

11 Dost thou unto the dead declare
thy wondrous works of fame?
Shall dead to life again repair,
and praise thee for the same?

12 Or shall thy loving kindness, Lord,
be preached in the grave?
Or shall with them that are destoy'd
thy truth her honour have?

13 Shall they that lie in dark full low
see all thy wonders great?

Or there shall they thy justice know
where men all things forget?

14 But I, O Lord, to thee always
do cry and call apace:
My pray'r also e're it be day
shall come before thy face.

15 Why dost thou, Lord, abhor my
in grief that seeketh thee: (soul,
And now, O Lord, why dost thou
thy face away from me? (hide

16 I am afflicted, dying still;
from youth many a year
Thy terrors, which do work me ill,
with troubled mind I bear.

17 The furies of thy wrathful rage
full sore upon me lie;
Thy terrors they do not aswage,
but press me heavily.

18 All day they compass me about,
as water at the tide:
And all at once with streams full
beset me on each side. (great

19 Thou settest far from me my
and lovers ev'ry one: (friends
Yea, and my old acquaintance all
out of my sight are gone.

Cantus & Bassus. PSALM LXXXIX. *Or to Martyrs Tune.*

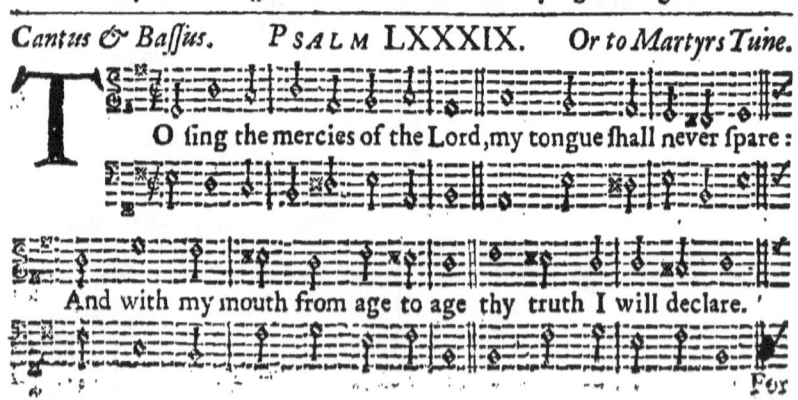

O sing the mercies of the Lord, my tongue shall never spare:
And with my mouth from age to age thy truth I will declare.

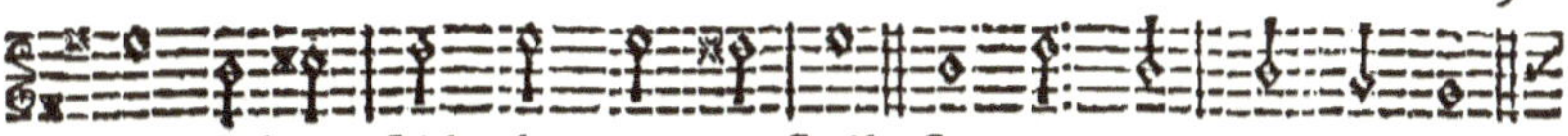

Psalm lxxxix. 151

For I have said, that mercy shall for e—ver--more remain:

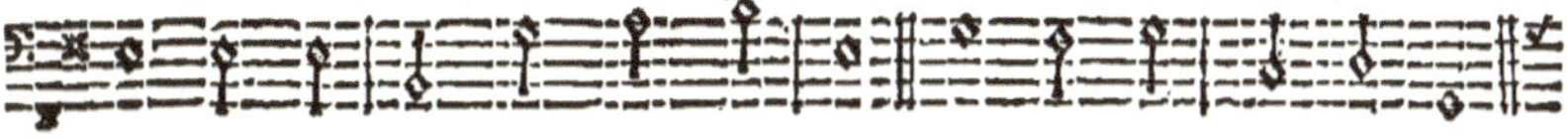

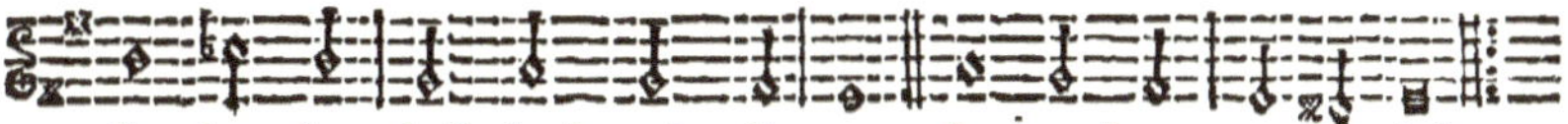

In that thou dost the heav'ns support, thy truth appeareth plain.

Medius.   P*salm* 89.   *A.* 3. *Voc.*

TO sing the mercies of the Lord, my tongue shall never spare:

And with my mouth from age to age thy truth I will declare.

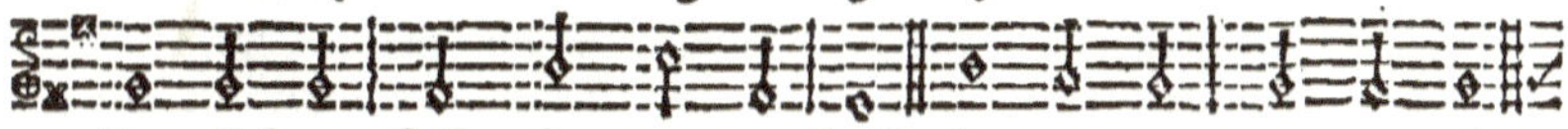

For I have said, that mercy shall for e—ver--more remain:

In that thou dost the heav'ns support, thy truth appeareth plain.

Bassus.   P*salm* 89.   *A.* 3. *Voc.*

TO sing the mercies of the Lord, my tongue shall never spare:

And with my mouth from age to age thy truth I will declare.

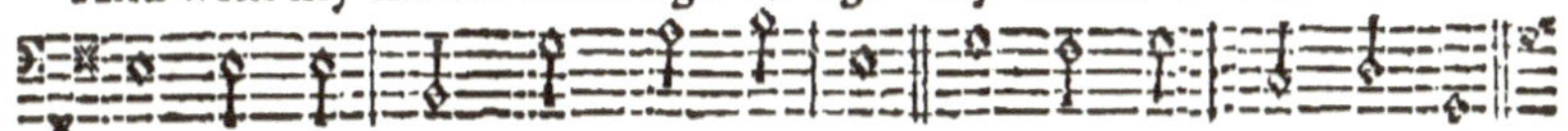

For I have said, that mercy shall for e—ver--more remain:

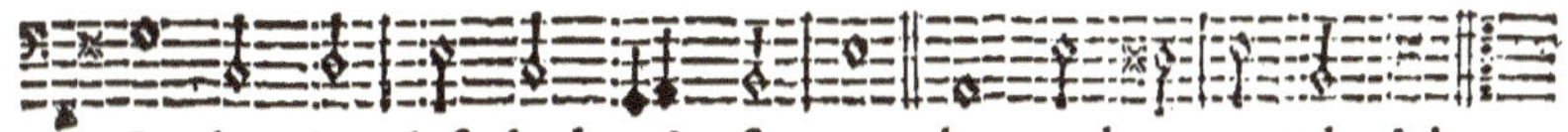

In that thou dost the heav'ns support, thy truth appeareth plain.

L 4   3 To

3 To mine elect, saith God, I made
  a cov'nant and beheſt:
My ſervant David to perſwade,
  I ſwore and did proteſt,
4 Thy ſeed for ever I will ſtay,
  and ſtabliſh it full faſt;
And ſtill uphold thy throne alway
  from age to age to laſt.
                           (mirth
5 The heav'ns do ſhew with joy and
  thy wondrous works, O Lord:
Thy ſaints within thy Church on
  thy faith and truth record. (earth
6 Who with the Lord is equal then
  in all the clouds abroad?
Among the ſons of all the gods,
  what one is like our God?

7 God in aſſembly of the ſaints
  is greatly to be dread:
And over all that dwell about
  in terror to be had.
8 Lord God of hoſts, in all the world
  what one is like to thee?
On ev'ry ſide, moſt mighty Lord,
  thy truth is ſeen to be.

9 The rage and fury of the ſea
  thou ruleſt at thy will:
And when the waves thereof ariſe,
  thou mak'ſt them calm and ſtill.
10 And Egypt, L^d, thou haſt ſubdu'd,
  thou haſt it quite deſtroy'd:
Yea, thou thy foes with mighty arm
  haſt ſcatter'd all abroad.
      The ſecond part.
11 The heav'ns are thine, & ſtill have
  likewiſe the earth & land: (been,
The world and all that is therein,
  thou foundedſt with thy hand.
12 Both north & ſouth, wth eaſt & weſt,
  thy ſelf didſt make and frame:
Both Tabor mount, and Hermon hill,
  rejoyce and praiſe thy Name.

13 Thine arm is ſtrong, and full of
  all might therein doth lie: (pow'r,
The ſtrength of thy right hand each
  thou lifteſt up on high.   (hour
14 In right'ouſneſs and equity
  thou haſt thy ſeat and place:
Mercy and truth are ſtill with thee,
  and go before thy face.

15 That folk is bleſt that knows a-
  the joyful ſound, O God: (right
For in the favour of thy ſight
  they walk full ſafe abroad.
16 For in thy Name throughout the
  they greatly do rejoyce: (day
And through thy right'ouſneſs have
  a pleaſant fame and noiſe. (they

17 For why? their glory, ſtrength, and
  in thee alone doth lie: (aid,
And thy goodneſs that hath us ſtaid,
  ſhall lift our horn on high.
18 Our ſtrength that doth defend us
  the Lord to us doth bring: (well,
The holy one of Iſrael,
  he is our Guide and King.

19 Sometimes thy will unto thy ſaints
  in viſions thou didſt ſhow:
And thus then didſt thou ſay to them,
  thy mind to make them know:
20 A man of might I have erect,
  your king and guide to be:
And ſet him up whom I elect
  among the folk to me.
      The third part.
21 My ſervant David I have found,
  for he doth pleaſe me well:
And have anointed him King of
  my people Iſrael.
22 For why? my hand is ready ſtill
  with him for to remain:
And with mine arm alſo I will
  him ſtrengthen and ſuſtain.

23 The

Psalm lxxxix.

23 The enemies shall not oppress,
  they shall him not devour:
Nor shall the sons of wickedness
  on him have any pow'r.
24 His foes likewise I will destroy
  before his face in sight:
And those that hate him I will plague
  and strike them with my might.

25 My truth and mercy also shall
  upon him ever lie:
And in my Name his horn shall be
  exalted very high.
26 His kingdom I will set to be
  upon the sea and land:
Also the running floods shall he
  embrace with his right hand.

27 He shall depend with all his heart
  on me, and this shall say,
My father and my God thou art,
  my rock of health and stay.
28 As my first-born I will him take
  of all on earth that springs:
His might and honour I will raise
  above all earthly kings.

29 My mercy shall be with him still,
  as I my self have told:
My faithful cov'nant to fulfil,
  my mercy I will hold.
30 Also his seed I will sustain
  for ever strong and sure:
So that his seat shall still remain
  while heav'n and earth endure.

The fourth part.

31 If that his sons forsake my law,
  and so begin to swerve:
And of my judgments have no aw,
  nor will not them observe.
32 Or if they do not use aright
  my laws for them prepar'd:
But set all my commandments light,
  and will them not regard.

33 Then with the rod will I begin
  their doings to amend,
And so will scourge them for their
  whenever they offend.   (sin
34 But yet thy mercy and goodness
  I will not take away
From him, nor let thy faithfulness
  in any wise decay.

35 But sure my cov'nant I will hold,
  with all that I have spoke:
No word the which my lips have
  shall alter or be broke.   (told,
36 Once sware I by my holiness,
  and that perform will I:
With David I shall keep promise,
  to him I will not lie.

37 His seed for evermore shall reign,
  also his throne of might:
As doth the sun, it shall remain
  for ever in my sight.
38 And as the moon within the sky
  for ever standeth fast
A faithful witness from on high,
  so shall his kingdom last.
               (ject,
29 But, Lord, thou dost him now re-
  and put him in great fear:
Yea, thou art wroth with thine elect,
  thine own anointed dear. (made,
40 The cov'nant with thy servant
  Lord, thou hast quite undone:
And down upon the ground also
  hath cast his royal crown.

The fifth part.   (might,
41 Thou pluck'st his hedges up with
  his walls thou dost confound:
Thou beatest all his bulwarks down,
  casting them to the ground.
42 That he is sore destroy'd & torn
  of comers by throughout:
And so is made a mock and scorn
  to all that dwell about.

43 Thou

Pſalm lxxxix, xc.

43 Thou their right hand haſt lifted up,
 that him ſo ſore annoy:
And all his foes that him devour,
 lo, thou haſt made to joy. (way,
44 His ſword's edge thou doſt take a-
 that ſhould his foes withſtand:
To him in war no victory
 thou giv'ſt, nor upper hand.

45 His glory thou doſt alſo waſte,
 his throne, his joy, his mirth,
By thee is overthrown and caſt
 full low upon the earth. (ſhort
46 Thou haſt cut off and made full
 his youth and joyful days:
And rais'd of him an ill report,
 with ſhame and great diſpraiſe.

47 How long away from me, O Lord,
 for ever wilt thou turn?
And ſhall thine anger ſtill alway
 as fire conſume and burn?
48 O call to mind, remember then
 my time conſumeth faſt:
Why haſt thou made the ſons of men
 as things in vain to waſte?

49 What man is he that liveth here,
 and death ſhall never ſee?
Or from the hand of hell, his ſoul
 ſhall he deliver free? (neſs
50 Where is, ô Lord, thine own good-
 ſo oft declar'd before,
Which by thy truth & uprightneſs
 to David thou haſt ſwore?

51 The great rebukes to mind I call
 that on thy ſervants lie:
The railings of the people all,
 born in my breaſt have I,
52 Wherewith, ô Lord, thine enemies
 blaſphemed have thy Name:
The ſteps of thine anointed one
 they ceaſe not to defame.

53 All praiſe be given unto Thee,
 O God the Lord moſt high,
From this time forth for evermore
 Amen, Amen, ſay I.
All Glory, Honour, Pow'r, and Praiſe
 to the Myſterious Three:
As at the firſt beginning was,
 may now and ever be.

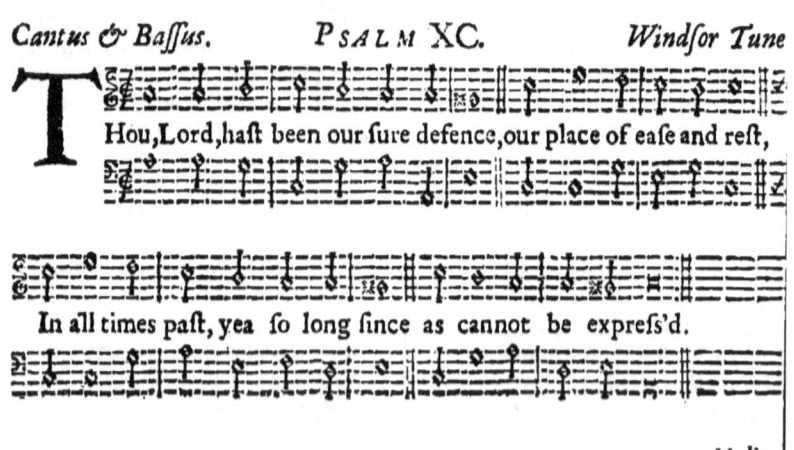

Cantus & Baſſus.   PSALM XC.   Windſor Tune

Thou, Lord, haſt been our ſure defence, our place of eaſe and reſt,

In all times paſt, yea ſo long ſince as cannot be expreſs'd.

M. dius.

Psalm xc.

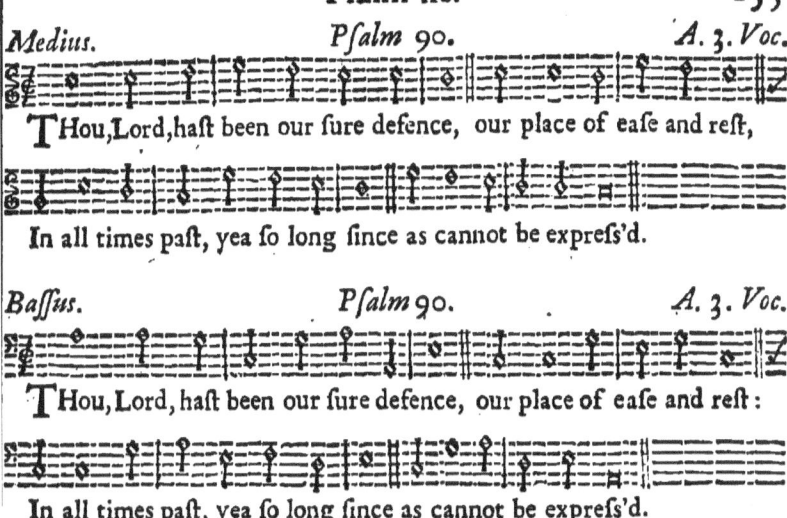

2 E're there was made mountain or
  the earth and world abroad: (hill,
From age to age, and always still,
  for ever thou art God.
                    (and pain
3 Thou grindest man through grief
  to dust or clay, and then
Thou unto them again dost say,
  Return ye sons of men.

4 The lasting of a thousand years,
  what is it in thy sight?
As yesterday it doth appear,
  or as a watch by night.

5 So soon as thou dost scatter them,
  then is their life and trade
Ev'n as a sleep, or like the grass,
  whose beauty soon doth fade:
                    (bright,
6 Which in the morning shines full
  but fadeth by and by:
And is cut down e're it be night,
  all wither'd, dead, and dry.

7 For thrô thine anger we consume,
  our might is much decay'd:
And of thy fervent wrath, O Lord,
  we are full sore afraid.
                    (wrought,
8 The wicked works that we have
  thou sett'st before thine eye:
Our privy faults, yea all our thoghts,
  thy countenance doth spy.
                    (waste,
9 For through thy wrath our days do
  thereof doth nought remain:
Our years consume as doth a blast,
  and are not call'd again.

13 The time of our abode on earth
  is threescore years and ten:
But if we come to fourscore years,
  our life is grievous then.
                The second part.
11 For of this time the strength and
  we dote so much upon,   (chief
Is nothing else but pain and grief,
  and we as blasts are gone.

12 What

156   Pſalm xc, xci.

12 What man doth know what power
  what might thine anger hath? (and
Or in his heart who doth thee fear
  according to thy wrath?

13 Inſtruct us, Lord, to know and try
  how long our days remain:
That ſo we may our hearts apply
  true wiſdom to attain.
                          (thou
14 Return, O Lord, how long wilt
  in thy great wrath proceed?
Shew favour to thy ſervants now,
  and help them at their need.

15 Refreſh us with thy mercy ſoon,
  and then moſt chearfully
All times ſo long as life doth laſt,
  in heart rejoyce will we.

16 As thou haſt plagued us before,
  now alſo make us glad:
And for the years wherein full ſore
  affliction we have had.

17 O let thy work and pow'r appear,
  and on thy ſervants light:
And ſhew unto thy children dear
  thy glory and thy might.

18 Lord, let thy grace and glory ſtand
  on us thy ſervants thus:
Confirm the works we take in hand,
  and proſper them to us.
            Gloria Patri.
To Father, Son, and Holy Ghoſt,
  immortal Glory be:
As was, is now, and ſhall be ſtill,
  to all Eternitie.

Cantus & Baſſus.   PSALM XCI.   St. Mary's Tune.

HE that within the ſecret place of God moſt high doth dwell
In ſhadow of the mighti'ſt grace, at reſt ſhall keep him well.

Medius.   Pſalm 91.   A. 3. Voc

HE that within the ſecret place of God moſt high doth dwell:
In ſhadow of the mighti'ſt grace, at reſt ſhall keep him well.

Baſſus

Pſalm xci. 157

Baſſus.   *Pſalm 91.*   *A. 3. Voc:*

HE that within the ſecret place of God moſt high doth dwell:

In ſhadow of the mighti'ſt grace, at reſt ſhall keep him well.

2 Thou art my hope, and my ſtrong
I to the Lord will ſay :   (hold,
My God is he, in him will I
my whole affiance ſtay.

3 He ſhall defend thee from the ſnare
the which the hunter laid:
And from the deadly plague & care
whereof thou art afraid.

4 And with his wings ſhall cover
and keep thee ſafely there : (thee,
His faith & truth thy fence ſhall be,
as ſure as ſhield and ſpear.

5 So that thou never ſhalt have cauſe
to fear or be affright,
For all the ſhafts that flie by day,
or terrors of the night:

6 Nor of the plague that privily
doth walk in dark ſo faſt :
Nor yet of that which doth deſtroy,
and at noon-day doth waſte.

7 Yea, at thy ſide as thou doſt ſtand,
a thouſand dead ſhall be :
Ten thouſand more at thy right
and yet ſhalt thou be free. (hand,

8 But thou ſhalt ſee it for thy part,
thine eyes ſhall well regard,
According unto their deſert
the wicked have reward.

9 For why, O Lord, I only reſt
and ſtay my hope on thee:

In the moſt High I put my truſt,
my ſure defence is he.

10 No evil thou ſhalt need to fear,
with thee it ſhall go well:
No plague ſhall ever once come near
the houſe where thou doſt dwell.

11 For why? unto his angels all
with charge commanded he,
That ſtill in all thy ways they ſhall
preſerve and proſper thee.

12 And in their hands ſhall bear thee
ſtill waiting thee upon;   (up,
So that thy foot ſhall never chance
to daſh againſt a ſtone.

13 Upon the lion thou ſhalt go,
the adder fell and long:
And tread upon the lions young,
with dragons ſtout and ſtrong.

14 Becauſe he ſets his love on me,
I'll ſave him by my might,
And him advance, becauſe that he
doth know my Name aright.

15 When he for help to me doth cry,
an anſwer I will give:
And from his grief take him will I
in glory for to live.

16 With length of years, and days of
I will fulfil his time :   (wealth,
The goodneſs of my ſaving health
I will declare to him.

P S A L M

Psalm xcii.

Cantus & Bassus.   **P SALM XCII.**   *Martyrs Tune.*

IT is a thing both good and meet to praise the highest Lord:

And to thy Name, O thou most High, to sing with one accord:

Medius.   *Psalm 92.*   *A. 3. Voc.*

IT is a thing both good and meet to praise the highest Lord:

And to thy Name, O thou most High, to sing with one accord :

Bassus.   *Psalm 92.*   *A. 3. Voc.*

IT is a thing both good and meet to praise the highest Lord :

And to thy Name, O thou most High, to sing with one accord:

2 To shew the kindness of the Lord,
 betime e're day be light:
And to declare his truth abroad,
 when it doth draw to night.

3 Upon ten-stringed instrument,
 or lute and harp so sweet :
With all the mirth you can invent
 of instruments most meet.

4 For thou hast made me to rejoyce
 in things so wrought by thee :

That I have joy in heart and voice
 thy handy-works to see.

5 O Lord, how glorious & how great
 are all thy works so stout !
So deeply are thy counsels set,
 that none can find them out.

6 The man unwise hath not the wit
 this work to pass to bring :
And all such fools are nothing fit
 to understand this thing.

7 When

Pſalm xcii, xciii.   159

7 When as the wicked at their will
like graſs do ſpring full faſt,
And when they flouriſh in their ill,
they ſhall for ever waſte.
                (high,
8 But thou art mighty, Lord, moſt
and thou doſt reign therefore
In ev'ry time eternally,
both now and evermore.

9 Behold, O Lord, thine enemies
ſhall be deſtroy'd alway :
And all that work iniquity
ſhall periſh and decay.

10 But thou, like as an unicorn,
ſhall lift mine horn on high :
With freſh and new-prepared oyl
anointed king am I.

11 And of my foes before mine eyes
ſhall ſee the fall and ſhame :

Of all that up againſt me riſe,
mine ears ſhall hear the ſame.

12 The juſt ſhall flouriſh up on high
as palm-trees bud and blow :
And as the cedars multiply
in Libanus that grow.

13 For they are planted in the place
and dwelling of our God :
Within his courts they ſpring apace,
and flouriſh all abroad.
                (bring,
14 And in their age much fruit ſhall
both fat and well beſeen :
And pleaſantly both bud and ſpring
with boughs and branches green.

15 To ſhew that God is good & juſt,
and upright in his will :
He is my rock, my hope, and truſt,
in him there is none ill.

Cantus & Baſſus.   PSALM XCIII.   *London new Tune.*

THE Lord doth reign, and cloathed is with majeſty moſt bright :

And to declare his ſtrength likewiſe, hath girt himſelf with might.

Medius.   *Pſalm 93.*   *A. 3. Voc.*

THE Lord doth reign, and cloathed is with ma-je--ſty moſt bright :

And to declare his ſtrength likewiſe, hath girt himſelf with might.
                                        Baſſus.

Psalm xciii, xciv.

Bassus.   **Psalm 93.**   *A. 3. Voc.*

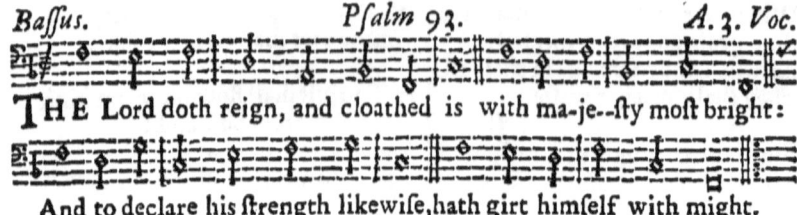

THE Lord doth reign, and cloathed is with ma-je--sty most bright:

And to declare his strength likewise, hath girt himself with might.

2 The Lord likewise the earth hath made,
and shaped it so sure,
No might can make it move or fade,
at stay it doth endure.

3 E're that the world was made or wrought,
thy seat was set before:
Beyond all time that can be thought,
thou hast been evermore.

4 The floods, O Lord, the floods do rise,
they roar and make a noise:
The floods, I say, did enterprise,
and lifted up their voice.

5 Yea thô the storms arise in sight,
thô seas do rage and swell:
The Lord is strong & more of might,
for he on high doth dwell.

6 O Lord, thy testimonies great
are very sure: therefore
Doth holiness right well become
thy house for evermore.

Cantus & Bassus.   PSALM XCIV.   *Peterborough Tune.*

O Lord, thou dost revenge all wrong, veng'ance belongs to thee:

Since then it doth to thee belong, declare that all may see.

Medius.   **Psalm 94.**   *A. 3. Voc.*

O Lord, thou dost revenge all wrong, veng'ance belongs to thee:

Since then it doth to thee belong, declare that all may see.

Psalm xciv.

Bassus.   Psalm 94.   *A. 3. Voc.*

O Lord, thou dost revenge all wrong, veng'ance belongs to thee:
Since then it doth to thee belong, declare that all may see.

2 Set forth thy self, for thou of right
the earth dost judge and guide:
Reward the proud and men of might
according to their pride.
                  (sway
3 How long shall wicked men bear
with lifting up their voice?
Shall proud and wicked men alway
thus triumph and rejoyce?
                  (burst out,
4 How long shall they with brags
and proudly prate their fill?
Shall they rejoyce that be so stout,
whose works are ever ill?

5 Thy flock, O Lord, thine heritage
they spoil and vex full sore:
Against thy people they do rage
still daily more and more.

6 The widows which are comfortless,
and strangers they destroy:
They slay the children fatherless,
and none doth put them by.
                  (in hand,
7 And when they take these things
this talk they have of thee;
Can Jacob's God this understand?
Tush, no, he cannot see.

8 O folk unwise, and people rude,
some knowledge now discern:
Ye fools among the multitude,
at length begin to learn.
                  (man,
9 The Lord which made the ear of
he needs of right must hear:

He made the eye, all things must then
before his sight appear.
                  (rect,
10 The Lord doth all the world cor-
and make them understand:
Shall he not then your deeds detect?
how can ye scape his hand?

The second part.
11 The L^d doth know the thoughts of
his heart he sees full plain: (man,
And he their very thoughs doth scan,
and findeth them but vain.

12 But, Lord, that man is happy sure
whom thou dost keep in aw,
And through correction dost procure
to teach him in thy law.

13 Whereby he shall in quiet rest
in time of trouble sit:
When wicked men shall be suppress,
and fall into the pit.

14 For sure the Lord will not refuse
his people for to take:
His heritage whom he did chuse,
he will no time forsake.

15 Until that judgment be decreed
to justice to convert:
That all may follow her with speed
that are of upright heart.

16 But who upon my part shall stand
against the cursed train?
Or who shall rid me from their hand
that wicked works maintain?

M   17 Except

Pſalm xciv, xcv.

17 Except the Lord had been mine aid,
  mine enemies to quell:
My ſoul and life had now been laid
  almoſt as low as hell.

18 When I did ſay, My foot doth ſlide,
  before that I could call:
Thy mercy, Lord, moſt ready was,
  to ſave me from the fall.

19 When with my ſelf I muſed much,
  and could no comfort find:
Then, Lord, thy goodneſs did me
  & that did eaſe my mind. (touch,

20 Wilt thou accuſtom, Lord, thy ſelf
  with wicked men to ſit,
Who with pretence, in ſtead of law,
  much miſchief do commit?

21 For they conſult againſt the life
  of right'ous men and good:
And in their counſels they are rife
  to ſhed the guiltleſs blood.

22 But yet the Lord is unto me
  a ſure and ſtrong defence:
To him I flee, becauſe he is
  my ſtrength and confidence.

23 And he ſhall cauſe their miſchiefs (all,
  themſelves for to annoy:
And in their malice they ſhall fall,
  our God ſhall them deſtroy.

Gloria Patri.

To Father, Son, and Holy Ghoſt,
  immortal Glory be:
As was, is now, and ſhall be ſtill,
  to all Eternitie.

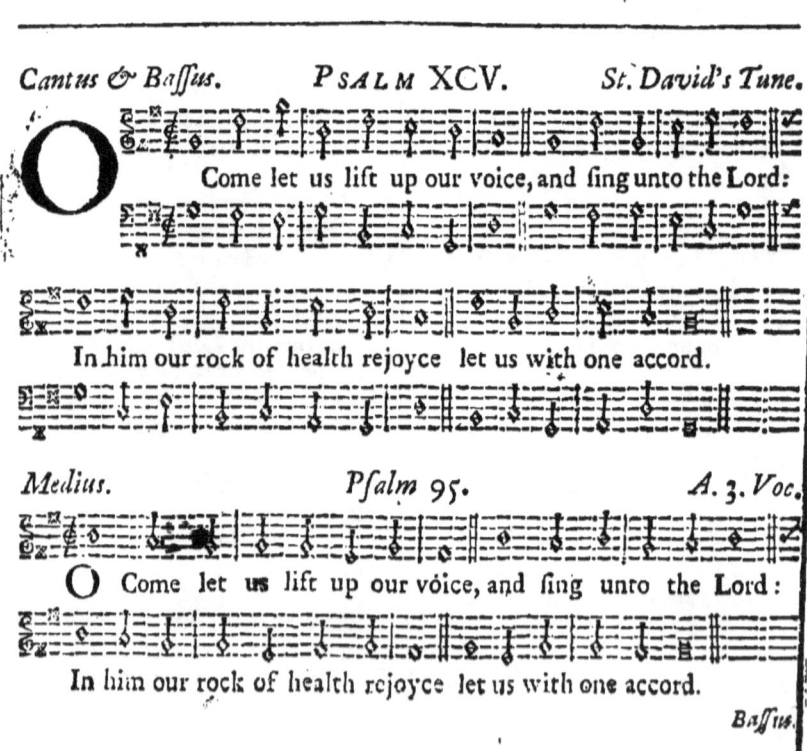

Cantus & Baſſus.   PSALM XCV.   St. David's Tune.

O Come let us lift up our voice, and ſing unto the Lord:
In him our rock of health rejoyce let us with one accord.

Medius.   Pſalm 95.   A. 3. Voc.

O Come let us lift up our vóice, and ſing unto the Lord:
In him our rock of health rejoyce let us with one accord.

Baſſus.

In him our rock of health rejoyce let us with one accord.

Yea, let us come before his face
to give him thanks and praise:
a singing Psalms unto his grace,
let us be glad always.
For why? the Lord he is no doubt
a great and mighty God,
King above all gods throughout,
in all the world abroad.

The secrets of the earth so deep,
and corners of the land,
the tops of hills that are so steep,
he hath them in his hand.
The sea and waters all are his,
for he the same hath wrought:
the earth and all that therein is,
his hand hath made of nought.
Come let us bow & praise the Lord,
before him let us fall:
and kneel to him with one accord,
the which hath made us all.

7 For why? he is the Lord our God;
for us he doth provide:
We are his flock, he doth us feed;
his sheep, and he our Guide.
8 To day if ye his voice will hear,
then harden not your heart:
As ye with grudging many year
provok'd me in desart.
9 Whereas your fathers tempted me,
my power for to prove: (see,
My wondrous works when they did
yet still they would me move:
10 Twice twenty years they did me
and I to them did say, (grieve,
They err in heart, and not believe,
they have not known my way.
11 Wherefore I sware when that my
was kindled in my breast, (wrath
That they should never tread the
to enter in my rest. (path;

Cantus & Bassus.   PSALM XCVI.   *Winchester Tune.*

Sing ye with praise unto the Lord new songs with joy and mirth:

Psalm xcvi.

Medius.   *Psalm 96.*   A. 3. Voc.

Sing ye with praise un--to the Lord new songs with joy and mirth:

Sing un--to him with one accord all people on the earth.

Bassus.   *Psalm 96.*   A. 3. Voc.

Sing ye with praise un--to the Lord new songs with joy and mirth:

Sing un--to him with one accord all people on the earth.

2 Yea, sing unto the Lord alway,
praise ye his holy Name:
Declare and shew from day to day
salvation by the same.

3 Among the heathen all declare
his honour round about:
To shew his wonders do not spare
in all the world throughout.

4 For why? the Lord is much of might,
and worthy of all praise:
And he is to be dread of right,
above all gods always.

5 For all the gods of heathen folk
are idols that will fade:
But yet our God he is the Lord
that hath the heavens made.

6 All praise and honour also dwell
ever before his face:
Both pow'r and might likewise excel
within his holy place.

7 Ascribe unto the Lord therefore,
all men with one accord:

All might and worship evermore
ascribe unto the Lord.

8 Ascribe unto the Lord also
the glory of his Name:
Also into his courts do go
with gifts unto the same.

The second part.

9 Fall down and worship ye the Lord
within his temple bright:
Let all the people of the world
be fearful at his sight.

10 Tell all the world, be not afraid,
the Lord doth reign above:
Yea, he the earth so fast hath stay'd,
that it can never move.

11 And that it is the Lord alone
that rules with princely might,
To judge the nations ev'ry one
with equity and right.

12 The heav'ns shall joyfully begin,
the earth likewise rejoyce:
The sea, with all that is therein,
shall shout and make a noise.

13 The

Psalm xcvi, xcvii.

13 The fields shall joy, & ev'ry thing
that springeth on the earth:
The wood and ev'ry tree shall sing
with gladness and with mirth.

14 Before the presence of the Lord,
and coming of his might:
When he shall justly judg the world,
and rule his folk with right.

Cantus & Bassus.   PSALM XCVII.   *Westminster Tune.*

THE L^d doth reign, whereat the earth may joy wth pleasant voice:

Also the iles with joyful mirth may triumph and rejoyce.

Medius.   Psalm 97.   *A. 3. Voc.*

THe Lord doth reign, whereat the earth may joy with pleasant voice:

Also the iles with joyful mirth may triumph and rejoyce.

Bassus.   Psalm 97.   *A. 3. Voc.*

THe Lord doth reign, whereat the earth may joy with pleasant voice:

Also the iles with joyful mirth may triumph and rejoyce.

2 Both clouds and darkness likewise
and round about him beat: (swell,
Yea, right and justice ever dwell
and 'bide about his seat.

3 Yea, fire and heat at once do run,
and go before his face:

Which all his enemies shall burn
abroad in ev'ry place.
(blaze,
4 His lightnings great full bright did
and to the world appear:
Whereat the earth did look and gaze
with dread and deadly fear.

5 The

Psalm xcvii, xcviii.

5 The hills like wax did melt in fight
 and presence of the Lord:
They fled before that Ruler's might
 which guideth all the world.
                              (show
6 The heav'ns likewise declare and
 his justice forth abroad,
That all the world may see & know
 the glory of our God.

7 Confusion sure shall come to such
 as worship idols vain:
Also to those that glory much
 dumb pictures to maintain.

8 For all the idols of the world,
 which they their gods do call,
Shall feel the power of the Lord,
 and down to him shall fall.

9 With joy shall Sion hear this thing,
 and Judah shall rejoyce:

For at thy judgments they shall sing,
 with a most chearful voice.

10 For thou, O Lord, art set on high
 in all the earth abroad:
And art exalted wondrously
 above each other god.

11 All ye that love the Lord, do this,
 Hate all things that are ill:
For he doth keep the souls of his
 from such as would them spill.
                              (just,
12 And light doth spring up to the
 with pleasure for his part:
Gladness and joy likewise to them
 that are of upright heart.

13 Ye right'ous, in the Lord rejoyce,
 his holiness proclaim:
And thankfully with heart & voice,
 be mindful of the same.

Cantus & Bassus.   PSALM XCVIII. *Or to London new Tune.*

O Sing ye now unto the Lord a new and pleasant song:

For he hath wrought throughout the world his wonders great and strong.

With his right hand full wor--thi---ly he doth his foes devour,

And

Psalm xcviii. 167

And gets himself the vi—cto—ry with his own arm and pow'r.

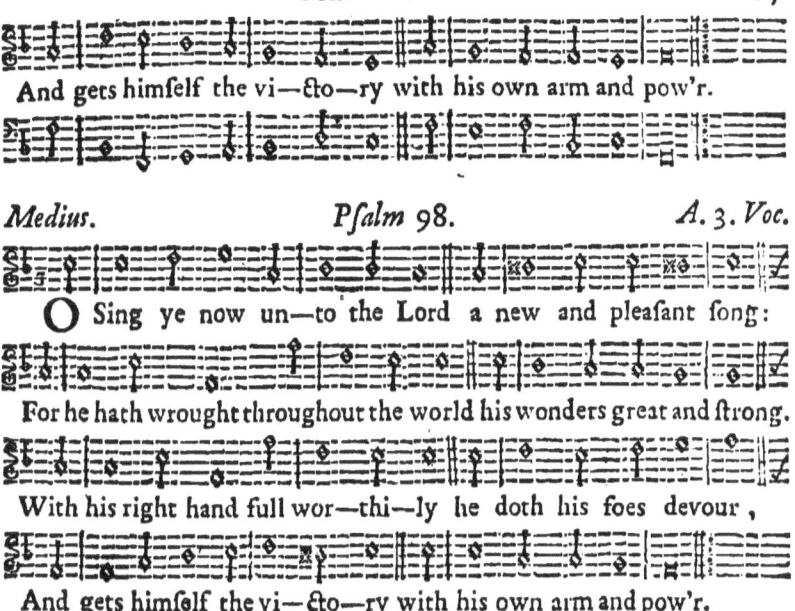

Medius.   Psalm 98.   *A. 3. Voc.*

O Sing ye now un—to the Lord a new and pleasant song:

For he hath wrought throughout the world his wonders great and strong.

With his right hand full wor—thi—ly he doth his foes devour,

And gets himself the vi—cto—ry with his own arm and pow'r.

Bassus.   Psalm 98.   *A. 3. Voc.*

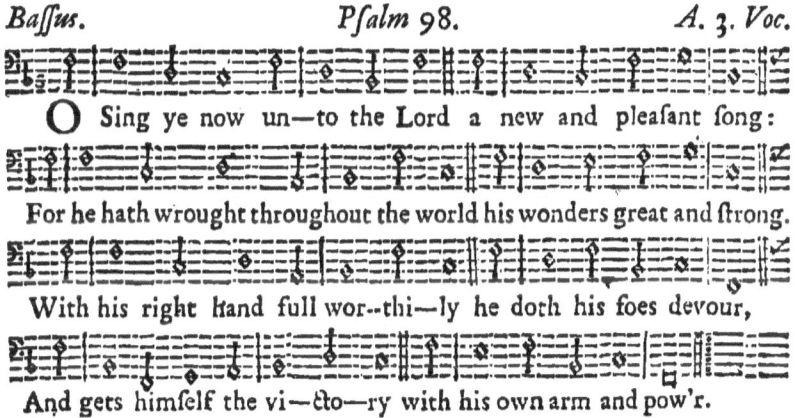

O Sing ye now un—to the Lord a new and pleasant song:

For he hath wrought throughout the world his wonders great and strong.

With his right hand full wor--thi—ly he doth his foes devour,

And gets himself the vi—cto—ry with his own arm and pow'r.

3 The L^d doth make the people know
his saving health and might:
And also doth his justice show
in all the heathens sight.

4 His grace and truth to Israel
in mind he doth record:
And all the earth hath seen right well
the goodness of the Lord.

168　Pſalm xcviii, xcix.

5 Be glad in him with joyful voice,
　all people of the earth :
Give thanks to God, ſing and rejoyce
　to him with joy and mirth.

6 Upon the harp unto him ſing,
　give thanks to him always :
Rejoyce before the Lord our King,
　with trumpets ſound his praiſe.

7 Yea, let the ſea, with all therein,
　for joy both rore and ſwell :
The earth likewiſe let it begin,
　with all that therein dwell.

8 And let the floods rejoyce their fills,
　and clap their hands apace :
Yea, let the mountains and the hills
　triumph before his face.

9 For he ſhall come to judge and try
　the world and ev'ry wight :
And rule the people mightily
　with juſtice and with right.

To Father, Son, and Holy Ghoſt,
　all glory be therefore :
As in beginning was, is now,
　and ſhall be evermore.

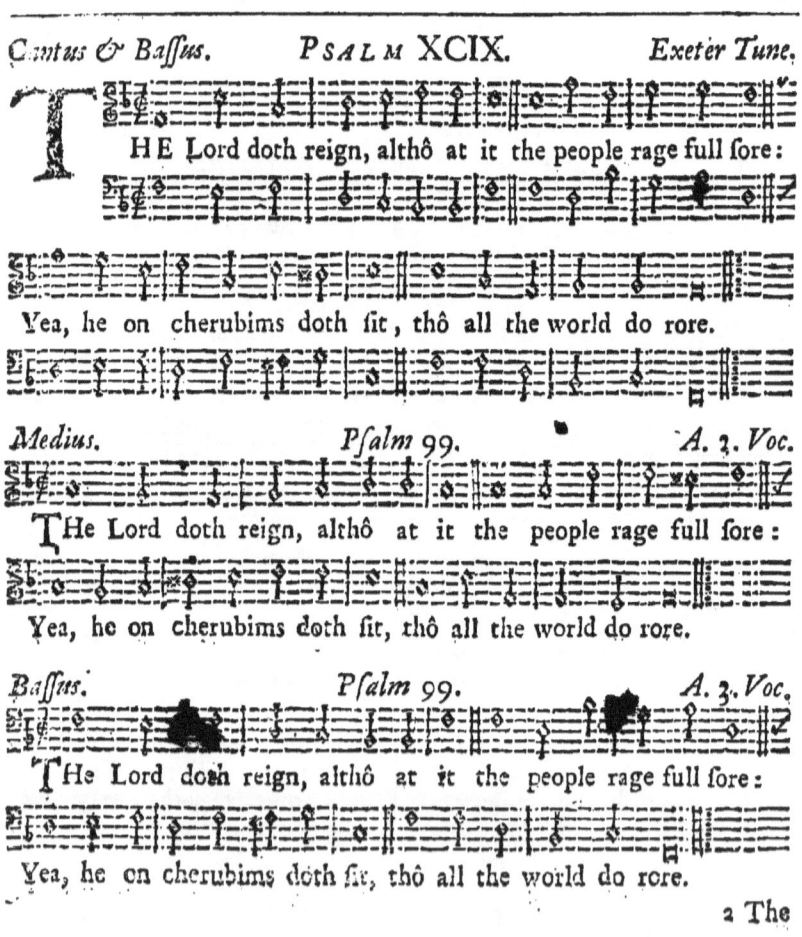

Cantus & Baſſus.　　PSALM XCIX.　　Exeter Tune.

THE Lord doth reign, althô at it the people rage full ſore :
Yea, he on cherubims doth ſit, thô all the world do rore.

Medius.　　Pſalm 99.　　A. 3. Voc.

THe Lord doth reign, althô at it the people rage full ſore :
Yea, he on cherubims doth ſit, thô all the world do rore.

Baſſus.　　Pſalm 99.　　A. 3. Voc.

THe Lord doth reign, althô at it the people rage full ſore :
Yea, he on cherubims doth ſit, thô all the world do rore.

Psalm xcix, c.   169

2 The Lord that doth in Sion dwell,
is high and wondrous great:
Above all folk he doth excel,
and he aloft is set.
                        (Name,
3 Let all men praise thy mighty
for it is fearful sure:
And let them magnifie the same,
that holy is and pure.

4 The princely power of our King
doth love judgment and right:
Thou rightly rulest ev'ry thing
in Jacob through thy might.

5 To praise the Lord our God devise,
all honour to him shew:
And at his footstool worship him
that holy is, and true.

6 Moses, Aaron, and Samuel,
as priests on him did call: (well,
When they did pray, he heard them
and gave them answer all.

7 Within the cloud to them he spake,
then did they labour still
To keep such laws as he did make,
according to his will.
                        (hear,
8 O Lord our God, thou didst them
and answer'dst them again:
But their inventions punished
which foolish were, and vain.
                        (fore
9 O praise our God and Lord there-
within his holy hill:
For why? our God whom we adore
is holy ever still.

Cantus & Bassus.   PSALM C.   Proper Tune.

ALL people that on earth do dwell, sing to the L^d wth chearful voice:

Him serve with fear, his praise forth tell, come ye before him and rejoyce.

Medius.   Psalm 100.   A. 3. Voc.

ALL people that on earth do dwell, sing to the L^d with chearful voice:

Him serve with fear, his praise forth tell, come ye before him and rejoyce.

Bassus.

170 **Pſalm c, ci.**

Baſſus.　　　　*Pſalm* 100.　　　　*A.* 3. *Voc.*

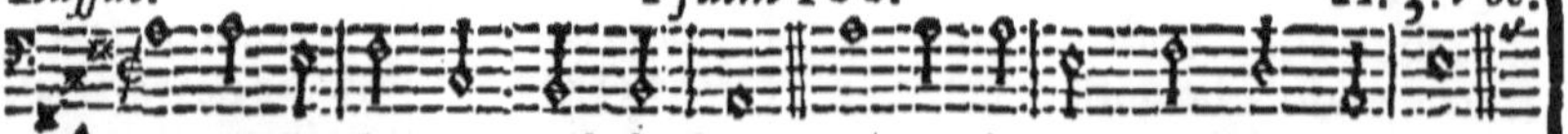

[music]

A LL people that on earth do dwell, ſing to the L^d with chearful voice:

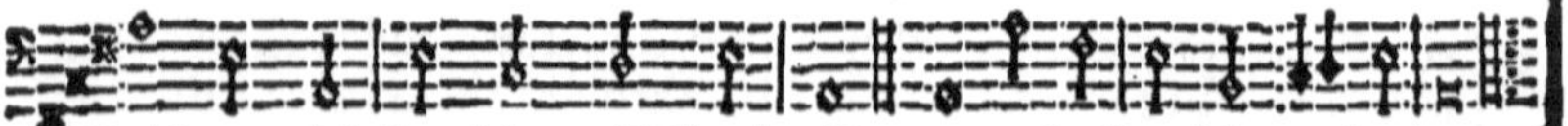

[music]

Him ſerve with fear, his praiſe forth tell, come ye before him and rejoyce.

3 The Lord ye know is God indeed,
 without our aid he did us make:
We are his flock, he doth us feed,
 and for his ſheep he doth us take.

4 O enter then his gates with praiſe,
 approach with joy his courts unto:

Praiſe, laud, & bleſs his Name always,
 for it is ſeemly ſo to do.

5 For why? the Lord our God is good,
 his mercy is for ever ſure:
His truth at all times firmly ſtood,
 and ſhall from age to age endure.

Pſalm 100.　　*Another of the ſame.*　　*St. Mary's Tune.*

IN God the Lord be glad & light,
 praiſe him throughout the earth:
2 Serve him, and come before his ſight
 with ſinging and with mirth.

3 Know that the Lord our God he is,
 he did us make and keep,
Not we our ſelves: for we are his
 own flock and paſture-ſheep.

4 O go into his gates always,
 give thanks within the ſame:
Within his courts ſet forth his praiſe,
 and laud his holy Name.

5 For why? the goodneſs of the Lord
 for evermore doth reign: (world
From age to age throughout the
 his truth doth ſtill remain.

Cantus & Baſſus.　　**P**ſ**ALM CI.**　　*London Tune.*

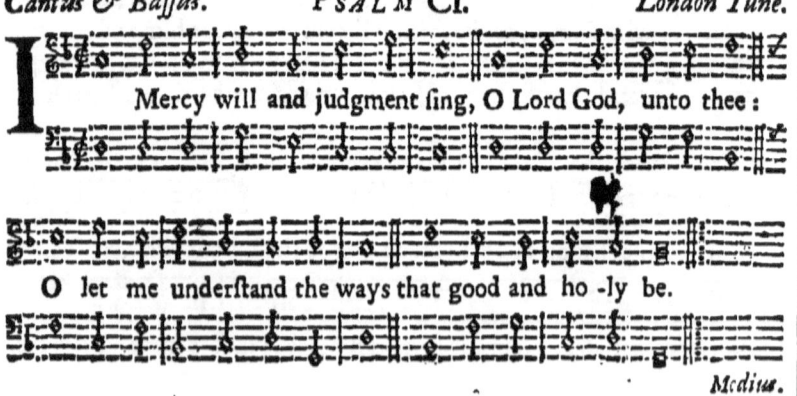

I Mercy will and judgment ſing, O Lord God, unto thee:

O let me underſtand the ways that good and ho-ly be.

Medius.

Pſalm ci. 171

Medius.   Pſalm 101.   *A. 3. Voc.*

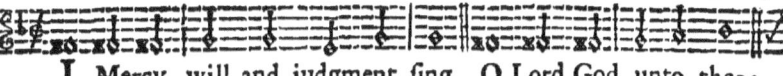
I Mercy will and judgment ſing, O Lord God, unto thee:

O let me underſtand the ways that good and holy be.

Baſſus.   Pſalm 101.   *A. 3. Voc.*

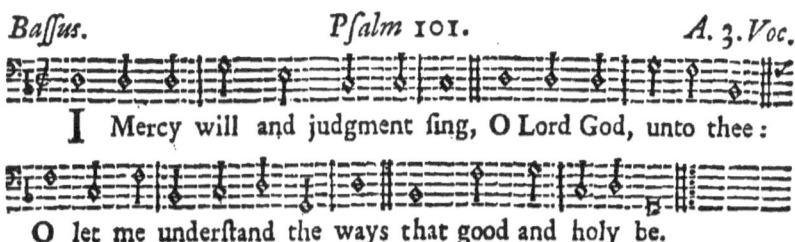
I Mercy will and judgment ſing, O Lord God, unto thee:

O let me underſtand the ways that good and holy be.

Within my houſe I'll daily walk
with heart pure and upright:
3 And I no kind of wicked thing
will ſet before my ſight.

I hate their works that fall away,
they ſhall not cleave to me:
4 From me ſhall part the froward
none evil will I ſee.   (heart,

5 Him I'll deſtroy that ſlandereth
his neighbour privily:
The lofty heart I cannot bear,
nor him that looketh high.

6 Mine eyes ſhall be on them within
the land that faithful be:

In perfect way who walketh, ſhall
be ſervant unto me.

7 I will no guileful perſon have
within my houſe to dwell:
And in my preſence he ſhall not
remain that lies doth tell.

8 Betimes I will deſtroy ev'n all
the wicked of the land:
That I may from God's city cut
the wicked worker's hand.

Gloria Patri.
*To Father, Son, and Holy Ghoſt,
all glory be therefore:
As in beginning was, is now,
and ſhall be evermore.*

Psalm cii.

Cantus & Bassus.   PSALM CII.   *Manchester Tune*

Hear thou my pray'r, O Lord, and let my cry come unto thee

In time of trouble do not hide thy face away from me.

Medius.   Psalm 102.   *A. 3. Voc.*

Hear thou my pray'r, O Lord, and let my cry come unto thee:

In time of trouble do not hide thy face away from me.

Bassus.   Psalm 102.   *A. 3. Voc.*

Hear thou my pray'r, O Lord, and let my cry come unto thee:

In time of trouble do not hide thy face away from me.

3 Incline thine ear to me, make haste
  to hear me when I call :
For as the smoke doth fade, so do
  my days consume and fall.
4 And as an hearth my bones are
  my heart is smitten dead, (burnt,
And withers like the grass, that I
  forget to eat my bread.
5 By reason of my groaning voice
  my bones cleave to my skin :
6 As pelican in wilderness,
  such case now am I in.

And as an Owl in desart is,
  lo, I am such an one :
7 I watch, and as a sparrow on
  the house-top am alone.
8 Lo, daily in reproachful wise
  my foes they ● ● scorn :
And them that ● against me rage,
  against me they have sworn.
9 Surely with ashes as with bread,
  my hunger I have fill'd :   (tears
And mingled have my drink with
  that from mine eyes distill'd.

10 Be-

Psalm cii.

10 Becaufe of thy difpleafure, Lord,
 thy wrath and thy difdain:
For thou haft lifted me aloft,
 and caft me down again.

11 The days wherein I pafs my life,
 are like the fleeting fhade:
And I am wither'd like the grafs
 that foon away doth fade.

12 But thou, O Lord, for ever doft
 remain in fteady place:
And thy remembrance ever doth
 abide from race to race.

The fecond part.

13 Thou wilt arife, and mercy thou
 to Sion wilt extend:
The time of mercy, now the time
 forefet is come to end.

14 For in the very ftones thereof
 thy fervants do delight:
And on the duft thereof they have
 compaffion in their fight.

15 Then fhall the heathen people fear
 the Lord's moft holy Name:
And all the kings on earth fhall
 thy glory and thy fame. (dread

16 Then when the Lord, the mighty
 again fhall Sion rear: (God,
And then when he moft nobly in
 his glory fhall appear.

17 To pray'r of the poor defolate
 when he himfelf fhall bend:
When he fhall not difdain unto
 their pray'rs for to attend.

18 This fhall be written for the age
 that after fhall fucceed:
The people that are yet unborn,
 the Lord's renown fhall fpread.

19 From his high fanctuary he
 hath looked down below:
And out of heav'n moft high he hath
 beheld the earth alfo.

20 That of the mourning captive he
 might hear the woful cry:
And that he might deliver thofe
 that were condemn'd to die.

21 That they in Sion may declare
 the Lord's moft holy Name:
And in Jerufalem fet forth
 the praifes of the fame.

22 Then when the people of the land
 and kingdom with accord
Shall be affembled to perform
 their fervice to the Lord.

The third part.

24 My former force and ftrength he
 abated in the way: (hath
And fhorter he did cut my days;
 thus I therefore did fay,

24 My God, in midft of all my days
 now take me not away:
Thy years endure eternally,
 and never do decay.

25 Thou the foundations of the earth
 before all time haft laid:
The heav'ns alfo, they are the work
 wch thine own hands have made.

26 They all fhall perifh and decay,
 but thou remaineft ftill:
And they fhall all in time wax old,
 ev'n as a garment will.

27 Thou as a garment fhalt them
 & changed fhall they be: (change,
But thou doft ftill abide the fame,
 thy years do never flee.

28 The children of thy fervants fhall
 continually endure:
And in thy fight their happy feed
 for ever fhall ftand fure.

To Father, Son, and Holy Ghoft,
 One God in Perfons Three:
All Honour, Praife, and Glory moft,
 both now and ever be.

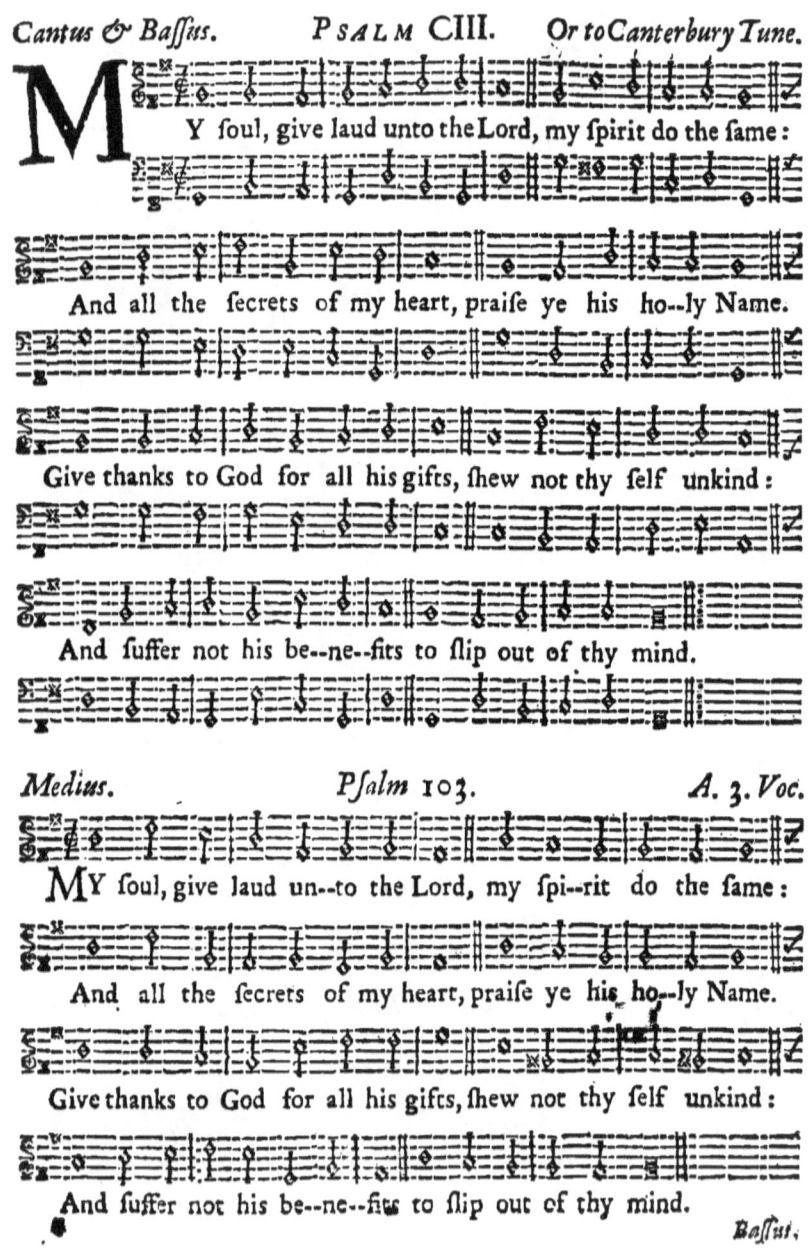

And all the secrets of my heart, praise ye his ho--ly Name.

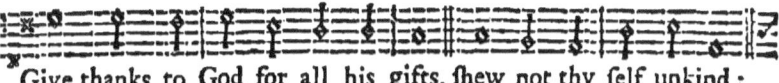

Give thanks to God for all his gifts, shew not thy self unkind:

And suffer not his be--ne--fits to slip out of thy mind.

3 That gave thee pardon for thy
and thee restor'd again: (faults,
From all thy weak and frail disease,
and heal'd thee of thy pain.
4 That did redeem thy life from death
from which thou couldst not flee:
His mercy and compassion both
he did extend to thee.

5 That fill'd with goodness thy desire,
and did prolong thy youth:
Like as the eagle casts her bill,
whereby her age renew'th.
6 The Lord with justice doth repay
all such as be opprefs'd:
So that their suff'rings and their
are turned to the best. (wrongs

7 His ways & his commandments all
to Moses he did shew:
His counsels and his valiant acts
the Isra'lites did know.
8 The Lord is kind and merciful
when sinners do him grieve:
The slowest to conceive a wrath,
and readi'st to forgive.

9 He chides not us continually,
thô we be full of strife:
Nor keeps our faults in memory
for all our sinful life.
10 Nor yet according to our sins
the Lord doth us regard:
And after our iniquities
he doth us not reward.

11 But as the space is wondrous great
'twixt earth and heav'n above:
So is his goodness much more large
to them that do him love.
12 God doth remove our sins from us,
and our offences all,
As far as the sun-rising is
full distant from his fall.

The second part.

13 And look what pity parents dear
unto their children bear:
Like pity beareth God to such
as worship him in fear. (shape,
14 The Lord that made us knows our
our mould and fashion just:
How weak and frail our nature is,
and how we are but dust.

15 And

15 And how the time of mortal men
    is like the with'ring hay :
Or like the flow'r right fair in field,
    that fades full soon away.
16 Whose gloss and beauty stormy
    do utterly disgrace :   (winds
And make that after their assaults
    such blossoms have no place.

17 But yet the goodness of the Lord
    with his shall ever stand :
Their childrens children do receive
    his right'ousness at hand.
18 I mean, which keep his covenant
    with all their whole desire :
And not forget to do the thing
    that he doth them require.

19 The heav'ns most high are made the
    and footstool of the Lord : (seat
And by his pow'r imperial
    he governs all the world.
20 Ye angels wch are great in pow'r,
    praise ye and bless the the Lord:
Which to obey and do his will
    immediately accord.

21 Ye noble hosts and ministers,
    cease not to laud him still :
Which ready are to execute
    his pleasure and his will.
22 Yea, all his works in ev'ry place,
    praise ye his holy Name :
My thankful heart, my mind & soul,
    praise ye also the same.

Cantus & Bassus.   P s a l m CIV.   *Proper Tune.*

MY soul, praise the Lord, speak good of his Name:
O Lord, our great God, how dost thou ap—pear,
So pas—sing in glo—-ry, that great is thy fame?
Honour and ma--je--sty in thee shine most clear.

Medius

Psalm civ.

Psalm 104.

Medius. A. 3. Voc.

MY soul, praise the Lord, speak good of his Name,

O Lord, our great God, how dost thou ap—pear,

So pas—sing in glo——ry, that great is thy fame?

Honour and ma--je--sty in thee shine most clear.

Bassus. Psalm 104. A. 3. Voc.

MY soul, praise the Lord, speak good of his Name:

O Lord, our great God, how dost thou ap—pear,

So pas—sing in glo——ry, that great is thy fame?

Honour and ma--je--sty in thee shine most clear.

2 With light as a robe,
 thou hast thy self clad,
Whereby all the earth
 thy greatness may see:
The heavens in such sort
 thou also hast spread,
That it to a curtain
 compared may be.

3 His chamber-beams lie
 in the clouds full sure,
Which as his chariots,
 are made him to bear:

And there with much swiftness
 his course doth endure,
Upon the wings riding
 of winds in the air.

4 He maketh his spirits
 as heralds to go:
And lightnings to serve
 we see also prest:
His will to accomplish
 they run to and fro,
To save or consume things,
 as seemeth him best.

5 He groundeth the earth
   so firmly and fast,
That it once to move
   none shall have such pow'r.
6 The deep a fair covering
   for it made thou hast:
Which by its own nature
   the hills would devour.

7 But at thy rebuke
   the waters do flee:
And so give due place
   thy word to obey.
At thy voice of thunder
   so fearful they be,
That in their great raging
   they haste soon away.

8 The mountains full high
   they then up ascend:
If thou do but speak,
   thy word they fulfil.
So likewise the valleys
   most quickly descend,
Where thou them appointest
   remain they do still.

9 Their bounds thou hast set
   how far they shall run,
So that in their rage
   not that pass they can:
For God hath appointed
   they shall not return
The earth to destroy more,
   which made was for man.

The second part.
10 He sendeth the springs
   to strong streams or lakes,
Which run do full swift
   among the huge hills:
11 Where both the wild asses
   their thirst oft-times slakes,
And beasts of the mountains
   thereof drink their fills.

12 By these pleasant springs
   of fountains full fair,
The fowls of the air
   abide shall and dwell:
Who moved by nature
   to hop here and there,
Among the green branches
   their songs shall excel.

13 The mountains to moist
   the clouds he doth use:
The earth with his works
   is wholly repleat.
14 So as the brute cattle
   he doth not refuse:
But grass doth provide them,
   and herb for man's meat.

15 Yea, bread, wine, and oyl,
   he made for man's sake,
His face to refresh,
   and heart to make strong.
16 The cedars of Liban
   this great Lord did make:
Which trees he doth nourish
   that grow up so long.

17 In these may birds build
   and make there their nests:
In fir-trees the storks
   remain and abide.
18 The high hills are succours
   for wild goats to rest:
Also the rock stony
   for conies to hide.

19 The moon then is set
   her seasons to two:
The days from the nights
   thereby to discern:
And by the descending
   also of the sun,
The cold from heat alway
   thereby we do learn.

Psalm civ.

20 When darkness doth come
   by God's will and pow'r,
Then creep forth do all
   the beasts of the wood.
21 The lions range roring
   their prey to devour:
But yet it is thou, Lord,
   which givest them food.

22 Assoon as the sun
   is up, they retire:
To couch in their dens
   then are they full fain:
23 That man to his work may,
   as right doth require,
Till night come and call him
   to take rest again.

The third part.

24 How sundry, O Lord,
   are all thy works found!
With wisdom full great
   they are indeed wrought:
So that the whole world
   of thy praise doth sound:
And as for thy riches,
   they pass all men's thought.

25 So is the great sea,
   which large is and broad,
Where things that creep swarm,
   and beasts of each sort.
26 There mighty ships sail,
   and some lie at rode:
The whale huge and monstrous
   there also doth sport.

27 All things on thee wait,
   thou dost them relieve;
And thou in due time
   full well dost them feed.
28 Now when it doth please thee
   the same for to give,
They gather full gladly
   those things which they need.

Thou open'st thy hand,
   and they find such grace,
That they with good things
   are filled we see.
29 But sore are they troubled
   if thou turn thy face:
For if thou their breath take,
   vile dust then they be.

30 Again, when thy Spirit
   from thee doth proceed
All things to appoint,
   and what shall ensue:
Then are they created
   as thou hast decreed:
And dost by thy goodness
   the dry earth renew.

31 The praise of the Lord
   for ever shall last,
Who may in his works
   by right well rejoyce.
32 His look can the earth make
   to tremble full fast,
And likewise the mountains
   to smoke at his voice.

33 To this Lord and God
   sing will I always:
So long as I live,
   my God praise will I.
34 Then am I most certain
   my words shall him please:
I will rejoyce in him,
   to him will I cry.

35 The sinners, O Lord,
   consume in thine ire:
Also the perverse,
   them root out with shame:
But as for my soul now,
   let it still desire,
And say with the faithful,
   Praise ye the Lord's Name.

Psalm cv.

Cantus & Bassus.   **PSALM CV.**   *Canterbury Tune.*

Give praises unto God the Lord, and call upon his Name:

Among the people all declare his works to spread his fame.

Medius.   *Psalm 105.*   *A. 3. Voc.*

Give praises un--to God the Lord, and call upon his Name:

Among the people all declare his works to spread his fame.

Bassus.   *Psalm 105.*   *A. 3. Voc.*

Give praises un--to God the Lord, and call upon his Name:

Among the people all declare his works to spread his fame.

2 Sing joyfully unto the Lord,
  yea, Sing unto him praise:
And talk of all his wondrous works
  that he hath wrought always.

3 In honour of his holy Name,
  rejoyce with one accord:
And let the heart also be glad
  of them that seek the Lord.
              (strength
4 Seek ye the Lord, and seek the
  of his eternal might:

And seek his face continually,
  and presence of his sight.
              (hath done,
5 The wondrous works which he
  keep still in mindful heart:
Let not the judgments of his mouth
  out of your mind depart.

6 Ye that of faithful Abraham
  his servants are the seed:
Ye his elect, the children that
  of Jacob do proceed.

                                              7 For

Psalm cv.

7 For why? 'tis he alone that
the mighty Lord our God:
And his most right'ous judgments are
through all the earth abroad.

8 His promise and his covenant
which he hath made to his,
He hath remember'd evermore
to thousands of degrees.

The second part.

9 The covenant which he hath made
with Abraham long ago,
And faithful oath which he hath
to Isaac also: (sworn

10 And did appoint it for a law,
that Jacob should obey;
And for eternal covenant
to Israel alway.

11 When thus he said, Lo, I to you
all Canaan land will give,
The lot of your inheritance,
wherein your seed shall live.

12 Altho' their number at that time
did very small appear:
Yea, very small, and in the land
they then but strangers were.

13 While yet they walk'd from land
without a sure abode, (to land
And while from sundry kingdoms
did wander all abroad. (they

14 Yet wrong at no oppressor's hand
he suffer'd them to take:
But ev'n the great and mighty kings
reproved for their sake.

15 And thus he said, Touch ye not
that mine anointed be: (those
Nor do the prophets any harm
that do pertain to me.

16 He call'd a dearth upon the land,
of bread destroy'd the store:
But yet against the time of need
did send a man before,

(is
The third part.

17 Ev'n Joseph wch had once been sold
to live a slave in wo:
Whose feet they hurt in stocks, whose
the irons pierc'd into. (soul

18 Until the time came when his
was known apparently, (cause
The mighty word of God the Lord
his faultless truth did try.

19 The king sent and deliver'd him
from prison where he was:
20 The ruler of the people then
did freely let him pass.

21 And over all his house he made
him lord, to bear the sway:
And of his substance made him have
the rule and all the stay.

22 That he might to his will instruct
the princes of the land:
And wisdom teach his senators
rightly to understand.

23 Then into the Egyptian land
came Israel also:
And Jacob in the land of Ham
did sojourn to and fro.

24 His people he exceedingly
in number made to flow;
And over all their enemies
in strength he made them grow.

25 Whose heart he turned, that with
they did his people treat: (hate
And did his servants wrongfully
abuse with false deceit.

The fourth part.

26 His faithful servant Moses then,
and Aaron whom he chose,
He did command to go to them,
his message to disclose.

27 His wonderful and mighty signs
among them he did show:
And wonders in the land of Ham
then did they work also.

28 Dark-

Psalm cv, cvi.

28 Darkness he sent, and made it dark
in stead of brighter day:
And his commission and his word
they did not disobey.

29 He turn'd their waters into blood,
and did their fishes slay: (place
30 Their land broght frogs ev'n in the
where their king Pharaoh lay.

31 He spake, & at his voice there came
great swarms of noisom flies:
And all the quarters of the land
were fill'd with crawling lice.

32 He gave them cold and stony hail
in stead of milder rain:
And fiery flames within their land
he sent unto their pain.

33 He smote their vines, & all the trees
whereon their figs did grow:
And all the trees within their coasts
also did overthrow.

34 He spake, then caterpillars did
and grashoppers abound:
35 Eating the grass in all their land,
and fruit of all their ground.

The fifth part.

36 The first-begotten in their land
with death did likewise smite:
Yea, the beginning and first-fruit
of all their strength and might.

37 With gold and silver caused them
from Egypt land to pass:
And in the number of their tribes
no feeble one there was.

38 Egypt was glad and joyful then
when they did thence depart:
For terrour and the fear of them
was fall'n upon their heart.

39 To shroud them from the parching
a cloud he did display: (heat,
And fire he sent to give them light
when night had hid the day.

40 They asked, and he caused quails
to rain at their request:
And fully with the bread of heav'n
their hunger he represt.

41 He opened the stony rock,
and waters gushed out:
Also the dry and parched ground
like rivers ran about.

42 For of his holy cov'nant he
was mindful evermore:
Which to his servant Abraham
he plighted long before.

43 He brought his people forth with
and his elect with joy, (mirth,
Out of the cruel land where they
had liv'd in great annoy.

44 And of the heathen men he gave
to them the fruitful lands:
The labours of the people did
they take into their hands.

45 That they his holy statutes might
observe for evermore,
And faithfully obey his laws:
Praise ye the Lord therefore.

Cantus & Bassus.   **PSALM CVI.**   *St. David's Tune.*

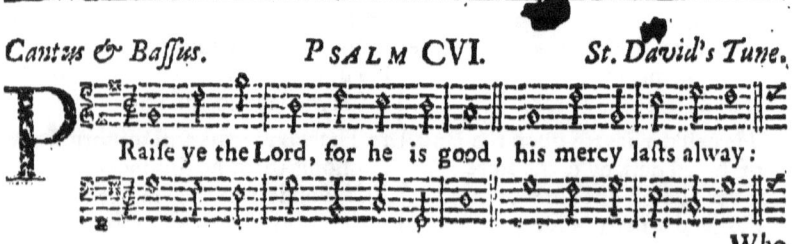

Raise ye the Lord, for he is good, his mercy lasts alway:

Who

Psalm cvi. 183

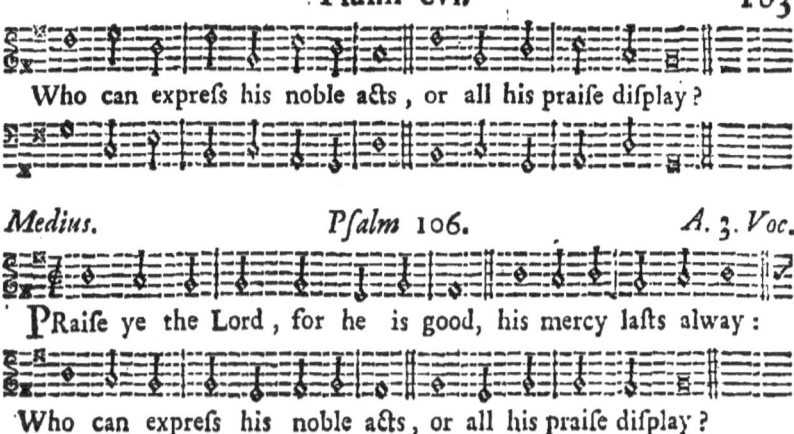

Who can express his noble acts, or all his praise display?

Medius. Psalm 106. *A. 3. Voc.*

PRaise ye the Lord, for he is good, his mercy lasts alway:
Who can express his noble acts, or all his praise display?

Bassus. Psalm 106. *A. 3. Voc.*

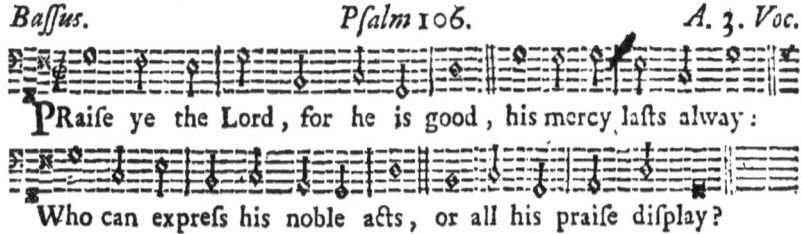

PRaise ye the Lord, for he is good, his mercy lasts alway:
Who can express his noble acts, or all his praise display?

3 They blessed are that judgment
and justly do alway: (keep,
4 With favour of thy people, Lord,
remember me, I pray:
And with thy saving health, ô Lord,
vouchsafe to visit me:
5 That I the great felicity
of thine elect may see:
And with thy people's joy I may
a joyful mind possess;
And may with thine inheritance
a chearful heart expr
6 Both we and our forefathers all
have sinned ev'ry one:
We have committed wickedness,
and very lewdly done.
7 The wonders great which thou, O
hast done in Egypt land, (Lord,

Our fathers thô they saw them all,
yet did not understand:
Nor they thy mercies multitude
did keep in thankful mind:
But at the sea, yea, the Red-sea,
rebelled most unkind.
8 Nevertheless he saved them
for honour of his Name:
That he might make his power
& spread abroad his fame. (known
9 The Red-sea he did then rebuke,
and forthwith it was dri'd:
And as in wilderness, so through
the deep he did them guide.
10 He sav'd them from the cruel hand
of their despiteful foe,
And from their enemies he did
deliver them also.

The second part.

11 The waters did them overwhelm,
   not one was left alive:
12 Then they believ'd his word, and
   in song they did him give. (praise
13 But very soon unthankfully
   his works they clean forgat:
And for his counsel and his will
   they did neglect to wait:
14 But sinned in the wilderness
   with fond and greedy lust:
And in the desarts tempted God,
   the stay of all their trust.
15 Who then their wanton minds de-
   did suffer them to have: (sire
But wasting leanness therewithal
   into their souls he gave.
16 Then when they lodged in their
   at Moses they did grutch: (tents,
Aaron the holy of the Lord
   they also envy'd much.
17 Therfore the earth did open wide,
   and Dathan did devour:
And all Abiram's company
   did cover in that hour.
18 In their assembly kindled was
   a hot consuming fire:
And wasting flame did then burn up
   the wicked in his ire.
19 Upon the hill of Horeb they
   an idol-calf did frame:
And there the molten image they
   did worship of the same.
20 Thus to the likeness of a calf
   which feedeth on the grass,
They turned all their glory, and
   their honour did deface.
21 And God their only Saviour
   unthankfully forgot,
Which many great & mighty things
   in Egypt land had wrought.

The third part.

22 And in the land of Ham for them
   most wondrous works had done,
And by the Red-sea dreadful things
   performed long agone.
23 Therefore because they shew'd
   forgetful & unkind, (themselves
To bring destruction on them all
   he purpos'd in his mind:
Had not his chosen Moses stood
   before him in the way,
To turn away his wrath, lest he
   should them destroy and stay.
24 They did despise the pleasant land
   that he to them did give:
Yea, and the words that he had spoke
   they did no whit believe.
25 But in their tents with grudging
   they wickedly repin'd, (heart
Nor to the voice of God the Lord
   did give an heark'ning mind.
26 Therefore against them lifted he
   his strong revenging hand,
Them to destroy in wilderness
   e're they should see the land:
27 And to destroy their seed among
   the nations with his rod,
And through the kingdoms of the
   to scatter them abroad. (world
28 To Baal-peor they did joyn
   themselves most wickedly:
The sacrifices of the dead
   eating most greedily.
29 Thus they with their inventions
   his anger did provoke:
And in his sore enkindled wrath
   the plague upon them broke.
30 But Phinehas stood up with zeal
   the sinners vile to slay:
And judgment he did execute,
   and then the plague did stay.

Pſalm cvi.

ʾrth part.	41 Into the hands of heathen men
ɩd unto him	he gave them for a prey,
ɩfs that day:	And made their foes their lords,
ɩforth ſo counted is	were forced to obey. (whom they
ɩce alway.	*The fifth part.*
lled Meribah	42 Yea, and their hateful enemies
ɩngry make:	oppreſs'd them in the land:
that Moſes then	And they were humbly made to ſtoop
or their ſake:	as ſubjects to their hand.
ɩex'd his ſpirit ſo,	43 Full oftentimes from thrall had he
ent heat	deliver'd them before:
ɩadviſedly,	But with their counſels they to wrath
ɩs ſo great.	provok'd him evermore.
l commanded them,	Therefore they by their wickedneſs
eople ſlay:	were brought full low to lie:
g the heathen mixt,	44 Yet when he ſaw them in diſtreſs,
eir wicked way:	he hearken'd to their cry.
ɩ idols ſerve, which	45 He call'd to mind his covenant
decay: (was	which he to them had ſwore:
ſons and daughters	And by his mercies multitude
ɩd ſlay. (they	repented him therefore.
ɩind and murd'ring	46 And favour he them made to find
ɔd they ſpilt: (knife	before the ſight of thoſe (land,
ſons and daughters	That led them captive from their
ɩfe of guilt. (blood	thô they had been their foes.
ɩanaan idols then	47 Save us,ô Lord,that art our God,
icked hand:	ſave us, O Lord, we pray:
ɔd of innocents	And from among the heathen folk,
ɩ land.	Lord, gather us away.
ɩy ſtained with the	48 That we may triumph & rejoyce
ɩlthy way: (works	in thy moſt holy Name:
ɔwn inventions	That we may glory in thy praiſe
ɩt aſtray.	and ſounding of thy fame.
inſt his people was	49 The Lord the God of Iſrael
led ſore:	be bleſt for evermore:
ɩ inheritance	Let all the people ſay, Amen,
herefore.	Praiſe ye the Lord therefore.

P S A L M

186   Pſalm cvii.

Cantus & Baſſus.   P SALM CVII.   *Wincheſter Tune.*

Give thanks unto the Lord our God, for gra--ci--ous is he:

And that his mercy hath no end all mortal men may ſee.

Medius.   Pſalm 107.   *A. 3. Voc.*

GIve thanks unto the Lord our God, for gra—ci—ous is he:

And that his mercy hath no end all mortal men may ſee.

Baſſus.   Pſalm 107.   *A. 3. Voc.*

GIve thanks unto the Lord our God, for gra—ci—ous is he:

And that his mercy hath no end all mortal men may ſee.

2 Such as the Lord redeemed hath,
   with thanks ſhall praiſe his Name:
And ſhew how they from foes were
   & how he wrought the ſame. (freed,

3 He gather'd them forth of the lands
   that lay ſo far about :   (ſouth,
From eaſt to weſt, from north to
   his hand did find them out.

4 They wander'd in the wilderneſs,
   and ſtrayed from the way :

And found no city where to dwell,
   that ſerve might for their ſtay.

5 Whoſe thirſt & hunger was ſo great
   in thoſe deſarts ſo void :
That faintneſs them aſſaulted, and
   their ſouls greatly annoy'd.

6 Then did they cry in their diſtreſs
   unto the Lord for aid :   (ſtate,
Who did remove their troublous
   according as they pray'd.

7 And

Pſalm cvii.

And by that way which was moſt right,
he led them like a guide:
That they might to their city go,
and there alſo abide.

Let them therefore before the Lord
confeſs his goodneſs then:
And ſhew the wonders that he doth
before the ſons of men.

For he their empty ſouls ſuſtain'd,
whom thirſt had made to faint:
Their hungry ſouls wᵗʰ goodneſs fed,
and heard their ſad complaint.

oSuch as do dwell in darkneſs deep,
where they on death do wait:
Faſt bound to bear ſuch troublous ſtorms
as iron chains do threat.

The ſecond part.

1 Becauſe againſt the words of God
they proudly did rebel:
Eſteeming light his counſels high,
which do ſo far excel.

2 But when he humbl'd them full low,
they then fell down with grief:
And none was found that could them help,
or give them ſome relief.

3 Then did they cry in their diſtreſs
unto the Lord for aid:
Who did remove their troublous ſtate
according as they pray'd.

4 For he from darkneſs broght them out,
and from death's dreadful ſhade:
Burſting with force the iron bands
which them before did lade.

5 Let men therefore before the Lord
confeſs his kindneſs then:
And ſhew the wonders that he doth
before the ſons of men.

6 For he threw down the gates of braſs
with ſtrong and mighty hand:
The iron bars in ſunder brake,
nothing could him withſtand.

17 The fooliſh folk great plagues do feel,
by reaſon of their ſin:
And for their great tranſgreſſion
which they continue in.

18 Their ſoul abhor'd all ſorts of meat,
no reliſh they could have:
Whereby death had them almoſt
unto the very grave.

19 Then did they cry in their diſtreſs
unto the Lord for aid:
Who did remove their troublous ſtate
according as they pray'd.

20 For then he ſent to them his word, brought
which health did ſoon reſtore:
And broght them from thoſe dangers
wherein they were before.

The third part.

21 Let them therfore before the Lord
confeſs his kindneſs then:
And ſhew the wonders that he doth
before the ſons of men.

22 And let them offer ſacrifice
to him moſt thankfully:
And ſpeak of all his wondrous works
with gladneſs and with joy.

23 Such as in ſhips and brittle barks
into the ſea deſcend,
Their merchandiſe through fearful floods
to compaſs and to end:

24 Thoſe men are forced to behold
the Lord's works what they be:
And in the dang'rous deep, the ſame
moſt marvellous they ſee.

25 For at his word the ſtormy wind
ariſeth in his rage,
And ſtirreth up the ſurges ſo,
that nought can them aſſwage.

26 Then are they lifted up ſo high,
the clouds they ſeem to gain:
And plunging down the depth until
their ſouls conſume with pain.

27 And

Psalm cvii.

27 And like a drunkard to and fro
  now here now there they reel,
As men who had their reason lost,
  and had no sense to feel.

28 Then did they cry in their distress
  unto the Lord for aid: (state,
Who did remove their troublous
  according as they pray'd.
                                (make
29 For with his word the Lord doth
  the sturdy storms to cease: (rage
So that the waves from their great
  are brought to rest and peace.
                                (come,
30 Then are they glad when rest is
  which they so much did crave:
And to the haven by him are broght,
  which they so fain would have.

The fourth part.

31 Let men therefore before the Lord
  confess his kindness then:
And shew the wonders that he doth
  before the sons of men.

32 Let them in presence of the folk
  with praise extol his Name:
And where the elders do convent,
  there let them do the same.

33 The wilderness he often makes
  with waters to abound:
And water-springs he often turns
  to dry and parched ground.
                                (deck'd
34 A fruitful land with pleasures
  full barren doth he make:
When on their sins that dwell there-
  he doth just veng'ance take. (in

35 Again the wilderness full rude
  he maketh fruit to bear:
W^th pleasant springs of waters clear,
  thô none before were there.

36 Wherein such hungry souls are
  as he doth freely chuse:
That they a city may them build
  to dwell in for their use.
                                (lan
37 That they may sow their pleasa
  and vineyards also plant,
To yield them fruits of such increase
  that they may have no want.

38 They multiply exceedingly,
  the Lord doth bless them so:
Who also maketh the brute beasts
  in numbers great to grow.
                                (low
39 But when the faithful are brough
  by the oppressors stout,
Diminishing through many plague
  that compass them about:
                                (shame
40 Then doth he princes bring to
  which did them sore oppress,
And likewise caused them to err
  within the wilderness.

41 But yet the poor he raiseth up
  out of his troubles deep:
And oft-times doth his train augmen
  much like a flock of sheep.
                                (sight
42 The right'ous shall behold this
  and also much rejoyce:
Whereas the wicked and perverse
  with grief shall stop their voice.
                                (wel
43 But who is wise, that now full
  he may these things record?
For certainly such shall perceive
  the kindness of the Lord.

Gloria Patri.

To Father, Son, and Holy Ghost,
  immortal Glory be:
As was, is now, and shall be still,
  to all Eternitie.

Pſalm cviii.   189

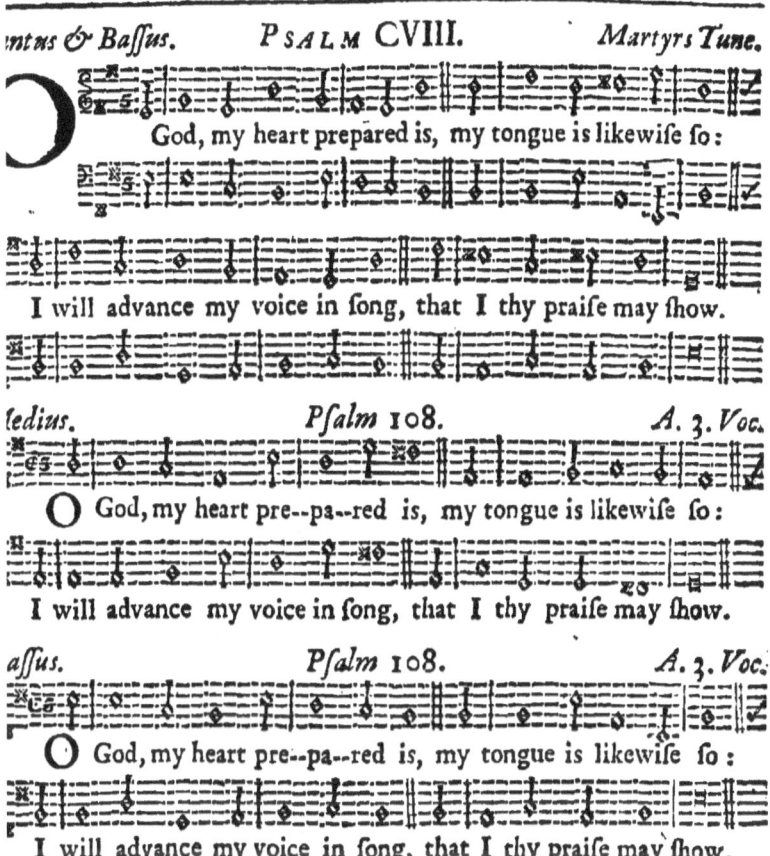

Awake my viol and my harp,
ſweet melody to make:
and in the morning I my ſelf
right early will awake.
By me among the people, Lord,
ſtill praiſed ſhalt thou be:
And I among the heathen folk
will praiſes ſing to thee:
Becauſe thy mercy doth aſcend
above the heavens high:
Alſo thy truth doth reach the clouds
within the lofty sky.

5 Above the ſtarry heavens high
exalt thy ſelf, O God:
Diſplay likewiſe upon the earth
thy glory all abroad.
6 That thy dearly beloved may
be ſet at liberty, (hand,
Help, O my God, with thy right
and hearken unto me.
7 God in his holineſs hath ſpoke,
wherefore my joys abound:
Sichem I will divide, and mete
the vale of Succoth's ground.

8 And

Pſalm cviii, cix.

8 And Gilead ſhall be mine own,
  Manaſſes mine ſhall be:
My head-ſtrength Ephraim, and law
  ſhall Judah give to me.

9 Moab my waſhpot, and my ſhoe
  on Edom will I throw:
Upon the land of Paleſtine
  in triumph will I go.

10 Who to the city ſtrong ſhall be
  leader and guide to me?
Alſo by whom to Edom's land
  conveyed ſhall I be?

11 Is it not thou, O Lord, which lat
  hadſt us forſaken quite?
And thou alſo, which with our hoſt
  didſt not go forth to fight?

12 Give us, O Lord, thy ſaving ai
  when troubles do aſſail:
For all the help of man is vain,
  and can no whit avail.

13 Through God we ſhall do valiar
  and worthy of renown: (act
He ſhall ſubdue our enemies,
  yea, he ſhall tread them down.

Cantus & Baſſus.   PSALM CIX.   *Norwich Tun*

IN ſpeechleſs ſilence do not hold, O God, thy tongue always:

Ev'n thou, O Lord, becauſe thou art the God of all my praiſe.

Medius.   Pſalm 109.   A. 3. Vo

IN ſpeechleſs ſilence do not hold, O God, thy tongue always:

Psalm cix.

2 The wicked and the guileful (mouths
of me disclosed be:
And they with false & lying tongues
have spoken unto me.

3 They did beset me round about
with words of hateful spight:
Without all cause of my desert
against me they did fight.

4 For my good will they were my
then I began to pray: (foes,
5 My good with ill, my friendliness
with hate they did repay.

6 Set thou the wicked over him
to have the upper hand:
At his right hand, Lord, suffer thou
his hateful foe to stand.

7 When he is judged, let him then
condemned be therein:
And let the pray'r that he doth make
be turned into sin.

8 Few be his days, his charge also
let thou another take:
9 His children let be fatherless,
his wife a widow make.

10 Let his offspring be vagabonds,
and ever beg their bread:
In places desolate and waste,
let them seek to be fed.

11 Let covetous extortioners
get all his goods in store:
And let the stranger spoil the fruit
of all his toil before.

12 Let there be none to pity him,
let there be none at all,
That on his children fatherless
will let their mercy fall.

The second part.

13 Let his posterity be quite
destroy'd, and never breed:
Their name out-blotted in the age
that after shall succeed.

14 Let not his father's wickedness
from God's remembrance fall:
And never let his mother's sin
be done away at all.

15 But in the presence of the Lord,
let them for ever stay:
That from the earth their memory
he may cut clean away.

16 Since mercy he forgot to shew,
but did pursue with spight
The troubled man, & sought to slay
the woful-hearted wight.

17 As he did cursing love, it shall
happen unto him so:
And as he did not blessing love,
far from him it shall go.

18 As he with cursing clad himself,
so it like water shall
Enter his bowels, and like oyl
into his bones shall fall.

19 As garment let it be to him,
to cover him withal:
And as a girdle wherewith he
always be girded shall.

20 Let this be the reward from God,
of him that is my foe:
Yea, and of those that evil speak
against my soul also.

21 But thou, O Lord, that art my God,
deal graciously with me:
Deliver me for thy Name's sake,
for great thy mercies be.

22 Be-

Pſalm cix, cx.

22 Becauſe in depth of great diſtreſs
I needy am, and poor:
Alſo within my pained breaſt,
my heart is wounded ſore.

The third part.

23 Ev'n ſo do I depart away,
as doth declining ſhade:
And as the graſhopper, ſo I
am ſhaken off and fade.

24 With faſting long from needful
my bones enfeebled are: (food
And all the fatneſs of my fleſh
is gone with grief and care.

25 And I alſo a vile reproach
to them am made to be:
And they that did upon me look,
did ſhake their heads at me.

26 Therefore, O God my Saviour,
mine aid and ſuccour be:
According to thy mercies great,
ſave and deliver me.

27 And they ſhall know thereby, that
is thy moſt mighty hand: (this
And that 'tis thou that haſt it done,
they well ſhall underſtand.

28 Althô they curſe with ſpite, yet
ſhalt bleſs with loving voice: (thou
When they riſe up, & come to ſhame,
thy ſervant ſhall rejoyce.

29 Let them with ſhame be cloathed
that are mine enemies: (all
And with confuſion as a cloak
be covered likewiſe.

30 But greatly I will with my mouth
give thanks unto the Lord:
And I among the multitude
his praiſes will record.

31 For he with help at his right hand
will ſtand the poor man by:
To ſave him from the man that
condemn his ſoul to die. (would

Cantus & Baſſus.   **PSALM CX.**   *London Tune.*

THE Lord did ſay unto my Lord, ſit thou on my right hand:
Till I have made thy foes a ſtool whereon thy feet ſhall ſtand.

Medius.   *Pſalm 110.*   *A. 3. Voc.*

THE Lord did ſay un--to my Lord, ſit thou on my right hand:
Till I have made thy foes a ſtool whereon thy feet ſhall ſtand.

Psalm cx, cxi. 193

Bassus.   *Psalm* 110.   *A. 3. Voc.*

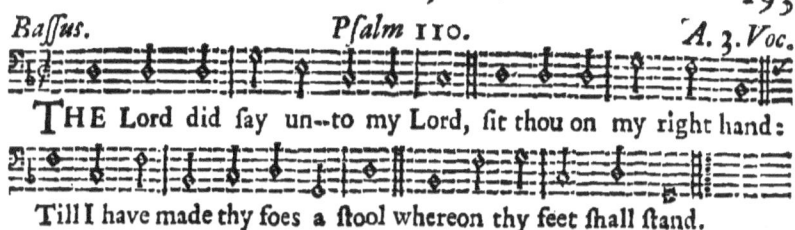

THE Lord did say un--to my Lord, sit thou on my right hand:

Till I have made thy foes a stool whereon thy feet shall stand.

2 The Lord shall out of Sion send
the scepter of thy might:
Amidst thy mortal foes be thou
the ruler in their fight.
3 And in the day on which thy reign
and power they shall see:
Then hereby freewill-off'rings shall
the people offer thee.
Yea, with an holy worshipping
then shall they offer all:
The births-dew is the dew that doth
from womb of morning fall.
4 The Lord hath sworn, & never will
repent what he doth say:

By th'order of Melchisedech
thou art a Priest alway.
5 The L^d thy God on thy right hand
that standeth for thy stay,
Shall wound for thee the stately kings
upon his wrathful day.
6 The heathen he shall judge, and fill
the place with bodies dead:
And over divers countries shall
in sunder smite the head.
7 And he shall drink out of the brook
that runneth in the way:
Wherefore he shall lift up on high
his royal head that day.

Cantus & Bassus.   PSALM CXI.   *Or to* 120 *Psalm Tune.*

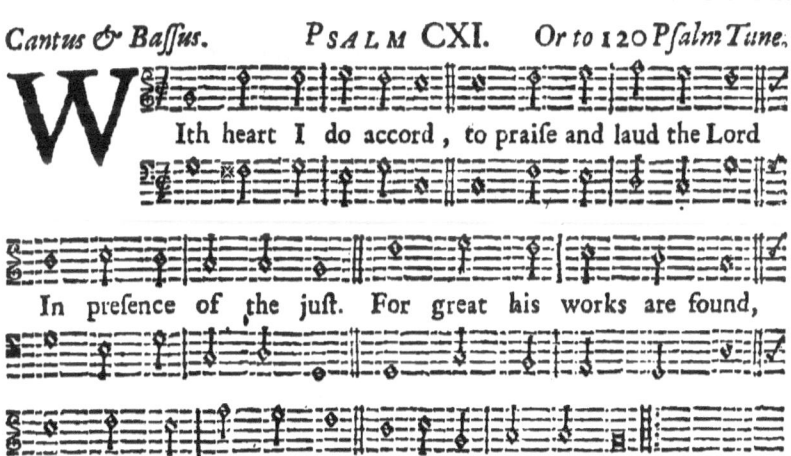

With heart I do accord, to praise and laud the Lord

In presence of the just. For great his works are found,

To search them such are bound as do him love and trust.

Psalm cxi.

Medius. Psalm 111. *A. 3. Voc.*

With heart I do accord, to praise and laud the Lord
In presence of the just. For great his works are found,
To search them such are bound as do him love and trust.

Bassus. Psalm 111. *A. 3. Voc.*

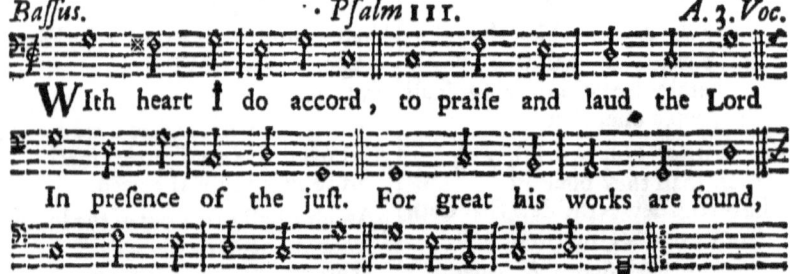

With heart I do accord, to praise and laud the Lord
In presence of the just. For great his works are found,
To search them such are bound as do him love and trust.

3 His works are glorious,
Also his right'ousness
  It doth endure for ever.
4 His wondrous works he would
We still remember should,
  His mercy faileth never.

5 Such as to him love bear,
A portion full fair
  He hath up for them laid:
For this they shall well find,
He will them have in mind,
  And keep them as he said.

6 For he did not disdain
His works to shew them plain,
  By lightnings and by thunders:
When he the heathens land
Did give into their hand,
  Where they beheld his wonders.

7 Of all his works ensu'th
Both judgment, right and truth,
  Whereto his statutes tend:
8 They are decreed sure
For ever to endure,
  Which equity doth end.

Redemption he gave
His people for to save:
9 And hath also requir'd
His promise not to fail,
But always to prevail;
  His holy Name be fear'd.

10 Whoso with heart full fain
True wisdom would attain,
  The Lord fear and obey:
Such as his laws do keep,
Shall knowledge have full deep,
  His praise shall last alway.

PSALM

Psalm cxii. 195

Cantus & Bassus.   PSALM CXII.   *Proper Tune.*

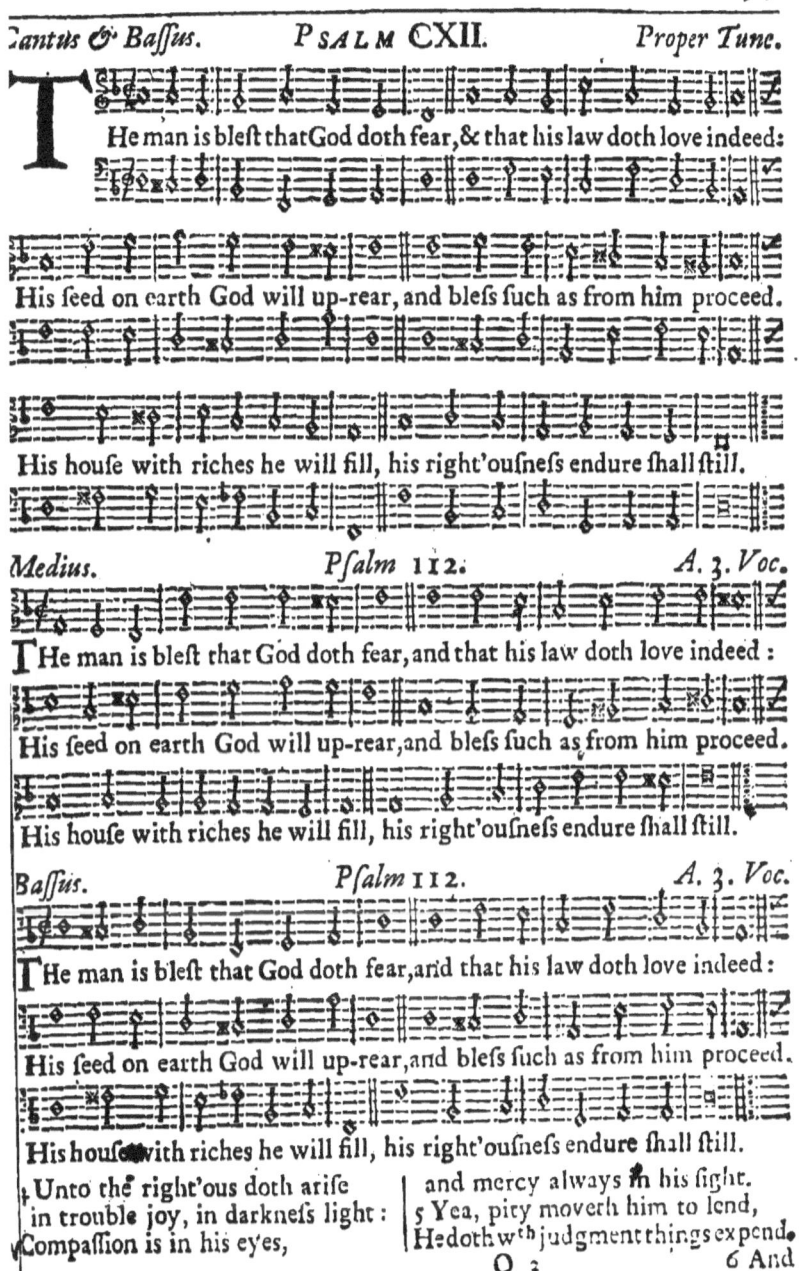

THe man is blest that God doth fear, & that his law doth love indeed:

His seed on earth God will up-rear, and bless such as from him proceed.

His house with riches he will fill, his right'ousness endure shall still.

Medius.   Psalm 112.   *A. 3. Voc.*

THe man is blest that God doth fear, and that his law doth love indeed:

His seed on earth God will up-rear, and bless such as from him proceed.

His house with riches he will fill, his right'ousness endure shall still.

Bassus.   Psalm 112.   *A. 3. Voc.*

THe man is blest that God doth fear, and that his law doth love indeed:

His seed on earth God will up-rear, and bless such as from him proceed.

His house with riches he will fill, his right'ousness endure shall still.

4 Unto the right'ous doth arise
in trouble joy, in darkness light:
Compassion is in his eyes,

and mercy always in his sight.
5 Yea, pity moveth him to lend,
He doth wth judgment things expend.

O 2   6 And

Psalm cxii, cxiii.

6 And surely such shall never fail,
  for in remembrance had is he:
7 Nor tidings ill his mind assail,
  who in the Lord sure hope doth see.
8 His heart is firm, his fear is past,
For he shall see his foes down cast.

9 He did well for the poor provide,
  his right'ousness shall still remain:
And his estate with praise abide,
  wch wicked men behold with pain.
10 Yea, gnash their teeth thereat shall
And so consume & melt away. (they

Cantus & Bassus.   PSALM CXIII.   *Proper Tune.*

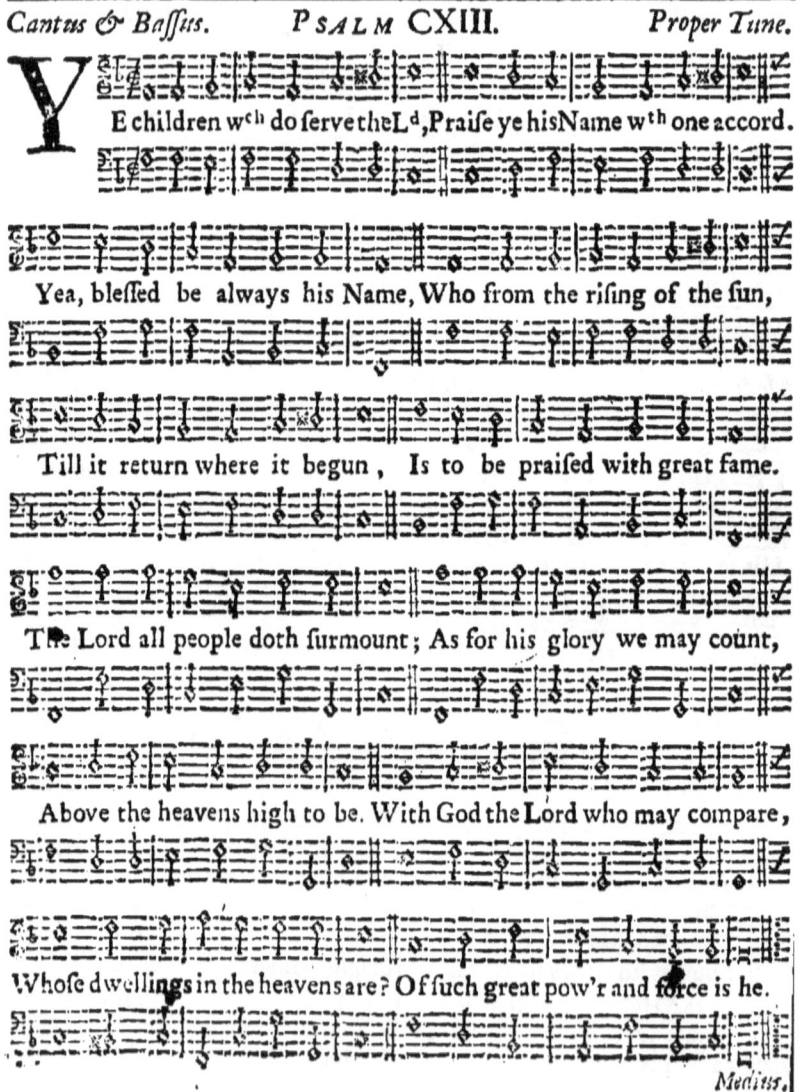

Ye children wch do serve the L^d, Praise ye his Name wth one accord.

Yea, blessed be always his Name, Who from the rising of the sun,

Till it return where it begun, Is to be praised with great fame.

The Lord all people doth surmount; As for his glory we may count,

Above the heavens high to be. With God the Lord who may compare,

Whose dwellings in the heavens are? Of such great pow'r and force is he.

Medius.

Psalm cxiii.

Medius.   Psalm 113.   *A. 3. Voc.*

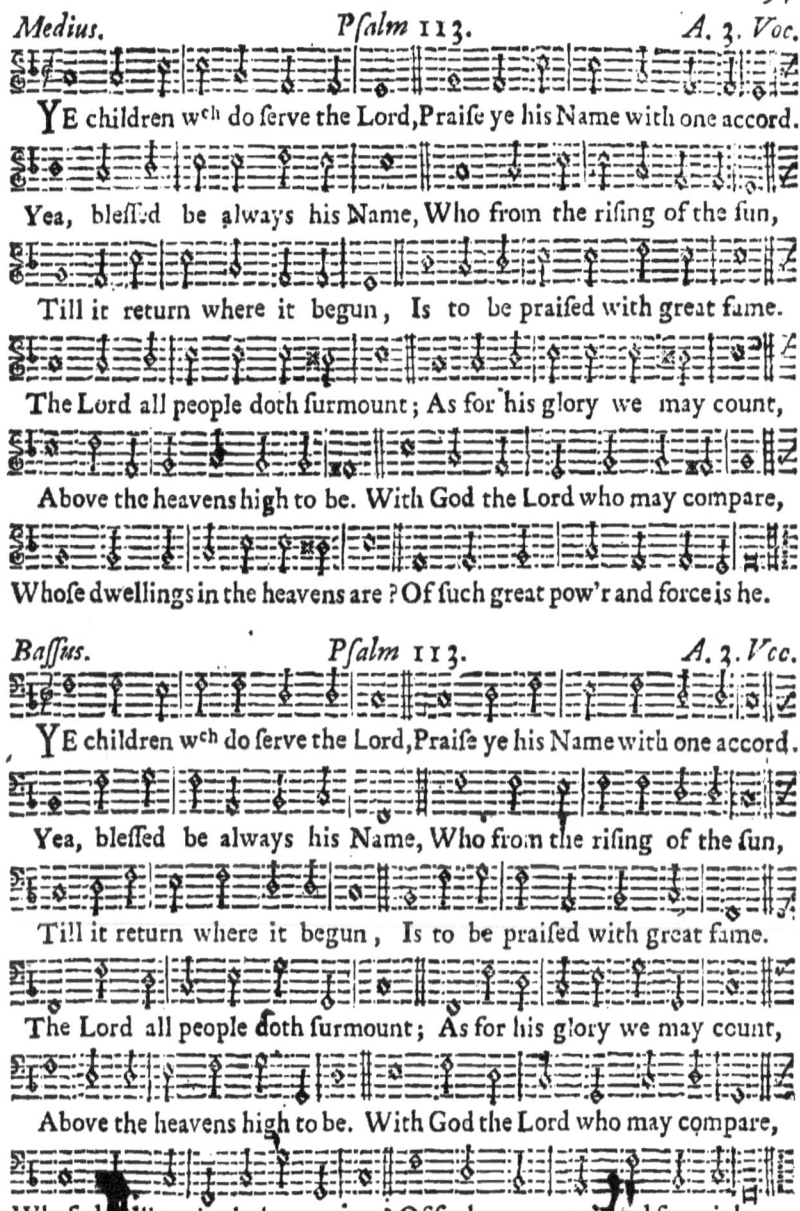

YE children wch do serve the Lord, Praise ye his Name with one accord.

Yea, blessed be always his Name, Who from the rising of the sun,

Till it return where it begun, Is to be praised with great fame.

The Lord all people doth surmount; As for his glory we may count,

Above the heavens high to be. With God the Lord who may compare,

Whose dwellings in the heavens are? Of such great pow'r and force is he.

Bassus.   Psalm 113.   *A. 3. Voc.*

YE children wch do serve the Lord, Praise ye his Name with one accord.

Yea, blessed be always his Name, Who from the rising of the sun,

Till it return where it begun, Is to be praised with great fame.

The Lord all people doth surmount; As for his glory we may count,

Above the heavens high to be. With God the Lord who may compare,

Whose dwellings in the heavens are? Of such great pow'r and force is he.

198   Pſalm cxiii, cxiv.

6 He doth abaſe himſelf we know,
Things to behold on earth below,
And alſo in heaven above.
7 The needy out of duſt to draw,
Alſo the poor which help none ſaw,
His only mercy did him move.

8 And ſo him ſet in high degree
With Princes of great dignity,
That rule his people wth great fame.
9 The barren he doth make to bear,
And with great joy her fruit do rear:
Therefore praiſe ye his holy Name.

Cantus & Baſſus.   PSALM CXIV.   *Worceſter Tune.*

Hen Iſrael by God's command from Pharaoh's land was bent;

And Jacob's houſe the ſtrangers left, and in the ſame train went:

Medius.   Pſalm 114.   A. 3. Voc.

When Iſ--ra--el by God's command from Pharaoh's land was bent;

And Jacob's houſe the ſtrangers left, and in the ſame train went:

Baſſus.   Pſalm 114.   A. 3. Voc.

When Iſ--ra--el by God's command from Pharaoh's land was bent;

And Jacob's houſe the ſtrangers left, and in the ſame train went:

Pfalm cxiv, cxv.   199

2 In Judah God his glory fhew'd,
his holinefs moft bright:
So did the Ifra'lites declare
his kingdom, pow'r, and might.

3 The fea it faw, and fuddenly
as all amaz'd did flee:
The roring ftreams of Jordan's flood
gave back immediately.

4 As rams afraid, the mountains skipt,
their ftrength did them forfake:
And as the filly trembling lambs,
their tops did beat and fhake.

5 What ailed thee, O fea, that thou,
fo fuddenly didft flee?

Ye rolling waves of Jordan's flood,
Why turn'd ye fo fwiftly?

6 Ye mountains, ev'n as rams afraid,
Why did your ftrength fo fhake?
Why did your tops, as trembling
for fear quiver & quake? (lambs,

7 O earth, confefs thy fov'reign Lord,
and dread his mighty hand:
Before the face of Jacob's God
fear ye both fea and land.
                                (rocks
8 I mean, the God, which from hard
doth caufe floods to appear:
And from the ftony flint doth fend
fountains of waters clear.

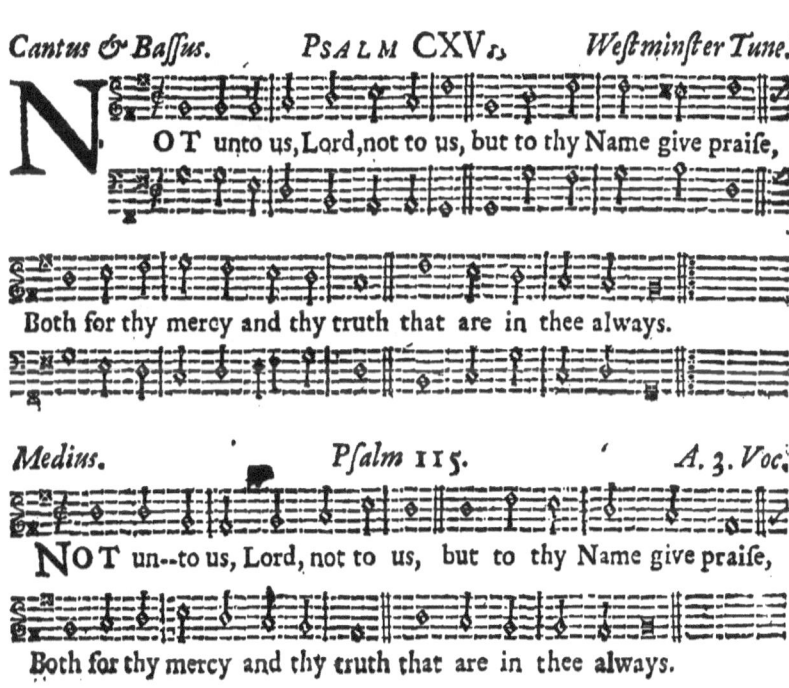

Cantus & Baffus.   Psalm CXV.   *Weftminfter Tune.*

NOT unto us, Lord, not to us, but to thy Name give praife,

Both for thy mercy and thy truth that are in thee always.

Medius.   *Pfalm 115.*   *A. 3. Voc.*

NOT un--to us, Lord, not to us, but to thy Name give praife,

Both for thy mercy and thy truth that are in thee always.

Psalm cxv.

Bassus.   Psalm 115.   A. 3. Voc.

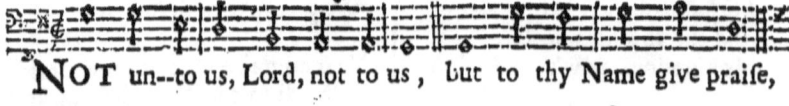
NOt un--to us, Lord, not to us, but to thy Name give praise,

Both for thy mercy and thy truth that are in thee always.

2 Why shall the heathen scorners say,
Where is their God become?
3 Our God he is in heav'n, and what
he will'd, that hath he done.

4 Their idols silver are and gold,
works of men's hands they be:
5 They have a mouth, & do not speak;
and eyes, but do not see.
               (heads,
6 And they have ears joyn'd to their
but do not hear at all:
Noses also they formed have,
but not to smell withal.
              (not;
7 And hands they have, but handle
and feet, but cannot go: (same
A throat they have, yet through the
they make no sound to blow.

8 They and their makers are alike.
and those whose trust they be:
9 O Israel, trust in the Lord,
thy help and shield is he.

10 O Aaron's house, trust in the Lord,
that still defendeth thee:
11 Ye that do fear him, trust in him,
your sure defence is he.

12 The Lord hath mindful been of us,
and will us bless also:

On Isr'el and on Aaron's house
his blessings he will show.

13 Them that be fearers of the Lord,
the Lord will bless them all:
Yea, he will bless them ev'ry one,
the great and also small.

14 To you alway the living Lord
will multiply his grace:
And also to the children that
shall follow of your race.

15 Ye are the blessed of the Lord,
ev'n of the Lord most high:
Which both the heav'n and earth did
and fix immoveably.   (make

16 The heavens, yea, the highest
belong unto the Lord: (heav'ns
The earth unto the sons of men
he gave of free accord.
              (praise
17 They that be dead do not with
set forth the Lord's renown:
Nor any that into the place
of silence do go down.
              (God
18 But we will praise the Lord our
henceforth for evermore:
He only worthy is of Praise;
Praise ye the Lord therefore.

Psalm cxvi. 201

Cantus & Bassus.   PSALM CXVI.   *Or to Windsor Tune.*

I Love the Lord, because my voice and prayer heard hath he:

I'll e—ver call on him, because he bow'd his ear to me.

Ev'n when the snares of cru—el death a--bout be—set me round:

When pains of hell me caught, and when I wo and sorrow found.

Medius.   *Psalm* 116.   *A. 3. Voc.*

I Love the Lord, because my voice and prayer heard hath he:

I'll e—ver call on him, because he bow'd his ear to me.

Ev'n when the snares of cruel death a--bout be—set me round:

When pains of hell me caught, and when I wo and sorrow found.

Bassus.

Psalm cxvi.

Bassus. Psalm 116. A. 3. Voc.

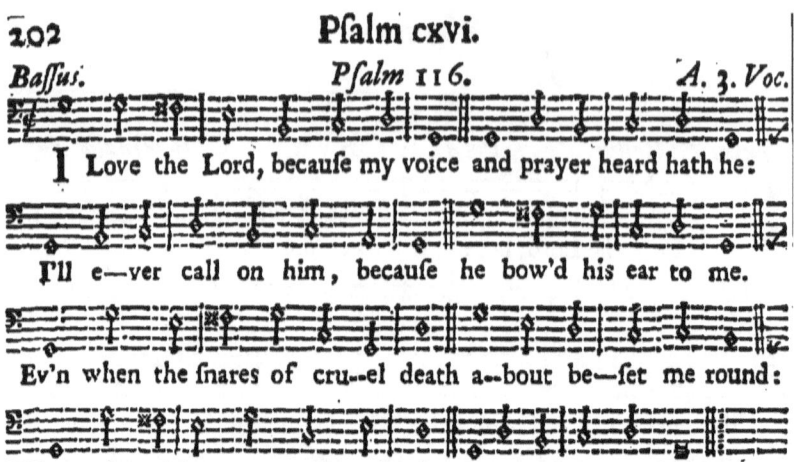

I Love the Lord, because my voice and prayer heard hath he:

I'll e—ver call on him, because he bow'd his ear to me.

Ev'n when the snares of cru--el death a--bout be—set me round:

When pains of hell me caught, and when I wo and sorrow found.

               (Lord,
4 Upon the Name of God my
   then did I call, and say,
Deliver thou my soul, O Lord,
   I do thee humbly pray.
5 The Lord is very merciful,
   and just he is also:
And in our God compassion
   doth plentifully flow.

6 The Lord in safety doth preserve
   all those that simple be:
I was in woful misery,
   and he deliver'd me. (safe,
7 And now, my soul, since thou art
   return unto thy rest :
For largely, lo, the Lord to thee
   his bounty hath express'd.

8 Because thou hast delivered
   my soul from deadly thrall:
My moisten'd eyes from mournful
   my sliding feet from fall. (tears,
9 Before the Lord I in the land
   of life will walk therefore :
10 I did believe, therefore I spake,
   for I was troubled sore.

The second part.
11 I said in my distress and fear,
   that all men liars be:
12 What shall I pay the Lord for all
   his benefits to me ?
13 The wholsom cup of saving health
   I thankfully will take:
And on the Lord's Name I will call
   when I my prayers make.

14 I to the Lord will pay my vows
   with joy and great delight:
Ev'n at this very present time
   in all his people's sight.
15 Right dear and precious in his sight
   he always doth esteem
The death of all his holy ones,
   whatever men do deem.

16 Thy servant, Lord, thy servant, lo,
   I do my self confess,
Son of thy handmaid, thou hast broke
   the bonds of my distress.
17 Therefore I'll offer up to thee
   a sacrifice of praise:
And I will call upon the Name
   of God the Lord always.

Psalm cxvi, cxvii.

18 I to the Lord will pay my vows
within his temple bright,
Ev'n at this very present time
in all his people's sight.

19 Yea, in the courts of God's own
and in the midst of thee, (house,
O thou Jerusalem: Therefore
the Lord our God praise ye.

Cantus & Bassus.   PSALM CXVII.   *Cambridge Tune.*

O All ye nations of the world, praise ye the Lord always:
And all ye people ev'ry where set forth his noble praise.

Medius.   *Psalm* 117.   *A. 3. Voc.*

O All ye nations of the world, praise ye the Lord always:
And all ye people ev'ry where set forth his noble praise.

Bassus.   *Psalm* 117.   *A. 3. Voc.*

O All ye nations of the world, praise ye the Lord always:
And all ye people ev'ry where set forth his noble praise.

2 For great his kindness is to (us,
his truth doth not decay:

Wherefore praise ye the Lord our (God,
praise ye the Lord alway.

Pſalm cxviii.

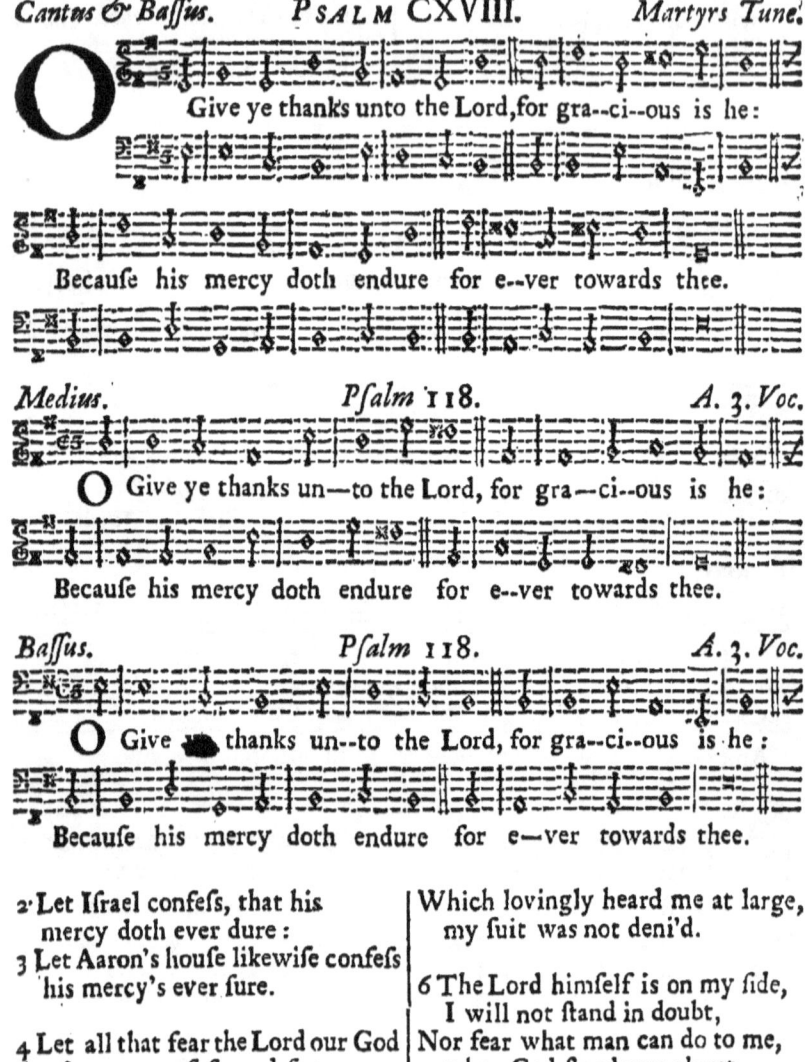

Cantus & Baſſus. PSALM CXVIII. *Martyrs Tune.*

O Give ye thanks unto the Lord, for gra--ci--ous is he:
Becauſe his mercy doth endure for e--ver towards thee.

Medius. Pſalm 118. *A. 3. Voc.*

O Give ye thanks un—to the Lord, for gra—ci--ous is he:
Becauſe his mercy doth endure for e--ver towards thee.

Baſſus. Pſalm 118. *A. 3. Voc.*

O Give ye thanks un--to the Lord, for gra--ci--ous is he:
Becauſe his mercy doth endure for e—ver towards thee.

2 Let Iſrael confeſs, that his
  mercy doth ever dure:
3 Let Aaron's houſe likewiſe confeſs
  his mercy's ever ſure.

4 Let all that fear the Lord our God
  ev'n now confeſs, and ſay,
  The mercy of the Lord our God
  endureth ſtill alway.

5 In trouble and in heavineſs
  unto the Lord I cri'd:

Which lovingly heard me at large,
  my ſuit was not deni'd.

6 The Lord himſelf is on my ſide,
  I will not ſtand in doubt,
  Nor fear what man can do to me,
  when God ſtands me about.

7 The Lord doth take my part with them
  that help to ſuccour me:
  Therefore I ſhall ſee my deſire
  upon mine enemy.

8 Better

Psalm cxviii.

8 Better it is to trust in God,
   than in man's mortal seed:
9 Or to put confidence in kings
   or princes in our need.
10 All nations have enclosed me,
   and compassed me round:
But in the Name of God shall I
   mine enemies confound.
11 They kept me in on ev'ry side,
   and did me quite surround:
But in the Lord's most mighty Name
   I'll cast them to the ground.
12 They came about me all like bees,
   but in the Lord's great Name
I quench'd their thorns that were on
   and will destroy the same. (fire,

The second part.

13 They did with force thrust sore at
   that I indeed might fall: (me,
But thrô the Lord I found such help,
   that they were vanquish'd all.
14 The Lord is my defence & strength,
   my joy, my mirth, and song:
He is become for me indeed
   a Saviour most strong.
15 The right hand of the Lord our God
   doth bring to pass great things:
He causeth voice of joy and health
   in right'ous men's dwellings.
16 The right hand of the Lord doth
   most mighty things to pass: (bring
His hand hath the preheminence,
   his force is as it was.
17 I shall not die, but ever live
   to utter and declare
The mighty power of the Lord,
   his works, and what they are.
18 The Lord himself hath chastened,
   and hath corrected me:
But not me given over yet
   to death, as ye may see.

19 Set open unto me the gates
   of truth and right'ousness:
That I may enter into them,
   the Lord's praise to express.
20 This is the gate ev'n of the Lord,
   which open shall be set:
For good and right'ous men alway
   shall enter into it.

The third part.

21 I will give thanks to thee, O Lord,
   and ever will praise thee,
Who hast me heard, and art become
   a Saviour unto me.
22 The stone which e're this time a-
   the builders was refus'd, (mong
Is now become the corner-stone,
   and chiefly to be us'd.
23 This was the mighty work of God,
   this was the Lord's own fact:
And it is wondrous to behold
   with eyes that noble act.
24 This is the joyful day indeed,
   which God himself hath wrought:
Let us be glad and joy therein
   in heart, in mind, and thought.
25 Now help us, Lord, & prosper us,
   we wish with one accord:
26 Blessed is he that comes to us
   in the Name of the Lord.
27 God is the L^d that shews us light,
   bind ye therefore with cord
Your sacrifice to the altar,
   and give thanks to the Lord.
28 Thou art my God, I will confess,
   and render thanks to thee:
Thou art my God, and I will praise
   thy mercy towards me.
29 O give ye thanks unto the Lord,
   for gracious is he:
Because his mercy doth endure
   for ever towards me.

Pſalm cxix.   207
aſſus.   *Pſalm* 119.   *A.* 3. *Voc.*

Bleſſed are they that perfect are, and pure in mind and heart:

Whoſe lives and con--ver--ſa--ti--ons from God's laws never ſtart.

Bleſſed are they that give themſelves his ſtatutes to obſerve:

Seeking the Lord with all their heart, and never from him ſwerve.

                           (ſtray,
Doubtleſs ſuch men go not a-
  nor do no wicked thing;
but ſtedfaſtly walk in his way
  without any wandring.
'Tis thy commandment & thy will,
  that with attentive heed
Thy noble and divine precepts
  we learn and keep indeed.
                     (pleaſe
5 O would to God it might thee
  my ways ſo to direct,
That I might always keep thy laws,
  and never them reject.
6 So ſhould no ſhame my life attaint,
  whilſt I thus ſet mine eyes,
And bend my mind always to muſe
  on thy ſacred decrees.
                     (heart,
7 Then will I praiſe with upright
  and magnifie thy Name, (juſt,
When I ſhall learn thy judgments
  and likewiſe prove the ſame.
8 And wholly will I give my ſelf
  to keep thy laws moſt right:
Forſake me not for ever, Lord,
  but ſhew thy grace and might.

Beth.   *The ſecond part.*
9 By what means may a young man
  his life learn to amend? (beſt
If that he mark and keep thy word,
  and therein his time ſpend.
10 Unfeignedly I have thee ſought,
  and thus ſeeking abide:
O never ſuffer me, O Lord,
  from thy precepts to ſlide.
11 Within my heart and ſecret
  thy words I have hid ſtill,
That I might not at any time
  offend thy godly will.
12 We magnifie thy Name, O Lord,
  and praiſe thee evermore:
Thy ſtatutes of moſt worthy fame,
  O Lord, teach me therefore.
13 My lips have never ceas'd to preach
  and publiſh day and night,
The judgments all wch did proceed
  from thy mouth full of might.
14 Thy teſtimonies and thy ways
  much more my heart rejoyce,
Than all the treaſures of the earth
  wch worldlings make their choice.

                                        15 On

Pſalm cxix.

(muſe,
15 On thy precepts I will ſtill
and thereto frame my talk:
As at a mark, ſo will I aim
how I thy ways may walk.
16 My only joy ſhall be ſo fix'd,
and on thy laws ſo ſet:
That nothing ſhall me ſo far blind,
that I thy words forget.

Gimel. *The third part.*
17 Grant to thy ſervant now ſuch
as may my life prolong: (grace,
Thy holy word then will I keep,
both in my heart and tongue.
18 Mine eyes wch were dim & ſhut up,
ſo open and make bright,
That of thy law & wondrous works
I may have the clear ſight.

19 I am a ſtranger in this earth,
wandring now here now there:
Thy word therefore to me diſcloſe,
my footſteps for to clear.
20 My ſoul is raviſh'd with deſire,
and never is at reſt: (high,
But ſeeks to know thy judgments
and what may pleaſe thee beſt.

21 The proud men and malicious
thou haſt deſtroy'd each one:
And curſed are ſuch as do not
thy laws attend upon. (ſhame
22 Lord, turn from me rebuke and
which wicked men conſpire:
For I have kept thy covenants
with zeal as hot as fire.

23 The princes great in council ſat,
and did againſt me ſpeak:
But then thy ſervant thought how he
thy ſtatutes might not break.
24 For why? thy cov'nants are the joy
and ſolace of my heart:
They are my faithful counſellors,
from them I'll not depart.

Daleth. *The fourth part.*
25 I am, alas, as brought to grave,
and almoſt turn'd to duſt:
Reſtore therefore my life again,
as thy promiſe is juſt.
26 My ways when I acknowledged,
with mercy thou didſt hear:
Hear now alſo, and me inſtruct
thy laws to love and fear.

27 Make me, O Lord, to underſtand
thy precepts evermore:
Then on thy works I'll meditate,
and lay them up in ſtore.
28 My ſoul I feel ſo ſore oppreſs'd,
that it doth melt for grief:
According to thy word therefore
haſte, Lord, to ſend relief.

29 From lying and deceitful lips
let thy grace me defend:
And that I may learn thee to love,
thy holy law me ſend.
30 The way of truth both ſtraight &
I choſen have and found: (ſure
Before me I thy judgments ſet,
which keep me ſafe and ſound.

31 Since then, O Lord, I readily
thy covenants embrace:
Let me therefore have no rebuke,
nor check in any caſe.
32 Then will I run moſt joyfully
where thy word doth me call:
When thou haſt ſet my heart at
and rid me out of thrall. (large

He. *The fifth part.*
33 Inſtruct me, Lord, in the right way
of thy ſtatutes divine:
And them to keep unto the end,
my heart will I incline.
34 Grant me the knowledge of thy
and I ſhall it obey: (law
With heart & mind, & all my might
I will it keep alway.

35 In

Psalm cxix.

5 In the right paths of thy precepts
 guide me, Lord, I require:
None other pleasure do I wish,
 nor greater thing desire.
6 Incline my heart thy laws to keep,
 and cov'nants to embrace:
And from all filthy avarice,
 Lord, shield me with thy grace.
               (lusts
7 From vain desires and worldly
 turn back mine eyes and sight:
Give me the sp'rit of life and pow'r,
 to walk thy ways aright.
8 Confirm thy gracious promise, L^d,
 which thou hast made to me,
Which am thy servant, and do love
 and fear nothing but thee.
               (fear,
9 Reproach and shame which I so
 from me, O Lord, expel:
For thou dost judge with equity,
 and therein dost excel.
10 Behold, my heart's desire is bent
 thy laws to keep alway:
Lord, strengthen me so with thy
 that it perform I may. (grace,

Tau. *The sixth part.*

11 Thy mercies great and manifold
 let me obtain, O Lord:
Thy saving health let me enjoy,
 according to thy word.
12 So shall I stop the sland'rous
 of lewd men and unjust: (mouth
For in thy faithful promises
 stands my comfort and trust.
               (mou
13 The word of truth within my
 let ever still be prest:
For in thy judgments wonderful
 my hope doth stand and rest.
14 And whilst that breath within me
 this natural life preserve, (doth
Yea, till this world shall be dissolv'd,
 thy law will I observe.

45 So walk will I as set at large
 from dread and danger free,
Because I study how to keep
 thy precepts faithfully.
46 Thy noble acts I will describe,
 as things of most great fame:
Ev'n before kings I will them blaze,
 and shrink no whit for shame.
47 I will rejoyce then to obey
 thy just commands and will,
Which evermore I have lov'd best,
 and so will love them still.
48 My hands I will lift to thy laws
 which I have dearly sought:
And practise thy commandements
 in will, in deed, and thought.

Zain. *The seventh part.*

49 Thy promise which thou madst to
 remember, Lord, I pray: (me,
For therein have I put my trust
 and confidence alway.
50 It is my comfort and my joy
 when troubles me assail:
For were my life not by thy word,
 it suddenly would fail.
51 The proud & such as God contemn
 still made of me a scorn:
Yet would I not thy law forsake,
 as if I were forlorn: (works
52 But call'd to mind, Lord, thy great
 shew'd to our fathers old:
Whereby I feel my joy surmount
 my grief an hundred fold.
53 Horror hath taken hold on me,
 because the wicked do
Forsake thy right'ous law, and will
 have no regard thereto.
54 But as for me, I fram'd my songs
 thy statutes to exalt,
When I among the strangers dwell,
 and grief did me assault.

(Lord,

55 I thought upon thy Name, O
    by night when others sleep:
Thy law also I kept always,
    and ever will it keep.
56 This grace I did obtain, because
    thy covenants most dear
I did embrace, and also keep
    with reverence and fear.

Cheth. *The eighth part.*

57 O God, which art my part & lot,
    my comfort and my stay,
I have decreed and promised
    thy laws to keep alway.
58 Mine earnest heart did humbly sue
    in presence of thy face:
As thou therefore hast promised,
    Lord, grant to me thy grace.

59 My life I have examined,
    and tri'd my secret heart:
Which to thy statutes caused me
    my feet straight to convert.
60 I did not stay nor linger long,
    as they that slothful are:
But hastily thy laws to keep
    I did my self prepare.

61 The cruel bands of wicked men
    have made of me their prey:
Yet would I not thy law forget,
    nor from thee go astray.
62 The right'ous laws and judgments
    so very great and high, (are
That ev'n at midnight I will rise
    thy Name to magnifie.

63 I am companion to all them
    which fear thee in their heart:
And never will for love nor dread
    from thy commandments start.
64 Thy mercies, L^d, most plenteously
    the earth throughout doth fill:
O teach me how I may obey
    thy statutes and thy will.

Teth. *The ninth part.*

65 According to thy promise, Lord,
    so hast thou with me dealt:
For of thy grace in sundry sorts
    have I thy servant felt.
66 Teach me to judge always aright,
    and give me knowledge sure:
For certainly I do believe
    thy precepts are most pure.

67 Before that I afflicted was,
    I err'd and went astray:
But now I keep thy holy word,
    and make it all my stay.
68 Thou art both good and gracious
    giving most lib'rally:
Thine ordinances how to keep
    therefore, O Lord, teach me.

69 The proud and the ungodly have
    against me forg'd a lie:
Yet thy commandments still observe
    with all my heart will I.
70 Their hearts are swoln wth world
    they are exceeding fat. (ly wealth
But in thy law do I delight,
    and nothing seek but that.

71 O happy time, may I well say,
    when thou didst me correct:
For as a guide to learn thy laws
    thy rod did me direct.
72 So that to me thy word and law
    is dearer manifold
Than thousands of gold and silver
    or ought that can be told.

Jod. *The tenth part.*

73 Thy hands have made & fashion'd
    thy creature for to be: (me
Make me to understand thy law,
    and keep it faithfully.
74 So they that fear thee shall rejoyce
    whenever they may see:
Because I have learn'd by thy word
    to put my trust in thee.

75 When

Psalm cxix.

75 When with thy rods the world is
    (plagu'd,
  I know the cause is just:
So when thou dost correct me, Lord,
  the cause right needs be must.
76 Now of thy goodness I thee pray
  some comfort to me send:
And as thou hast me hitherto,
  O Lord, still me defend.

77 Thy tender mercies pour on me,
  and I shall surely live:
For joy and consolation both
  thy law to me doth give.
78 Confound the proud, who do me
  perversly to destroy: (seek
But as for me, thy laws to know
  I will my self employ.

79 Whoso with rev'rence do thee
  (fear,
  to me let them retire:
And such as do thy cov'nants know,
  and them alone desire.
80 My heart without all wavering
  let on thy laws be bent:
That no confusion come to me,
  nor any discontent.

Caph. *The eleventh part.*

81 My soul doth faint, & ceaseth not
  thy saving health to crave:
And for thy words sake still I trust
  my heart's desire to have.
82 Mine eyes do fail with looking for
  thy word, and thus I say,
Oh when wilt thou me comfort?
  Why dost thou thus delay?

83 Like as a bottle in the smoke,
  so am I parch'd and dry'd:
Yet will I not out of my heart
  let thy commandments slide.
84 How long, O Lord, shall I yet
  before I see the hour, (live,
That on my foes which me torment,
  thy veng'ance thou wilt pour.

85 Presumptuous men have digged
  (pits
  thinking to make me sure:
Thus contrary unto thy law
  my hurt they do procure. (true
86 But thy commandments are all
  and causeless they me grieve:
To thee therefore I do complain,
  that thou may'st me relieve.

87 Almost they had me clean de-
  (stroy'd,
  and brought me quite to ground:
Yet by thy statutes I abide,
  and therein succour found.
88 Restore me, Lord, again to life,
  for thy mercies excel:
And so shall I thy cov'nants keep,
  till death my life expel.

Lamed. *The twelfth part.*

89 In heav'n, O Lord, where thou dost
  thy word is stablish'd sure: (dwell,
And shall to all eternity
  fast settled there endure.
90 From age to age thy truth abides,
  as doth the earth witness:
Whose ground-work thou hast laid
  as no tongue can express. (so sure,

91 Ev'n to this day we may well see
  how thou dost them preserve,
According to thine ordinance,
  for all things do thee serve.
92 Had it not been that in thy law
  my soul had comfort sought,
Long time e're now in my distress
  I had been brought to nought.

93 Therefore will I thy precepts keep
  in memory full fast:
Because that thou by them, O Lord,
  my life restored hast.
94 No man to me can title make,
  for I am only thine:
Save me therefore, for to thy laws
  mine ears and heart incline.

95 The

bane,
95 The wicked men that seek my
   for me do lie in wait:
But I will meditate upon
   thy testimonies great.
96 For nothing in this world I see
   which hath at length no end:
But thy commandment and thy word
   beyond all time extend.

Mem. *The thirteenth part.*

97 What great desire & fervent love
   unto thy law I bear:
On it my daily study is,
   that so I may thee fear.
98 Thy word hath taught me to ex-
   in wisdom all my foes: (ceed
For they are ever with me, and
   do daily me oppose.

99 My teachers which did me in-
   in knowledge I excel: (struct,
Because I do thy cov'nants keep,
   and them to others tell.
100 In wisdom I do far surpass
   the ancient men also:
And that because I keep thy laws,
   and so resolve to do.

101 My feet I have refrain'd likewise
   from ev'ry evil way,
That so I might thy word observe,
   and keep without delay. (swerv'd
102 I have not from thy judgments
   nor shrunk, as thou canst tell:
For why? thou hast me taught thereto live godly and well. (by

103 O Lord, how sweet unto my taste
   I find thy words alway!
Doubtless no honey in my mouth
   doth taste so sweet as they.
104 Thy laws have me such wisdom
   that utterly I hate (learn'd,
All wicked and ungodly ways
   in ev'ry kind or rate.

Nun. *The fourteenth part.*

105 Ev'n as a lantern to my feet,
   so doth thy word shine bright:
And to my paths where-e're I go,
   it is a flaming light. (form
106 I have both sworn and will per-
   in truth and faithfulness,
That I will keep thy judgments just,
   and them in life express.

107 Affliction hath me sore oppress'd,
   and brought me to death's door:
O Lord, as thou hast promised,
   so me to life restore. (and voice
108 The off'rings which with heart
   most freely I thee give,
Accept, and teach me how I may
   after thy judgments live.

109 My soul is ever in my hand,
   great danger me assail:
Yet do I not thy law forget,
   nor it to keep will fail.
110 Altho the wicked laid their nets
   to make of me a prey,
Yet did I not from thy precepts
   once swerve or go astray.

111 Thy law, O Lord, I taken have
   mine heritage to be:
Because such great delight and joy
   it doth afford to me.
112 For evermore I have been bent
   thy statutes to fulfil:
Ev'n so likewise unto the end
   I will continue still.

Samech. *The fifteenth part.*

113 All thoughts that vain & wicked
   I do always detest: (are
But for thy precepts and thy laws,
   I love them ever best.
114 Thou art my hid and secret place,
   my shield and strong defence:
Therefore have I thy promises
   look'd for with patience.

115 There-

Psalm cxix.

115 Therefore ye evil-doers all
   away from me be gone:
For the commandments will I keep
   of God my Lord alone.
116 As thou hast promis'd, so perform,
   that I may live, and be
Never ashamed of the hope
   which thou hast given me.

117 Uphold me, and I shall be safe
   for ought they do or say:
And in thy statutes pleasure take
   will I both night and day.
118 Thou hast trod such under thy feet
   as do thy statutes break:
For nought avails their subtilty,
   their counsel is too weak.
                              (out
119 Like dross thou casts the wicked
   where-e'er they go or dwell:
Therefore can I as thy statutes
   love nothing half so well. (thee,
120 My flesh doth quake for fear of
   my soul is much dismay'd:
By reason of thy judgments great
   my heart is sore afraid.

Jin.   *The sixteenth part.*
121 I do the thing that lawful is,
   and give to all men right:
Resign me not to them that would
   oppress me with their might.
122 But for thy servant surety be
   in that thing which is right:
And never let the proud oppress
   me with their rage and spight.
                              (for
123 Mine eyes do fail with waiting
   thy health, which I do crave:
And for thy right'ous promise, Lord,
   whereby thou wilt me save.
124 Entreat thy servant lovingly,
   and favour to him show:
And thy statutes most excellent
   teach me also to know.

125 Thy humble servant, Lord, I am,
   grant me to understand,
How by thy statutes I may know
   best what to take in hand.
126 It is now time, Lord, to begin,
   for truth doth quite decay:
Thy law likewise they have made
   and none doth it obey.   (void,

127 This is the cause wherefore I love
   thy laws much more than gold,
Or Jewels fine which are esteem'd
   most costly to be sold.   (just,
128 I thought thy precepts all most
   and so them kept in store:
All crafty and malicious ways
   I greatly do abhor.

Pe.   *The seventeenth part.*
129 Thy cov'nants are most wonder-
   and full of things profound: (ful,
My soul therefore doth keep them
   when they are tri'd & found. (sure,
130 The entrance of thy word doth
   to men a light most clear: (give
The simple likewise understand
   when they it read or hear.

131 My mouth I open'd, & did pant,
   because my soul did long
For thy commandments, wch always
   do guide my heart and tongue.
132 With mercy & compassion, Lord,
   behold me from above,
As thou art wont such to behold
   as thy Name fear and love.

133 Direct my footsteps by thy word,
   that I thy will may know:
And never let iniquity
   thy servant overthrow.   (harms,
134 From slandrous tongues & deadly
   preserve and keep me sure:
Thy precepts then will I observe
   with heart upright and pure.

P 3   135 Thy

Pſalm cxix.

(ſurmount
135 Thy countenance which doth
 the ſun in his bright hue,
Let ſhine on me, and by thy law
 teach me what to eſchew.
136 Rivers of water from mine eyes
 continually do fall,
Becauſe I ſee how wicked men
 thy laws keep not at all.

Tzade. *The eighteenth part.*
137 In ev'ry point. Lord, thou art juſt,
 a'thô the wicked grudge:
And when thou doſt ſentence pro-
 ⸺ thou art a right'ous judg. (nounce,
138 To render right, & flee from guile,
 are two chief points moſt high:
And ſuch as thou haſt in thy law
 commanded us ſtraitly.

139 My zeal hath even conſum'd me,
 and I am pin'd away,
Becauſe my foes thy word forget,
 and will it not obey.
140 Thy word's ſo very pure, that it
 doth much my heart rejoyce:
Therefore thy ſervant nothing more
 can love or make my choice.

141 And thô I be nothing ſet by,
 as one of baſe degree:
Yet do I not thy laws forget,
 nor ſhrink away from thee.
142 Thy truth and right'ouſneſs, O
 for ever ſhall endure: (Lord,
Alſo thy law is truth it ſelf,
 moſt conſtant and moſt pure.
                            (me,
143 Trouble and grief have ſeiz'd on
 and brought me wondrous low:
Yet do I ſtill of thy precepts
 delight to hear and know.
144 The right'ouſneſs of thy judg-
 doth laſt for evermore: (ments
Then teach them me, becauſe in them
 my life lies up in ſtore.

Koph. *The nineteenth part.*
145 With fervent heart I call'd and
 now anſwer me, O Lord: (cri'd,
That thy commandments to obſerve
 I fully may accord.
146 To thee, my God, I make my ſuit,
 ſave me, I humbly pray:
Thy teſtimonies then will I
 always keep and obey.

147 To thee I cry, ev'n in the morn
 before the day appear:
Becauſe I hoped in thy word,
 and thee alone do fear. (watches
148 Mine eyes prevent the night-
 before they call, I wake:
That meditating on thy word,
 I might ſome comfort take.
                          (voice,
149 Incline thine ears to hear my
 and pity on me take:
As thou waſt wont, ſo quicken me,
 leſt life ſhould me forſake.
150 My foes draw near, & greedily
 do after miſchief run:
From thy law they are far gone back,
 and wickedly it ſhun.
                          (near,
151 Therefore, O Lord, approach thou
 for need doth ſo require:
For all thy precepts are moſt true,
 then help, I thee deſire,
152 Concerning thy command-
 have learned long ago, (ments, I
That they remain for evermore,
 thou haſt them grounded ſo.

Reſch. *The twentieth part.*
153 My trouble and affliction
 conſider and behold:
Deliver me, for of thy law
 I ever take faſt hold.   (cauſe,
154 Defend my good and right'ous
 with ſpeed ſome ſuccour ſend:
From death as thou haſt promiſed,
 Lord, ever me defend.

155 As

Pſalm cxix.

155 As for the wicked, far are they
from ſaving health and grace:
Becauſe the way thy laws to know
they enter not the trace. (grant,
156 Great are thy mercies, Lord, I
What tongue can them explain?
According to thy judgments good,
let me my life obtain.

157 Thô many men did trouble me,
and perſecute me ſore:
Yet from thy laws I never ſhrunk,
nor went aſide therefore.
158 The great tranſgreſſors I beheld
with great anxiety:
Becauſe they did not keep thy word,
nor ever ſeek to thee.

159 Behold, how I do love thy laws
with a moſt upright heart:
Then quicken me, O Lord, for thou
moſt good and gracious art.
160 Thy word from the beginning
been ever true and juſt. (hath
Thy right'ous judgments ev'ry one
always continue muſt.

Schin. *The twenty firſt part.*
161 Princes have perſecuted me
without a cauſe, but ſaw
It was in vain; for of thy word
my heart did ſtand in aw.
162 And ſurely of thy word I was
more joyful and more glad,
Than he that of rich ſpoils and prey
great ſtore and plenty had.

163 But as for lies and falſities,
them I hate and deteſt:
Becauſe thy holy law I do
above all things love beſt. (Lord,
164 Ten times a day I praiſe the
ſinging with heart and voice:
Becauſe thy right'ous judgments do
greatly my heart rejoyce.

165 Great peace and reſt ſhall all ſuch
as do thy ſtatutes love: (have
No danger ſhall their quiet ſtate
impair or once remove.
166 My only health and comfort, L^d,
I look for at thy hand: (things
And therefore have I done thoſe
which thou didſt me command.

167 Thy laws have been my exerciſe,
which my ſoul moſt deſir'd:
So much to them my love was bent,
that nought elſe I requir'd.
168 Thy ſtatutes & commandments I
have kept with heart upright:
For all my dangers and my ways
are preſent in thy ſight.

Tau. *The twenty ſecond part.*
169 O Lord, let my complaint & cry
before thy face appear:
And as thou haſt me promiſe made,
ſo teach me thee to fear.
170 O let my ſupplication
have free acceſs to thee:
And grant me, Lord, deliverance,
as thou haſt promis'd me.
(ſpeak
171 Then ſhall my lips thy praiſes
after moſt ample ſort: (taught,
When thou thy ſtatutes haſt me
wherein ſtands my comfort.
172 My tongue ſhall freely preach
and evermore confeſs, (thy word,
Thy famous acts and noble laws
are truth and right'ouſneſs.
(ſeech,
173 Stretch out thy hand, I thee be-
and ſpeedily me ſave:
For thy commandments to obſerve
choſen, O Lord, I have.
174 Of thee alone, L^d, I crave health,
for other I know none:
And in thy law and nothing elſe
I do delight alone.

Psalm cxix, cxx.

175 Grant me therefore long days to live
thy Name to magnifie:
And of thy judgments merciful
let me the favour try.

176 For I was lost and went astray
much like a wandring sheep:
Oh! seek me, for I have not fail'd
thy statutes for to keep.

Cantus & Bassus. PSALM CXX. *Proper Tune.*

IN trouble, & in thrall, unto the Lord I call, & he doth me comfort:
De-li-ver me, I say, from liars lips alway, and tongues of false report.

Medius. Psalm 120. A. 3. Voc.

IN trouble, and in thrall, unto the Lord I call, & he doth me comfort:
De-li-ver me, I say, from liars lips alway, and tongues of false report.

Bassus. Psalm 120. A. 3. Voc.

IN trouble, and in thrall, unto the Lord I call, & he doth me comfort:
De-li-ver me, I say, from liars lips alway, and tongues of false report.

3 What vantage, or what thing,
Gett'st thou thus for to sting,
Thou false and flatt'ring liar?

4 Thy tongue doth hurt, I ween,
No less than arrows keen,
Or hot consuming fire.

5 Alas!

Psalm cxx, cxxi. 217

5 Alas! too long I flack
Within thefe tents fo black,
 Which Kedars are by name.
By whom the flock elect,
And all of Ifaac's fect,
 Are put to open fhame.

6 With them that peace did hate
I came a peace to make,
 And fet a quiet life:
7 But when my tale was told,
Caufelefs I was controul'd
 By them that would have ftrife.

Cantus & Baffus.   PSALM CXXI.   Proper Tune.

Lift mine eyes to Sion hill, From whence I do attend
That fuccour God me fend. The mighty God me fuccour will,
Which heaven and earth hath framed, And ev'ry thing therein named.

Medius.   Pfalm 121.   A. 3. Voc.

I Lift mine eyes to Sion hill, From whence I do attend

Psalm cxxi, cxxii.

Bassus. Psalm 121. A. 3. Voc.

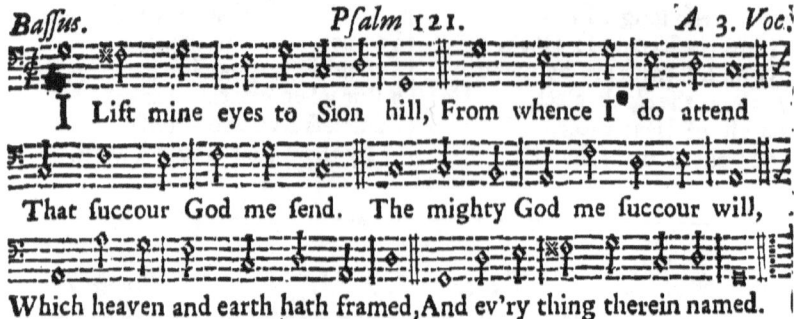

I Lift mine eyes to Sion hill, From whence I do attend
That succour God me send. The mighty God me succour will,
Which heaven and earth hath framed, And ev'ry thing therein named.

3 Thy foot from slip he will preserve,
And will thee safely keep,
For he will never sleep.
4 Lo he that Isr'el doth conserve,
No sleep at all that can him catch,
But that his eyes shall ever watch.

5 The Lord is thy warrant alway,
The Lord he doth thee cover
As at thy right hand ever.

6 The sun shall not thee parch by day,
Nor the moon that's not half so bright
Shall wth the cold thee hurt by night.

7 The Lord will keep thee from di-
And will thy life sure save: (stress,
8 And thou shalt also have
In all thy business good success.
Wherever thou go'st in or out,
God sure will thy things bring a-
(bout.

Cantus & Bassus. PSALM CXXII. *Proper Tune.*

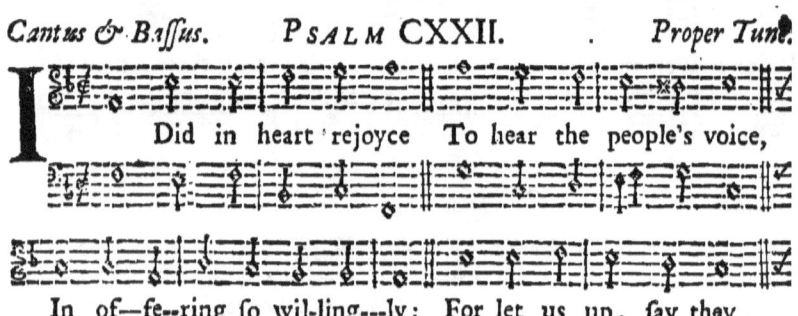

I Did in heart rejoyce To hear the people's voice,
In of--fe--ring so wil-ling---ly: For let us up, say they,

Psalm cxxii.

Our feet that wander'd wide Shall in thy Gates a—bide

O thou Je—ru—sa--lem full fair, Which art so seemly set

such like a Ci--ty neat, The like whereof is not elsewhere.

Medius.   *Psalm 122.*   *A. 3. Voc.*

I Did in heart re—joyce To hear the peo--ple's voice,

In of—fe—ring so wil--ling-ly : For let us up, say they,

And in the Lord's house pray : Thus spake the folk full lovingly.

Our feet that wander'd wide Shall in thy Gates a—bide,

O thou Je—ru—sa--lem full fair, Which art so seemly set

ich like a Ci--ty neat, The like whereof is not elsewhere.

Bassus.

Psalm cxxii, cxxiii.

Bassus.   **Psalm 122.**   A. 3. Vo

I Did in heart re—joyce To hear the peo—ple's voice,

In of—fe—ring so wil—ling-ly: For let us up, say they,

And in the Lord's house pray: Thus spake the folk full lovingly.

Our feet that wander'd wide Shall in thy Gates a—bide,

O thou Je—ru—sa—lem full fair, Which art so seemly set

Much like a Ci--ty neat, The like whereof is not elsewhere.

4 The tribes with one accord,
The tribes of God the Lord
  Are thither bent their way to take:
So God before did tell,
That there his Israel   (make.
  Their prayers should together

5 For there are thrones erect,
And that for this respect,
  To set forth justice orderly:
Which thrones right to maintain
To David's house pertain,
  His folk to judge accordingly.

6 To pray let us not cease
For Jerusalem's peace,
  Thy friends God prosper might:
7 Peace be thy walls about,
And prosper thee throughout
  Thy palaces continually.

8 I wish thy prosp'rous state
For my poor brethren's sake,
  That comfort have by means
9 God's house doth me allure, (th
Thy wealth for to procure
  So much as lies in me.

Cantus & Bassus.   **PSALM CXXIII.**   *Windsor Tne.*

O Thou that in the heav'ns dost dwell, I lift mine eyes to the

Ev'n as a servant lifteth his, his master's hands to see.

Medi

Psalm cxxiii, cxxiv.   221

Tedius.   *Psalm 123.*   *A. 3. Voc.*

O Thou that in the heav'ns doft dwell, I lift mine eyes to thee:
Ev'n as a fervant lifteth his, his mafter's hands to fee.

Baſſus.   *Psalm 123.*   *A. 3. Voc.*

O Thou that in the heav'ns doft dwell, I lift mine eyes to thee:
Ev'n as a fervant lifteth his, his mafters hands to fee.

As handmaids watch their miftrefs
 fome grace for to achieve: (hand
So we behold the Lord our God,
 till he do us forgive.
3 Lord, grant us thy compaſſion,
 and mercy in thy fight:

For we are fill'd and overcome
 with hatred and defpight.
4 Our minds are ſtuff'd with great re-
 the rich and worldly wife (buke,
Do make of us their mocking-ſtock,
 the proud do us defpiſe.

Cantus & Baſſus.   **PSALM CXXIV.**   *Proper Tune.*

NOW If—ra—el may fay, and that tru--ly, If that the
Lord had not our caufe maintain'd, If that the Lord had not our
righ fuftain'd, When all the world againſt us fu—riouſ—ly

Psalm cxxiv.

Medius.   Pſalm 124.   A. 3. V.

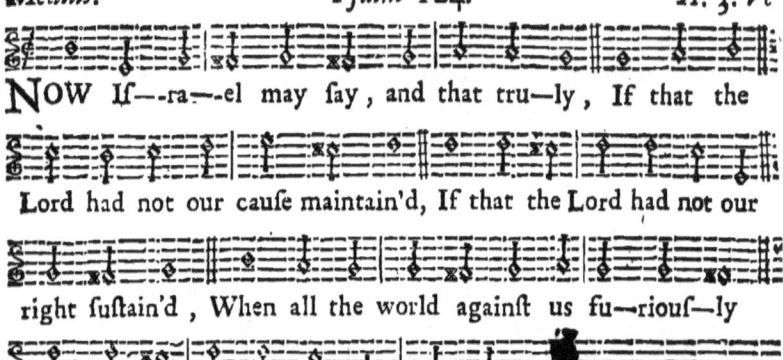

Now Iſ—ra—el may ſay, and that tru—ly, If that the Lord had not our cauſe maintain'd, If that the Lord had not our right ſuſtain'd, When all the world againſt us fu—riouſ—ly Made their uproars, and ſaid, We ſhould all die.

Baſſus.   Pſalm 124.   A. 3. Vo

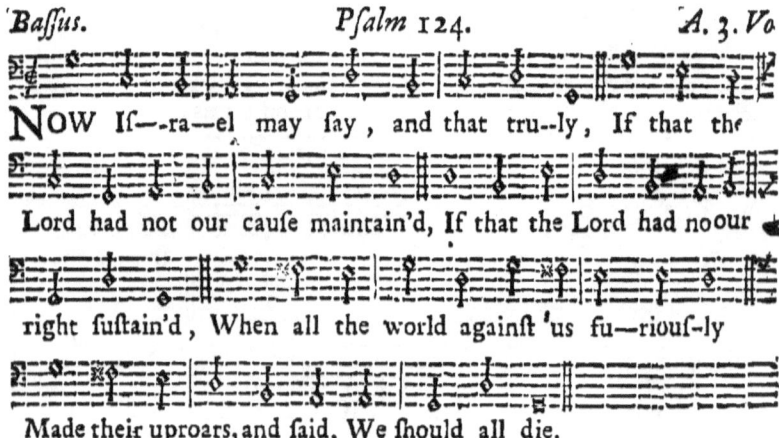

Now Iſ—ra—el may ſay, and that tru--ly, If that the Lord had not our cauſe maintain'd, If that the Lord had no our right ſuſtain'd, When all the world againſt 'us fu—riouſ-ly Made their uproars, and ſaid, We ſhould all die.

3 Now long ago
  they had devour'd us all,
And ſwallow'd quick,
  for ought that we could deem:
Such was their rage,
  as we might well eſteem.
4 And as the floods
  with mighty force do fall:
So had they now
  our lives ev'n brought to thrall.

5 The raging ſtreams,
  moſt proud in roring noiſe
Had long ago
  o'erwhelm'd us in the deep:
6 But lov'd be God,
  which doth us ſafely keep
From bloody teeth,
  and their moſt cruel voice
Which as a prey,
  to eat us would rejoyce.

7 Ev'n

Psalm cxxiv, cxxv. 223

7 Ev'n as a bird
out of the fowler's gin
Escapes away,
right so it fares with us:
Broke are their nets,

and we have scaped thus.
8 God that made Heav'n
and Earth is our help then:
His Name hath sav'd
us from these wicked men.

Cantus & Bassus.   PSALM CXXV.   *Proper Tune.*

Such as in God the L^d do trust, As mount Sion shall firmly stand,

And be removed at no hand. The Lord will count them right and just:

So that they shall be sure For ever to endure.

Medius.   Psalm 125.   *A. 3. Voc.*

Such as in God the Lord do trust, As mount Si--on shall firmly stand,

And be removed at no hand. The Lord will count them right and just:

So that they shall be sure For ever to endure.

Bassus.

Psalm cxxv.

Bassus. *Psalm 125.* *A. 3. Voc.*

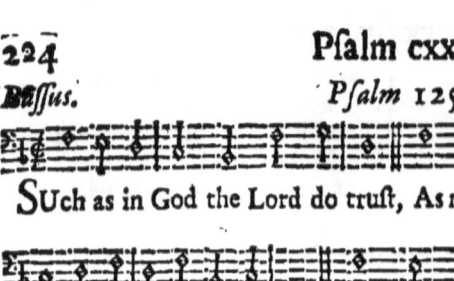

SUch as in God the Lord do trust, As mount Si--on shall firmly stand,

And be removed at no hand. The Lord will count them right and just:

So that they shall be sure For ever to endure.

2 As mighty mountains huge & great
Jerusalem about do close:
So will the Lord do unto those
Who on his godly will do wait:
Such are to him so dear,
They never need to fear.

3 For thô the right'ous try doth he
By making wicked men his rod,
Lest they thrô grief forsake their God,

It shall not as their lot still be.
4 Give, Lord, to us thy light,
Whose hearts are true and right.

5 But as for such as turn aside (sought,
By crooked ways which they out
The L^d will surely bring to noght,
With workers vile they shall abide:
But peace with Israel
For evermore shall dwell.

Cantus & Bassus. *Another of the same.* *Or to 100 Psalm Tune.*

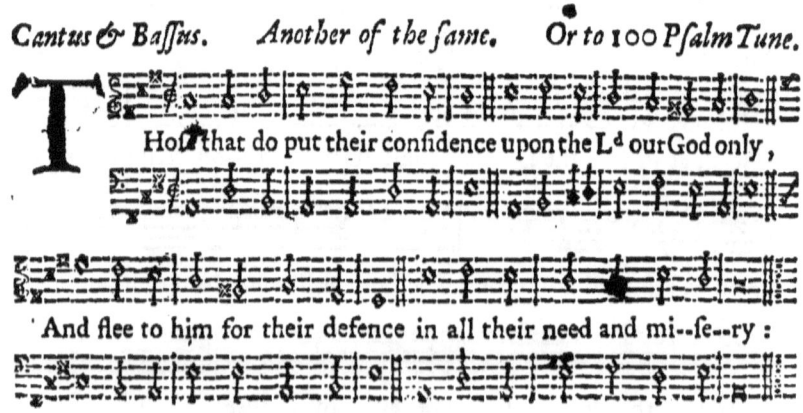

THose that do put their confidence upon the L^d our God only,

And flee to him for their defence in all their need and mi--se--ry:

Medius.

Psalm cxxv. 225

Medius. Psalm 125. *A. 3. Voc.*

THose that do put their confidence upon the Lord our God only,

And flee to him for their defence in all their need and mi--se--ry:

Bassus. Psalm 125. *A. 3. Voc.*

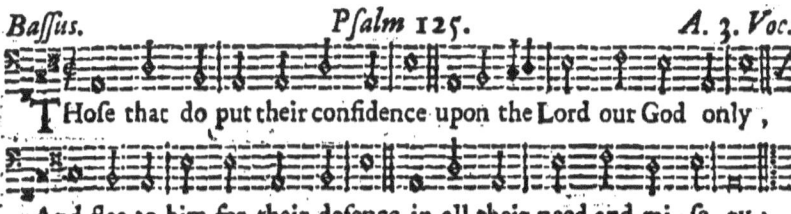

THose that do put their confidence upon the Lord our God only,

And flee to him for their defence in all their need and mi--se--ry:

    Their faith is sure
    Still to endure,
Grounded on Christ the corner-stone;
Mov'd with none ill,
    But standeth still
Stedfast like to the Mount Sion.

And as about Jerusalem
The mighty hills do it compass,
So that no en'mies come to them
To hurt that town in any case:
    So God indeed
    In ev'ry need
His faithful people doth defend,
Standing them by
    Assuredly   (end.
From this time forth world without

Right wise and good is our Ld God,
And will not suffer certainly
The sinners and ungodlies rod
To rest upon his family:
    Lest they also
    From God should go,
Falling to sin and wickedness.

    O Lord, defend
    World without end   (ness.
Thy Christian flock thrô thy good-

O Lord, do good to Christians all
That stedfast in thy word abide:
But such as from the Lord do fall,
And to false doctrine daily slide,
    Them will the Lord
    Scatter abroad   (hell,
With hypocrites thrown down to
    God will them send
    Pains without end:
But, Lord, grant peace to Israel.
    Gloria Patri.

*Glory to God the Father of might,
And to the Son our Saviour;
And to the Holy Ghost, whose light
Shine in our hearts, and us succours
That the right way
From day to day
We may walk, and him glorifie:
With heart's desire
All that are here
Worship the Lord, and say, Amen.*

226   Psalm cxxvi.

Cantus & Bassus.   PSALM CXXVI.   *Proper Tune.*

WHen that the Lord again his Si—on had forth brought

From bondage great, and al—so servitude extream; His work was

such as did surmount man's heart & thoght: So that we were much like to

them that use to dream. Our mouths all were with laughter filled then;

Also our tongues did shew us joyful men.

Medius.   Psalm 126.   A. 3. Voc.

WHen that the Lord again his Si—on had forth brought

From bondage great, and al—so servitude extream; His work was

such as did surmount man's heart & thoght: So that we were much like to

them

Pfalm cxxvi.

them that ufe to dream. Our mouths all were with laughter filled then,

Alfo our tongues did fhew us joyful men.

Baſſus.   *Pſalm* 126.   *A. 3. Voc.*

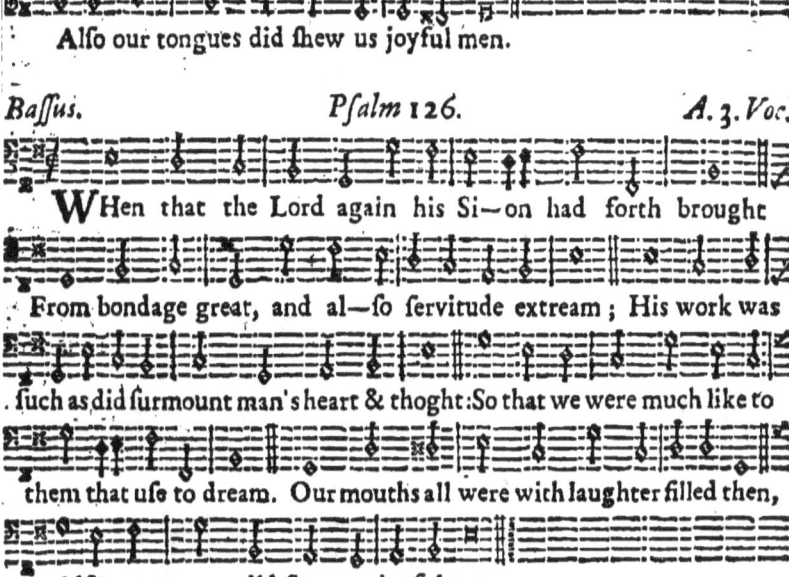

WHen that the Lord again his Si—on had forth brought

From bondage great, and al—fo fervitude extream ; His work was

fuch as did furmount man's heart & thoght:So that we were much like to

them that ufe to dream. Our mouths all were with laughter filled then,

Alfo our tongues did fhew us joyful men.

The heathen folk
  were forced then this to confefs,
How that the Lord
  for them alfo great things had
3 But much more we,   (done.
  and therefore can confefs no lefs:
Wherefore to joy
  we have good caufe as we begun.
4 O Lord, go forth,
  thou canft our bondage end:
As to defarts
  the flowing rivers fend.

5 Full true it is,
  that they which fow with tears in-
A time will come   (deed,
  when they fhall reap with mirth &
6 They went and wept   (joy:
  in bearing of their precious feed,
For that their foes
  full oftentimes did them annoy.
But their return
  with joy they fhall furely fee,
Their fheaves home bring,
  and not impaired be.

Psalm cxxvii.

Cantus & Bassus.   PSALM CXXVII.   112 *Psal. Tune.*

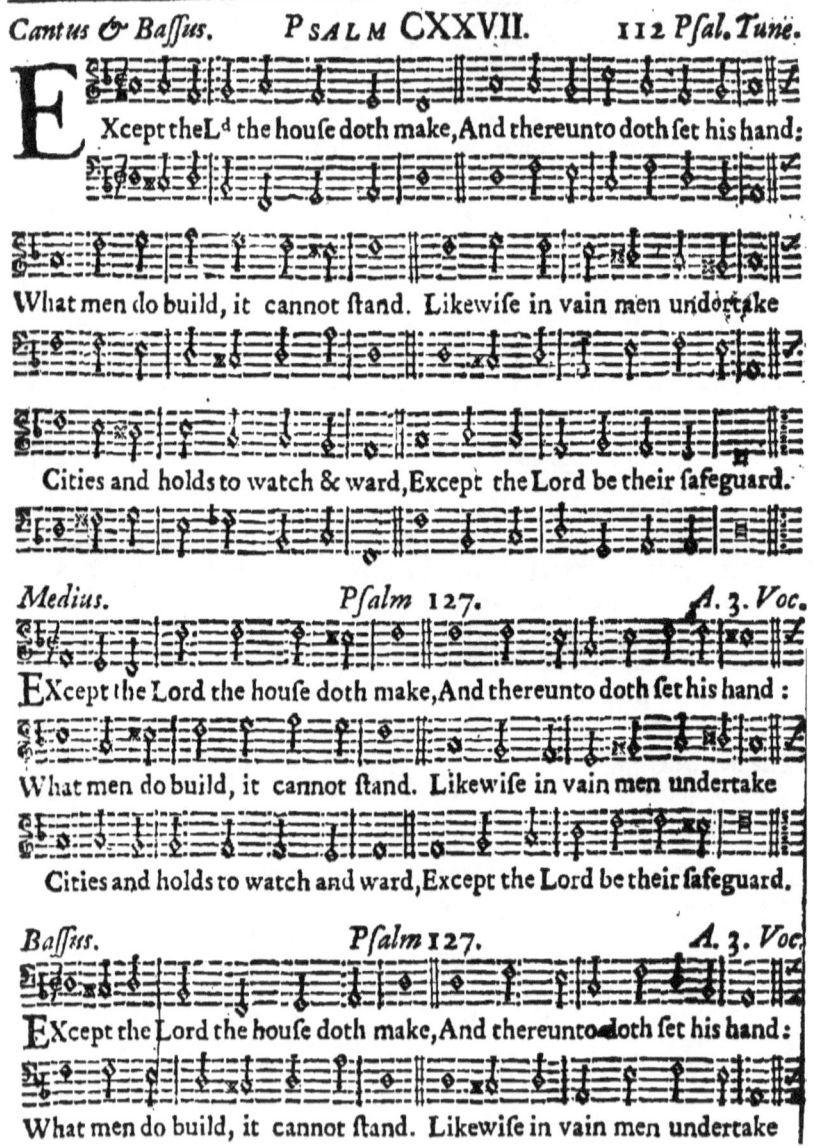

Except the L^d the house doth make, And thereunto doth set his hand:

What men do build, it cannot stand. Likewise in vain men undertake

Cities and holds to watch & ward, Except the Lord be their safeguard.

Medius.   Psalm 127.   *A. 3. Voc.*

EXcept the Lord the house doth make, And thereunto doth set his hand :

What men do build, it cannot stand. Likewise in vain men undertake

Cities and holds to watch and ward, Except the Lord be their safeguard.

Bassus.   Psalm 127.   *A. 3. Voc.*

EXcept the Lord the house doth make, And thereunto doth set his hand:

What men do build, it cannot stand. Likewise in vain men undertake

Psalm cxxvii, cxxviii.

2 Thô ye rise early in the morn,
And so at night go late to bed,
Feeding full hardly wth brown bread,
  Yet were your labour lost & worn:
But they whom God doth love & keep,
Receive all things with quiet sleep.
  (you see
3 Therefore mark well whene'er
That men have heirs t'enjoy ther land,
It is the gift of God's own hand:
For God himself doth multiply
Of his great liberality
The blessing of posterity.

4 And when the children com to age
They grow in strength & activeness,
In person and in comeliness:
  So that a shaft shot with courage
Of one that hath a most strong arm,
Flies not so swift, nor doth like harm.

5 Oh well is he that hath his quiv'r
Furnish'd with such artillery:
For when in peril he shall be, (shiv'r
  Such one shall never quake nor
When that he pleads before the judg
Against his foes that bear him grudg.

Cantus & Bassus.   PSALM CXXVIII.   *London Tune.*

Blessed art thou that fearest God, and walkest in his ways:
For of thy labour thou shalt eat, happy shall be thy days.

Medius.   Psalm 128.   *A. 3. Voc.*

Blessed art thou that fearest God, and walkest in his ways:
For of thy labour thou shalt eat, happy shall be thy days.

Bassus.   Psalm 128.   *A. 3. Voc.*

Blessed art thou that fearest God, and walkest in his ways:
For of thy labour thou shalt eat, happy shall be thy days.

Psalm cxxviii, cxxix.

3 Like fruitful vines on thy house-
  so doth thy wife spring out: (side,
Thy children stand like olive-plants
  thy table round about.
4 Thus art thou bless'd that fearest
  and he shall let thee see (God,
5 The promised Jerusalem,
  and her felicity.
6 Thou shalt thy children's children
  to thy great joy's increase: (see,
And likewise grace on Israel,
  prosperity and peace.

Cantus & Bassus.   PSALM CXXIX.   *Norwich Tune.*

OFT they, now Is—ra—el may say, me from my youth assail'd:
Oft they assail'd me from my youth, yet never have prevail'd.

Medius.   Psalm 129.   A. 3. Voc.

OFT they, now Is—ra—el may say, me from my youth assail'd:
Oft they assail'd me from my youth, yet never have prevail'd.

Bassus.   Psalm 129.   A. 3. Voc.

OFT they, now Is—ra—el may say, me from my youth assail'd:
Oft they assail'd me from my youth, yet never have prevail'd.

3 Upon my back the plowers plow'd,
  and furrows long did cast:
4 The right'ous Lord hath cut the
  of wicked men at last. (cords
5 They that hate me shall be asham'd,
  and turned back also:
6 And made as grass upon the house,
  which with'reth e're it grow:
7 Whereof the mower cannot find
  enough to fill his hand:
Nor can he fill his lap, that goes
  to glean upon the land.
8 Nor passers by, pray God on them
  to let his blessing fall:
Nor say, We bless you in the Name
  of God the Lord at all.

PSALM

Pſalm cxxx.

Cantus & Baſſus.   PSALM CXXX.   *Proper Tune.*

Lord, to thee I make my mone when dangers me oppreſs:

I call, ſigh, complain and grone, truſting to find releaſe.

Hear now, O Lord, my requeſt, for it is full due time:

Let thine ears always be preſt unto this pray'r of mine.

Medius.   *Pſalm* 130.   *A.* 3. *Voc.*

Lord, to thee I make my mone when dangers me oppreſs:

I call, ſigh, complain and grone, truſting to find releaſe.

Hear now, O Lord, my requeſt, for it is full due time:

Let thine ears always be preſt unto this pray'r of mine.

Q 4   *Baſſus*

Psalm cxxx, cxxxi.

Bassus. **Psalm 130.** **A. 3. Voc.**

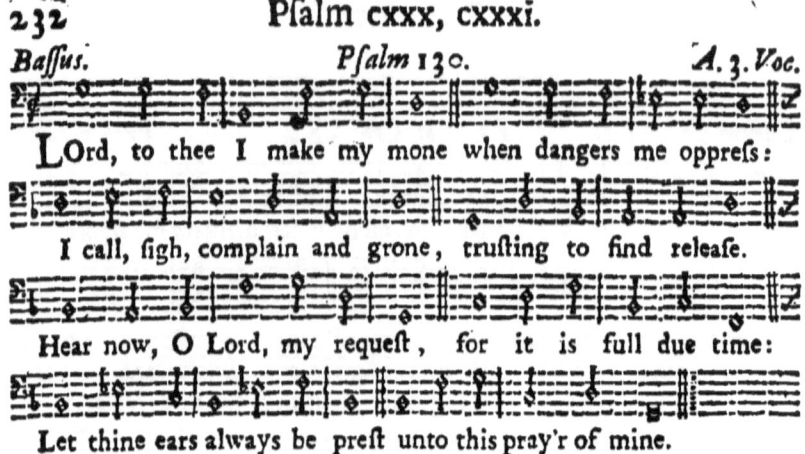

LOrd, to thee I make my mone when dangers me oppress:

I call, sigh, complain and grone, trusting to find release.

Hear now, O Lord, my request, for it is full due time:

Let thine ears always be prest unto this pray'r of mine.

3 O Lord our God, if thou weigh
  our sins, and them peruse:
Who shall then escape, and say,
  I can my self excuse?
4 But, Lord, thou art merciful,
  and turn'st to us thy grace,
That we with hearts most careful
  should fear before thy face.

5 In God I put my whole trust,
  my soul waits on his will:
For his promise is most just,
  and I hope therein still.

6 My soul to God hath regard,
  wishing for him alway,
More than they that watch and ward
  to see the dawning day.

7 Let Israel then boldly
  in the Lord put his trust:
He is that God of mercy
  that his deliver must.
8 For he it is that must save
  Israel from his sin,
And all such as surely have
  their confidence in him.

Cantus & Bassus. **PSALM CXXXI.** *Windsor Tune.*

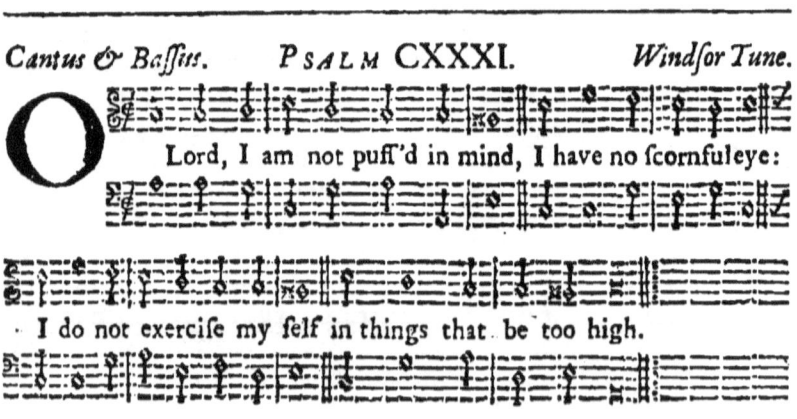

O Lord, I am not puff'd in mind, I have no scornful eye:

I do not exercise my self in things that be too high.

Medius.

Psalm cxxxi, cxxxii. 233

Medius.   Psalm 131.   *A. 3. Voc.*

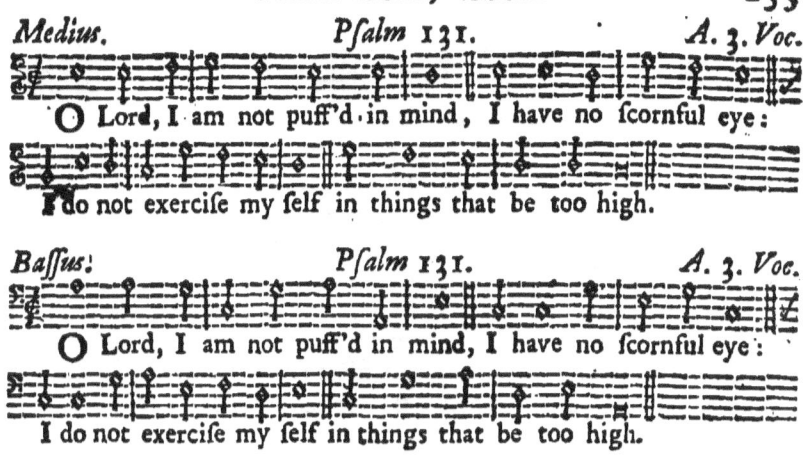

O Lord, I am not puff'd in mind, I have no scornful eye:
I do not exercise my self in things that be too high.

Bassus.   Psalm 131.   *A. 3. Voc.*

O Lord, I am not puff'd in mind, I have no scornful eye:
I do not exercise my self in things that be too high.

2 But as a child that weaned is
ev'n from his mother's breast:
So have I, Lord, behav'd my self
in silence and in rest.

3 O Israel, trust in the Lord,
let him be all thy stay,
From this time forth for evermore,
from age to age alway.

Cantus & Bassus.   PSALM CXXXII.   *Or to York Tune.*

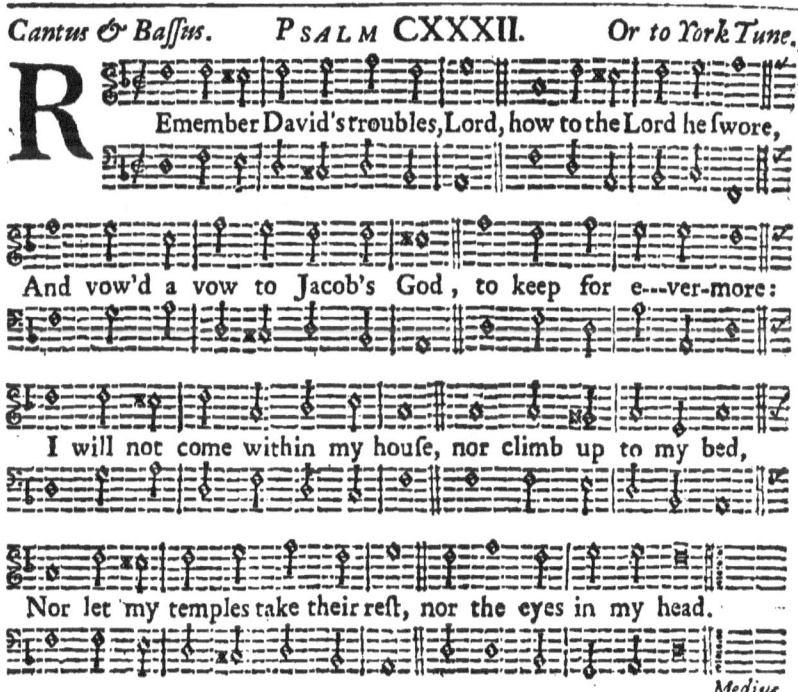

Remember David's troubles, Lord, how to the Lord he swore,
And vow'd a vow to Jacob's God, to keep for e---ver-more:
I will not come within my house, nor climb up to my bed,
Nor let my temples take their rest, nor the eyes in my head.

Medius.

5 Till I have found out for the Lord
   a place to sit thereon:
An house for Jacob's God to be
   an habitation.
6 We heard of it at Ephrata,
   there did we hear this found:
And in the fields and forests there
   these voices first were found.

7 We will essay, and go into
   his tabernacle there,
Before his footstool to fall down,
   and worship him in fear.

8 Arise, O Lord, arise, I pray,
   into thy resting-place:
Thou & the ark of thy great strength,
   the presence of thy grace.

9 Let all thy priests be clothed, Lord,
   with truth and right'ousness:
Let all thy saints and holy men
   sing with great joyfulness.
10 And for thy servant David's sake,
   refuse not, Lord, I pray,
The face of thine anointed, and
   turn not thy face away.

Psalm cxxxii, cxxxiii.   235

The second part.
11 The Lord to David swore in truth,
and will not shrink from it,
Saying, The fruit of thy body
upon thy seat shall sit.
12 And if thy sons my cov'nant keep,
That I shall learn each one:
Then shall their sons for ever sit
upon thy princely throne.
13 The Lord himself hath Sion chose,
and loves therein to dwell,
14 Saying, this is my resting-place,
I love and like it well.
15 And I will bless with great increase
her victuals ev'ry where:
And I will satisfie with bread
the needy that be there.

(cloath
16 With my salvation I will
her priests for evermore:
And all her saints likewise shall sing
and shout for joy therefore.
17 There will I surely make the horn
of David for to bud:
For there I have ordain'd for mine
a lantern bright and good.
18 As for his foes, I will them cloath
with shame for evermore:
But I will cause his crown to shine
more fresh than heretofore.
*To Father, Son, and Holy Ghost,
all glory be therefore:
As in beginning was, is now,
and shall be evermore.*

Cantus & Bassus.   PSALM CXXXIII.   *Winchester Tunc.*

O How happy a thing it is, and joyful for to see,

Brethren together fast to hold the band of a---mi---ty!

Medius.   *Psalm* 133.   *A. 3. Voc.*

O How happy a thing it is, and joyful for to see,

Brethren together fast to hold the band of a---mi---ty!

Bassus.   *Psalm* 133.   *A. 3. Voc.*

O How happy a thing it is, and joyful for to see,

Brethren together fast to hold the band of a---mi---ty!

2 It calls to mind that sweet perfume,
 and that costly ointment,
Which on the sacrificer's head
 by God's command was spent.
It wet not Aaron's head alone,
 but on his beard did fall:
And finally it did run down
 on his rich garments all.

3 And as the lower ground doth
 the dew of hermon hill, (drink
And Sion with his silver drops
 the fields with fruit doth fill:.
4 Ev'n so the Lord doth pour on them
 his blessings manifold, (guile
Whose hearts and minds without all
 this knot doth keep and hold.

Cantus & Bassus. PSALM CXXXIV. *Southwel Tune.*

BEhold and have regard, ye servants of the Lord,
Which in his house by night do watch: Praise him with one accord.

Medius. Psalm 134. A. 3. Voc.

BEhold and have regard, ye servants of the Lord,
Which in his house by night do watch: Praise him with one accord.

Bassus. Psalm 134. A. 3. Voc.

BEhold and have regard, ye servants of the Lord,
Which in his house by night do watch: Praise him with one accord.

2 Lift up your hands on high
 unto his holy place.
And give the Lord his praises due,
 his benefits embrace.

3 For why? the Lord, who did
 both earth and heaven frame,
Doth Sion bless, and will conserve
 for evermore the same.

PSALM

Pſalm cxxxv. 237

Cantus & Baſſus.   PSALM CXXXV. *Or to St.David's Tune.*

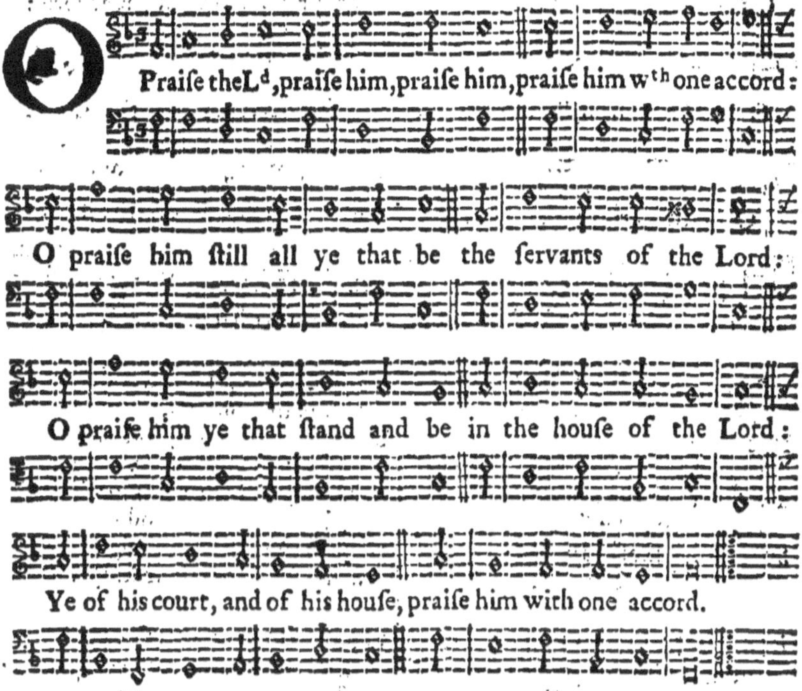

Praiſe the L^d, praiſe him, praiſe him, praiſe him wth one accord:

O praiſe him ſtill all ye that be the ſervants of the Lord:

O praiſe him ye that ſtand and be in the houſe of the Lord:

Ye of his court, and of his houſe, praiſe him with one accord.

Medius.   *Pſalm 135.*   *A. 3. Voc.*

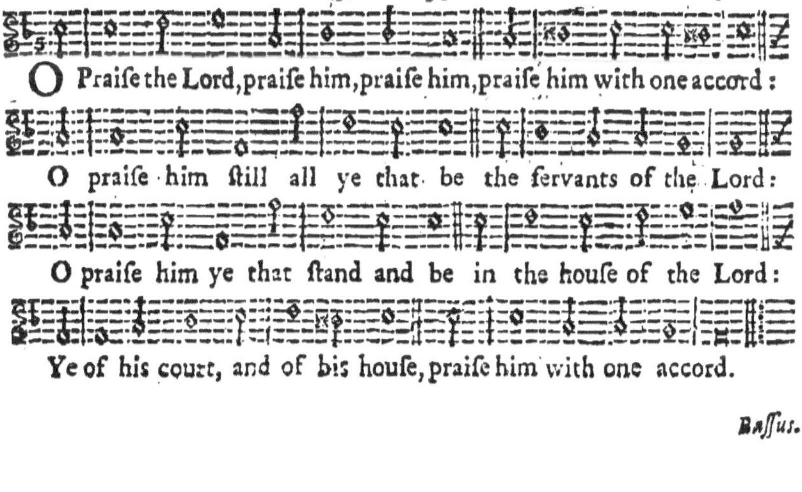

O Praiſe the Lord, praiſe him, praiſe him, praiſe him with one accord:

O praiſe him ſtill all ye that be the ſervants of the Lord:

O praiſe him ye that ſtand and be in the houſe of the Lord:

Ye of his court, and of his houſe, praiſe him with one accord.

Baſſus.

238   Psalm cxxxv.

Bassus.   Psalm 135.   A. 3. Voc.

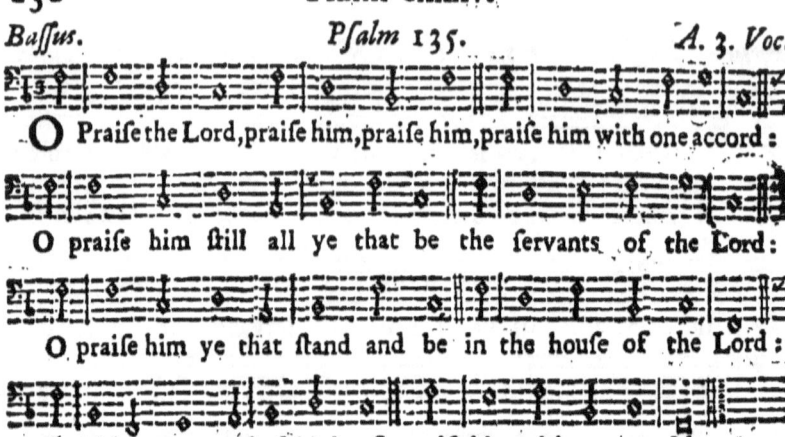

O Praise the Lord, praise him, praise him, praise him with one accord:

O praise him still all ye that be the servants of the Lord:

O praise him ye that stand and be in the house of the Lord:

Ye of his court, and of his house, praise him with one accord.

3 Praise ye the Lord, for he is good,
  sing praises to his Name:
It is a comely and good thing
  always to do the same.   (chose,
4 For why? the Lord hath Jacob
  his very one ye see:
So hath he chosen Israel
  his treasure for to be.

5 For this I know, and am right sure,
  the Lord is very great:
He is indeed above all gods
  most easie to intreat.
6 For whatsoever pleased him,
  all that full well he wrought,
In heav'n, in earth, and in the sea,
  which he hath made of nought.
                (earth,
7 He lifts up clouds ev'n from the
  he makes lightnings and rain:
He bringeth forth the winds also,
  and nothing made in vain.
8 He smote the first-born of each
  in Egypt that took rest: (thing
He spared there no living thing,
  the man, nor yet the beast.

9 He did likewise shew wonders great
  on his inhabitants,
Upon king Pharaoh, and also
  on his severe servants.
10 He smote then many nations,
  and did great acts and things:
He slew the great and mightiest
  and chiefest of their kings.

11 Sehon king of the Amorites,
  and Og king of Basan:
He slew also the kingdoms all
  that were of Canaan:
12 And gave their land to Israel,
  an heritage we see,
To Israel his own people
  an heritage to be.

The second part.

13 Thy Name shall still endure, and
  memorial likewise   (thy
Throughout all generations
  that are, or shall arise.
14 The Lord will surely now avenge
  his people all indeed:
And to his servants he will shew
  favour in time of need.

15 The

Psalm cxxxv, cxxxvi.   239

15 The idols of the heathen which
  are in the coasts and lands,
Of silver and of gold they be,
  the work ev'n of men's hands.
16 They have their mouths but cannot
  & eyes that have no sight : (speak,
17 And they hav ears but hear nothing,
  their mouths are breathless quite.

18 Wherefore all they are like to them
  that so do set them forth:
And likewise those that trust in them,
  or think they be ought worth.

19 O all ye house of Israel,
  see that ye praise the Lord :
And ye that be of Aaron's house,
  praise him with one accord.

20 And ye that be of Levi's house,
  praise ye likewise the Lord :
And ye that stand in awe of him,
  praise him with one accord.

21 And out of Sion sound his praise,
  the great praise of the Lord,
Which dwelleth in Jerusalem :
  Praise him with one accord.

Cantus & Bassus.   PSALM CXXXVI.   100 Psal. Tune.

Praise ye the Lord, for he is good, for his mercy endur'th ever.

Give praise unto the God of gods, for his mercy endur'th ever.

Medius.   Psalm 136.   A. 3. Voc.

Praise ye the Lord, for he is good, for his mercy endur'th ever.

Give praise unto the God of gods, for his mercy endur'th ever.

Bassus.   Psalm 136.   A. 3. Voc.

Praise ye the Lord, for he is good, for his mercy endur'th ever.

Give praise unto the God of gods, for his mercy endur'th ever.

3 Give

Psalm cxxxvi.

3 Give praise unto the Lord of lords,
for his mercy endur'th ever.
4 Which only doth great wondrous
for his mercy, &c.   (works,
5 Which by his wisdom made the
for his mercy, &c.   (heav'ns,
6 Which on the waters stretch'd the
for his mercy, &c.   (earth,
7 Which made great lights to shine
for his mercy, &c.   (abroad,
8 As sun to rule the lightsom day,
for his mercy, &c.
9 The moon and stars to guide the
for his mercy, &c.   (night,
10 W^{ch} smote Egypt with their first-
for his mercy, &c.   (born,
11 And Israel brought out from
for his mercy, &c.   (thence,
12 With mighty hand and stretched
for his mercy, &c.   (arm,
13 Which cut the Red-sea in two
for his mercy, &c.   (parts,
14 And Isr'el made to pass there-
for his mercy, &c.   (through,
15 And drowned Pharoah and his
for his mercy, &c.   (host,

16 Through wilderness his people
for his mercy, &c.   (led,
17 He which did smite great noble
for his mercy, &c.   (kings,
18 And which hath slain the mighty
for his mercy, &c.   (kings,
19 As Sehon king of th' Amorites,
for his mercy, &c.
20 And Og the king of Basan land,
for his mercy, &c.
21 And gave their land for heritage,
for his mercy, &c.
22 Ev'n to his servant Israel,
for his mercy, &c.
23 Remembring us in base estate,
for his mercy, &c.
24 And from oppressors rescu'd us,
for his mercy, &c.
25 Which giveth food unto all flesh,
for his mercy, &c.
26 Praise ye the Lord of heav'n a-
for his mercy, &c.   (bove,
27 Give thanks unto the Lord of
for his mercy, &c.   (lords,
All that hath breath praise ye the L^d,
for his mercy endur'th ever.

Cantus & Bassus.   *Another of the same.*   **148 Psalm Tune.**

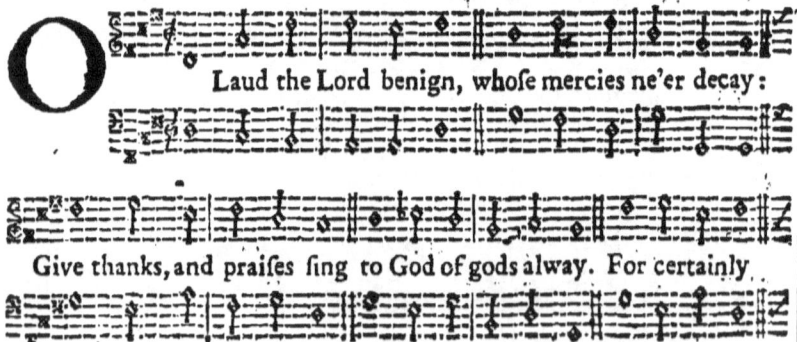

O Laud the Lord benign, whose mercies ne'er decay:
Give thanks, and praises sing to God of gods alway. For certainly

His

Psalm cxxxvi.

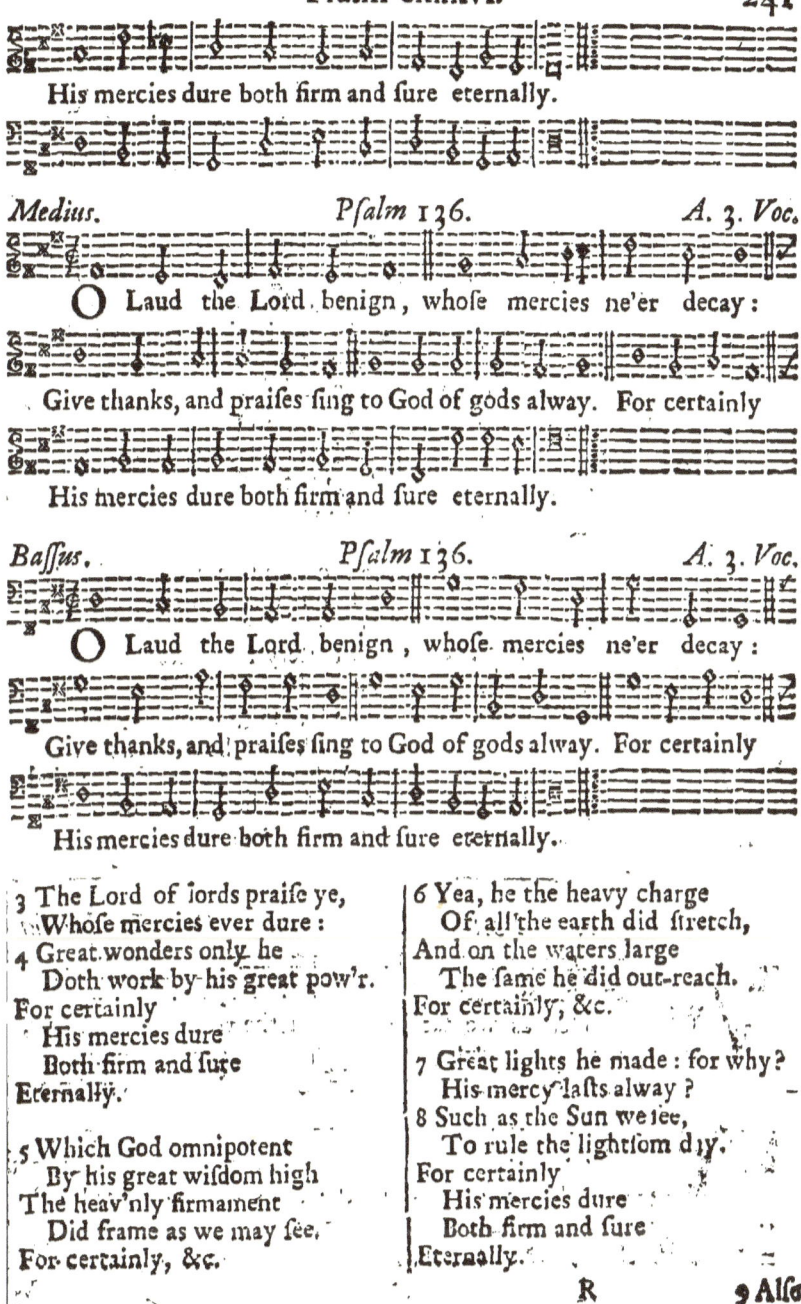

His mercies dure both firm and sure eternally.

Medius.   Psalm 136.   *A. 3. Voc.*

O Laud the Lord benign, whose mercies ne'er decay:

Give thanks, and praises sing to God of gods alway. For certainly

His mercies dure both firm and sure eternally.

Bassus.   Psalm 136.   *A. 3. Voc.*

O Laud the Lord benign, whose mercies ne'er decay:

Give thanks, and praises sing to God of gods alway. For certainly

His mercies dure both firm and sure eternally.

3 The Lord of lords praise ye,
  Whose mercies ever dure:
4 Great wonders only he
  Doth work by his great pow'r.
For certainly
  His mercies dure
  Both firm and sure
Eternally.

5 Which God omnipotent
  By his great wisdom high
The heav'nly firmament
  Did frame as we may see,
For certainly, &c.

6 Yea, he the heavy charge
  Of all the earth did stretch,
And on the waters large
  The same he did out-reach.
For certainly, &c.

7 Great lights he made: for why?
  His mercy lasts alway?
8 Such as the Sun we see,
  To rule the lightsom day.
For certainly
  His mercies dure
  Both firm and sure
Eternally.

Pſalm cxxxvi, cxxxvii.

9 Alſo the Moon ſo clear,
  Which ſhineth in our ſight,
And Stars that do appear,
  To guide the darkſom night.
For certainly, &c.

10 With grievous plagues and ſore
  All Egypt ſmote ye then:
The firſt-born leſs and more
  He ſlew of beaſts and men.
For certainly, &c.

11 And from amidſt their land
  His Iſrael forth brought:
12 Which he with mighty hand
  And ſtretched arm hath wrought.
For certainly, &c.

13 The ſea he cut in two,
  Which ſtood up like a wall:
14 And made through it to go
  His choſen children all.
For certainly, &c.

15 But there o'erwhelmed then
  The proud king Pharaoh,
With his huge hoſt of men,
  And chariots alſo.
For certainly, &c.

16 Who led through wilderneſs
  His people ſafe and ſound:

17 And for his love endleſs
  Great kings he brought to ground.
For certainly, &c.

18 And with puiſſant hand
  Slew kings of mighty fame:
19 As of Amorites land
  Sehon the king by name.
For certainly, &c.

20 And Og (the giant large)
  Of Baſan king alſo:
21 Whoſe land for heritage
  He gave his people to.
For certainly, &c.

22 Ev'n unto Iſrael
  His ſervant dear, I ſay,
He gave the ſame to dwell,
  And there abide alway.
For certainly, &c.

23 To mind he did us call
  In our moſt baſe degree:
24 And from oppreſſors all
  In ſafety ſet us free.
For certainly, &c.

25 All fleſh in earth abroad
  With food he doth fulfill:
26 Wherefore of heav'n the God
  To laud be it your will.
For certainly, &c.

Cantus & Baſſus.   Pſalm CXXXVII.   *Or to London Tune.*

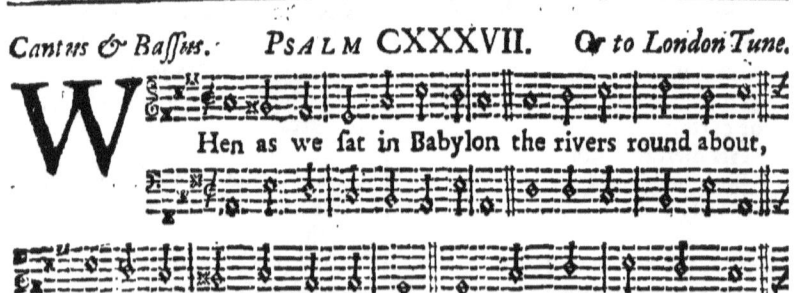

Hen as we ſat in Babylon the rivers round about,

Pſalm cxxxvii. 243

We hang'd our harps and inſtruments the willow-trees upon :

For in that place men for their uſe had planted many one.

Medius. *Pſalm 137.* *A. 3. Voc.*

WHen as we ſat in Ba—by—lon the rivers round about,

And in remembrance of Si—on the tears for grief burſt out.

We hang'd our harps and inſtruments the willow-trees upon :

For in that place men for their uſe had planted many one.

Baſſus. *Pſalm 137.* *A. 3. Voc.*

WHen as we ſat in Ba—by—lon the rivers round about,

And in remembrance of Si—on the tears for grief burſt out.

We hang'd our harps and inſtruments the willow-trees upon :

For in that place men for their uſe had planted many one.

R 2 3 Then

Psalm cxxxvii, cxxxviii.

3 Then they to whom we pris'ners
   said to us tauntingly, (were,
Now let us hear your Hebrew songs,
   and pleasant melody.
4 Alas! said we, who can once frame
   his heavy heart to sing
The praises of our loving God
   thus under a strange king?

5 But yet if I Jerusalem
   out of my heart let slide,
Then let my fingers quite forget
   the warbling harp to guide.
6 And let my tongue within my
   be ti'd for ever fast, (mouth
If that I joy before I see
   thy full deliv'rance past.

5 Therefore, O Lord, remember now
   the cursed noise and cry
That Edom's sons against us made,
   when they ras'd our City.
Remember, Lord, their cruel words,
   when as with mighty sound
They cried, Down, yea, down with it
   unto the very ground.

8 Ev'n so shalt thou, O Babylon,
   at length to dust be brought:
And happy shall that man be call'd,
   that our revenge hath wrought.
9 Yea, blessed shall that man be call'd
   that takes thy little ones,
And dasheth them in pieces small
   against the very stones.

Cantus & Bassus.   PSALM CXXXVIII.   Martyrs Tune.

Hee will I praise wth my whole heart, my L^d my God always:

Ev'n in the presence of the gods I will advance thy praise.

Medius.   Psalm 138.   A. 3. Voc.

Thee will I praise with my whole heart, my Lord my God, always:

Ev'n in the presence of the gods I will advance thy praise.

Bassus.

Psalm cxxxviii, cxxxix. 245

Bassus.   *Psalm* 138.   *A. 3. Voc.*

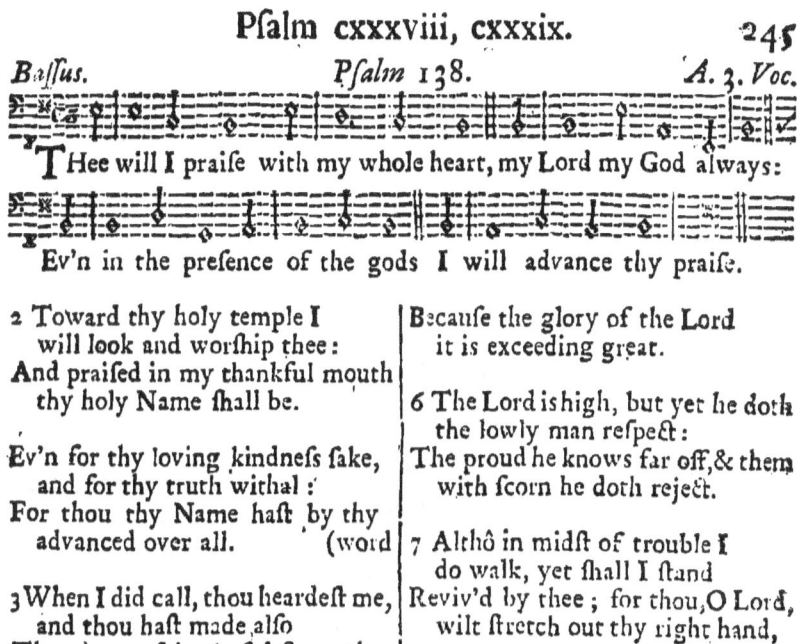

THee will I praise with my whole heart, my Lord my God always:

Ev'n in the presence of the gods I will advance thy praise.

2 Toward thy holy temple I
will look and worship thee:
And praised in my thankful mouth
thy holy Name shall be.

Ev'n for thy loving kindness sake,
and for thy truth withal:
For thou thy Name hast by thy
advanced over all.   (word

3 When I did call, thou heardest me,
and thou hast made also
The power of increased strength
within my soul to grow.
                    (shall

4 Yea, all the kings on earth they
give praise to thee, O Lord:
For they of thy most holy mouth
have heard the mighty word.

5 They of the ways of God the Lord
in singing shall entreat,

Because the glory of the Lord
it is exceeding great.

6 The Lord is high, but yet he doth
the lowly man respect:
The proud he knows far off, & them
with scorn he doth reject.

7 Altho in midst of trouble I
do walk, yet shall I stand
Reviv'd by thee; for thou, O Lord,
wilt stretch out thy right hand,

Upon the wrath of all my foes,
and saved shall I be
By thy right hand. The Lord God
perform his work to me.   (will

8 Thy mercy lasts for evermore,
Lord, do me not forsake:
Forsake me not that am the work
which thine own hand did make.

Cantus & Bassus.   P SALM CXXXIX.   *Rochester Tune,*

O Lord, thou hast me tri'd & known, my sitting down dost know,

My rising up, and thoughts far off, thou understand st al--so.

Psalm cxxxix.

Medius.   Psalm 139.   A. 3. Voc.

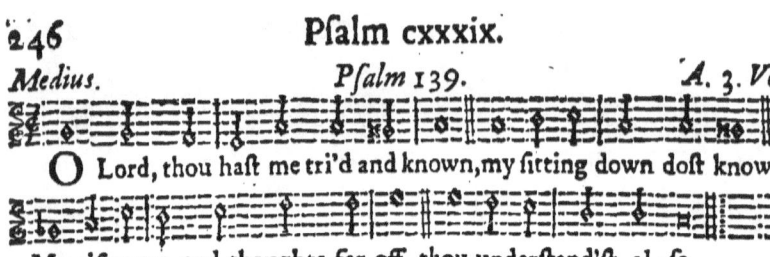

O Lord, thou hast me tri'd and known, my sitting down dost know, My rising up, and thoughts far off, thou understand'st al-so.

Bassus.   Psalm 139.   A. 3. Voc.

O Lord, thou hast me tri'd and known, my sitting down dost know, My rising up, and thoughts far off, thou understand'st al-so.

3 My paths, yea, and my lying down
  thou compassest always:
And by familiar custom art
  acquainted with my ways.

4 No word is in my tongue, O Lord,
  that is not known to thee:
5 Thou hast beset me round about,
  and laid thy hand on me.

6 Such knowledge is too wonderful,
  and past my skill to gain:
It is so high, that I unto
  the same cannot attain.

7 From sight of thy all-seeing Sp'rit,
  Lord, whither shall I go?
Or whither shall I fly away
  from thy presence also?

8 To heav'n if I do mount aloft,
  lo, thou art present there:
In hell if I lie down below,
  ev'n there thou dost appear.

9 Yea, let me take the morning wings,
  and let me go and dwell
Ev'n in the very utmost parts
  where flowing sea doth swell:

10 Yet certainly there also shall
  thy hand me lead and guide:
And thy right hand shall hold me fast,
  and make me to abide.

11 Or if I say, The darkness shall
  shroud me quite from thy sight:
Ev'n then the night that is most dark,
  about me shall be light.

12 The darkness hideth not from thee,
  but night doth shine as day:
To thee the darkness and the light
  are both alike alway.

The second part.

13 For thou possessed hast my reins,
  and thou hast cover'd me
When I within my mother's womb
  enclosed was by thee.

14 Thee will I praise, made fearfully
  and wondrously I am:
Thy works are marvellous, right well
  my soul doth know the same.

15 My bones they are not hid from thee,
  altho' in secret place
I have been made, and in the earth
  beneath I shaped was.

16 When

Psalm cxxxix, cxl. 247

16 When I was formless, then thine
faw me: for in thy book (eye
Were written all, nought was before
that after fashion took.

17 The thoughts therefore of thee, O
how dear are they to me! (God,
And of them all how passing great
the endless number be!

18 If I should count them, lo, their sum
more than the sand I see:
And whensoever I awake,
yet am I still with thee.

19 The wicked and the ungodly
most surely thou wilt slay:
Therefore now all ye bloody men,
depart from me away.

20 For they against thee, O my God,
do speak full wickedly:
They take thy Name in vain, and
great enemies to thee. (are

21 Hate I not them that hate thee, L^d,
and that in earnest wise?
Am I not grieved with all those
that up against thee rise?

22 I hate them with a perfect hate,
ev'n as my utter foes: (heart,
23 Try me, O God, and know my
my thoughts prove and disclose.

24 Consider, Lord, if wickedness
in me there any be:
And in thy ways, O God my guide,
for ever lead thou me.

Cantus & Bassus.   PSALM CXL.   *Glocefter Tune.*

LOrd, save me from the evil man, and from his pride and spight,

And from all those also which do in vi--o--lence delight.

Medius.   Psalm 140.   A. 3. Voc.

LOrd, save me from the e—vil man, and from his pride and spight,

And from all those also which do in vi--o--lence delight.

Bassus.   Psalm 140.   A. 3. Voc.

LOrd, save me from the e—vil man, and from his pride and spight,

And from all those also which do in vi--o--lence delight.

Pſalm cxl, cxli.

Which make on me continual war,
their tongues, lo, they have whet
3 Like ſerpents; underneath their
is adders poiſon ſet.   (lips

4 Keep me, O Lord, from wicked
preſerve me to abide   (hands,
Free from the cruel man,that means
to cauſe my ſteps to ſlide.

5 The proud have laid a ſnare for me,
and they have ſpread a net
With cords in my path-way, & gins
for me alſo have ſet.

6 Therefore I ſaid unto the Lord,
Thou art my God alone :
Hear me, O Lord, O hear the voice
wherewith I pray and mone.

7 O Lord my God, thou alone art
the ſtrength that ſaveth me :
My head in day of battel hath
been cover'd ſtill by thee.

8 Let not,O Lord, the wicked have
the end of his deſire :

Perform not his ill thought, leſt he
with pride be ſet on fire.

9 Of them that compaſs me about,
the chiefeſt of them all,
Lord, let the miſchief of their lips
upon their own heads fall.

10 Let coals fall on them, let them be
caſt in conſuming flame,
And in deep pit, ſo as they may
not riſe out of the ſame.

11 For no backbiter ſhall on earth
be ſet in ſtable plight :
And evil to deſtruction ſtill
ſhall hunt the cruel wight.

12 I know the Lord th'afflicted will
revenge, and judge the poor :
13 The juſt ſhall praiſe thy Name,&
dwell with thee evermore. (ſhall
    Gloria Patri.
*All Glory, Honour, Pow'r, and Praiſe,
to the Myſterious Three :
As at the firſt beginning was,
may now and ever be.*

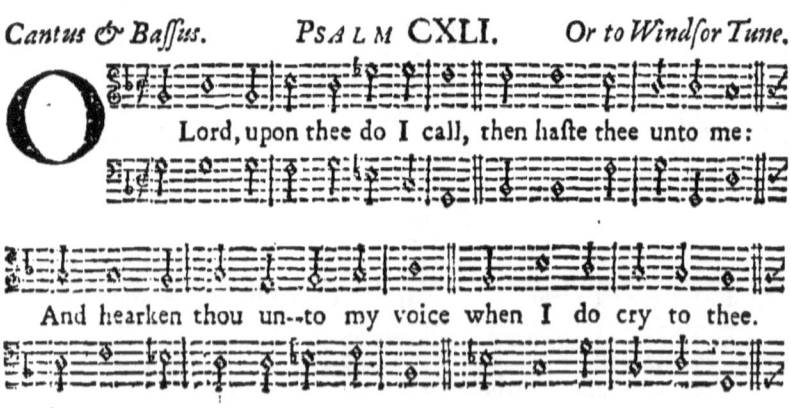

Cantus & Baſſus.   PSALM CXLI.   *Or to Windſor Tune.*

O Lord, upon thee do I call, then haſte thee unto me:

And hearken thou un--to my voice when I do cry to thee.

As

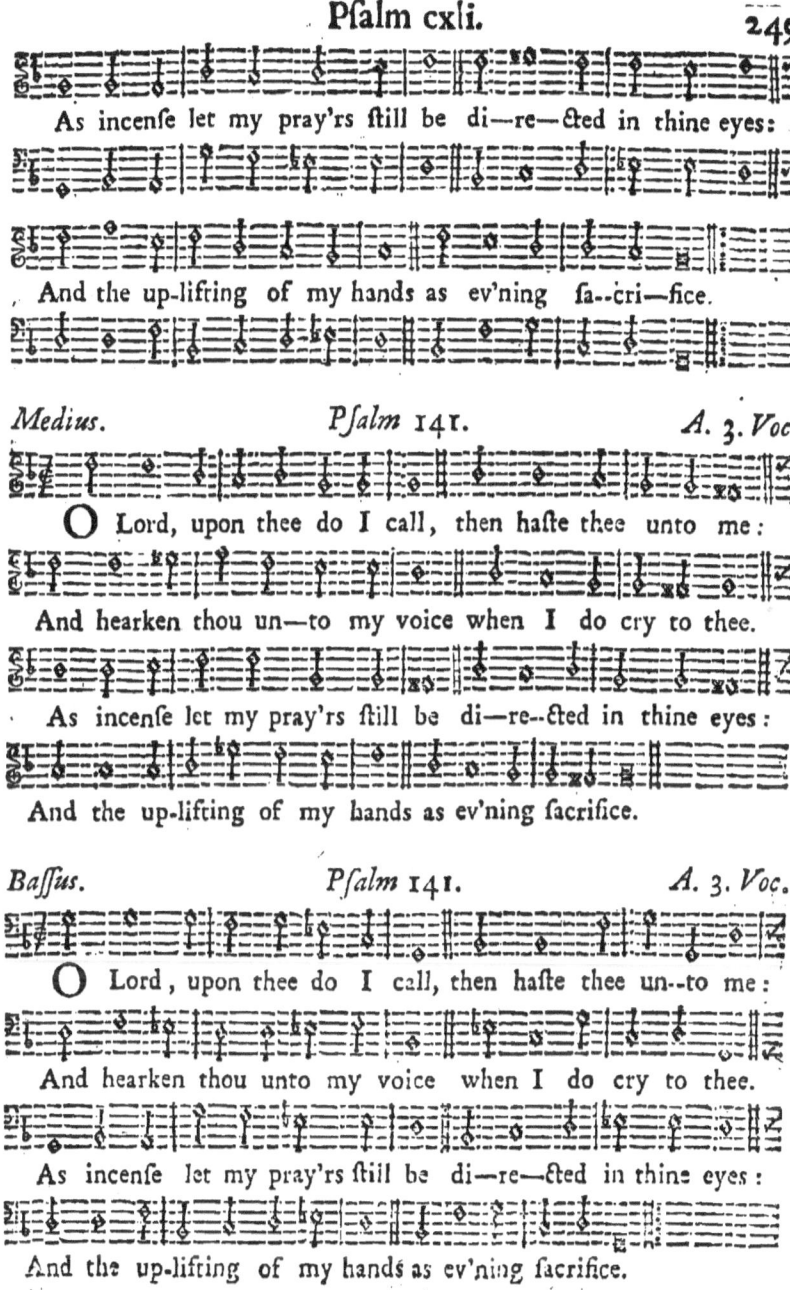

250 Pſalm cxli, cxlii.

3 For guiding of my mouth,ô Lord,
  ſet thou a watch before:
And alſo of my moving lips,
  O Lord, keep thou the door.
4 That I ſhould wicked works com-
  incline thou not mine heart: (mit,
With ill men of their delicates,
  Lord, let me eat no part.
                        (Lord,
5 But let the right'ous ſmite me,
  for that is good for me:
Let him reprove me, and the ſame
  a precious oyl ſhall be.
Such ſmiting ſhall not break my
  the time ſhall ſhortly fall, (head,
When I ſhall in their miſery
  make prayers for them all.

6 And when in ſtony places down
  their judges ſhall be caſt: (cauſe
Then ſhall they hear my words, be-
  they have a pleaſant taſte.

7 Our bones about the graves mouth
  all ſcattered and found: (are
As he that heweth wood, or he
  that diggeth up the ground.
                          (eyes
8 But, O my Lord my God, mine
  do look up unto thee:
In thee is all my truſt, let not
  my ſoul forſaken be.
9 Keep & preſerve me from the ſnare
  which they for me have laid:
And from the gins of wicked men,
  whereof I am afraid.

10 The wicked into their own nets
  together let them fall:
While I do by thy help eſcape
  the danger of them all.

To Father, Son, and Holy Ghoſt,
  immortal Glory be:
As was, is now, and ſhall be ſtill,
  to all Eternitie.

Cantus & Baſſus.   P s a l m CXLII.   *St. Mary's Tune.*

UN--to the Lord God with my voice I did ſend out my cry:

And with my ſtrained voice unto the Lord God prayed I.

Medius.   Pſalm 142.   *A. 3. Voc.*

UNto the Lord God with my voice I did ſend out my cry:

And with my ſtrained voice unto the Lord God prayed I.

Baſſus.

Psalm cxlii, cxliii. 251

Bassus.   *Psalm* 142.   *A. 3. Voc.*

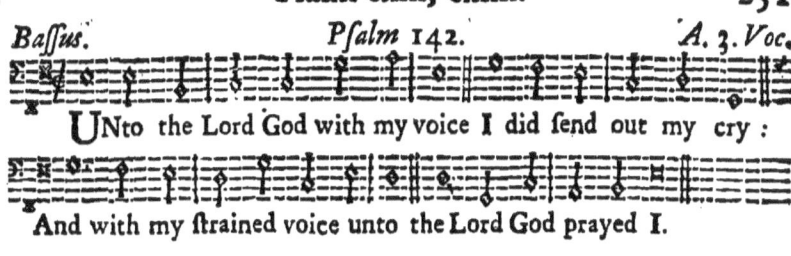

UNto the Lord God with my voice I did send out my cry:

And with my strained voice unto the Lord God prayed I.

2 My meditation in his sight
to pour I did not spare:
And in the presence of the Lord
my trouble did declare.

3 Altho perplexed was my soul,
my path was known to thee:
In way where I did walk, a snare
they slily laid for me.

                         (hand,
4 I look'd and view'd on my right
but none there would me know:
All refuge failed me, and for
my soul none cared now.

5 Then cried I to thee, and said,
O Lord, my hope thou art:
And in the land of the living,
my portion and my part.

6 Heark to my cry, for I am brought
full low, deliver me
From them that do me persecute,
for me too strong they be.

                         (soul
7 That I may praise thy Name, my
from prison, Lord, bring out:
When thou art good to me, the just
shall press me round about.

Cantus & Bassus.   PSALM CXLIII.   *Manchester Tune.*

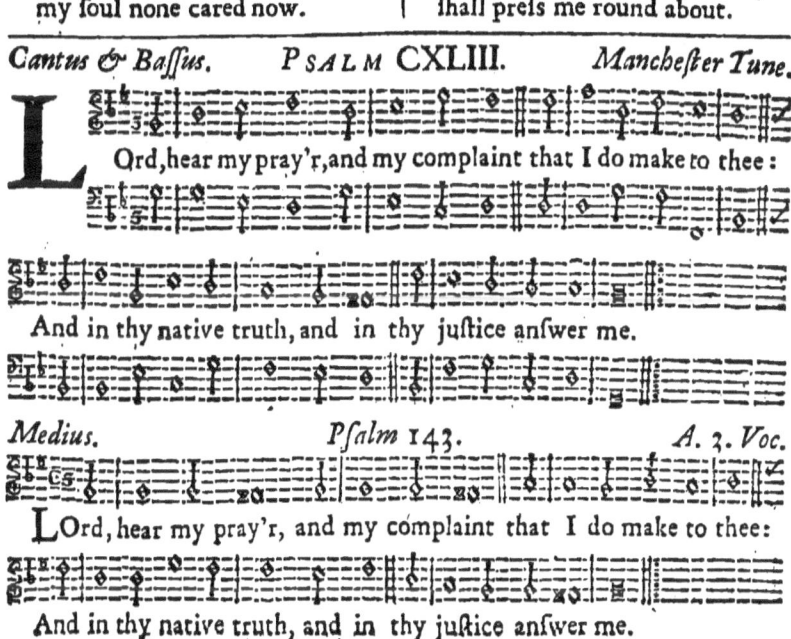

LOrd, hear my pray'r, and my complaint that I do make to thee:

And in thy native truth, and in thy justice answer me.

Medius.   *Psalm* 143.   *A. 3. Voc.*

LOrd, hear my pray'r, and my complaint that I do make to thee:

And in thy native truth, and in thy justice answer me.

Bassus.

Psalm cxliii, cxliv.

Bassus. **Psalm 143.** *A. 3. Voc.*

LOrd, hear my pray'r, and my complaint that I do make to thee:
And in thy native truth, and in thy justice answer me. 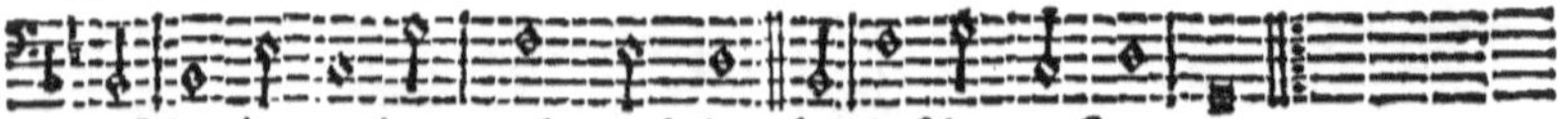

2 In judgment with thy servant, L^d,
O enter not at all:
For justifi'd be in thy sight
not one that liveth shall.

3 The enemy pursu'd my soul,
my life to ground hath thrown,
And laid me in the dark, like them
that dead are long agone.

4 Within me in perplexity
was my afflicted sp'rit:
And in me was my troubled heart
amazed and affright.

5 Yet I record time past, and on
thy works I meditate:
Yea, I do muse upon thy works
that thy hands have create.

6 To thee, O Lord my God, do I
stretch forth my craving hands:
My soul desireth after thee,
as do the thirsty lands.

7 Hear me with speed, my spirit fails,
hide not thy face, lest I

Be like to them that in the pit
sink down, and there do lie.

8 Let me thy loving kindness in
the morning hear and know,
For in thee is my trust; shew me
the way where I shall go.

9 For I lift up my soul to thee,
O Lord, deliver me
From all mine enemies: for I
have hidden me with thee.

10 Teach me to do thy will, for thou,
thou art my God alway:
Let thy good spirit to the land
of mercy me convey.

11 For thy Names sake with quickning
alive do thou me make: (grace
And out of trouble bring my soul
ev'n for thy justice sake.

12 And of thy mercy slay my foes,
O Lord, destroy them all
That do oppress my soul, for I
thy servant am, and shall.

Cantus & Bassus. **PSALM CXLIV.** *York Tune.*

BLest be the Lord my strength, that doth instruct my hands to fight:
The Lord that doth my fingers frame to battel by his might.

Psalm cxliv.

Medius.   Pſalm 144.   *A. 3. Voc.*

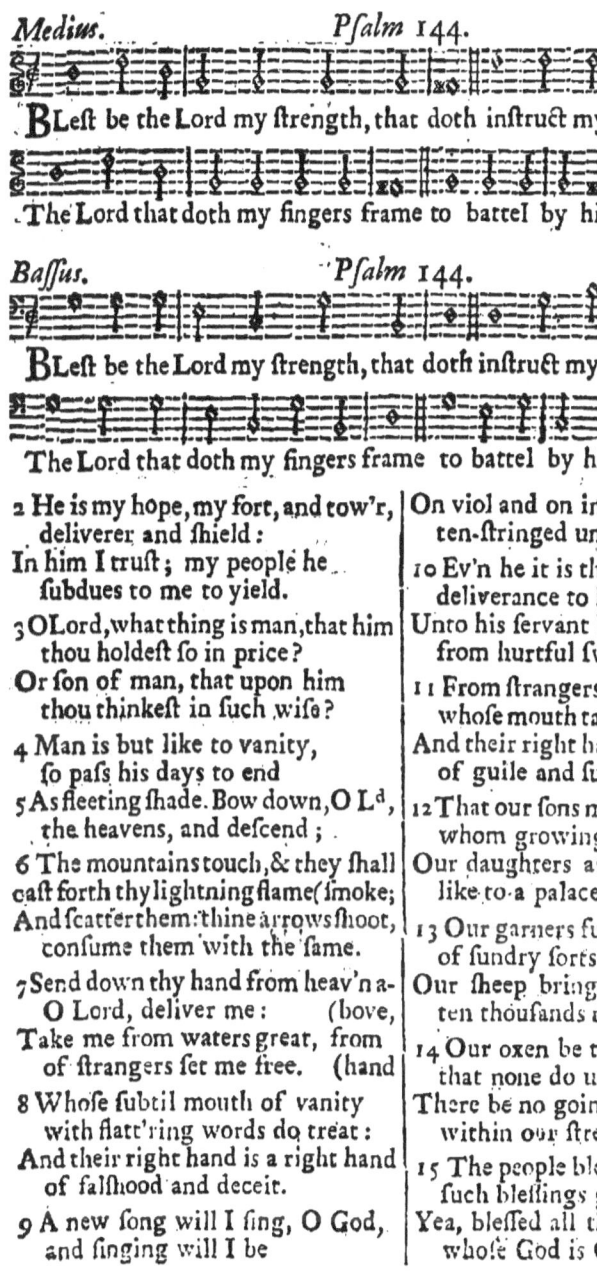

BLeſt be the Lord my ſtrength, that doth inſtruct my hands to fight:
The Lord that doth my fingers frame to battel by his might.

Baſſus.   Pſalm 144.   *A. 3. Voc.*

BLeſt be the Lord my ſtrength, that doth inſtruct my hands to fight :
The Lord that doth my fingers frame to battel by his might.

2 He is my hope, my fort, and tow'r,
   deliverer and ſhield:
In him I truſt; my people he
   ſubdues to me to yield.
3 O Lord, what thing is man, that him
   thou holdeſt ſo in price?
Or ſon of man, that upon him
   thou thinkeſt in ſuch wiſe?
4 Man is but like to vanity,
   ſo paſs his days to end
5 As fleeting ſhade. Bow down, O L^d,
   the heavens, and deſcend;
6 The mountains touch, & they ſhall
caſt forth thy lightning flame (ſmoke;
And ſcatter them: thine arrows ſhoot,
   conſume them with the ſame.
7 Send down thy hand from heav'n a-
   O Lord, deliver me: (bove,
Take me from waters great, from
   of ſtrangers ſet me free.   (hand
8 Whoſe ſubtil mouth of vanity
   with flatt'ring words do treat :
And their right hand is a right hand
   of falſhood and deceit.
9 A new ſong will I ſing, O God,
   and ſinging will I be

On viol and on inſtrument
   ten-ſtringed unto thee.
10 Ev'n he it is that only gives
   deliverance to kings:
Unto his ſervant David help
   from hurtful ſword he brings.
11 From ſtrangers hand me ſave and
   whoſe mouth talks vanity: (ſhie'ld,
And their right hand is a right hand
   of guile and ſubtilty.
12 That our ſons may be as the plants
   whom growing youth doth rear:
Our daughters as carv'd corner-
   like to a palace fair.   (ſtones,
13 Our garners full, and plenty may
   of ſundry ſorts be found : (ſtreets
Our ſheep bring thouſands, in our
   ten thouſands may abound.
14 Our oxen be to labour ſtrong,
   that none do us invade :
There be no goings out, nor cries
   within our ſtreets be made.
15 The people bleſſed are that with
   ſuch bleſſings great are ſtor'd:
Yea, bleſſed all the people are
   whoſe God is God the Lord.

PSALM

Psalm cxlv.

Bassus.   *Psalm* 145.   A. 3. *Voc.*

THee will I laud, my God and King, and bless thy Name alway:

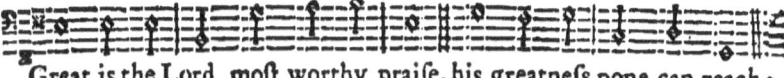

For e—ver will I praise thy Name, and bless thee day by day.

Great is the Lord, most worthy praise, his greatness none can reach:

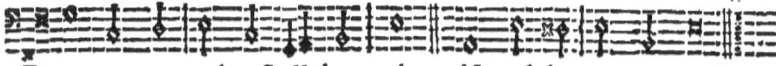

From race to race they shall thy works praise, and thy power preach.

5 I of thy glorious majesty
  thy beauty will record:
And meditate upon thy works
  most wonderful, O Lord.
6 And they shall of thy pow'r, and of
  thy fearful acts declare:
And I to publish all abroad
  thy greatness will not spare.

7 And they into the mention shall
  break of thy goodness great:
And I aloud thy right'ousness
  in singing shall repeat.
8 The Lord our God is gracious,
  and merciful also:
Of great abounding mercy, and
  to anger he is slow:

9 Yea, good to all; and all his works
  his mercy doth exceed:
10 Lo, all thy works do praise thee, L^d,
  and do thy honour spread.
11 Thy saints do bless thee, & they do
  thy kingdom's glory show:
12 And blaze thy pow'r, to cause the (sons
  of men thy pow'r to know.

The second part.
And of his kingdom's majesty
  to spread the glorious praise.
13 Thy kingdom, Lord, a kingdom is
  that doth endure always:
And thy dominion through each age
  endures without decay.
14 The Lord upholdeth them that
  their sliding he doth stay. (fall,

15 The eyes of all do wait on thee,
  thou dost them all relieve:
And thou to each sufficing food
  in season due dost give.
16 Thou openest thy plenteous hand,
  and bounteously dost fill
All things whatever that do live,
  with gifts of thy good will.

17 The Lord is just in all his ways,
  his works are holy all:
18 And he is near all those that do
  in truth upon him call.
19 He the desires which they require
  that fear him will fulfil:
And he will hear them when they
  and save them all he will. (cry,

Psalm cxlv, cxlvi.

        (him | (speak
20 The Lord preserves all those to | 21 My thankful mouth shall gladly
 that bear a loving heart: | the praises of the Lord:
But he them all that wicked are | All flesh to praise his holy Name
 will utterly subvert. | for ever shall accord.

Cantus & Bassus.   PSALM CXLVI.   *Canterbury Tune.*

MY soul, praise thou the L^d always, my God I will confess:
While breath and life prolong my days, my tongue no time shall cease.

Medius.   Psalm 146.   *A. 3. Voc.*

MY soul, praise thou the Lord always, my God I will confess:
While breath and life prolong my days, my tongue no time shall cease.

Bassus.   Psalm 146.   *A. 3. Voc.*

MY soul, praise thou the Lord always, my God I will confess:
While breath and life prolong my days, my tongue no time shall cease.

      (then, | (depart,
3 Trust not in worldly princes | 4 For why? their breath doth soon
 tho they abound in wealth: | to earth anon they fall:
Nor in the sons of mortal men, | And then the counsels of their heart
 in whom there is no health. | decay and perish all.

              5 Blessed

Pſalm cxlvi, cxlvii. 257

5 Bleſſed, and happy is that (man,)
whom Jacob's God doth aid:
And he whoſe hope doth not decay,
but on the Lord is ſtay'd.

6 Who made the earth and waters (deep,)
the heavens high withal:
Which doth his word and promiſe
in truth, and ever ſhall. (keep)

7 With right always doth he proceed
for ſuch as ſuffer wrong:
The poor and hungry he doth feed,
and looſe the fetters ſtrong.

8 The Lord doth ſend the blind their (ſight,)
the lame to limbs reſtore:
And he doth love the righteous,
and juſt man evermore.

9 He doth defend the fatherleſs,
and ſtranger ſad in heart:
And quit the widow from diſtreſs,
and ill men's ways ſubvert.

10 Thy Lord and God eternally,
O Sion, ſtill ſhall reign,
In time of all poſterity
for ever to remain.

Cantus & Baſſus.   PSALM CXLVII.   *St. David's Tune.*

PRaiſe ye the Lord, for it is good unto our God to ſing:
For it is pleaſant, and to praiſe it is a comely thing.

Medius.   Pſalm 147.   *A. 3. Voc.*

PRaiſe ye the Lord, for it is good un—to our God to ſing:
For it is pleaſant, and to praiſe it is a comely thing.

S   *Baſſus.*

Bassus. Psalm 147. A. 3. Voc.

Praise ye the Lord, for it is good un—to our God to sing:

For it is pleasant, and to praise it is a comely thing.

2 The Lord his own Jerusalem
  he buildeth up alone:
And the dispers'd of Israel
  doth gather into one.

3 He heals the broken in their heart,
  their sores up doth he bind:
4 He counts the number of the stars,
  and names them in their kind.
            (pow'r,
5 Great is the Lord, great is his
  his wisdom infinite.   (throws
6 The Lord relieves the meek, and
  to ground the wicked wight.
            (praise,
7 Sing unto God the Lord with
  unto the Lord rejoyce:
And to our God upon the harp
  advance your singing voice.
            (for
8 He covers heav'n with clouds, and
  the earth prepareth rain:
And on the mountains he doth make
  the grass to grow again.

9 He gives to beasts their food,
  young Ravens wh—   ,and to
10 His pleas—   en they cry:
         e not in strenth of horse,
  nor in man's legs doth lie.

11 But in all those that fear the Lord,
  the Lord hath his delight,
And such as do attend upon
  his mercies shining light.

The second part.
12 O praise the Lord, Jerusalem,
  thy God, O Sion, praise:
13 For he the bars hath forged strong,
  wherewith thy gates he stays.

14 Thy children he hath blest in thee,
  and in thy borders he
Doth settle peace, and with the flour
  of wheat he filleth thee.

15 And his commandement upon
  the earth he sendeth out:
Also his word with speedy course
  doth swiftly run about.

16 He giveth snow like wooll, & frost
  like ashes scatt'reth wide:
17 Like morsels casts his ice, thereof
  the cold who can abide?

18 He sendeth forth his mighty word,
  and melteth them again:
His wind he makes to blow, and then
  the waters flow amain.

19 The doctrine of his holy word
  to Jacob he doth show:
His statutes and his judgments he
  gives Israel to know.

20 With ev'ry nation he hath not
  so dealt, nor have they known
His secret judgments; ye therefore
  praise ye the Lord alone.

PSALM

Pſalm cxlviii. 259

Psalm cxlviii.

3 Praise him both moon and sun,
  Which are so clear and bright:
The same of you be done,
  Ye glistring stars of light:
4 And you no less,
  Ye heavens fair,
  And clouds of th' air,
His laud express.

5 For at his word they were
  All formed as we see:
At his voice did appear
  All things in their degree,
6 Which he set fast;
  To them he made
  A law and trade
Always to last.

7 Extol and praise God's Name
  On earth ye dragon's fell:
All deeps do ye the same,
  For it becomes ye well.
8 Him magnifie,
  Fire, hail, ice, snow,
  And storms that blow
At his decree.

9 The hills and mountains all,
  And trees that fruitful are,
The cedars great and tall,
  His worthy praise declare.
10 Beasts and cattel,
  Yea, birds flying,
  And worms creeping,
That on earth dwell.

11 All kings both more and less,
  With all their pompous train,
Princes and all judges
  That in the world remain,
Exalt his Name.
12 Young men and maids,
  Old men and babes,
Do ye the same.

13 For his Name shall we prove
  To be most excellent,
Whose praise is far above
  The earth and firmament.
14 For sure he shall
  Exalt with bliss
  The horn of his,
And help them all.

15 His saints all shall forthtell
  His praise and worthiness,
The children of Isr'el
  Each one both more and less:
16 And also they
  That with good will
  His words fulfil,
And him obey.

Gloria Patri.

Unto the Three in One,
  That bear Record above,
The Father, and the Son,
  And Holy Sp'rit of Love,
Be Glory high:
  As first begun,
  So shall be done
Eternally.

Pſalm cxlix.

2 Let Iſrael rejoyce in him
that made him of nothing:
And let the Children of Sion
be joyful in their King.
3 Let them ſound praiſe with voice
unto his holy Name: (lute
And with the timbrel and the harp
ſing praiſes to the ſame.
4 For why? the Lord his pleaſure all
hath in his people ſet:
And by deliv'rance he will raiſe
the meek to glory great.
5 With glory and with honour now
let all his ſaints rejoyce:

And now aloud upon their beds-
advance their ſinging voice.
6 And in their mouths let be the high
praiſes of God the Lord:
And in their hands likewiſe a ſharp
and double-edged ſword;
7 To plague the heathen, and correct
the people with their hands:
To bind their ſtately kings in chains,
their lords in iron bands:
8 To execute on them the doom
that written was before,
This honour all his ſaints ſhall have:
Praiſe ye the Lord therefore.

S 3   PSALM

2 Advance his Name, and praise him
   his mighty acts always:
According to his excellence
   and greatness give him praise.

3 His praises with the princely noise
   of sounding trumpets blow:
Praise him upon the viol, and
   upon the harp also.

                 (in
4 Praise him with timbrel and with
   organs and virginals: (him,
5 With sounding cymbals praise ye
   praise him with loud cymbals.

6 Whatever hath the benefit
   of breathing praise the Lord:
To praise his great & mighty Name,
   agree with one accord.

The End of the Psalms of David *in Metre.*

The

The Divine Hymns.

Cant. & Baſſ. At Conſecration of Prieſts. *Or to 100 Pſ.Tune.*

Come Holy Ghoſt, our Souls inſpire, & lighten wᵗʰ celeſtial fire!

Thou the Anointing Spirit art, who doſt thy ſev'nfold Gifts impart.

Medius. Hymn. *A. 3. Voc.*

Come Holy Ghoſt, our Souls inſpire, and lighten with celeſtial fire!

Thou the Anointing Spirit art, who doſt thy ſev'nfold Gifts impart.

Baſſus. Hymn. *A. 3. Voc.*

Come Holy Ghoſt, our Souls inſpire, and lighten with celeſtial fire!

Thou the Anointing Spirit art, who doſt thy ſev'nfold Gifts impart.

Thy bleſſed Unction from above
Is Comfort, Life, and Fire of Love:
Enable with perpetual light,
The dulneſs of our blinded ſight.
Anoint and cheer our ſoiled face
With the abundance of Thy Grace.
Keep far our foes, keep peace at home;
Wher Thou art guide, no ill can come.

Teach us to know the Father, Son,
And Thee, of both to be but One;
That through the Ages all along,
This ſtill may be our endleſs Song:
Praiſe to Thy Eternal Merit,
Father, Son, and Holy Spirit:
Hallelujah, Hallelujah,
Hallelujah, Hallelujah.

S 4 Veni

(264)

Cantus & Bassus.   Veni Creator.   Or to 119 *Ps. Tune.*

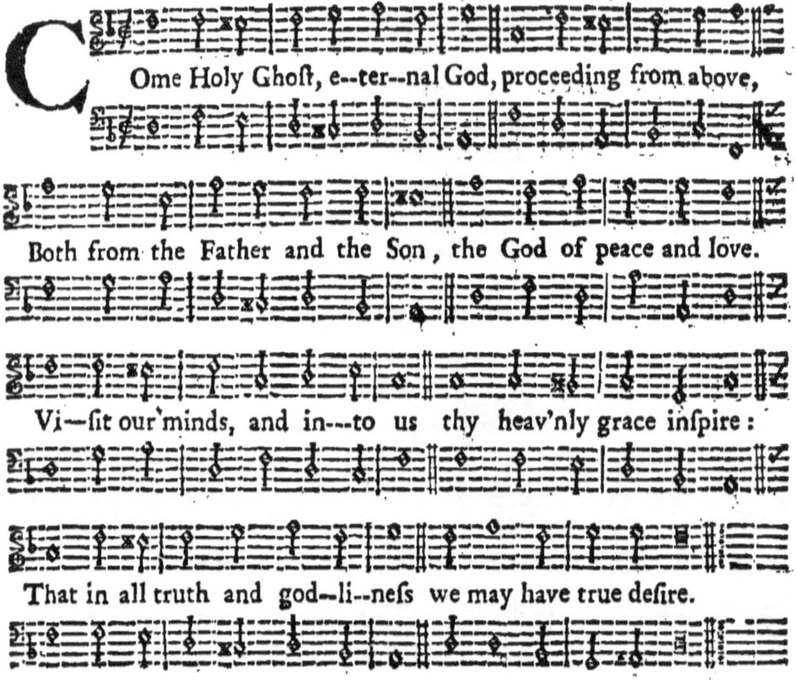

COme Holy Ghoſt, e--ter--nal God, proceeding from above,

Both from the Father and the Son, the God of peace and love.

Vi—ſit our minds, and in---to us thy heav'nly grace inſpire:

That in all truth and god--li--neſs we may have true deſire.

Medius.   Veni Creator.   *A. 3. Voc.*

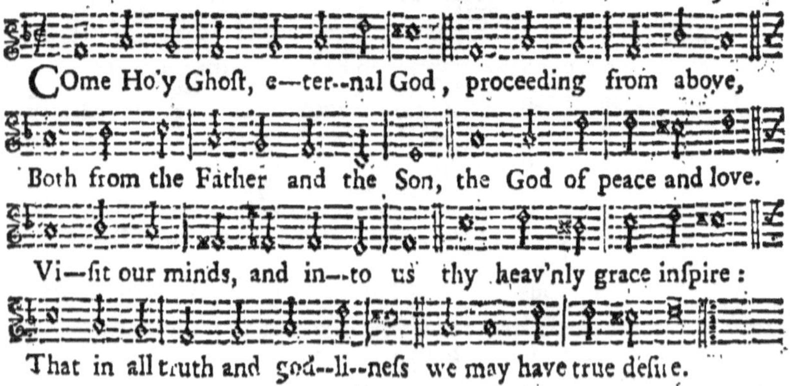

COme Holy Ghoſt, e---ter--nal God, proceeding from above,

Both from the Father and the Son, the God of peace and love.

Vi—ſit our minds, and in--to us thy heav'nly grace inſpire:

That in all truth and god--li--neſs we may have true deſire.

Baſſus.

(265)

Bassus.   Veni Creator.   A. 3. Voc.

COme Holy Ghost, e--ter--nal God, proceeding from above,

Both from the Father and the Son, the God of peace and love.

Vi—sit our minds, and in---to us thy heav'nly grace inspire:

That in all truth and god--li---ness we may have true desire.

Thou art the very Comforter
  in all wo and distress:
The heav'nly gift of God most high,
  which no tongue can express:
The fountain and the lively spring
  of joy celestial:
The fire so bright, the love so clear,
  and unction spiritual.
Thou in thy gifts art manifold,
  whereby Christ's Church doth stand:
In faithful hearts writing thy law,
  the finger of God's hand.
According to thy promise made,
  thou givest speech of grace:
That thrô thy help the praise of God
  may stand in ev'ry place.
O Holy Ghost, into our souls
  send down thy Heav'nly light:
Kindle our hearts with fervent love
  to serve God day and night.
Strengthen & stablish our weakness,
  so feeble and so frail:
That neither devil, world, nor flesh,
  against us may prevail.
Our enemies put far from us,
  and grant us to obtain
Peace in our hearts with God & man,
  without grudge or disdain.

And grant, O Lord, that thou being
  our leader and our guide,
We may eschew the snares of sin,
  and from thee never slide.
To us such plenty of thy grace,
  good Lord, grant we thee pray,
That thou may'st be our Comforter
  at the last dreadful day.
Of all strife and dissention,
  O Lord, dissolve the bands:
Make fast the knots of peace & love
  throughout all Christian lands.
Grant us, O Lord, thrô thee to know
  the father most of might:
That of his dear beloved Son
  we may attain the sight:
And that with perfect faith also
  we may acknowledge thee,
The Spirit of them both alway
  one God in Persons three.
All laud and praise to the Father,
  and to the Son equal,
And to the Holy Ghost also,
  one God coeternal.
And pray we that the only Son
  vouchsafe his Sp'rit to send
To all that do profess his Name,
  ev'n unto the world's end.

Te

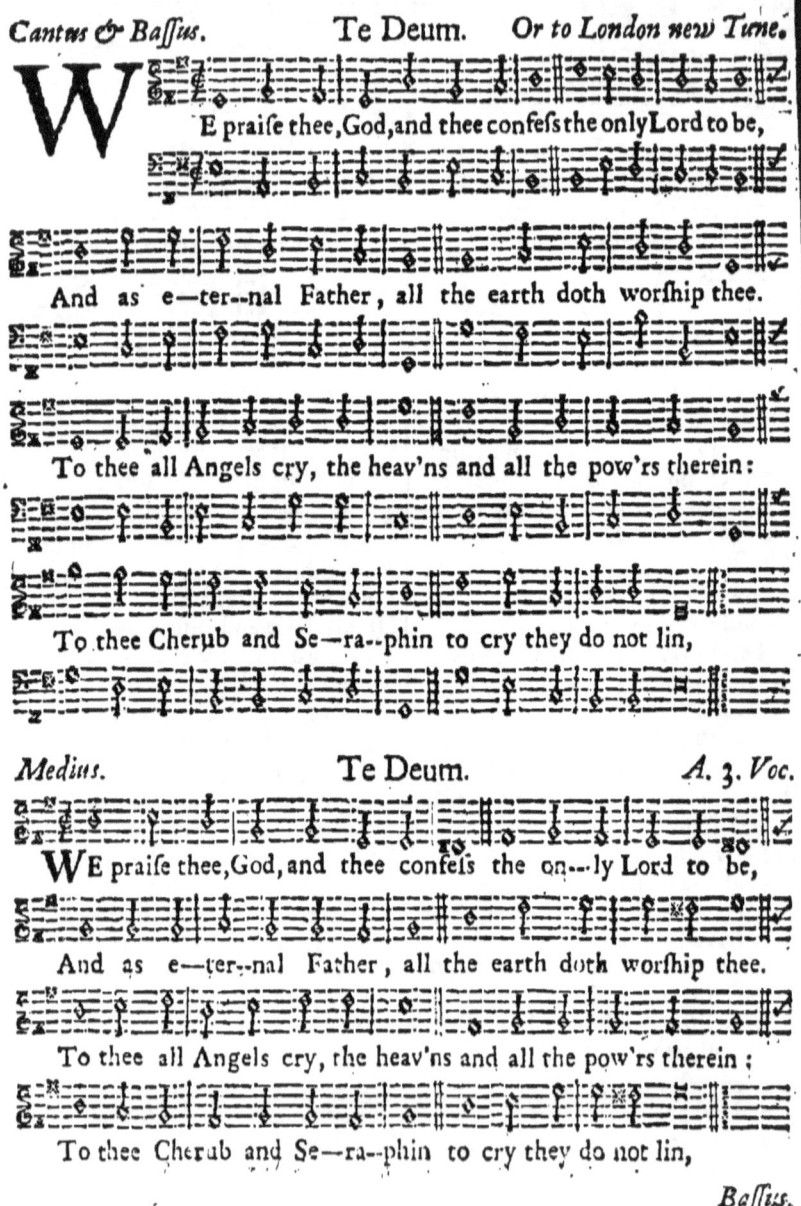

(267)

Bassus.   Te Deum.   *A.* 3. *Voc.*

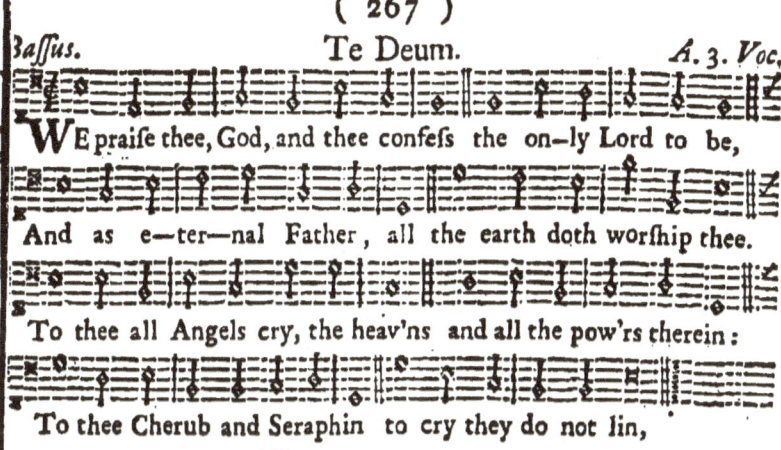

WE praise thee, God, and thee confess the on—ly Lord to be,

And as e—ter—nal Father, all the earth doth worship thee.

To thee all Angels cry, the heav'ns and all the pow'rs therein:

To thee Cherub and Seraphin to cry they do not lin,

O holy, holy, holy Lord,
  of Sabbath Lord the God;
Through heav'n & earth thy praise
  and glory all abroad is spread,
Th' Apostles glorious company
  yield praises unto thee:
The Prophets goodly fellowship
  praise thee continually.
The noble and victorious host
  of Martyrs found thy praise:
The holy Church thrô-out the world
  acknowledge thee always.
Father of endless Majesty
  they do acknowledge thee:
Thy Christ thine honourable, true,
  and only Son to be,
The holy Ghost the Comforter;
  of glory thou art King,
O Christ, and of the Father art
  the Son everlasting.
When sinful man's decay in hand
  thou tookest to restore,
To be inclos'd in virgin's womb
  thou diddest not abhor.
When thou hadst overcome of death
  the sharp and cruel might,
Then heav'ns kingdom didst open
  to each believing wight.   (let

In glory of the Father thou
  dost sit on God's right hand:
We trust that thou shalt come our
  our cause to understand. (Judge,
L^d, help thy servants whom thou hast
  bought with thy precious blood,
And in eternal glory set
  them with thy saints so good.
O Lord, do thou thy people save,
  bless thine inheritance:
Lord, govern them, and also do
  for ever them advance.
We magnifie thee day by day,
  and world without an end
Adore thy holy Name: O Lord,
  vouchsafe us to defend
From sin this day: have mercy, L^d,
  have mercy on us all:
And on us, as we trust in thee,
  Lord, let thy mercy fall.
O Lord, I have reposed all
  my confidence in thee:
Therfore let no confounding shame
  my portion ever be.
All Glory, Honour, Pow'r, and Praise,
  to the Mysterious Three;
As at the first beginning was,
  may now and ever be.

Bene-

(263)

Cantus & Bassus.   Benedictus.   *Or to Martyrs Tune.*

THE only Lord of Is--ra--el be praised e--ver--more:

For through his vi--si--ta--ti--on and mercy kept in store,

His people now he hath redeem'd that long have been in thrall;

And spread abroad his saving health upon his servants all.

Medius.   Benedictus.   *A. 3. Voc.*

THE only Lord of Is--ra--el be praised e--ver--more:

For through his vi--si--ta--ti--on and mercy kept in store,

His people now he hath redeem'd that long have been in thrall:

And spread abroad his saving health upon his servants all.

Bassus.

(269)
Benedictus. *A. 3. Voc.*

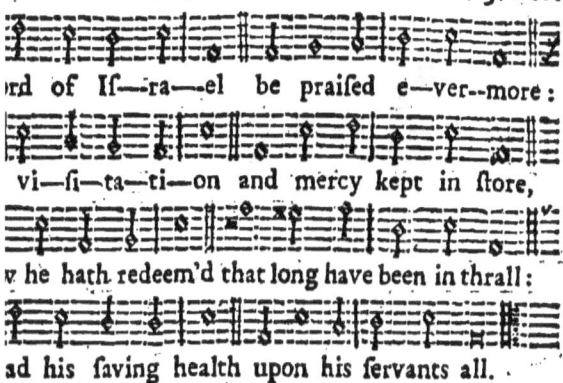

rd of If—ra—el be praifed e—ver--more:

vi—fi—ta—ti—on and mercy kept in ftore,

v he hath redeem'd that long have been in thrall:

ad his faving health upon his fervants all.

fervant true,	And that without all kind of fear,
ind,	alfo in right'oufnefs:
d King,	And alfo for to lead our lives
e find.	in fteadfaft holinefs. (born,
iets all	And thou, O child, which now art
eclare,	and of the Lord elect,
e the world be-	Shalt be the Prophet of the High'ft,
epare. (gan,	his ways for to direct.

elivered	For thou fhalt go before his face
ake debate,	for to prepare his ways,
m the hands	And alfo for to teach his will
late.	and pleafure all thy days.
e promifed	To give them knowledge how that
fil,	Salvation is near: (their
cov'nant made	And that remiffion of their fins
vill.	is through his mercy dear.

the oath	Whereby the day-fpring from on
iad fworn	is come us to vifit, (high
ther dear,	And thofe for to illuminate
orlorn:	which do in darknefs fit.
himfelf for us,	To lighten thofe that fhadow'd be
age bring	with death, and are oppreft:
f all our foes,	And alfo for to guide our feet
nly King.	the way to peace and reft.

Magni-

(270)

Cantus & Bassus.   Magnificat.   *Or to St. David's Tune.*

MY soul doth magnifie the Lord, my spirit evermore

Rejoyceth in the Lord my God, which is my Sa—vi—our.

And why? because he did regard, and gave respect unto

The low estate of his handmaid, and let the mighty go.

Medius.   Magnificat.   *A. 3. Voc.*

MY soul doth mag—ni—fie the Lord, my spi—rit e—ver-more

Rejoyceth in the Lord my God, which is my Sa—vi—our.

And why? because he did regard, and gave respect unto

The low estate of his handmaid, and let the mighty go.

Bassus.

(271)

Bassus.   Magnificat.   *A. 3. Voc.*

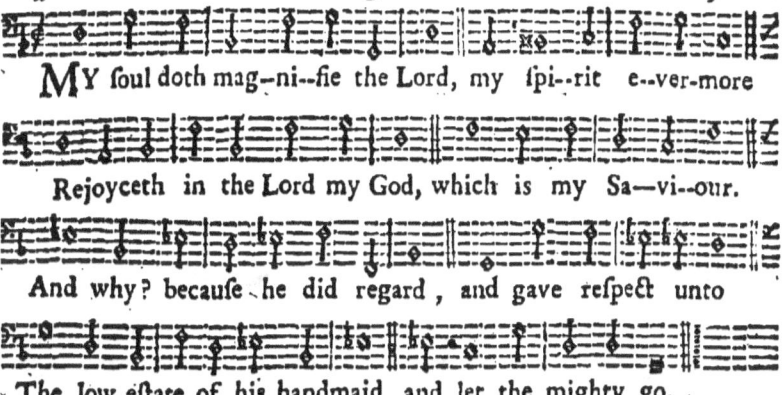

My soul doth mag-ni--fie the Lord, my spi--rit e--ver-more

Rejoyceth in the Lord my God, which is my Sa—vi--our.

And why? because he did regard, and gave respect unto

The low estate of his handmaid, and let the mighty go.

For now behold, all nations
and generations all,
From this time forth for evermore
shall me right blessed call:
Because he hath me magnifi'd,
which is the Lord of might;
Whose Name be ever sanctifi'd,
and praised day and night.

For with his mercy and his grace
all men he doth inflame,
Throughout all generations
to such as fear his Name.
He shewed strength with his great (arm,
and made the proud to start,
With all imaginations
that they bear in their heart.

He hath put down the mighty ones
from their supernal seat,
And did exalt the meek in heart
as he hath thought it meet.
The hungry he replenished
with all things that were good,
And thrô his pow'r he made the rich
oft-times to want their food.

And calling to remembrance his
great mercy very well,
Hath holpen up assistantly
his servant Israel.
According to his promise made
to Abraham before,
And to his seed successively,
to stand for evermore.

Nunc

(272)

(273)

Bassus.   Nunc Dimittis.   *A. 3. Voc.*

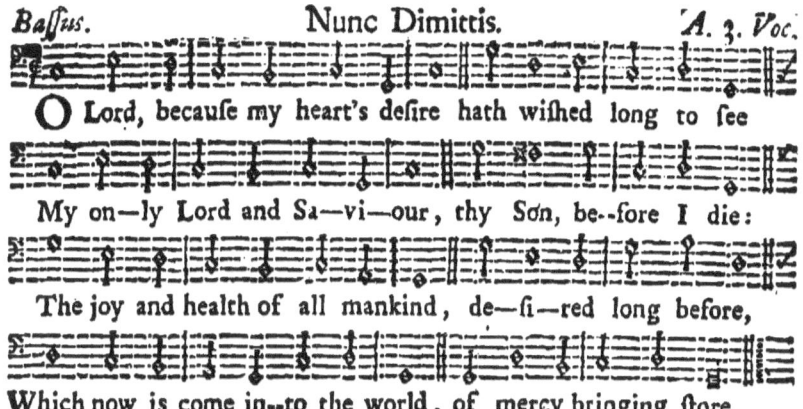

O Lord, becaufe my heart's defire hath wifhed long to fee

My on—ly Lord and Sa—vi—our, thy Son, be--fore I die:

The joy and health of all mankind, de—fi—red long before,

Which now is come in--to the world, of mercy bringing ftore.

Thou fuffereft thy fervant now	Whom thou haft mercifully fet,
in peace for to depart,	of thine abundant grace,
According to thy holy Word,	In open fight and vifible
which lighteneth my heart.	before all people's face,
Becaufe mine eyes which thou haft	The Gentiles to illuminate,
to give my body light, (made	and Satan over-quell;
Have now beheld thy faving health,	Alfo to be the glory of
which is the Lord of might.	thy people Ifrael.

Cantus & Bassus.   The LORD's Prayer.   112 *Pf. Tune.*

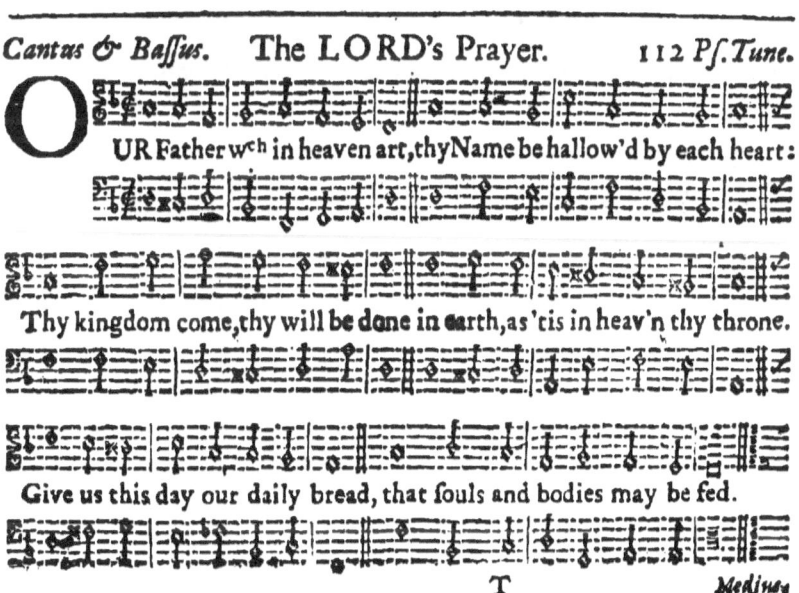

OUR Father wch in heaven art, thy Name be hallow'd by each heart:

Thy kingdom come, thy will be done in earth, as 'tis in heav'n thy throne.

Give us this day our daily bread, that fouls and bodies may be fed.

T   *Medius*

(274)

Medius.   The LORD's Prayer.   *A. 3. Voc.*

OUR Father which in heaven art, thy Name be hallow'd by each heart:

Thy kingdom come, thy will be done in earth, as 'tis in heav'n thy throne.

Give us this day our daily bread, that souls and bodies may be fed.

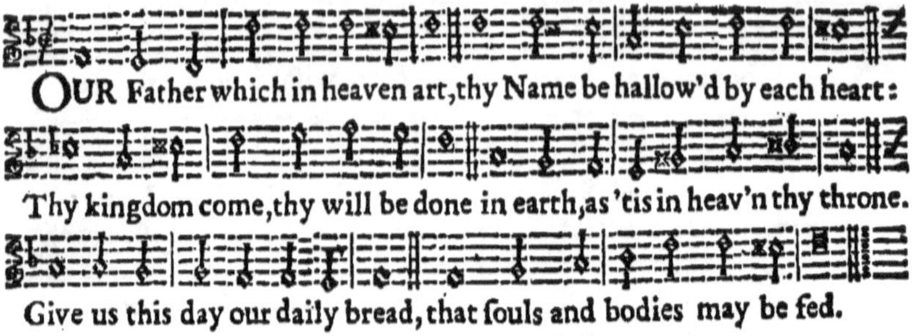

Bassus.   The LORD's Prayer.   *A. 3. Voc.*

OUR Father which in heaven art, thy Name be hallow'd by each heart:

Thy kingdom come, thy will be done in earth, as 'tis in heav'n thy throne.

Give us this day our daily bread, that souls and bodies may be fed.

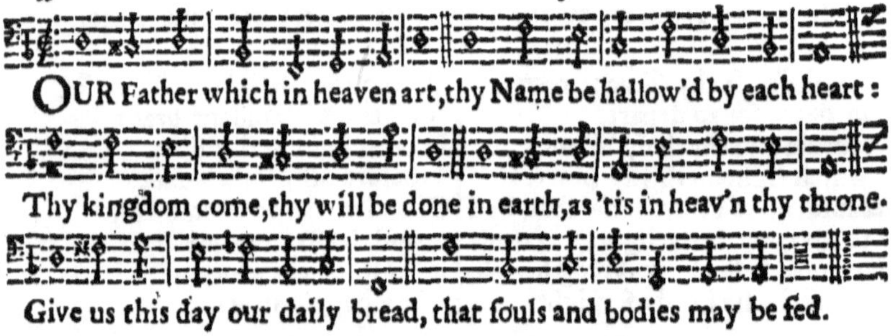

Forgive our trespasses, as we | But us deliver from all ill:
Forgive them where we trespass'd be: | For thine the kingdom, & the pow'r,
To no temptation lead our will, | And glory is for evermore.

Cantus & Bassus.   The Creed.   *St. Mary's Tune.*

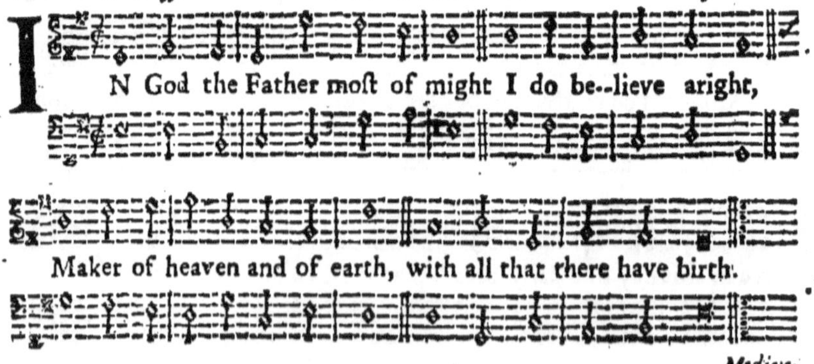

IN God the Father most of might I do be--lieve aright,

Maker of heaven and of earth, with all that there have birth.

(275)

Medius.   The Creed.   *A. 3. Voc.*

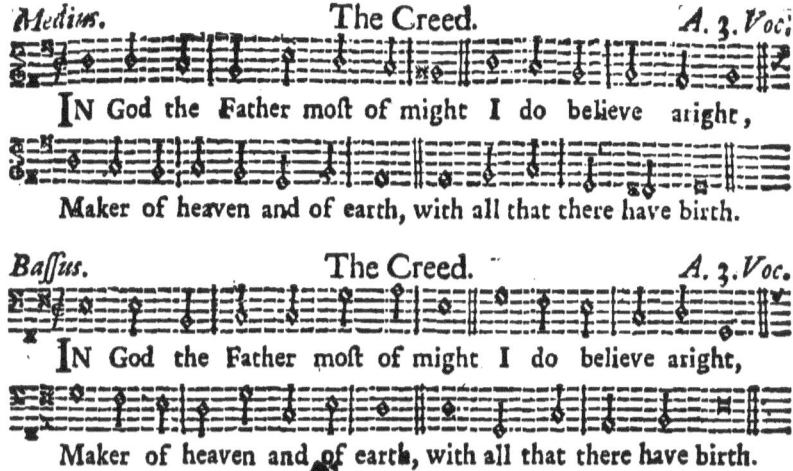

IN God the Father most of might I do believe aright,

Maker of heaven and of earth, with all that there have birth.

Bassus.   The Creed.   *A. 3. Voc.*

IN God the Father most of might I do believe aright,

Maker of heaven and of earth, with all that there have birth.

And Jesus Christ his only Son,
Whose pure conception
Did by the Holy Spirit come,
Born in the Virgin's womb.
He under Pilate crucifi'd,
Suffer'd for us, and di'd,
Was buri'd, went to hell beneath:
The third day rose from death:
He into heaven did ascend,
And sits at God's right hand:

From thence he shal come down with
To judge both quick & dead: (dread
I in the Holy Ghost believe:
The Cath'lick Church receive,
The Saints in one communion join'd:
That sins forgiveness find:
That these our bodies from the
A Resurrection have: (grave
And shall enjoy a life of bliss,
Which everlasting is.

Cant. & Bass.   The Ten Commandments.   *Or to* 100 *Ps. Tune.*

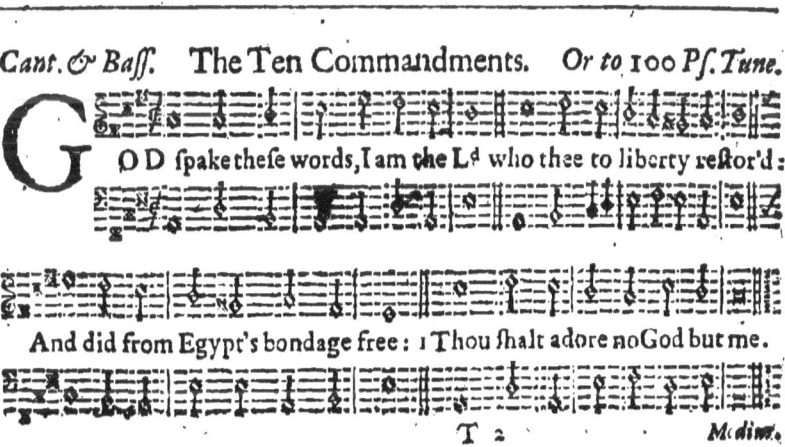

G OD spake these words, I am the L^d who thee to liberty restor'd:

And did from Egypt's bondage free: 1 Thou shalt adore no God but me.

T 2   *Medius.*

(276)

Medius.   The Ten Commandments.   *A. 3. Voc.*

GOD spake these words, I am the Lord who thee to liberty restor'd:

And did from Egypt's bondage free: 1 Thou shalt adore no God but me.

Bassus.   The Ten Commandments.   *A. 3. Voc.*

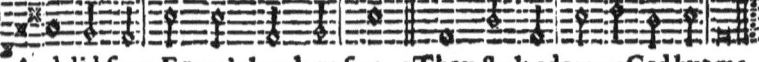

GOD spake these words, I am the Lord who thee to liberty restor'd:

And did from Egypt's bondage free: 1 Thou shalt adore no God but me.

2 Thou shalt no graven Image make,
Nor any other likeness take,
In heav'n or earth, or seas below,
To wch thou may'st fall down & bow.

For jealous of mine honour, I
Unto the fourth posterity
Visit the children for the sin
Which hath by Father's acted been.

Yet I my mercies heap in store
For thousand generations more
Of them that love me, whose intents
Walk after my commandements.

3 Thou shalt by swearing not profane
Nor take thy Maker's Name in vain;
For God will no man guiltless deem,
Who doth his sacred Name blasphem.

4 Remember that to rest and pray
Thou holy keep the Sabbath-day :
Six days thou labour shalt, but this
The Lord thy God's high Sabbath is:

No kind of work shall then be done
By thee, thy daughter, or thy son;

Nor servants, cattle, nor the late
Admitted stranger to thy gate.

For God in six days all things made,
And resting on the seventh stay'd :
The Sabbath-day he therefore blest,
Appointing it a Day of Rest.

5 Honour thy Parents, and obey
What just commands soe'er they lay,
That in the land thou longmaist live,
W^{ch} God doth for thy dwelling give.

6 From bloody Acts and Murder fly.
7 Commit no foul Adultery.
8 Thou shalt not steal. 9 Nor any where
False witness 'gainst thy Neibor bear.
(strife,
10 Thou shalt not, mov'd by lust or
Covet thy Neighbour's house or wife,
Nor man, nor maid, nor oxe of his,
Nor what to him belonging is.

The PRAYER.

THe Sp'rit of grace grant us, O L^d,
To keep these laws our hearts restore:
And cause us all with one accord
To magnifie thy Name therefore.

For

(277)

For of our selves no strength we have	Of thee to speed how should we miss,
To keep these laws after thy will:	In whom our treasure doth consist?
Thy might therfore, ô Christ, we crave	
That we in thee may them fulfil.	To thee for evermore be praise,
(this,	With the Father in each respect,
Lord, for thy Name's sake grant us	And with the Holy Sp'rit always,
Thou art our strength, ô Savior Christ:	The comforter of thine Elect.

The SONG of the Three Holy Children, *Shadrach, Meshach,* and *Abednego,* which were cast bound into the midst of the hot fiery Furnace by Command of King *Nebuchad-nezzar.*

Cantus & Bassus. *Proper Tune.*

O All ye works of God the Lord, bless ye the Lord;
Praise him, and magnifie him for ever.

Medius, Benedicite. *A. 3. Voc.*

O All ye works of God the Lord, bless ye the Lord:
Praise him, and magnifie him for ever.

Bassus. Benedicite. *A. 3. Voc.*

O All ye works of God the Lord, bless ye the Lord:
Praise him, and magnifie him for ever.

T 3

2 O ye Angels of the Lord,
bleſs ye the Lord : Praiſe him,
and magnifie him for ever.

3 O ye the ſtarry heavens high,
bleſs ye the Lord, &c.

4 O ye the waters 'bove the sky,
bleſs ye the Lord, &c.

5 O ye the powers of the Lord,
bleſs ye the Lord, &c.

6 O ye the ſhining Sun and Moon,
bleſs ye the Lord, &c.

7 O ye the gliſt'ring ſtars of heav'n,
bleſs ye the Lord, &c.

8 O ye the ſhow'rs & dropping dew,
bleſs ye the Lord, &c.

9 O ye the blowing winds of God,
bleſs ye the Lord, &c.

10 O ye the fire and warming heat,
bleſs ye the Lord, &c.

11 Ye winter and the ſummer tide,
bleſs ye the Lord, &c.

12 O ye the dews and binding froſts,
bleſs ye the Lord, &c.

13 O ye the froſts and chilling cold,
bleſs ye the Lord, &c.

14 O ye congealed ice and ſnow,
bleſs ye the Lord, &c.

15 O ye the nights & lightſom days,
bleſs ye the Lord, &c.

16 O ye the darkneſs and the light,
bleſs ye the Lord, &c.

17 O ye the lightnings & the clouds,
bleſs ye the Lord, &c.

18 O let the earth eke bleſs the Lord,
bleſs ye the Lord, &c.

19 O ye the mountains and the hills,
bleſs ye the Lord, &c.

20 O all ye green things on the earth,
bleſs ye the Lord, &c.

21 O ye the ever-ſpringing wells,
bleſs ye the Lord, &c.

22 O ye the ſeas, and eke the floods,
bleſs ye the Lord, &c.

23 Whales, and all that in the waters
bleſs ye the Lord, &c.   (move,

24 O all ye flying fowls of th' air,
bleſs ye the Lord, &c.

25 O all ye beaſts and cattle eke,
bleſs ye the Lord, &c.

26 O ye children of mankind,
bleſs ye the Lord, &c.

27 Let Iſrael eke bleſs the Lord,
bleſs ye the Lord, &c.

28 O ye the prieſts of God the Lord,
bleſs ye the Lord, &c.

29 O ye the ſervants of the Lord,
bleſs ye the Lord, &c.

30 Ye ſp'rits and ſouls of right'ous
bleſs ye the Lord, &c.   (men,

31 Ye holy, and the meek of heart,
bleſs ye the Lord, &c.

32 O Ananias bleſs the Lord,
bleſs thou the Lord, &c.

33 O Azarias bleſs the Lord,
bleſs thou the Lord, &c.

34 And Miſael bleſs thou the Lord,
bleſs thou the Lord : Praiſe him,
and magnifie him for ever.

(279)

Cantus & Bassus. Humble Suit of a Sinner. *Or to Windsor Tune.*

O Lord, on whom I do depend, behold my careful heart:

And when thy will and pleasure is, releafe me of my smart.

Thou fee'ft my forrows what they are, my grief is known to thee:

And there is none that can remove, or take the fame from me;

Medius. An Hymn. *A. 3. Voc.*

O Lord, on whom I do depend, behold my careful heart:

And when thy will and pleasure is, releafe me of my smart.

Thou fee'ft my forrows what they are, my grief is known to thee:

And there is none that can remove, or take the fame from me ;

T 4 *Bassus.*

(280)

Baſſus. An Hymn. *A. 3. Voc.*

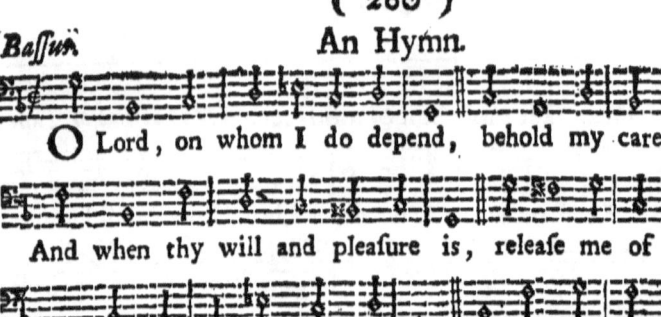

O Lord, on whom I do depend, behold my careful heart:

And when thy will and pleaſure is, releaſe me of my ſmart.

Thou ſee'ſt my ſorrows what they are, my grief is known to thee:

And there is none that can remove, or take the ſame from me ;

But only thou, whoſe aid I crave,
  whoſe mercy ſtill is preſt.
To eaſe all thoſe that come to thee
  for ſuccour and for reſt.
And ſince thou ſee'ſt my reſtleſs eyes,
  my tears and grievous groan ;
Attend unto my ſuit, O Lord,
  mark my complaint and moan:

For ſin hath ſo incloſed me,
  and compaſs'd me about,
That I am now remedileſs,
  if mercy help not out.
For mortal man cannot releaſe,
  or mitigate this pain :
But ev'n thy Chriſt, my L^d and God,
  who for my ſins was ſlain.

Whoſe bloody wounds are yet to ſee,
  thô not with mortal eye :
Yet do thy ſaints behold them all,
  and ſo I truſt ſhall I.
Thô ſin doth hinder me a while,
  when thou ſhalt ſee it good
I ſhall enjoy the ſight of him
  who ſhed for me his blood.

And as thine angels and thy ſaints
  do now behold the ſame :
So truſt I to poſſeſs that place,
  with them to praiſe thy Name.
But whilſt I live here in this vale
  where ſinners do frequent,
Aſſiſt me ever with thy grace,
  my ſins ſtill to lament : -

Leſt that I tread the ſinners trace,
  and give them my conſent
To dwell with them in wickedneſs,
  whereto nature is bent.
Only thy grace muſt be my ſtay,
  let that with me remain :
For if I fall, then of my ſelf
  I cannot riſe again.

Wherefore this is yet once again
  my ſuit and my requeſt,
To grant me pardon for my ſin,
  that I in thee may reſt.
Then ſhall my heart & tongue alſo
  be inſtruments of praiſe,
And in thy Church & houſe of ſaints
  ſing Pſalms to thee always.

Lamen-

(281)

Cantus & Bassus.   Lamentation of a Sinner.   *Martyrs Tune.*

O Lord, turn not thy face away from him that lies proſtrate,

Lamenting ſore his ſinful life before thy mercy gate.

Medius.   An Hymn.   *A. 3. Voc.*

O Lord, turn not thy face away from him that lies proſtrate,

Lamenting ſore his ſinful life before thy mercy gate.

Bassus.   An Hymn.   *A. 3. Voc.*

O Lord, turn not thy face away from him that lies proſtrate,

Lamenting ſore his ſinful life before thy mercy gate.

W^{ch} gate thou open'ſt wide to thoſe
that do lament their ſin:
Shut not that gate againſt me, Lord,
but let me enter in.

And call me not to ſtrict account
how I have lived here:
For then I know right well, O Lord,
how vile I ſhall appear.

I need not to confeſs my life,
I am ſure thou canſt tell:

What I have been, and what I am,
I know thou know'ſt it well.
        (be paſt,
O Lord, thou know'ſt what things
alſo the things that be:
Thou know'ſt alſo what is to come,
nothing is hid from thee.
        (made
Before the heav'ns and earth were
thou knowſt what things were then,
And all things elſe that have been
among the ſons of men. (ſince

And

And can the things that I have done
  be hidden from thee then?
No, no, thou know'ſt them all, ô Lord,
  where they were done, and when.

Wherefore with tears I come to thee
  to beg and to intreat,
Ev'n as the child that hath done ill,
  and feareth to be beat.

So come I to thy mercy gate,
  where mercy doth abound,
Deſiring mercy for my ſin,
  to heal my deadly wound.

O Lord, I need not to repeat
  what I do beg or crave:
Thou know'ſt, O Lord, before I ask,
  the thing that I would have.

Mercy, good Lord, mercy I ask,
  this is the total ſum:
For mercy, Lord, is all my ſuit,
  Lord, let thy mercy come.

Cantus & Baſſus.   A Penitential Hymn.   *Or to 51 Pſ. Tune.*

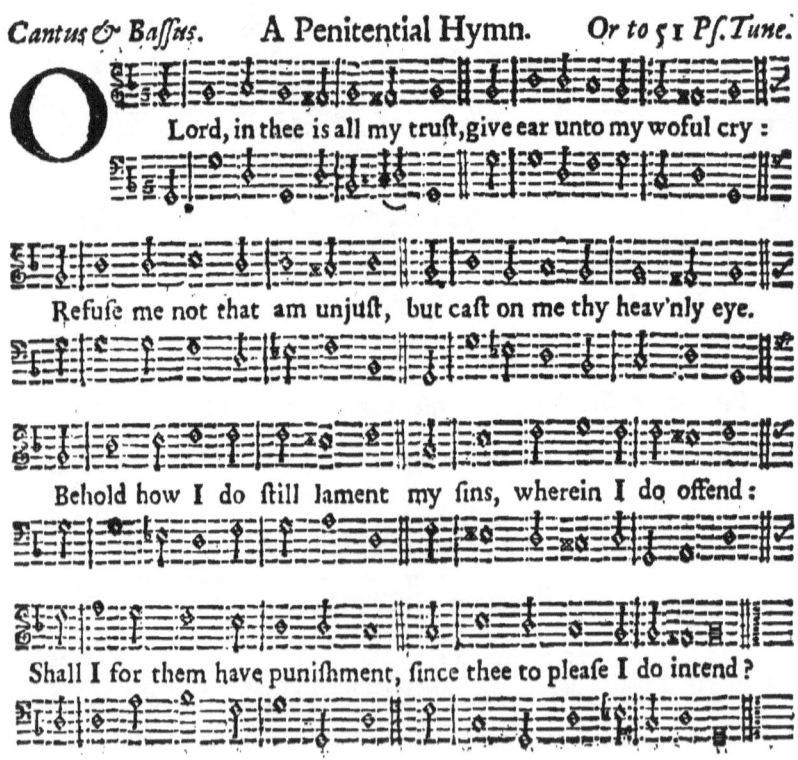

O Lord, in thee is all my truſt, give ear unto my woful cry:

Refuſe me not that am unjuſt, but caſt on me thy heav'nly eye.

Behold how I do ſtill lament my ſins, wherein I do offend:

Shall I for them have puniſhment, ſince thee to pleaſe I do intend?

Medius.

(283)

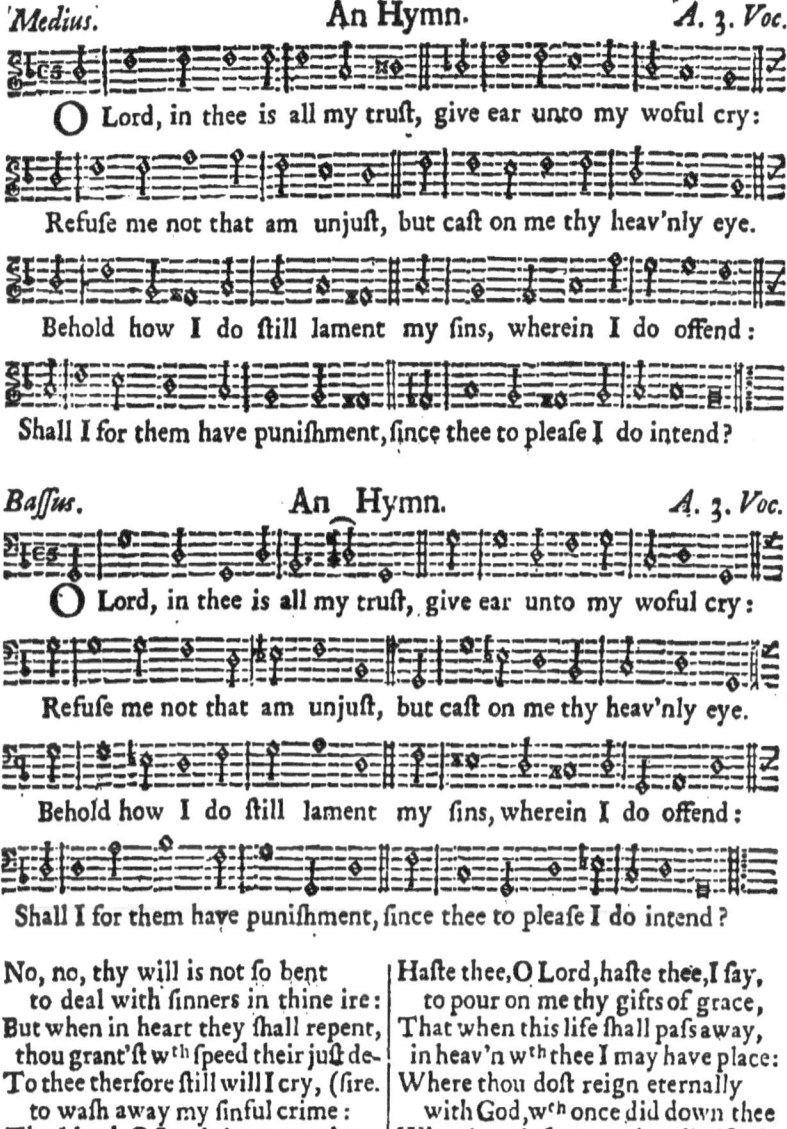

Medius. An Hymn. *A. 3. Voc.*

O Lord, in thee is all my trust, give ear unto my woful cry:

Refuse me not that am unjust, but cast on me thy heav'nly eye.

Behold how I do still lament my sins, wherein I do offend:

Shall I for them have punishment, since thee to please I do intend?

Bassus. An Hymn. *A. 3. Voc.*

O Lord, in thee is all my trust, give ear unto my woful cry:

Refuse me not that am unjust, but cast on me thy heav'nly eye.

Behold how I do still lament my sins, wherein I do offend:

Shall I for them have punishment, since thee to please I do intend?

No, no, thy will is not so bent
  to deal with sinners in thine ire:
But when in heart they shall repent,
  thou grant'st wth speed their just de-
To thee therfore still will I cry, (sire.
  to wash away my sinful crime:
Thy blood, O Lord, is not yet dry,
  but that it may help me in time.

Haste thee, O Lord, haste thee, I say,
  to pour on me thy gifts of grace,
That when this life shall pass away,
  in heav'n wth thee I may have place:
Where thou dost reign eternally
  with God, wch once did down thee
Wher Angels sing continually (send,
  to thee be praise world without end.

After

(284)

Cantus & Bassus.   After the H. Communion.   Or *to Martyrs Tune.*

ALL glory be to God on high, and peace on earth likewise,

Good will to men e--ter-nal-ly, by Christ his sacrifice.

Medius.   An Hymn.   *A. 3. Voc.*

ALL glo--ry be to God on high, and peace on earth likewise,

Good will to men e--ter-nal-ly, by Christ his sacrifice.

Bassus.   An Hymn.   *A. 3. Voc.*

ALL glory be to God on high, and peace on earth likewise,

Good will to men e--ter-nal-ly, by Christ his sacrifice.

O God the Father, heav'nly King,
  we praise, we worship thee :
We glorifie thee, we give thanks,
  Lord, for thy great glory.

O Lord, Lord God, O Jesu Christ,
  the Father's only Son :
Only begot, the Wisdom true,
  by whom all things were done.

O Lamb of God that tak'ft away
  the sins of all the world,

By guiltless death on cursed cross,
  have mercy on us, Lord.

O thou that tak'ft away the sins
  and errors of the world,
By guiltless death on cursed cross,
  have mercy on us, Lord.

O thou that tak'ft away the sins
  and errors of the world,
By guiltless death on cursed cross,
  receive our Pray'rs, O Lord.

O thou

(285)

O thou that fit'st on God's right hand, the Father eternal,
And dost our weakness understand, have mercy on us all.

For thou only deserv'st the Name of Israel's Holy One;

Thou holy art, thou art the Lord, thou, even thou alone.

And thou only, O Jesu Christ, thou with the Holy Ghost,
In glory of the Father, art highly advanced most.

Cantus & Bassus. An Hymn for Sunday. *Or to St. David's Tune.*

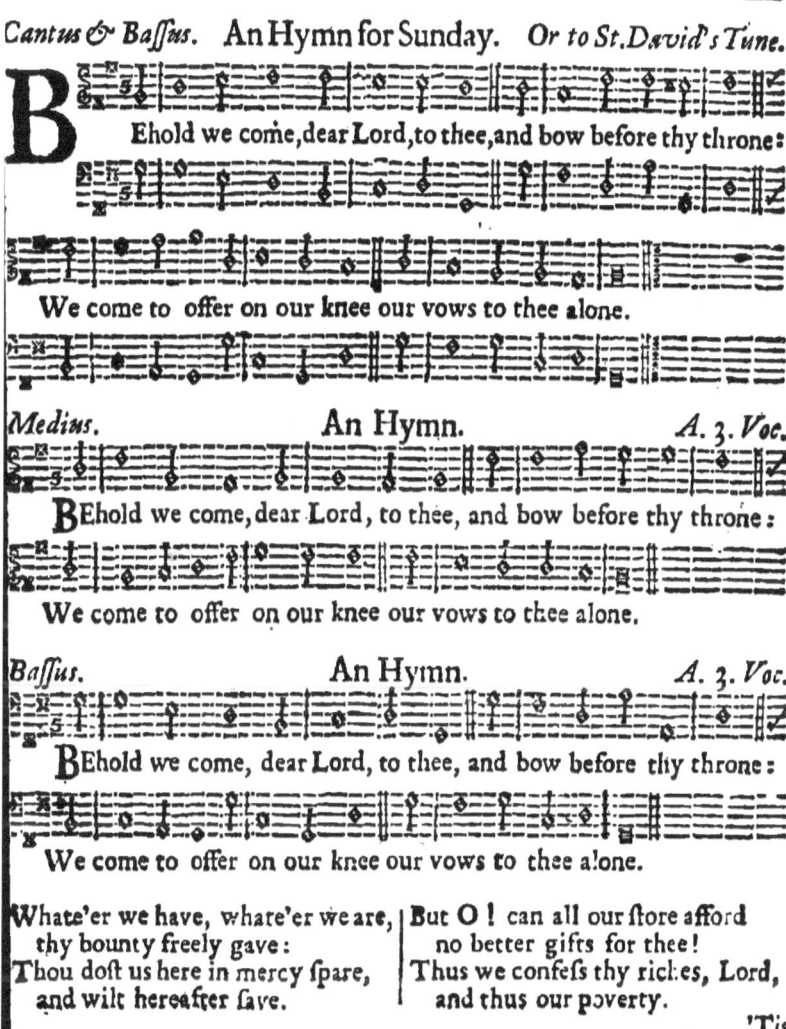

Behold we come, dear Lord, to thee, and bow before thy throne:

We come to offer on our knee our vows to thee alone.

Medius. An Hymn. *A. 3. Voc.*

Behold we come, dear Lord, to thee, and bow before thy throne:

We come to offer on our knee our vows to thee alone.

Bassus. An Hymn. *A. 3. Voc.*

Behold we come, dear Lord, to thee, and bow before thy throne:

We come to offer on our knee our vows to thee alone.

Whate'er we have, whate'er we are, thy bounty freely gave:
Thou dost us here in mercy spare, and wilt hereafter save.

But O! can all our store afford no better gifts for thee!
Thus we confess thy riches, Lord, and thus our poverty.

'Tis

(286)

'Tis not our tongue or knee can pay
 the mighty debt we owe:
Far more we should than we can say,
 far lower than we bow.
         (pow'rs,
Come then, my soul, bring all thy
 and grieve thou hast no more:
Bring ev'ry day thy choicest hours,
 and thy Great G O D adore.

But above all, prepare thy heart
 on this his own blest Day,
In its sweet task to bear thy part,
 and Sing, and Love, and Pray.
           Gloria Patri.
To God the Father, and the Son,
 and Holy Ghost therefore ;
Eternal Honour let be done
 henceforth for evermore.

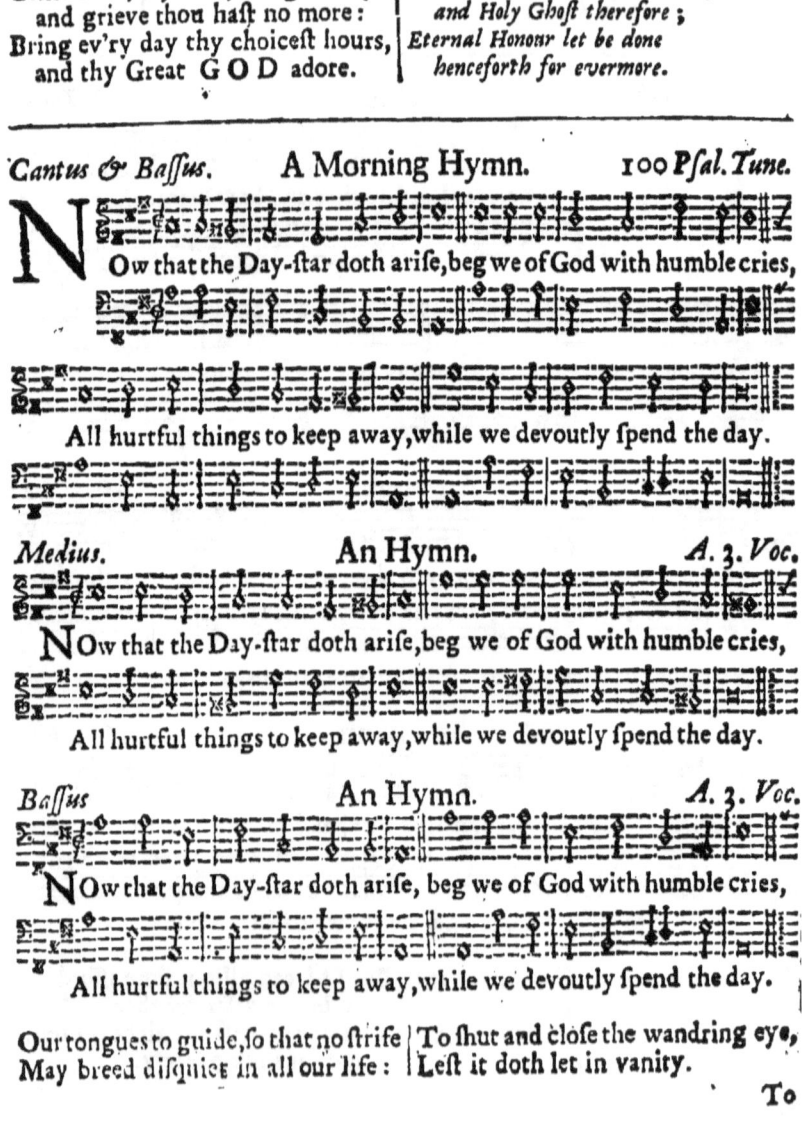

Cantus & Bassus.   A Morning Hymn.   100 *Psal. Tune.*

Now that the Day-star doth arise, beg we of God with humble cries,

All hurtful things to keep away, while we devoutly spend the day.

Medius.   An Hymn.   *A. 3. Voc.*

Now that the Day-star doth arise, beg we of God with humble cries,

All hurtful things to keep away, while we devoutly spend the day.

Bassus   An Hymn.   *A. 3. Voc.*

Now that the Day-star doth arise, beg we of God with humble cries,

All hurtful things to keep away, while we devoutly spend the day.

Our tongues to guide, so that no strife
May breed disquiet in all our life :

To shut and close the wandring eye,
Lest it doth let in vanity.

To

(287)

To keep the heart moſt pure & free
From fond and troubled fantaſie ;
To tame proud fleſh, while we deny't
A too full cup and wanton diet.

That when the day-light ſhall go out,
Time bringing on the night about,

We may, by leaving worldly ways,
Neglect no time our God to praiſe.
  Gloria Patri.
To Father, Son, and Holy Ghoſt,
  One bleſſed conſubſtantial Three :
All higheſt Praiſe, all humbleſt Thanks,
May now, and ſtill for ever be.

Cant. & Baſſ.   On the Divine Uſe of Muſick.   Or to 100 Pſ. Tune.

WE ſing to thee, whoſe Wiſdom form'd the curious Organ of the Ear :

And thou who gav'ſt us Voices, Lord, our grateful Songs in kindneſs bear.

Medius.   *An Hymn.*   *A. 3. Voc.*

WE ſing to thee, whoſe Wiſdom form'd the curious Organ of the Ear :

And thou who gav'ſt us Voices, Lord, our grateful Songs in kindneſs hear.

Baſſus.   *An Hymn.*   *A. 3. Voc.*

WE ſing to thee, whoſe Wiſdom form'd the curious Organ of the Ear :

And thou who gav'ſt us Voices, Lord, our grateful Songs in kindneſs hear.

We'l joy in God, who is the ſpring
 of lawful Joy and harmleſs Mirth :
Whoſe boundleſs Love is fitly call'd,
 The Harmony of Heav'n and Earth.

Thoſe Praiſes, deareſt Lord, aloud
 our humbleſt Sonnets ſhall rehearſe ;
Which rightly Tun'd, are rightly ſtyl'd,
 The MUSICK of the Univerſe.

And

And whilst we sing, we'l consecrate
that too too much prophaned Art,
By off'ring up with ev'ry Tongue
in ev'ry Song a flaming Heart.

We'l hallow Pleasure, and redeem
from vulgar use our precious Voice:
Those Lips which wantonly have sung,
shall serve our turn for nobler Joys.

Thus we will imitate on Earth
poor Mortals, still the heav'nly Quires:

And with high Notes, above the Clouds
we'l send with words more rais'd desires.

And that Above we may be sure,
when we come there, our part to know;
Whilst we live here, at Home and Church
we'l practise Singing oft below.

Gloria Patri.

Glory and Praise be given most,
To Father, Son, and Holy Ghost:
Hallelujah, Hallelujah,
Hallelujah, Hallelujah.

FINIS.

Books of *DIVINE MUSICK* Printed for Henry Playford *at his Shop near the* Temple Church.

Cantica Sacra; the first Set in Latin, the second in English and Latin, containing *Hymns* for 2 and 3 Voices to the *Organ*. Price of each 3 s.

Harmonia Sacra, in two Books; containing *Divine Hymns* and *Dialogues* lately set to Musick by Dr. *John Blow*, Mr. *Henry Purcell*, and several other eminent Masters. Price of the first Book stitch'd 7 s. the second 4 s.

The *Psalms* of *David* in 4 Parts, in Folio. Price stitch'd 2 s. 6 d.

The *Introduction to the Skill of Musick*, both Vocal and Instrumental, by *John Playford*. The 12th Edition corrected and amended. To which is added, several new Rules for Composing 2, 3, 4, and 5 Parts, by Mr. *Henry Purcell*. Price bound 2 s.

Also a large Sheet of *Directions* for the *Bass-Viol*. Price 1 s.

☞ Likewise all sorts of *MUSICK Books*, both Vocal and Instrumental; and all sorts of *Ruled Paper*, and *Ruled Books of Musick* of several sizes; with Books on all other Subjects, and all sorts of *Stationary Ware*, are to be sold at the same Shop.

www.ingramcontent.com/pod-product-compliance
Lightning Source LLC
Chambersburg PA
CBHW032048230426
43672CB00009B/1513